RESTORATIVE JUVENILE JUSTICE:
Repairing the Harm of Youth Crime

D0556205

Gordon Bazemore
and
Lode Walgrave
Editors

Criminal Justice Press
Monsey, New York USA
1999

ISBN: 1-881798-13-5

Contents

Introduction: Restorative Justice and the International Juvenile
Justice Crisis
Gordon Bazemore and Lode Walgrave 1

Part One: Key Principles 15

Rehabilitation, Retribution and Restorative Justice: Alternative
Conceptions of Juvenile Justice
Barry C. Feld 17

Restorative Juvenile Justice: In Search of Fundamentals and an
Outline for Systemic Reform
Gordon Bazemore and Lode Walgrave 45

The History of Restorative Justice
Elmar G.M. Weitekamp 75

Restorative Justice Is Republican Justice
John Braithwaite and Christine Parker 103

Part Two: Process, Programs and Practices 127

Community Service as a Cornerstone of a Systemic Restorative
Response to (Juvenile) Crime
Lode Walgrave 129

After Shaming, Whither Reintegration: Restorative Justice
and Relational Rehabilitation
Gordon Bazemore 155

Protecting Community: The Public Safety Role in a Restorative
Juvenile Justice
Susan Guarino-Ghezzi and Andrew Klein 195

Avoiding the Marginalization and "McDonaldization" of Victim-Offender
Mediation: A Case Study in Moving Toward the Mainstream
Mark S. Umbreit 213

continued

Contents

Part Three: Implementation Issues 235

Implementing Restorative Youth Justice: A Case Study in
Community Justice and the Dynamics of Reform
  Curt Taylor Griffiths and Ray Corrado 237

Legal Issues of Restorative Justice
  Daniel W. Van Ness 263

**Part Four: Research — Impact on Victim, Offender
and Community** 285

Punitive Attitudes of the Public: Reality and Myth
  Klaus Sessar 287

Restorative Justice, Juvenile Offenders and Crime Victims:
A Review of the Literature
  Russ Immarigeon 305

The Impact of Restorative Interventions on Juvenile Offenders
  Mara Schiff 327

Part Five: Toward the Future 357

Reflections on the Future of Restorative Justice for Juveniles
  Lode Walgrave and Gordon Bazemore 359

FOREWORD

Initial drafts of the chapters in this book were discussed by the authors in a workshop, held at the first International Conference on Restorative Justice for Juveniles, in Leuven, Belgium, in May 1997. The conference was organized by the International Network for Research on Restorative Justice for Juveniles, funded by the Fund for Scientific Research-Flanders (Belgium). The conference resulted in the publication of a selection of papers by prominent scholars, and of the Declaration of Leuven on the Advisability of Promoting Restorative Responses to Juvenile Crime, all appearing in L. Walgrave (ed.) (1998), *Restorative Justice for Juveniles: Potentialities, Risks and Problems* (Leuven, Belgium: Leuven University Press.

Author Affiliations

Gordon Bazemore (editor), Florida Atlantic University, Department of Criminal Justice, University Tower, 220 SE 2nd Avenue, 612C, Fort Lauderdale, Florida 33301-1905. *E-mail* <bazemor@fau.edu>.

Lode Walgrave (editor), Catholic University of Leuven, Research Group on Juvenile Criminology, Hooverplein 10, 3000, Leuven, Belgium. *E-mail* <lode.walgrave@law.kuleuven.ac.be>.

★   ★   ★

John Braithwaite, Australian National University, Department of Social Research, GPO Box 4, Canberra ACT 2601, Australia. *E-mail* <jbb304@coombs.anu.edu.au>.

Ray Corrado, Simon Fraser University, School of Criminology, Burnaby, British Columbia, V5A 1S6, Canada. *E-mail* <corrado@sfu.ca>.

Barry C. Feld, University of Minnesota, 285 Law Center, 229-19th Avenue South, Minneapolis, Minnesota 55455. *E-mail* <bfeld000@counsel.com>.

Curt Taylor Griffiths, Simon Fraser University, School of Criminology, Burnaby, British Columbia, V5A, 1S6, Canada.

Susan Guarino-Ghezzi, Stonehill College, 320 Washington Street, North Easton, Massachusetts 02357. *E-mail* <Guarino@stonehill.edu>.

Russ Immarigeon, 563 Route 21, Hillsdale, New York 12529. *E-mail* <russ.immarigeon@taconic.net>.

Andrew Klein, Quincy District Court, 1 Dennis Ryan Parkway, Quincy, Massachusetts 02169. *E-mail* <klein122@concentric.net>.

Christine Parker, Law School, University of New South Wales, Kensington 2052, Australia. *E-mail* <C.Parker@unsw.edu.au>.

Mara F. Schiff, Florida Atlantic University, Department of Criminal Justice, University Tower, Department of Criminal Justice, 220 SE 2nd Avenue, 613F, Fort Lauderdale, Florida 33301-1905. *E-mail* <mschiff@acc.fau.edu>.

Klaus Sessar, Seminar for Jugendrecht und Jugendhilfe, Universität Hamburg, Schlütersstrasse 28, 20146, Hamburg, Germany. *E-mail* <seszar@aol.com>.

Mark S. Umbreit, University of Minnesota, School of Social Work, 400 Ford Hall, 224 Church Street S.E., Minneapolis, Minnesota 55455. *E-mail* <ctr4rjm@che2.che.umn.edu>.

Daniel W. Van Ness, Prison Fellowship International, P.O. Box 17434, Washington, DC. *E-mail* <dvanness@pfi.org>.

Elmar G.M. Weitekamp, Institute of Criminology, University of Tübingen, Correnstrasse 34, D-72076, Tübingen, Germany. *E-mail* <elmar.weitekamp@uni-tuebingen.de>.

Introduction: Restorative Justice and the International Juvenile Justice Crisis

by

Gordon Bazemore

and

Lode Walgrave

Virtually unknown to all but a small group of academics at the beginning of the 1990s, restorative justice is now part of the national and international criminal justice reform dialogue. In some countries, as well as in individual states and provinces, it is also becoming an important focus of the criminal justice policy agenda. While there are now common international themes, actual practices and policies take quite different forms both within and between countries, and implementation varies even more significantly. In Australia, New Zealand, and Canada, for example, the term restorative justice is used to describe a variety of ancient indigenous dispute resolution practices associated with Aboriginal groups. These practices are now being updated and somewhat cautiously integrated into dominant European-style criminal and juvenile justice systems. In the U.S. and Europe, restorative justice has been associated primarily with one practice, victim-offender mediation, but is gradually being viewed as encompassing a much more diverse range of practices and processes that share a common focus on repairing the harm crime causes (Zehr, 1990; Van Ness and Strong, 1997).

Nowhere has the intensity of activity around restorative justice been greater than in juvenile justice and the response to youth crime. In fact, some of the most significant innovations in recent years have been developed and implemented as strictly youth justice alternatives. In New Zealand, for example, family group conferencing (Maxwell and Morris, 1993; Hudson and Galaway, 1996) has become the most strongly institutionalized restorative justice practice, now serving as the dominant dispositional option for all but the most serious and chronic juvenile offenders. A large number of victim-offender mediation programs are primarily or exclusively focused on juvenile crime (Umbreit, 1994). In several countries, special initiatives are underway for juvenile justice systems that have sparked legislation and policy encouraging and supporting pilot restorative justice projects. Juvenile justice professionals and youth advocates around the world are beginning to view what was once a set of marginalized practices as a possible "third way" to aid their beleaguered juvenile justice systems. In many countries, these systems have come to an impasse between the traditional social welfare or individual treatment focus on the needs and "best interests" of juveniles and a new punitive, "criminalized" approach (Feld, this volume).

The interest in restorative justice is in large part enhanced by the crisis facing juvenile justice systems globally. With few exceptions, nations and states are considering harsher, more adult-like penalties for juvenile offenders, and reconsidering the extent to which their governments remain committed to an individual treatment or social welfare mission for juvenile court intervention (Bazemore, 1996; Junger-Tas, 1994; Feld, 1993). The movement toward a punitive/retributive model is most extreme in the U.S., although individual states vary significantly in the way and extent to which this movement is affecting policy and actual practice. But the movement to in some way "criminalize" the juvenile court can also be seen in Canada, in virtually every European country, and indeed in almost every nation where the separation between juvenile and criminal court has existed historically.

Support for punishment has gained new legitimacy in the past two decades as evidenced by the rise in popularity of just deserts philosophies (von Hirsch, 1976, 1997; McAnany et al., 1984), which signaled judges, prosecutors and other decision makers that retribution was indeed an appropriate, even politically correct, response to delinquent behavior. In addition to pure just deserts alternatives for juvenile justice, a more generic crime control agenda has exerted strong influence in countries such as the U.S. and Canada, and a variety of models that seek to combine elements of retribution, risk management, and due process with treatment or social welfare overlays have been proposed and at least partially implemented in the past decade (Corrado et al., 1992; Guarino-Ghezzi and Loughran, 1995; Torbet et. al., 1996).

Unfortunately, the only opposition to the punitive/ retributive transformation of the juvenile court has been from those who in one form or another propose a revitalization or reaffirmation of the individual treatment or social welfare mission of the court (Krisberg, 1988; McAllair, 1993). Down in the trenches, judges, prosecutors, probation supervisors and other juvenile justice decision makers struggle daily with practical responses to hundreds of juvenile offenses, knowing that the real choice is often a limited one between, as one U.S. judge puts it, "sending the kid to jail or sending him to the beach." Faced with the choice between approaches that seem to provide only benefits to offenders while requiring little other than their participation in counseling or remedial services, and punitive sanctions that at least seem to provide consequences and affirm community standards, average citizens, policy makers, and crime victims will choose the latter. On the one hand, those trying to preserve a separate and distinct juvenile court and justice system by trying to make the case for a return to the treatment/best interests mission thus have a seemingly impossible task. On the other hand, those in favor of some modified form of just deserts model find it increasingly difficult to justify the need for *juvenile* justice at all (see Feld, this volume).

In this introduction to the chapters in this volume, we briefly consider the opportunities and obstacles facing advocates of systemic restorative justice reform in this larger context of an international crisis in juvenile justice. In doing so, we describe general dangers inherent in this context, and propose three challenges to restorative justice advocates hoping to develop a fully-fledged alternative response to youth crime. Addressing these challenges is itself controversial because those restorative justice proponents who are content with small-scale experiments that function as helpful, yet marginal, interventions may resist our proposal for systemic reform. We then present an overview of the structure of this volume and describe the general content of each chapter. It is difficult to ensure that any group of contributions representing perspectives as diverse as those of these authors is tightly focused around a few core themes. However, we believe that each chapter and each section addresses one or more of the challenges to restorative justice reform, and/or the controversies surrounding the restorative model as a genuine third way for juvenile justice.

WINDOW FOR RESTORATIVE JUSTICE REFORM

Pessimistically, prospects for implementing *any* significant juvenile justice reform that goes against the grain of dominant ideological and bureaucratic transformations of the past decade are far from promising. These changes have pushed juvenile justice systems, especially those in the U.S., so far down the road toward retribution that they are almost indistinguishable from most criminal justice systems. Moreover, a frightening prospect is that some advocates of the treatment model now seem extremely vulnerable to co-optation by retributive state systems driven primarily by the need to build more (and often larger) secure facilities operated by private-sector providers (Orlando, 1997).

More optimistically, the hope for reform based on restorative justice lies in its very *lack* of resonance with the concerns of the traditional treatment/punishment debate. By definition, an approach focused neither on punishment nor treatment of the offender, but on repairing harm and peaceful resolution of conflict, moves the dialogue about the response to youth crime to a different plane. The restorative dialogue necessarily challenges traditional political and criminal justice ideologies, as well as the assumptions of dominant youth justice paradigms. The appeal of restorative justice lies in its potential to change both the nature of juvenile justice intervention and the role of government and community in such intervention (Van Ness and Strong, 1997; Pranis, 1997). The current crisis in juvenile justice systems is in this sense an opportunity to mount a credible attempt to preserve juvenile justice while also demonstrating the viability of the restorative response.

Forced to compete for attention with far more "marketable" programs, it seems almost unfathomable that restorative justice ideas have fared as well as they have. If restorative justice has presented a less-than-formidable challenge as a serious, systemic alternative to the current array of trendy interventions that now often combine secure confinement, strict discipline and some treatment in secure facilities, it may be in part because most of its advocates are clearly not in the mainstream of the policy or practitioner communities. In addition, most restorative justice advocates have thus far refused to rely on gimmicks to pander to the demand for instant cures for youth crime. They should not begin to do so now. But, if restorative justice is to offer a viable, third way for juvenile justice, rather than an interesting yet irrelevant sideshow, supporters must face three related challenges.

First, precisely because of the newfound popularity of the term and the growing interest in some restorative practices, the most important challenge is to prevent restorative justice from becoming another trendy buzzword, or marketing tool, to increase the appeal of current policy and practice. Under the banner of restorative justice, for example, interventions such as mandatory adult sentencing for juvenile offenders could be packaged as part of a "crime victims' agenda." Similarly, offender-focused treatment programs with trendy new names could be sold as restorative responses, even in the absence of community and victim involvement in intervention. The danger today is that restorative justice is seldom *defined* in such a way that allows even astute juvenile justice policy makers and professionals to distinguish what are actually traditional practices from those that truly address the core agenda of restorative justice, i.e., to repair the harm crime causes (e.g., Zehr, 1990). Hence, a working definition is needed that is, on the one hand, specific enough about the parameters of restorative justice to guard against the bastardization of core principles and the mislabeling of various practices as restorative (Bazemore, 1997). On the other hand, such a definition must not be so restrictive as to limit creativity in what is still an emerging practice, which itself is helping to build stronger theory and criteria as it evolves (Daly, 1996).

Second, restorative justice must address the unique context of youth crime, and the assumptions behind a separate response to it. There are strong reasons to believe that juvenile justice systems remain the best "laboratory" for implementing restorative justice practices. In addition, even in the absence of principled rationales for retaining a separate juvenile justice system in the future, there are many strategic reasons to focus restorative justice reform on the juvenile justice system. This book is based on the premise that restorative justice can offer a viable alternative to current juvenile justice systems and can help to avoid the relapse into a punitive system. Thus, while most principles of restorative justice are universal in their implications for a generic response to crime, implementation strategies must take account of what is unique about youth crime. They must address both real and apparent differences between young people and adults, and between the courts and systems currently designed to respond to crimes by each.

The final challenge, and a key premise of this book, is that the future of a restorative juvenile justice depends on it becoming a fully-fledged, systemic alternative. That is, if the restorative justice response to youth crime is to become something other than a sideshow, it must resist the tendency to compartmentalize reforms as alternative programs, processes or ancillary policies. *Systemic reform* based on restorative justice implies that there can be a restorative response to any crime that community members or juvenile justice professionals may encounter. Restorative intervention will therefore not be limited to one type of offender, one type of victim or community, one program or part of the system, or one system objective or function (e.g., sanctioning, public safety).

Such systemic reform means also that in a given jurisdiction where restorative justice is fully implemented, one could observe clear differences in the response to youth crime compared with treatment/welfare or punishment-focused systems. These differences would be based on: a distinctive *context* for intervention (e.g., a new set of values/principles, new participants, new processes); a different *content* (e.g., new outcomes, new intervention practices); and a different *structure* (e.g., new roles for justice professionals and the agencies that support them). Moreover, not only explicitly reparative and mediative processes but *all system functions* would be based on restorative principles and focused on the common goal of repairing harm.

Meeting this third challenge is a tall order, and the challenge itself is one that is likely to provoke controversy and discussion around two criticisms. First, the quest for systemic reform may appear to promote an absolute distinction between a purely restorative system, and a complete surrender to retributive juvenile justice. Advocates of such a holistic, utopian restorative justice agenda would not be content until reforms had eliminated all remnants of retributive and welfare/treatment systems. Second, the proposal for systemic restorative justice reform as a long-term work in progress may appear to undervalue small-scale restorative reforms and programs in favor of a future "pie in the sky."

In answer to the first criticism, we do not view restorative justice, or any justice paradigm, as a monolithic system. It is therefore not necessary to challenge every feature of current juvenile justice systems to promote restorative alternatives. For example, a fully-fledged restorative justice system will have to give serious consideration to such issues as the role of coercion, the validity of public concerns about safety, the need to sanction crime and the need to devise better ways of rehabilitating offenders. While this view may be controversial among restorative justice proponents, even the most holistic and systemic application of restorative principles in the foreseeable future will still need to allow room for a range of treatment alternatives, relatively traditional risk management initiatives, adversarial processes, and the option of incapacitation for the most chronic and violent offenders. Restorative justice should also not limit the ability of justice systems to ensure fairness and protection of the rights of the accused. As advocates of just deserts have also argued, it is never a question of only one set of objectives or operating principles (von Hirsch, 1976; 1993). Rather, the key issue is which set of principles plays the *dominant* role in setting priorities for justice intervention, and which provide "limiting goals" that protect interests essential to guard against abuses that threaten individual liberties (Robinson, 1987; Walgrave, 1995).

In response to the second criticism, the choice is not between the small-scale restorative justice experiments being implemented around the world today, on the one hand, and the pursuit of a systemic, fully-fledged restorative justice reform on the other; both endeavors should be mutually reinforcing. Although most small experiments continue to operate with minimal impact on the "business" of the dominant retributive system, they are important for several reasons. First, and most important, they appear to be producing what a Canadian group of restorative justice advocates has begun to call "satisfying justice" for a number of victims, community members and offenders (Church Council on Justice and Corrections, 1996). Second, the experiments provide the necessary basis for developing restorative justice as a vision by demonstrating the practical potential of the model, and helping to refine emerging normative theory consistent with restorative principles. But we also believe a clear vision of a restorative system is necessary if reformers are to begin to alter those practices of retributive systems that minimize the prospects for even small-scale restorative processes and practices. It is, after all, the widespread dissatisfaction of the public and professionals with *current* inflexible and monolithic systems that has created the unexpected support for restorative justice. Experiences in the field should provide a primary focus for empirical research, and will form productive soil in which to grow and nurture new experimental initiatives.

But this is insufficient. Small-scale experiments that remain at the local level become vulnerable to being reintegrated into retributive or rehabilitative systems, or to being kept at the margins of these systems. Under these circumstances, the broader potential inherent in the restorative approach does not then become apparent, and theoretical development and methodological underpinnings do not evolve toward a coherent restorative justice paradigm and basic model for intervention. Hence, theoretical reflection and empirical research is needed in order to abstract and then synthesize the common elements in all these successful experiments, to facilitate comparisons, to provide protocols for evaluation, and to build a coherent vision that may become a strong countervailing force in the search for a constructive and satisfying systemic response to youth crime. Practical experiments and scientific research and reflection need each other. Practitioners must become primary partners in the discussion with researchers on desirable evolutions in theory and vision and on practical feasibility.

PURPOSE AND ORGANIZATION OF THE BOOK

The editors of this volume are researchers who have attempted to compile a collection of manuscripts that present an optimistic, yet critical and objective view of the prospects for a restorative juvenile justice. At the same time, we may be fairly labeled as proponents of restorative justice, in part because we believe that this new paradigm is unlikely to be given a chance unless it is presented in a way that clearly articulates the possibilities of restorative intervention based on theory and principles. While we insist that the new model must rise or fall based on the empirical evidence, practice and research thus far provide numerous indications that restorative justice is pointing the way to a more satisfying and constructive model for dealing with the aftermath of crime. But commitment and a positive vision have to be balanced by healthy skepticism. While belief can inspire a movement, critical empirical assessment must feed scientific questioning and guide implementation.

The major purpose of the book is to explore the potential of restorative justice as an overarching vision for the juvenile justice system, and to outline a research agenda to support its further theoretical and empirical development. There is a growing body of empirical, theoretical and ethical literature supportive of the idea that restorative principles could point the way toward a fully-fledged alternative model for responding to youth crime. Although some of our supporters have encouraged us to do nothing less than describe a complete alternative restorative system in detail, doing so is well beyond the scope of an edited volume that necessarily includes a diverse group of authors writing from a wide variety of perspectives and focal concerns. Rather, our more modest objective is to explore the parameters and components of this alternative for juvenile justice. In doing so, we hope to raise a number of questions and problems that require further reflection, experimentation and research.

To achieve these objectives, we have attempted to compile a coherent set of logically ordered chapters, each of which addresses a complementary aspect of what we will refer to as a "maximalist" agenda for restorative juvenile justice: an agenda that seeks to integrate restorative justice principles and practice at every level of the juvenile justice system. In preparation for this volume, after first discussing its structure, we prepared a brief programmatic summary and provided short outlines for each chapter. Only then did we invite authoritative scholars to prepare their contributions within our project structure, and according to the proposed outline. After receiving our comments and suggestions on their more detailed subsequent outlines, each author then prepared first drafts of their respective chapters. These initial versions were read and discussed by all authors, who gathered at a workshop in Leuven, Belgium, held at the first International Conference on Restorative Justice for Juveniles on May 12-14, 1997, and organized by the International Network for Research on Restorative Justice for Juveniles.[1] The meeting resulted in further suggestions for revision, aimed at improving each chapter separately and at promoting coherence of the book as a whole.

Of course, more than one opinion is presented here. Although specific positions of the authors differ on several important issues, a broad maximalist or holistic approach to restorative justice for juveniles provides a common ground on which readers can identify these differences and hopefully view them as constructive tensions in the development of a paradigm. We will engage some of the basic controversies directly, and have indeed chosen contributions that to some degree push the limits of the emerging restorative paradigm, or even question its viability. While none of these contributions, nor this volume as a whole, can solve all problems for those interested in a systemic alternative for juvenile justice, they do raise key questions that must be addressed in the continuing debate about a restorative justice future.

The chapters are organized around topics representing issue domains that must be addressed in the development of a systemic restorative juvenile justice. In Part One, basic principles underlying the restorative alternative are examined and considered in the context of competing models and sociolegal frameworks. In Chapter 1, Barry C. Feld describes the insoluble contradictions in the option for a treatment-oriented juvenile justice system, and concludes that a fundamental change is needed. His way out of the dilemma is the abolition of the juvenile justice system, in favor of a just deserts model that would safeguard the legal rights of juvenile offenders in a criminal court sentencing process that takes age into account. Moreover, Feld poses several provocative questions to restorative justice advocates and presents the strongest critical view of the emerging paradigm in this volume. In the second chapter, Gordon Bazemore and Lode Walgrave provide a provisional definition of restorative justice focused on the idea of repairing harm, propose core principles, and consider in detail the three challenges posed earlier to the development of restorative justice as a fully-fledged alternative. Next, Elmar G.M. Weitekamp's historical analysis demonstrates that the restorative approach is not new at all. In ancient societies, the primary concern was to restore peace to the community rather than mete out punishment in responding to crime. The conclusion that reparative and settlement-focused responses preceded the currently dominant punitive model is a harsh challenge to those who believe that punishment is in some way the natural human response to crime. Finally, John Braithwaite and Christine Parker broaden the perspective in a rare effort to apply a macro theory of justice, "republicanism" (Braithwaite and Petitt, 1990), to restorative interventions at the micro level. Using family group conferencing as a case study, the chapter addresses criticisms of restorative justice. In addition, it develops guidelines for guarding against power imbalances and ensuring that participants can opt out of an informal restorative process, or appeal sanctioning decisions that appear to be harsher than those that might have resulted from a court process. From the perspective of these authors, restorative justice is intrinsically linked to a unique value framework and social ethics, and it can only be fully actualized in a society based on a rule of law and rights that guarantee freedom as non-domination. Such a republican ideal presupposes a constant striving for greater equality and stronger communities, wherein lies the assurance against domination by others.

In Part Two, issues of consistency in practice and process are considered and a restorative agenda for addressing public safety, sanctioning and rehabilitation is explored. Walgrave argues that the maximalist approach to restorative justice will need to include the use of coercion, and a formalization of both procedures and the relationship between communities and society. The integration and formalization of community service is a cornerstone is this development. Gordon Bazemore then makes clear that restorative justice does not reject or minimize the need for a concern with the needs of offenders and their reintegration. On the contrary, a restorative, "naturalistic" approach to rehabilitation, focused on building — or rebuilding — relationships between young people and law-abiding adults, may offer greater opportunities for meaningful reintegration than do current highly profes-sionalized treatment modalities. Next, Susan Guarino-Ghezzi and Andrew Klein address a neglected issue in the restorative justice debate: its relevance for public safety. They advance convincing arguments and present practical examples to support the view that "protective restoration" may offer better outcomes with regard to peace and safety in the community than most traditional responses. In the final chapter in this section, Mark S. Umbreit describes how victim-offender mediation can offer satisfying outcomes for two parties or stakeholders in the crime, and documents the impressive expansion of this commonly used restorative justice process. While such expansion and more mainstream application of mediation is encouraging, Umbreit warns against the dangers of the proliferation of a kind of "fast-food" version of restorative justice, aimed more at meeting the needs of the system than those of victims and offenders. Benchmarks are outlined for assessing the extent to which the mediation process is being implemented in a manner con-sistent with restorative principles.

With its concern for integrity in expanding this now time-tested restorative process, Umbreit's chapter is also relevant to the contributions in Part Three, which address issues of implementation. Curt Taylor Griffiths and Ray Corrado examine the ethnic relevance of restorative justice, and address difficult issues associated with implementing informal community-centered restorative processes within highly centralized, bureaucratic state systems. While some have wondered whether such restorative responses have enough cultural resilience to meet the justice needs of oppressed minorities, it appears that, on the contrary, modern Westernized versions of restorative justice have much to learn from Aboriginal settlement processes that in many ways illustrate the full potential of a holistic restorative process. Unfortunately, the pretensions of industrialized states to "regulate" these responses in the name of uniformity may limit creativity and expansion of these restorative opportunities. Acknowledging that the informal character of many restorative negotiations and exchanges may threaten due process rights for all parties concerned, and thus the wider implementation of restorative justice, Daniel Van Ness reviews international conventions and guidelines in an examination of how juridical principles typical in constitutional democratic regimes can be safeguarded in a restorative juvenile justice system.

Part Four of the volume compiles and critiques available empirical research in an attempt to focus specifically on what is known about the impact of restorative interventions on these three primary stakeholders in the juvenile justice process. Because researchers have only very recently become "enlightened" about the need to move beyond examination of offender outcomes, assessing community and victim impact is no easy task — and research on restorative practices in general is in its infancy. In considering the impact on communities, for example, it is necessary provisionally to focus primarily on public opinion research that can only allow for inferences about how satisfied citizens *might be* with restorative versus traditional disposition options. Hence, in the first chapter in this section, Klaus Sessar reviews research on the public's attitude toward punitive sanctions and restorative justice alternatives. These data are promising with respect to the political feasibility of expanding restorative justice, and appear to suggest that the supposedly punitive attitude of the public is a myth. Russ Immarigeon reviews what is still a very limited body of research on victims' experiences and outcomes in restorative justice interventions. Generally, victims feel better, more respected, and that they are treated in a more equitable way after participation in a mediation program as compared to a traditional judicial procedure. Moreover, most restorative processes hold greater opportunities for peace making in the relationship between victim and offender, and Immarigeon suggests that the effects of mediation, conferencing, impact panels and other interventions on victims may become even more positive as restorative principles are applied with greater consistency. Finally, Mara F. Schiff outlines and classifies the larger body of research data on offender impact. Though results here are less ambiguous, methodological problems and a general absence of theoretical elaboration continue to limit the inferences that can be made. However, offender outcomes point in a surprisingly positive direction given the limited experience with restorative interventions relative to treatment practices. The least we can say is that there are no indications that restorative processes result in a more negative impact on offender reintegration and recidivism than traditional sanctions.

Finally, in Part Five the editors look to the future of restorative responses to youth crime. Based on the literature reviewed and the arguments and findings of preceding chapters, they conclude that restorative justice has the potential to become a fully-fledged systemic alternative to both rehabilitative and retributive youth justice systems. To strengthen this conclusion, the editors specifically revisit many of the criticisms and concerns — especially the often-persuasive arguments of critics such as Feld — and contend that inherent and irreconcilable contradictions in both competing models for the future (treatment and punishment) strengthen the case for at least further experimentation with restorative responses. Many questions have been raised that remain unanswered, and, toward this end, an agenda is proposed for critical examination, more rigorous research, and the development of both normative and ethological theory. Criminological research and theory can in this way contribute to a movement that currently seems capable of harnessing human creativity to engage community, victim and offender in an empowering effort to respond to the aftermath of crime.

REFERENCES

Bazemore, G. (1996). "Three Paradigms for Juvenile Justice." In: Joe Hudson and Burt Galaway (eds.) *Restorative Justice: International Perspectives*. Monsey, NY: Criminal Justice Press.

—— (1997a). "What's New About the Balanced Approach?" *Juvenile and Family Court Journal* 48(1):1-23.

Braithwaite, J. and P. Petitt (1990). *Not Just Desert. A Republican Theory of Criminal Justice*. Oxford, UK: Clarendon.

Church Council on Justice and Corrections (1996). *Satisfying Justice: Safe Community Options that Attempt to Repair Harm from Crime and Reduce the Use or Length of Imprisonment*. Ottawa, CAN: author.

Corrado R.R., N. Bala, R. Linden and M. LeBlanc (1992) *Juvenile Justice in Canada*. Toronto, CAN: Butterworths.

Daly, K. (1996). "Shaming Conferences in Australia: A Reply to the Academic Skeptics," Paper presented at the Annual Meeting of the American Society of Criminology, Chicago.

Feld, B. (1993). "The Criminal Court Alternative to Perpetuating Juvenile in Justice." In: *The Juvenile Court: Dynamic, Dysfunctional, or Dead?* Philadelphia, PA: Center for the Study of Youth Policy, School of Social Work, University of Pennsylvania.

Guarino-Ghezzi, S. and N. Loughran (1995). *Balancing Juvenile Justice.* New Brunswick, NJ: Transaction Publishers.

Hudson, J. and B. Galaway. (1996). "Introduction." In: J. Hudson and B. Galaway (eds.), *Restorative Justice: International Perspectives.* Monsey, NY: Criminal Justice Press.

Junger-Tas, J. (1994)."Will the Juvenile Justice System Survive?" *European Journal for Criminal Policy and Research* 2(2):76-91.

Krisberg, B. (1988). *The Juvenile Court: Reclaiming The Vision.* San Francisco, CA: National Council of Crime & Delinquency.

Maxwell, G. and A. Morris (1993). *Family Participation, Cultural Diversity and Victim Involvement in Youth Justice: A New Zealand Experiment.* Wellington, NZ: Victoria University.

McAllair, D. (1993). "Reaffirming Rehabilitation in Juvenile Justice." *Youth and Society* 25:104-125.

McAnany, P.D., D. Thompson and D. Fogel (1984). *Probation and Justice: Reconsideration of Mission.* Cambridge, MA: Oelgeschlager, Gunn & Hain.

Orlando, F. (1997) "More Grifs in the Mills." *Youth Today* (March/April):8.

Pranis, K. (1997). "From Vision to Action: Some Principles of Restorative Justice." *Church & Society: Presbyterian Church Journal* 87(4):32-42.

Robinson, P. (1987). "Hybrid Principles for the Distribution of Criminal Sanctions." *Northwest University Law Review* 19:34-36.

Torbet, P., R. Gable, H. Hurst, I. Montgomery, L. Szymanski and D. Thomas (1996). *State Responses to Serious and Violent Juvenile Crime.* Office of Juvenile Justice and Delinquency Prevention research report. Pittsburgh, PA: National Center for Juvenile Justice.

Umbreit, M. (1994). *Victim Meets Offender: The Impact of Restorative Justice and Mediation.* Monsey, NY: Criminal Justice Press.

Van Ness, D. and K.H. Strong (1997). *Restoring Justice.* Cincinnati, OH: Anderson.

von Hirsch, A. (1993). *Censure and Sanctions.* Oxford, UK: Clarendon.

—— (1997). "Penal Philosophy: How Much to Punish?" In: M. Tonry (ed.), *Oxford Crime and Justice Handbook.* New York, NY: Oxford University Press.

—— (1976). *Doing Justice.* New York, NY: Hill & Wang.

Walgrave, L., (1995). "Restorative Justice for Juveniles: Just a Technique or a Fully-fledged Alternative?" *Howard Journal of Criminal Justice* 34(3):228-249.

Zehr, H. (1990). *Changing Lenses: A New Focus for Crime and Justice.* Scottsdale, PA: Herald Press.

NOTES

1. At this conference, most of the provisional chapters were also presented to the audience. A selection of other presentations, received in response to the call for papers, appears in L. Walgrave (ed.) (1998), *Restorative Justice for Juveniles: Potentialities, Risks and Problems* (Leuven, Belgium: Leuven University Press). This volume contains contributions by, among others, Ezzat Fattah, Uberto Gatti, Klaus Hartmann, Kevin Haines, Guy Masters, Paul McCold, Jean Trépanier, Martin Wright and other prominent scholars, and the Declaration of Leuven on the Advisability of Promoting Restorative Responses to Juvenile Crime.

PART ONE:
KEY PRINCIPLES

1. Rehabilitation, Retribution and Restorative Justice: Alternative Conceptions of Juvenile Justice

by

Barry C. Feld

INTRODUCTION

Within the past three decades, judicial decisions, legislative amendments and administrative changes have transformed the juvenile court in the U.S. from a nominally rehabilitative social welfare agency into a scaled-down second-class criminal court that provides young offenders with neither therapy nor justice (Feld, 1984, 1988b, 1993a). The substantive and procedural convergence between juvenile and criminal courts eliminates virtually all of the conceptual and operational differences in strategies of criminal social control for youths and adults.

In reaction to this transformation, defenders of the juvenile court propose to rehabilitate the "rehabilitative ideal" and reinvigorate its social welfare role (Krisberg and Austin, 1993). On the other hand, critics of the juvenile court question whether any reasons exist to maintain a separate punitive youth court, propose to abolish juvenile courts, and advocate formal recognition of youthfulness as a mitigating factor when sentencing younger offenders (Feld, 1988b, 1995; Ainsworth, 1991). And, as the various chapters in this volume indicate, still others propose restorative justice as a new conceptual response to youth crime.

The present analyses focus only on the delinquency jurisdiction of juvenile courts because youth crime and violence provide the impetus for most of the current public debate and political response (Feld, 1995). This chapter will analyze the transformation of the juvenile court from a social welfare agency into a deficient criminal court for young offenders. Secondly, it analyzes the inherent and irreconcilable contradictions between attempting to combine treatment and punishment, social welfare and penal social control, in the juvenile court, and proposes a conceptual and administrative uncoupling of the two goals. Once states separate social welfare from criminal social control, no role remains for a separate juvenile delinquency court. However, if states try all offenders in one integrated criminal court, then they must formally recognize youthfulness as a mitigating factor when sanctioning younger offenders. Because I analyze youth justice from a neo-classical deserts perspective, in the concluding section, this chapter poses some questions that proponents of restorative justice should address in order to persuade skeptics that their proposals provide a viable alternative to the conceptual impasse of rehabilitation and retribution embedded in the contemporary juvenile court.

This chapter focuses on developments and discussions in the U.S., where the conflicts between treatment and punishment are the most clear and explicit. In other parts of the Western world, however, we can observe similar tendencies. In Europe, for example, the dominance of rehabilitative aims in juvenile justice has also been heavily criticized, because of its disregard for legal rights and failure to respond adequately to public safety concerns (Hudson, 1987; Booth, 1991; *European Journal on Criminal Policy and Research,* 1994; Walgrave, 1995). These criticisms have not led to proposals to abolish the juvenile court, but rather to strengthen its juridical framework and disciplinary approach.

1. Transformed But Unreformed: The Recent History of the Juvenile Court

1.1. The Rehabilitative Juvenile Court

The social history of the juvenile court is an oft-told tale (Platt, 1977; Ryerson, 1978; Rothman, 1980). Economic modernization and structural changes associated with the transition from a rural agrarian to an urban industrial economy fostered rapid social change, increased rates of immigration, changed the configuration of cities and altered family life. The separation of work from the home modified women's domestic roles and fostered a newer, more modern conception of children and childhood. Progressive performers combined positivistic theories of criminology with new ideas about childhood to create a social welfare alternative to criminal courts to treat and control criminal and non-criminal misconduct by youths. Juvenile court represented one of several state agencies that Progressives used to "Americanize" immigrants and the poor; it provided a coercive mechanism to discriminate between "our" children and "other people's children," those of other ethnic backgrounds, cultures and classes (Rothman, 1980; Platt, 1977).

At the turn of the century, the conjunction of positivist criminology and medical analogies to "treat" criminals provided the conceptual undergirding of the "Rehabilitative Ideal," a prominent feature of all Progressive criminal justice reforms. Positivist ideology attributed crime and delinquency to antecedent forces that "determined" offender's behavior, rather than to "free will" and responsible moral actors. "Scientific" explanations of criminality encouraged an activist intervention strategy. Progressives introduced a variety of criminal justice reforms — probation, parole, indeterminate sentences and juvenile courts — all of which emphasized open-ended, informal, flexible policies and a case-by-case approach to the delinquent or criminal (Rothman, 1980; Allen, 1964). Progressive criminal justice reforms maximized discretion and deference to professional expertise because diagnosing the causes of and prescribing the cures for delinquency precluded uniform treatment or standardized criteria.

The reformers who created the juvenile court embraced positivist theory and attempted to implement the Rehabilitative Ideal more completely than did any other criminal justice innovators. In part, their greater enthusiasm reflected the social construction of childhood and the apparent prospects it promised of greater success. The ideology of *adolescence* emphasized the plasticity and malleability of young people. The reformers conceived of juvenile court professionals using indeterminate procedures and substituting a scientific and preventative approach for the criminal law's punitive policies. Under the guise of *parens patriae*, the juvenile court emphasized treatment, supervision and control rather than punishment. The juvenile court's "rehabilitative ideal" envisioned a specialized judge trained in social science and child development whose empathic qualities and insight would enable him or her to make individualized dispositions in the "best interests" of the child (Platt, 1977; Ryerson, 1978; Rothman, 1980). Reformers individualized their solicitude to treat the "whole child," and intervened to assure youths' *future welfare* rather than to *punish* them for their *past offenses*. The medical model of delinquency rejected notions of *deserved punishment* because children did not bear responsibility for their social or developmental circumstances and, therefore, their conduct. The treatment model rejected the idea of individual responsibility or proportionality embodied in retributive criminal law. Because offenses constituted only symptoms of "real needs," a child's delinquency theoretically affected neither the degree nor the duration of intervention because each child differed. Judges imposed indeterminate and non-proportional sentences that potentially continued for the duration of minority. A similar perspective prevailed in Europe. For example, the Belgian Director General of the Administration for Juvenile Justice observed that there is "no need anymore to be puzzled by the circumstances or coincidences that have brought the child before the judge rather than before a psychiatrist" (Huynen, 1967:202).

A strong relationship exists between juvenile courts' substantive goals and their procedural strategies. The rehabilitative juvenile court, for example, emphasized informal, flexible and discretionary procedures to implement its therapeutic goals. By separating children from adults and providing a rehabilitative alternative to punishment, juvenile courts rejected both the criminal law's jurisprudence and procedural safeguards such as juries and lawyers. Juvenile court judges discarded their judicial robes and elevated bench, conducted informal confidential hearings in their chambers to make proceedings more personal and private, limited public access to court proceedings and records, eliminated any implication of a criminal prosecution, employed a euphemistic vocabulary to minimize stigma, and found youths to be "delinquent" rather than convicted them of crimes (Schlossman, 1977). States' juvenile codes classified delinquency as civil matters rather than criminal proceedings. Because the important issues involved a child's background and welfare rather than the commission of a specific crime, juvenile courts dispensed with juries, lawyers, rules of evidence and formal procedures (Rothman, 1980). After the establishment of the first juvenile court in Chicago (1899), European countries enthusiastically followed that example and inaugurated comparable specialized judiciaries (the Netherlands: 1905; England, Germany: 1908; France, Belgium:1912). Belgium was the most progressive and completely abolished punishment for young offenders until the age of 16 (Walgrave, 1993).

Progressives sited the juvenile court on a number of cultural, legal, and criminological faultlines, and institutionalized several binary conceptions for the respective justice systems: child or adult, determinism or free will, dependent or responsible, treatment or punishment, welfare or deserts, procedural informality or formality, and discretion or the rule of law. Recent increases in serious youth crime and the erosion of the rehabilitative underpinnings of the juvenile court challenge these dichotomous constructs. Contemporary changes in juvenile justice law, administration and policy represent efforts to modify and reduce the Progressives' radical bifurcation between these competing cultural conceptions of children and social control.

1.2. Constitutional Domestication of the Juvenile Court

Procedure and substance intertwine inextricably in juvenile courts. Progressives envisioned an informal court that acted in the child's best interests. The U.S. Supreme Court in *In re Gault* (1967), emphasized the disjunctions between rehabilitative rhetoric and punitive reality and required greater procedural safeguards in juvenile courts. Three decades ago, the Supreme Court, in *Kent v. United States* (383 U.S. 541, 556 [1966]), observed that "the child receives the worst of both worlds: he gets neither the protections accorded to adults nor the solicitous care and regenerative treatment postulated for children." In the "worst of both worlds" of juvenile justice today, youths continue to receive neither therapy nor procedural justice, but instead endure punishment without criminal due process.

The Warren Court's due process revolution in the 1960s responded to social structural changes that began several decades earlier and critically reassessed criminal and juvenile justice practices. Two crucial demographic forces combined in the 1960s to provide the impetus for the due process revolution, the constitutional domestication of the juvenile court, the restructuring of penal practices, and ultimately the increased punitiveness of juvenile courts. First, the "baby boom" generation born after World War II created a demographic bulge, and rates of crime and juvenile delinquency began to escalate in the 1960s and into the 1970s as these youths moved through the age structure. This created the political impetus to "get tough" and repress — rather than rehabilitate — young offenders, and these pressures in turn led the court to provide greater procedural protections for youths charged with crimes. Second, the migration of African Americans from the rural South to the industrial North and West in the decades before and during World War II increased the urbanization of blacks, and placed the issues of racial equality and civil rights on the national political agenda (Lemann, 1993; Massey and Denton, 1993). Criminal and juvenile justice reforms constituted part of a broader constitutional program to protect the civil rights of racial minorities. The synergy of campus youth rebellions, "baby boom" crime rates and urban racial disorders in the 1960s precipitated a crisis of "law and order" and brought issues of criminal justice administration and civil rights to the legal forefront. The legal recognition of racial divisions and diversity eroded the social consensus about means and ends that sustained the Progressives' Rehabilitative Ideal (Rothman, 1978; Allen, 1981. Race provided the impetus for the Supreme Court to focus on procedural rights in states' juvenile and criminal justice systems to protect minorities' liberty interests. By the late 1980s, urban racial segregation and concentrated poverty among African Americans and the rise in youth gun violence and homicide fostered political perceptions of juvenile crime primarily as black youth crime and sustained more punitive and repressive policies (Feld, 1999).

The Supreme Court in *Gault*, (1967), began to transform the juvenile court into a very different institution than the Progressives contemplated. In *Gault*, the Supreme Court engrafted some formal procedures at trial onto the juvenile court's individualized treatment sentencing schema. Although the court did not intend its decisions to alter juvenile courts' therapeutic mission, in the aftermath of *Gault*, judicial, legislative and administrative changes have fostered a procedural and substantive convergence with adult criminal courts (Feld, 1991, 1993a). *In re Winship* (1970), required states to prove delinquency by the criminal law's standard of proof "beyond a reasonable doubt." *Breed v. Jones* (1975) applied the constitutional ban on double jeopardy and posited a functional equivalence between criminal trials and delinquency proceedings.

Gault's emphasis on procedural formality altered the focus of delinquency proceedings from a child's "best interests" to proof of legal guilt in an adversary hearing, and shifted the spotlight from paternalistic assessments of a youth's "real needs" to proof that the youth committed a crime. By formalizing the connection between criminal conduct and coercive intervention, the court made explicit a relationship previously implicit, unacknowledged and deliberately obscured. And, ironically, *Gault*'s insistence on criminal procedural safeguards may have legitimated more punitive sanctions for young offenders.

The increased procedural formality since *Gault* coincides with changes in legal theory and administrative practice from therapeutic, individualized dispositions toward more punitive, offense-based sentences (Feld, 1984; 1988b). Although the formal procedures of juvenile and criminal courts have converged under *Gault's* impetus, a substantial gulf remains between theory and reality, between "law on the books" and "law in action," between legal "rhetoric" and administrative "reality." Despite the criminalizing of juvenile courts, most U.S. states provide neither special procedures to protect youths from their own immaturity nor the full panoply of adult procedural safeguards (Feld, 1984). Instead, states treat juveniles just like adult criminal defendants when formal equality places youths at a practical disadvantage, and use less adequate juvenile court safeguards when those deficient procedures provide an advantage to the state.

Procedural justice hinges fundamentally on access to and the assistance of counsel. Despite *Gault's* (1967) formal legal changes, the promise of quality legal representation remains unrealized for many juveniles (Feld 1993b; U.S. General Accounting Office, 1995; American Bar Association [ABA] 1995). In many states, half or fewer of all juveniles receive the assistance of counsel to which the U.S. Constitution and state statutes entitle them (Feld, 1988a). Moreover, rates of representation vary substantially within states and suggest that differences in rates of appointment of counsel reflect judicial policies to discourage representation. The most common explanation for why so many juveniles are unrepresented is that judges find that they "waived" their right to counsel. Courts typically use the adult legal standard of "knowing, intelligent, and voluntary" under the "totality of the circumstances" to gauge the validity of juveniles' waivers of rights (*Fare v. Michael C*, 1979). Because juveniles possess less ability than adults to deal effectively with the legal system (Grisso 1980), formal equality results in practical procedural inequality. Proponents of restorative justice in non-judicial settings necessarily will confront the reality that many states currently fail to provide adequate procedural justice for youths even within a formal judicial setting. How will youths' legal interests be protected in less legally structured environments such as family group conferences or mediation?

1.3. Punishment and the Juvenile Court

In the decades since *Gault*, legislative, judicial and administrative changes have modified juvenile courts' jurisdiction and jurisprudence, and furthered their convergence with criminal courts. These interrelated developments — removal of non-criminal status offenders from juvenile court jurisdiction, waiver of serious offenders to the adult system, and an increased emphasis on punishment in sentencing delinquents — constitute a form of criminological "triage," crucial components of the criminalizing of the juvenile court, and elements of the erosion of the theoretical and practical differences between the two systems (Feld, 1991, 1993a). This triage strategy removes many middle-class, white and female non-criminal status offenders from the juvenile court; simultaneously transfers persistent, violent and disproportionally minority youths to criminal court for prosecution as adults; and imposes increasingly punitive sanctions on those middle-range criminal delinquent offenders who remain under the jurisdiction of the juvenile court. These jurisdictional changes at the "soft" and "hard" ends of the youth continuum have transformed the juvenile court into a scaled-down criminal court.

Status Offenses

Legislative recognition that juvenile courts often failed to realize their benevolent purposes has led to a strategic retrenchment of juvenile courts' jurisdiction over non-criminal misconduct such as truancy or incorrigibility, behavior that would not be a crime if committed by an adult. In the 1970s, critics objected that juvenile courts' status jurisdiction treated non-criminal offenders indiscriminately like criminal delinquents, disabled families and other sources of referral through one-sided intervention, and posed insuperable legal issues for the court (Rubin, 1985). Judicial and legislative disillusionment with juvenile courts' responses to non-criminal youths led to diversion, deinstitutionalization and decriminalization reforms that have removed much of the "soft" end of juvenile court clientele (Klein, 1979; Schwartz, 1989). These reforms represent a strategic legislative and judicial withdrawal from "child saving," an acknowledgment of the limited utility of coercive intervention to provide for child welfare, a reduced judicial role in enforcing normative concepts of childhood and a diminished prevention mission. Many restorative justice proposals to divert youths to non-judicial settings on an informal basis may simply replicate the decades-long experience with "decriminalizing" status offenders and referring them to other agencies. Without adequate criteria or safeguards, such proposals may also repeat juvenile courts' net-widening experiences and subject to informal social control many youths who would never have entered the formal criminal justice system (Klein, 1979; Decker, 1985; Polk, 1984).

Waiver of Serious Juvenile Offenders to Adult Criminal Court

A second jurisdictional change entails the criminalizing of serious juvenile offenders, as courts and legislatures increasingly transfer chronic and violent youths from juvenile to criminal courts for prosecution as adults (Feld, 1987; 1995; Snyder and Sickmund, 1995). Transfer laws simultaneously attempt to resolve both fundamental crime control issues and the ambivalence embedded in our cultural construction of youth. The jurisprudential conflicts reflect many of the current sentencing policy debates: the tensions between rehabilitation or incapacitation and retribution, between basing decisions on characteristics of the individual offender or the seriousness of the offense, between discretion and rules, and between indeterminacy and determinacy. Waiver laws attempt to reconcile the contradiction posed when the child is a criminal and the criminal is a child, and to devise administrative procedures and substantive criteria to enable decision makers to select from among the competing cultural images of youths as responsible and culpable offenders, or as immature and salvageable children.

Changes in waiver laws also occur against the backdrop of the continuing structural transformation of cities, the shift from a manufacturing to a service and information economy increasingly located in suburbs, the rise of the urban "underclass," and the increase in youth violence, especially among minority juveniles (Massey and Denton, 1993; Katz, 1993; Wilson, 1987, 1996; National Research Council, 1993). Blumstein (1995) attributes the dramatic increase in homicide rates among adolescents and young adults to the proliferation of guns in the illegal drug industry beginning in the mid-1980s. The homicide rate for African Americans, which typically averaged about five time that of whites, increased even more sharply than did the white rate, doubling between 1987 and 1991 and tripling between 1984 and 1991 (Blumstein, 1995). The proportion of firearm homicides committed by youths aged 15 to 19 also increased from about 63% of all murders in the decade prior to the mid-1980s to 85% in 1992. Blumstein (1995) links the age-race-gun specific pattern homicides to the "crack cocaine" drug distribution industry that emerged in minority communities in large cities during the late 1980s. Others attribute minority youth violence to the structural transformation of cities, the de-industrialization of urban America, and racial hypersegregation and concentrated poverty (Wilson, 1996; Massey and Denton, 1993). The crack drug industry attracted many urban, African-American males who lacked alternative economic opportunities, and escalated patterns of violence.

In response to the rise in youth homicide and gun violence in the late 1980s, almost every state amended its waiver statutes and other provisions of its juvenile codes in a frantic effort to get tough and stem the rising tide of youth violence (Snyder and Sickmund, 1995; Torbet et al, 1996). In most states, judges decide whether a youth is a criminal or a child in a waiver hearing based on their discretionary assessment of youths' "amenability to treatment" or "dangerousness" (Snyder and Sickmund, 1995; Feld, 1995). The inherent subjectivity of waiver criteria permits a variety of racial inequalities and geographic disparities to occur when judges interpret and apply these vague laws (Feld, 1990; Podkopacz and Feld, 1995, 1996). Judicial discretion also frustrates rational social control and confounds criminal courts' response to young career criminals. A lack of fit between juvenile waiver decisions and criminal court sentencing practices often produces a "punishment gap" that allows many chronic and active young criminals to fall between the cracks when they make the transition between the two systems (Feld, 1987; 1995). By contrast, when judicial waiver decisions, legislatively excluded offenses or prosecutorial charging decisions target violent young offenders, these youths often receive substantially longer sentences than do their counterparts who remain in juvenile court simply because of their new found "adult" status (Podkopacz and Feld, 1995, 1996).

Recent changes in waiver statutes signal a fundamental inversion in juvenile court jurisprudence from treatment to punishment, from rehabilitation to retribution, from immature child to responsible criminal. The common over-arching legislative strategy reflects a jurisprudential shift from the *principle of individualized justice* to the *principle of offense*, from judges' clinical assessments of offenders' "amenability to treatment" to an emphasis on the seriousness of the offense. States use offense criteria as dispositional guidelines to structure and limit judicial discretion, to guide prosecutorial charging decisions, or to automatically exclude certain youths from juvenile court jurisdiction.

Regardless of the details of these legislative strategies, these efforts to crack down and get tough repudiate rehabilitation and judicial discretion, narrow juvenile court jurisdiction and reduce its clientele, base youths' "adult" status increasingly on the offense charged, and reflect a shift toward more punitive sentencing policies. Whether the legislature makes the forum decision by excluding offenses, or the prosecutor does so on a discretionary basis via concurrent jurisdiction, these laws reduce or remove both discretionary judicial authority and juvenile courts' clientele. Offense exclusion rejects the philosophical premise of juvenile courts that they can aid youths, and denies courts the opportunity to try to accomplish this without regard to the "real needs" of the offending youths. Because of differences in rates of violent offending by race, facially neutral policies that target violent crimes have a disproportionate impact on minority juveniles who increasingly find themselves prosecuted in criminal court as adults. Finally, the impetus to try more young offenders as adults exposes at least some youths to the possibility of capital punishment for the crimes they committed as juveniles.

Punishing Delinquent Offenders

The same public impetus and political pressures to waive the most serious young offenders to criminal courts impel juvenile courts to get tough and punish more severely those remaining criminal delinquents — the residual "less bad of the worst." Within the past two decades, offense-based strategies have increasingly displaced the offender-oriented rationales of rehabilitation and indeterminacy for sentencing both adult offenders and juveniles (Tonry, 1996; Cullen and Gilbert, 1982). Political pressures to get tough on youth crime and to control lenient judicial discretion provide legislative impetus to increase the certainty and predictability of juvenile sanctions, and to displace therapeutic, individualized dispositions with punitive sentences of incarceration. Both in legal theory and practice, many states use offense criteria — determinate or mandatory minimum sentencing statutes or administrative sentencing guidelines — to regulate juvenile court judges' sentencing decisions (Feld, 1988b). In actual practice, a youth's present offense and prior record dominate juvenile court sentencing decisions. Evaluation research of juvenile court sentencing practices, treatment effectiveness and conditions of confinement reveal increasingly punitive juvenile justice and corrections systems. These various indicators strongly suggest that despite juvenile courts' persisting rehabilitative rhetoric, the reality of *treating* juveniles closely resembles *punishing* adult criminals (Feld, 1988b). This jurisprudential and administrative convergence erodes the justifications for a separate justice system for younger offenders.

Several indicators reveal that juvenile court judges *punish* youths for their *past offense* rather than *treat* them for their *future welfare*. Currently, nearly half of states use determinate or mandatory minimum sentencing provisions that base a youth's disposition on the offense he or she committed, rather than his or her "real needs," to regulate at least some aspects of sentence duration, institutional commitment or release (Feld, 1988b; Sheffer, 1995; Torbet et al, 1996). These provisions use offense criteria to rationalize sentencing decisions, to increase the penal bite of juvenile court sanctions, and to enable legislators symbolically to demonstrate their "toughness" (Altschuler, 1994).

Two general conclusions emerge clearly from the empirical evaluations of juvenile court judges' sentencing practices. First, a youth's present offense and prior record account for most of the variance in juvenile court sentences that can be explained, and reinforce the criminal orientation of juvenile courts (Clarke and Koch, 1980; McCarthy and Smith, 1986; Feld, 1989). Second, after controlling for offense variables, juvenile courts' "individualized justice" often produces racial disparities in the sentencing of minority offenders (McCarthy and Smith, 1986; Krisberg et al., 1987). The individualized discretion inherent in the juvenile courts' treatment ideology is often synonymous with racial discrimination (see, for example, Kempf-Leonard et al.,1995; Bishop and Frazier, 1988; 1996; Pope and Feyerherm, 1992).

Evaluations of conditions of confinement and treatment effectiveness also dispute juvenile courts' therapeutic claims. Progressives expressed considerable optimism that delinquents' youthfulness and greater malleability would enable them to respond more readily to treatment. A comprehensive assessment of rehabilitation research conducted by the National Academy of Sciences questioned both the efficacy of juvenile justice interventions and the assumption that youths manifest greater treatment responsiveness than adults (Sechrest et al., 1979). Evaluations of juvenile rehabilitation programs provide scant support for the conclusion that juvenile institutions either effectively treat youths or lower recidivism rates (Lab and Whitehead, 1988; Whitehead and Lab, 1989). Martinson's (1974:25) generally negative observation that "[W]ith few and isolated exceptions, the rehabilitative efforts that have been reported so far have had no appreciable affect on recidivism," challenged the fundamental premise of the therapeutic juvenile court. More recent evaluations of the ability of juvenile correctional intervention to lower recidivism rates counsel skepticism about the availability of programs that consistently or systematically rehabilitate adult or serious juvenile offenders (Sechrest et al., 1979; Whitehead and Lab, 1989). One methodological strategy to identify "what works" entails meta-analysis, or studies of studies. A meta-analysis of juvenile correctional treatment evaluations meeting certain criteria of methodological rigor concluded that "[t]he results are far from encouraging for rehabilitation proponents (Lab and Whitehead, 1988:77)."

Despite the generally negative results, recent evaluation researchers continue the quest for the elusive "rehabilitative" grail. While proponents of "rehabilitation" have not persuasively refuted the general conclusion that "nothing works" in juvenile or adult corrections, they strenuously resist it. Advocates of "treatment" offer literature reviews, meta-analyses or program descriptions that stress that some types of intervention may have positive effects on selected clients under certain conditions (Greenwood and Zimring, 1985; Gendreau and Ross, 1987; Fagan, 1990). Other meta-analysts also report guardedly positive treatment effects (Garrett, 1985; Roberts and Camasso, 1991; Izzo and Ross, 1990; Andrews et al., 1990; Lipsey 1992). However, even Palmer's (1991:340) optimistic assessment of the rehabilitation of "rehabilitation" concludes only that "several methods seem promising, but none have been shown to usually produce major reductions [in recidivism] when applied broadly to typical composite samples of offenders."

There are a variety of reasons why juvenile courts' and correctional institutions' claims to rehabilitate young offenders remain unproven at best. Many evaluations of treatment effectiveness lack methodological rigor (Sechrest et al., 1979). Others may use insufficiently sensitive outcome measures (Fagan, 1990). Many treatment programs lack a theoretical rationale or consistent intervention strategies based upon that rationale. Some evaluation studies fail to assess whether the program staff actually implemented the prescribed treatment with integrity (Gendreau and Ross, 1987). Finally, even if viable rehabilitative strategies exist, clinicians lack techniques or tools with which to classify offenders for appropriate forms of intervention to maximize their "responsivity" (Sechrest, 1987). The failure to show treatment effects may reflect methodological flaws, poorly conceived or implemented programs, an inability to accurately match subjects with programs, or the absence of viable methods to successfully treat serious or chronic young offenders.

Although research on the elements of effective correctional programs for youths suggests some direction, either providing more humane, short-term institutional experiences or improving youths' long-term life chances, most states choose not to provide these types of programs or services. Rather, they incarcerate juveniles in euphemistically sanitized youth prisons. Thus, even if some "treatment" programs might work for some young offenders under some conditions, that theoretical possibility does not justify confining youths "for their own good" with fewer procedural safeguards than those provided to adults offenders, particularly when favorable outcomes remain far from certain. And, even if treatment programs may produce some marginal improvements for some young offenders, do those benefits sufficiently outweigh the inevitable racial disparities that result from the exercise of individualized discretion to classify for treatment? While some "model" programs may reduce recidivism rates somewhat, the likelihood seems remote that public officials actually will provide such treatment services for most delinquents when they confront fiscal constraints, budget deficits and competition from more politically potent interest groups. Rather, organizational imperatives to achieve "economies of scale" mandate confining ever-larger numbers of youths in institutions and thereby preclude the possibility of matching offenders with appropriate programs. Finally, if states do not appropriate significant resources and correctional administrators do not provide effective services in a responsive environment, then do any practical differences exist between treatment and punishment?

2. Inherent Contradiction of the Juvenile Court

The foregoing jurisdictional, jurisprudential and procedural changes have transformed the juvenile court from its original model as a social service agency into a deficient, second-rate criminal court that provides young people with neither positive treatment nor criminal procedural justice. It effectively punishes young offenders, but uses procedures under which no adult would consent to be tried if he or she faced the prospect of a term of confinement in a secure facility. The recent changes in procedures, jurisdiction and jurisprudence reflect confusion about the role of juvenile courts, ambivalence about the social control of young offenders, and the conflicted impulses engendered when a child is a criminal and a criminal is a child.

Juvenile court judges incarcerate youths in prison-like settings for substantial terms, but use procedures clearly inferior to those available to adult criminal defendants. Public and political concerns about drugs, youth crime, guns and violence sustain public policies to repress rather than rehabilitate young offenders. Politicians use simplistic slogans ("adult crime, adult time"), propose popular get tough policies, and pander to public fears rather than lead and educate the public about the structural roots and social complexity of crime and the limits of justice systems' ability to reduce it.

At the present time, European practices and legislations have not evidenced as punitive a reaction to juvenile crime as has occurred in the U.S. However, the increasing unemployment rate since the mid-1970s and the lack of successful integration strategies for immigrants — from Northern African countries, former colonies and, recently, Eastern European countries — have provoked a growing concern for public safety and a decreasing tolerance for deviance. This is certainly reflected in public discourse and in the media, although not yet manifest in daily juvenile justice practices and legislation. Some recent legislative modifications augur changes in a more punitive direction (e.g., in the Netherlands, in France and especially in England and Wales, after the Bulger case). Similarly, the use of waivers or of incarcerating sanctions has not grown dramatically (Mehlbye and Walgrave, 1998). Perhaps the more deeply rooted tradition of social welfare in Europe provides a buffer against the punitive tendency to "get tough" than in the U.S. (Messner and Rosenfeld, 1994). Europeans also appreciate the threats to juveniles' legal rights posed by the welfare-oriented juvenile justice systems (Van de Kerchove, 1997; Gatti and Verde, 1991; Doek, 1994). Proposals in many countries improve youths' legal position and several international guidelines affect the jurisdiction and treatment of juvenile offenders (Dünkel, 1991; Doek, 1994). However, these proposals fail to overcome the fundamental conflict between welfare concerns and legal principles, because they continue to emphasize the priority of rehabilitative purposes in juvenile justice systems.

The social welfare model of the traditional juvenile court, in the U.S. as well as in Europe, represents a failed policy strategy. The juvenile court's creators envisioned a social service agency in a judicial setting, and attempted to fuse its welfare mission with the power of state coercion. If we formulated a child social welfare policy *ab initio*, would we designate a court as the most appropriate agency through which to deliver social services *and* would we make criminality a condition precedent to the receipt of services? If we would not use a court to deliver social services, does the fact that a youth committed a crime confer any special competency on it as a welfare agency? Many young people who desperately need social services do not commit crimes, and many youths who commit crimes do not require or will not respond to social services. In short, criminality represents an inaccurate and haphazard criterion upon which to allocate social services. Because states deny adequate social welfare to meet the needs of *all* young people, juvenile courts' welfare and treatment ideology ultimately legitimate the exercise of judicial coercion of some youths *because of their criminality*.

Quite apart from its unsuitability as a social welfare agency, the individualized justice of a "rehabilitative" juvenile court fosters lawlessness and detracts from its utility as a court of law as well. Because each child's "real needs" differ, pursuit of the *idea* of treatment necessarily entails individualized discretion, indeterminacy, a rejection of proportionality, and a disregard of normative valuations of the seriousness of behavior. This chapter's earlier review of evaluations of the impact of "treatment" on recidivism rates questioned the availability of programs that consistently "rehabilitate" juvenile offenders *and* noted the discriminatory impact of discretionary decisions. Even if some programs produce modest incremental improvements in the lives of some young offenders, do those benefits justify the inevitable inequalities and racial disparities that result from the exercise of individualized discretion? Discrimination, abuses of discretion, and racial, gender, geographic and socioeconomic disparities constitute almost inevitable corollaries of a treatment ideology that lacks either a scientific basis or technical foundation. Juvenile courts' procedural deficiencies also reflect their continued adherence to a treatment ideology. The persisting absence or co-optation of defense counsel in many jurisdictions reduces the likelihood that courts will adhere to existing legal mandates. Closed, informal, and confidential delinquency proceedings reduce the visibility and accountability of the justice process, and preclude external checks on coercive interventions.

The fundamental shortcoming of the juvenile court's welfare *idea* reflects a failure of conception rather than simply a failure of implementation. Juvenile courts attempt to combine social welfare and penal social control functions in one agency, inevitably do both badly and, in practice, subordinate welfare concerns to crime control considerations. Providing for child welfare represents a societal responsibility rather than a judicial one. Juvenile courts lack adequate resources to meet child welfare needs, and may lack sufficient social services exactly because of the gender, class and racial characteristics of their clients (Krisberg and Austin, 1993; Grubb and Lazerson, 1982; van Sloun, 1988; Queloz, 1991; Walgrave, 1994). The conflict between concern for child welfare and punitive responses to violations of criminal law forms the root of the ambivalence embedded in the juvenile court. People experience hostile impulses toward "other peoples' children" whom they regard as a threat to themselves and their own children, and this reaction undermines benevolent aspirations and elevates concerns for their control.

The juvenile court inevitably subordinates social welfare to criminal social control because of its built-in penal focus. Legislatures do not define juvenile courts' social welfare jurisdiction on the basis of characteristics of children for which they are not responsible and for whom effective intervention could be beneficial. For example, juvenile court law does not define eligibility for services or create an enforceable right or entitlement based upon young people's lack of access to decent education, lack of adequate housing or nutrition, unmet health needs, or impoverished families, *none of which are their fault*. In all of these instances, children bear the social burdens of their parents' circumstances literally as innocent bystanders (Grubb and Lazerson, 1982; National Research Council, 1993; Braithwaite, 1989; Wiles, 1993). If states based juvenile courts' jurisdiction on young people's needs for social welfare, then such a policy would declare a broad category of "at-risk" children eligible for public assistance. Such a policy would require substantial social resources, structural changes and public commitment to children's welfare.

Instead, states' juvenile codes define juvenile courts' jurisdiction based on a youth committing a crime, a prerequisite that detracts from a compassionate response. Unlike disadvantaged social conditions, criminal behavior represents the one characteristic for which adolescent offenders do bear at least partial responsibility. As long as juvenile courts define eligibility for "services" in terms of criminality, they highlight those aspect of youths that rationally elicit the least sympathy and ignore environmental conditions that evoke a greater desire to help. Thus, the defining characteristic used by juvenile courts to determine eligibility simply reinforces the public's antipathy to young people by emphasizing that they are law violators. Recent changes in juvenile waiver and sentencing policies emphasize punishment, accountability and personal responsibility; re-enforce juvenile courts' penal foundations; and reduce the legitimacy of youths' claims to compassion or humanitarian assistance.

3. JUST DESERTS' RESPONSE WHEN THE CHILD IS A CRIMINAL AND THE CRIMINAL IS A CHILD: YOUTHFULNESS AS A FORMAL MITIGATING FACTOR IN SENTENCING

If we uncouple social welfare from penal social control, then no need remains for a separate juvenile court for young offenders. If the child is a criminal and penal social control constitutes the "real" reason for formal intervention, then we should abolish juvenile courts and try young offenders in criminal courts alongside their adult counterparts. But if the criminal is a child, then we must modify criminal courts' procedures and sentencing provisions to accommodate the youthfulness of some defendants. In particular, substantive justice requires a rationale to sentence younger offenders differently — and more *leniently* — than older defendants, a formal recognition of *youthfulness as a mitigating factor in sentencing*. Procedural justice requires providing youths with full procedural parity with adult defendants and additional safeguards to account for the disadvantages of youths in the justice system. In combination, these substantive and procedural modifications can avoid the "worst of both worlds," provide youths with protections functionally equivalent to those accorded adults, and "do justice" in sentencing.

A proposal to abolish juvenile courts constitutes neither an unqualified endorsement of punishment nor a primitive throw-back to earlier centuries' views of young people as miniature adults (Ainsworth, 1991; 1995; Feld, 1988b). Rather, it honestly acknowledges that juvenile courts currently engage in criminal social control, and asserts that younger offenders in a criminal justice system *deserve* less severe consequences for their misdeeds than do more mature offenders *simply* because they are *young*. Formulating a deserts-based youth sentencing policy entails two tasks: providing a rationale to sentence young offenders differently, and *more leniently*, than older defendants; and developing an administrative mechanism — what might be called a "youth discount" — to formally implement youthfulness as a mitigating factor in sentencing (Feld, 1988b, 1993a, 1996). Explicitly punishing younger offenders rests on the premise that adolescents possess sufficient moral reasoning, cognitive capacity, and volitional controls to hold them responsible and accountable for their behavior. But the younger offenders do not possess the same degree of criminal responsibility as adults. The social construction of adolescence represents a developmental moratorium during which young people require an opportunity to "learn to be responsible" without life-shattering consequences (Zimring, 1982). A youth discount constitutes one component of this moratorium, and provides a developmental sliding scale of criminal responsibility and sanctions.

To what extent does or should youthfulness mitigate the degree of consequences for engaging in criminal behavior? Should the criminal law treat a 14 year old as the moral equivalent of a 24 year old and impose an identical sentence? Elsewhere, I have argued that young people *do differ somewhat* from adults in ways that should affect criminal sentencing policies (Feld, 1988b, 1993a, 1996, 1999). These differences stem from physical, psychological or developmental characteristics of young people, and as by-products of the legal and social construction of youth. These structural and developmental factors affect young peoples' opportunity to learn to be responsible, to develop fully the ability to make mature, adult-like judgments, and thus the punishment they "deserve" for criminal choices.

Deserved punishment emphasizes censure and condemnation for blameworthy choices (von Hirsch 1976; 1986; 1993). As long as the criminal law rests on a moral foundation, the idea of blameworthiness remains central to ascribing guilt and allocating punishment. Penalties proportionate to the *seriousness* of the crime reflect the connection between the nature of the conduct and its blameworthiness. Because commensurate punishment proportions sanctions according to the seriousness of the offense, it shifts the analytical focus to the meaning of *seriousness*. Two elements — *harm* and *culpability* — define the seriousness of an offense. Evaluations of harm focus on the degree of injury inflicted, risk created or value taken. A perpetrator's age matters little when assessing the harm inflicted or the need for social defense.

The *seriousness* of a crime also includes the quality of the actor's *choice* to engage in the conduct that produced the harm. Just deserts theory and criminal law grading principles base the degree of punishment an actor deserves on culpability, rather than simply harm. For example, an actor may cause the death of another person with premeditation and deliberation, intentionally, "in the heat of passion," recklessly, negligently or accidentally. The criminal law treats the same objective consequence or harm, the death of another person, very differently depending upon the nature and quality of the choice made. In particular, because punishment entails censure for blameworthy choices, the *proportionality* of sentences reflects actors' culpability rather than just the harm their behavior caused.

It is with respect to the culpability of *choices* — the blameworthiness of acting in a particular harm-producing way — that the issue of youthfulness acquires special salience. When sentencing within a framework of deserved punishment, it would be fundamentally unjust to impose the same penalty upon offenders who do not share equal culpability. A person's responsibility as a moral agent for his or her actions provides the precondition to legally deserved consequences. But if young people are neither as fully responsible as nor the moral equals of adults, then they do not *deserve* the same legal consequences even for their blameworthy and harmful misconduct.

It is beyond the scope of this chapter to provide the jurisprudential and developmental psychological rationales for youthfulness as a mitigating factor in sentencing (Feld, 1996, 1999). Suffice it to say that the criminal law regards young actors differently from adults exactly because they have not yet had sufficient opportunity to fully internalize moral norms, to develop sufficient empathic identification with others, to acquire adequate moral appreciation, or to fully develop the ability to restrain their actions. They possess neither the rationality — cognitive capacity — nor the self-control — volitional capacity — to equate their criminal responsibility with that of adults. Developmental psychological research that analyzes the quality of judgment and self-control of adolescents indicates that youths differ from adults on a number of crucial dimensions relevant to criminal responsibility: breadth of experience; short-term versus long-term temporal perspective; attitude toward risk; impulsivity; and the importance attached to peer influence (Scott, 1992; Scott et al., 1995; Cauffman and Steinberg, 1995; Steinberg and Cauffman, 1996). Three developmentally unique attributes of youth — temporal perspective, attitudes toward and acceptance of risk, and susceptibility to peer influences — may affect young peoples' maturity of judgment in ways that distinguish them from adults and that affect their degree of criminal responsibility and deserved punishment. Adolescents' emotional and psychosocial developmental processes and life circumstances restrict their capacity fully to appreciate the consequences of their behavior or to exercise self-control. They simply have not had adequate opportunity to internalize restraints or to develop the capacity to make autonomous judgments. "Growing up" takes time and practice, and the chance to make occasional mistakes (Zimring 1982).

Shorter sentences for reduced responsibility represent a more modest and attainable reason to treat young people differently from adults than the rehabilitative justifications advanced by Progressive child savers. Exercising criminal social control while protecting young people from the full penal consequences of their poor judgment reflects a policy to preserve their life chances for the future, when they presumably will make more responsible choices. The law simultaneously holds young offenders accountable for their acts because they possess some criminal capacity, and yet mitigates the consequences because youths' choices entail less blameworthiness than do those of adults. Because criminal behavior represents the "real reason" youths appear in criminal court, they would receive the criminal procedural safeguards of all criminal defendants. Indeed, the developmental justifications for shorter sentences also provide rationales to provide youths with additional such safeguards that more adequately recognize their limitations in dealing with the justice system.

A criminal sentencing policy that integrates youths' lesser opportunity to learn to be responsible, reduced culpability and proportionality of sanctions would provide younger offenders with categorical fractional reductions of adult sentences. Treating youthfulness as a formal mitigating sentencing factor represents a social, moral and criminal policy judgment about *deserved punishment*. This categorical approach could take the form of an explicit youth discount at sentencing. Such fractional reductions already partly exist in several European countries, such as France, where the maximum possible detention for juvenile offenders from the ages of 13 to 17 is half of the duration for adults, and in Italy, where the maximum for the ages of 14 to 17 is two-thirds. Both countries, however, regard such penal incarcerations as exceptional, and give priority to measures with an explicit re-educative objective (Mehlbye and Walgrave, 1998).

The proposal here would adopt a punitive rationale as the basis for intervention, and explicitly provide for a differential scale based on age. A 14 year old offender, for example, might receive 25 to 33% of the adult penalty, a 16 year old defendant, 50 to 66%, and an 18 year old adult, the full penalty, as presently occurs. The "deeper discounts" for younger offenders correspond to the developmental continuum of responsibility, and the truncated opportunity to learn and develop a capacity for self-control. A youth discount functions as a sliding scale of criminal responsibility, so that 14 year old youths enjoy a greater mitigation of blameworthiness than 17 year olds.

Discounted sentences that preserve younger offenders' life chances require that the maximum sentences they receive remain considerably below those imposed on adults. Even explicitly punitive youth sentences do not require judges or correctional authorities to confine young people with adults in jails and prisons, or simply to warehouse them. States should maintain separate, age-segregated facilities for the protection of both younger offenders and older inmates. Because all youths eventually will return to the community, states should also provide youths with resources for voluntary self-improvement and "room to reform."

A proposal to abolish juvenile courts and to try all young offenders in an integrated justice system represents a commitment to honesty about state coercion.

States bring young offenders who commit crimes to juvenile court for social control and to punish them, not to deliver social services. Juvenile courts' rehabilitative claims fly in the face of reality, undermine their legitimacy and impair their ability to function as agents of criminal social control. Juvenile courts' fundamental flaw resides in the very *idea* that we can successfully combine criminal social control and social welfare in one system.

4. Is "Restorative Justice" an Oxymoron?

Previous sections of this chapter analyzed the theoretical and practical failures of the "rehabilitative" juvenile court, and sketched the bare outlines of an explicitly punitive justice system response to youth crime. This was done, in part, to provide a conceptual framework for a series of questions posed to proponents of restorative justice. The answers to these questions may indicate whether restorative justice constitutes: an attempt to revive rehabilitation; a return to an earlier, pre-*Gault* system of informal, discretionary coercive social control; a series of dispositional add-ons to current juvenile and criminal justice sentencing options; a fundamental threat to a liberal democracy's tenets of individual liberty and the rule of law; or an alternative conception of social control and a justice system.

What is restorative justice? In what ways do its "balanced" emphases on offenders, victims and communities differ from the traditional conception of a criminal violation as an offense against the state as the collective community (Bazemore and Umbreit, 1995)? Is restorative justice, as it is sometimes and variously described by its proponents a program, an idea, a policy, a strategy, a conceptual framework or a paradigm shift?

What is the relationship between the various conceptions of restorative justice and the juvenile justice system? Sometimes, proponents appear to envision victim-offender mediation or family group conferences as informal practices that occur outside of the formal justice system. To the extent that they constitute informal programs on the periphery of the system, in what ways do they differ from diversionary strategies that have been employed by the juvenile courts for nearly 25 years? To the extent that these informal programs resemble diversion conceptually, how do proponents of restorative justice propose to deal with the now-well-documented problems associated with those practices — net-widening, informal coercion exercised on a discretionary basis on the periphery, the absence of objective criteria for making routing decisions, and the discriminatory consequences of inclusion or exclusion?

On other occasions, proponents of restorative justice appear to locate their programs within the formal justice system. To the extent that restorative justice practitioners employ programs like restitution or community service, do they differ in any significant way from the array of intermediate sanctions currently available and used regularly in juvenile and criminal justice systems (Tonry and Morris 1994)? If restorative justice programs that resemble intermediate sanctions entail more than repackaging of familiar community-based dispositions, how do they provide a conceptual alternative to intermediate punishments?

Finally, some proponents envision restorative justice as "transformative," a "paradigm shift," and a replacement of traditional welfare or penal models of juvenile justice (Bazemore and Walgrave, this volume). To the extent that restorative justice constitutes something "really different," it too, must address fundamental issues of procedure and substance. In the rehabilitative juvenile court, procedural informality coexisted with substantive discretion to act in a child's best interests. Within a just deserts framework, procedural formality and the rule of law bolster substantive equality achieved through penal principles of determinacy and proportionality.

What rationale provides a procedural and substantive framework for a system of restorative justice? How do concepts like restoring offenders, restoring victims, community bonds, injury, dignity or the like provide a conceptual framework for structuring a justice process? Some restorative justice advocates recognize this fundamental problem and try to formulate responses to it (Van Ness and Strong, 1997; Walgrave and Geudens, 1996). However, many questions remain unresolved and a satisfying solution may not be found within the fully restorative conceptual framework. Do procedural informality and substantive discretion reflect restorative justice's communitarian roots? After *Gault*, the traditional rehabilitative juvenile court experienced considerable difficulty providing delinquents with access to, and defining the appropriate role for, defense counsel. Thus, the right to and role of defense counsel provides a useful test for thinking about the broader role of procedures within a restorative justice framework as well.

If we envision restorative justice as something "outside" the formal justice system, does any right to or role for counsel exist? In juvenile justice, the formal initiation of the legal process — the filing of a petition — provides the legal threshold for appointment of counsel. If a youth is dealt with informally in a mediation or conference without the filing of formal charges, what mechanism exists to trigger the right to counsel? And, if the outcome of a mediation or conference includes an imposition on a youth's liberty interests, (e.g. restitution, community service or other restrictions on autonomy), what mechanisms exist to protect him or her?

"Due process" safeguards and lawyers operate to protect citizens from impositions by the state. But what mechanisms exist to protect youths from impositions by the "community" acting in lieu of the state? Youths "in trouble," especially those from disadvantaged backgrounds, are especially vulnerable to imposition by adult authorities. Moreover, the research on police interrogation of juveniles strongly suggests that most parents cannot protect their children in the thralls of the law and often aggravate their plight (Grisso, 1980). What protections exist for a youth in mediation or a conference that may result in some type of coercive, i.e. non-voluntary, disposition? What does "voluntary" mean in this type of setting? And, what role, if any, can a lawyer play in this type of lawless proceeding, assuming an attorney is even available? In short, does restorative justice simply provide a rationale to reinvent the old, informal pre-*Gault* juvenile court that disregarded youths' procedural rights?

While some concede that a youth has a right to a formal proceeding if he or she denies involvement or wishes to appeal a community order, what mechanisms exist to inform youths of and implement that right? Juveniles have had a right to counsel for more than three decades, and many juvenile court judges simply ignored their constitutional and statutory rights with impunity (Feld, 1993b; ABA, 1995). The absence of lawyers at trial also limited juveniles' ability to appeal adverse decisions or dispositions. Within an informal procedural framework of restorative justice, do juveniles have a right to appeal a family-group-conference determination about restitution or community service? How will they know of a right to appeal? How will they perfect an appeal? To whom will they appeal? Will they receive a trial *de novo*, or simply a review of the conference proceedings? Will a record of those proceedings be maintained? Will admissions or statements made in the course of a mediation or group conference be admissible subsequently in formal legal proceedings? Will a youth receive the restorative justice equivalent of a *Miranda* warning advising them of the potential adverse legal consequences of participating in the informal process?

Issues of substantive justice also loom large within a framework of restorative justice and implicate the principle of legality and the rule of law. What are the norms of the "community" that a family group conference will invoke? Again, the threshold question of informal or formal norms arises. If restorative justice envisions informal enforcement of "community" norms, who defines the "community" or the "norms"? For example, Brown and Polk (1996) describe the "restorative" response of a Tasmanian community's fear of crime caused by disorderly youths in public spaces. Are other "disorderly" youths entitled to representation on a conference panel as representatives of their community? Who decides the makeup of a panel, and according to what criteria? Are members of inner-city street gangs also members of the community and entitled to representation and participation? What is a "community" in the anomic environs of many larger, disorganized crack-devastated urban milieus? To the extent that each panel creates its own norms to resolve the dispute presented by its unique offender-victim-community triad, does restorative justice amount to a jury system in which the members decide guilt and sanction without any instruction by a judge as to the law they apply? Is restorative justice the kadi justice that Matza (1964) described, in which every decision is unique and decided on its own "merits" but without defining the criteria of merit?

To the extent that restorative justice relies upon formal norms, i.e., the criminal law, as its defining characteristic, it encounters the same conceptual difficulties as the rehabilitative juvenile court. Of all of the indicators of breakdowns in a youth's relationship with other people and the community, why does offending take precedence? Youths who are homeless, hungry, pushed out of school, ill, or just desperately poor and disadvantaged seemingly would have greater claims to "restoration" than those who simply offend. Once restorative justice employs a penal premise, then issues of formal procedural justice immediately emerge as a prerequisite to all coercive impositions and we are back to the conceptual flaw of the traditional juvenile court.

Restorative justice must address substantive questions of proportionality or limits. Retributive proportionality uses the seriousness of a crime to define both the upper and lower limits of punishment, censure and blame. The juvenile court's rehabilitative ideology simply subordinated proportionality to a youth's best interests. To what scale does restorative justice refer to gauge too much or too little intervention? And, to the extent that every offender-victim-community triad differs, what role, if any, does the legal principle of equality — treating similarly-situated offenders similarly — have to play?

To the extent that restorative justice uses "harm" to define proportionality and limit intervention, it cuts the concept totally loose from its penal moorings. Again, the seriousness of a crime is the product of two components, harm and culpability. For purposes of gauging seriousness in penal law, culpability or the quality of choice may be the more important of the two because it is the factor over which the actor has greater control. The same "choice" to strike or "assault" another person and the exact same blow may result in minimal harm, minor bodily harm, grave injury or death, depending upon a host of fortuities beyond the contemplation of the actor, e.g., a loss of balance, a striking of the head while falling or the victim's proximity to a hospital trauma center. Earlier, it was argued that reduced culpability provides a rationale to justify a youth discount (shorter sentences for younger offenders). A restorative justice system that attends primarily to "harm" rather than culpability or deserts contains no similar limiting concept. And if restorative justice intervention is not punishment, then why should there be any proportionality limitations at all?

A restorative justice that attends more to the harm an offender causes than to the quality of the choice resembles more closely a tort system than a criminal law system. In tort law, the remedy is "restorative" — to make the victim "whole" — primarily through monetary compensation. And in tort, a very minor miscue or momentary lapse in attention potentially can produce a catastrophic harm, for example, negligence resulting in an automobile accident with all of its myriad consequences. Does proportionality in restorative justice subordinate culpability to consequences? And, if harm is the primary focus, then why limit it to penal harm?

Indeed, tort law provides many fruitful examples for restorative justice — alternative dispute resolution, mediation, arbitration, and restitution — in a non-judicial setting. But is a tort system without clear rules, normative standards, or structured procedures a criminal justice system? And, can its proponents reconcile restorative justice with justice?

★   ★   ★

REFERENCES

Ainsworth, J. E. (1991). "Re-imagining Childhood and Re-constructing the Legal Order: The Case for Abolishing the Juvenile Court." *North Carolina Law Review* 69:1083-1133.

—— (1995). "Youth Justice in a Unified Court: Response to Critics of Juvenile Court Abolition." *Boston College Law Review* 36:927-951.

Allen, F.A. (1964). "Legal Values and the Rehabilitative Ideal." In: *The Borderland of the Criminal Law: Essays in Law and Criminology*. Chicago, IL: University of Chicago Press.

—— (1981). *The Decline of the Rehabilitative Ideal: Penal Policy and Social Purpose*. New Haven, CT: Yale University Press.

Altschuler, D.M. (1994). "Tough and Smart Juvenile Incarceration: Reintegrating Punishment, Deterrence and Rehabilitation." *St. Louis University Public Law Review* 14:217-237.

American Bar Association (1995). *A Call For Justice: An Assessment of Access to Counsel and Quality of Representation in Delinquency Proceedings*. Washington DC: ABA Juvenile Justice Center.

Andrews, D.A., I. Zinger, R.D. Hoge, J. Bonta, P. Gendreau and F.T. Cullen (1990). "Does Correctional Treatment Work? A Clinically Relevant and Psychologically Informed Meta-Analysis." *Criminology* 28:369:404.

Bazemore, G. and M. Umbreit (1995). *Balanced and Restorative Justice: Program Summary*. Washington DC: U.S. Office of Juvenile Justice and Delinquency Prevention.

Bishop, D. M. and C. S. Frazier (1988). "The Influence of Race in Juvenile Justice Processing." *Journal of Research in Crime and Delinquency* 25:242-263.

—— and C.S. Frazier (1996). "Race Effects in Juvenile Justice Decision-Making: Findings of a Statewide Analysis." *Journal of Criminal Law and Criminology* 86:392-413.

Blumstein, A. (1995). "Youth Violence, Guns, and the Illicit-Drug Industry." *Journal of Criminal Law and Criminology* 86: 10-36 .

Booth, T. (ed.) (1991). *Juvenile Justice in the New Europe*. Sheffield, UK: Social Services Monographs.

Braithwaite, J. (1989). *Crime, Shame and Reintegration*. Cambridge, UK: Cambridge University Press.

Breed v. Jones (1975). 421 U.S. 519.

Brown, M. and K. Polk (1996). "Taking Fear of Crime Seriously: The Tasmanian Approach to Community Crime Prevention." *Crime & Delinquency* 42:398-420.

Cauffman, E. and L. Steinberg (1995). "The Cognitive and Affective Influences on Adolesent Decision-Making." *Temple Law Review* 68:1763-1789.

Clarke, Stevens H., and G.G. Koch (1980). "Juvenile Court: Therapy or Crime Control, and Do Lawyers Make a Difference?" *Law and Society Review* 14:263-308.

Cullen, F.T. and K.E. Gilbert (1982). *Reaffirming Rehabilitation*. Cincinnati, OH: Anderson.

Decker, S.H. (1985). "A Systematic Analysis of Diversion: Net Widening and Beyond." *Journal of Criminal Justice* 13:206-216.

Doek, J. (1994). "The Juvenile Court: An Endangered Species"? *European Journal on Criminal Policy* and *Research* 2(2): 42-56.

Dünkel, F. (1991). "Legal Differences in Juvenile Criminology in Europe." In: T. Booth (ed.), *Juvenile Justice in the New Europe*. Sheffield, UK: Social Services Monographs.

European Journal for Criminal Policy and Research (1994). "The Juvenile Justice System." Special issue 2(2):5-90.

Fagan, J. (1990). "Social and Legal Policy Dimensions of Violent Juvenile Crime." *Criminal Justice and Behavior* 17:93-133

Fare v. Michael C. (1979). 442 U.S. 707.

Feld, B.C. (1984). "Criminalizing Juvenile Justice: Rules of Procedure for Juvenile Court." *Minnesota Law Review* 69:141-276.

—— (1987). "Juvenile Court Meets the Principle of Offense: Legislative Changes in Juvenile Waiver Statutes." *Journal of Criminal Law and Criminology* 78:471-533.

—— (1988a). "*In re Gault* Revisited: A Cross-State Comparison of the Right to Counsel in Juvenile Court." *Crime & Delinquency* 34:393-424.

—— (1988b). "Juvenile Court Meets the Principle of Offense: Punishment, Treatment, and the Difference it Makes." *Boston University Law Review* 68:821-915.

—— (1989). "The Right to Counsel in Juvenile Court: An Empirical Study of When Lawyers Appear and the Difference They Make." *Journal of Criminal Law and Criminology* 79:1185-1346.

—— (1990). "Bad Law Makes Hard Cases: Reflections on Teen-Aged Axe-Murderers, Judicial Activism, and Legislative Default." *Journal of Law and Inequality* 8:1-101.

—— (1991). "The Transformation of the Juvenile Court." *Minnesota Law Review* 75:575-625.

—— (1993a). "Criminalizing the American Juvenile Court." In: M. Tonry (ed.), *Crime and Justice: A Review of Research*, vol. 17. Chicago, IL: University of Chicago Press.

—— (1993b). *Justice for Children: The Right to Counsel and the Juvenile Court.* Boston, MA: Northeastern University Press.

—— (1995). "Violent Youth and Public Policy: A Case Study of Juvenile Justice Law Reform." *Minnesota Law Review* 79:965-1128.

—— (1996). "Youthfulness, Criminal Responsibility, and Sentencing Policy." Paper presented at the annual meeting of the American Society of Criminology, Chicago.

—— (1999) *Bad Kids: Race and the Transformation of the Juvenile Court.* New York, NY: Oxford University Press.

Garrett, C. J. (1985). "Effects of Residential Treatment on Adjudicated Delinquents: A Meta-Analysis." *Journal of Research in Crime and Delinquency* 22:287-308.

Gatti, U. and Verde, A. (1991). "The Dividing Line Between Punishment and Help: New Questions, Old Answers. Observations on the Juvenile Procedural Penal Code in Italy." In: J. Junger-Tas, L. Boendermaker and P. van der Laan (eds.), *The Future of the Juvenile Justice System,* Leuven, Belgium: Acco.

Gendreau, P. and B. Ross (1987). "Revivification of Rehabilitation: Evidence from the 1980s." *Justice Quarterly* 4:349-407.

Greenwood, P. and F. Zimring (1985). *One More Chance: The Pursuit of Promising Intervention Strategies for Chronic Juvenile Offenders.* Santa Monica, CA: Rand.

Grisso, T. (1980). "Juveniles' Capacities to Waive *Miranda Rights*: An Empirical Analysis." *California Law Review* 68:1134-1166.

Grubb, W. N. and M. Lazerson (1982). *Broken Promises: How Americans Fail Their Children.* New York, NY: Basic Books.

Hudson, B. (1987). *Justice through Punishment.* London, UK: MacMillan.

Huynen, S. (1967). "De Nouveaux Horizons pour la Protection de la Jeunesse." (New Horizons for the Protection of Youth). *Revue de Droit Pénal et de Criminologie* 2:183-202.

In re Gault (1967). 387 U.S. 1.

In re Winship (1970). 397 U.S. 358.

Izzo, R. L., and R.R. Ross (1990). "Meta-Analysis of Rehabilitation Programs for Juvenile Delinquents." *Criminal Justice and Behavior* 17:134-142.

Katz, M. B. (ed.) (1993). *The "Underclass" Debate: Views from History.* Princeton, NJ: Princeton University Press.

Kempf-Leonard, K., C. Pope and W. Feyerher. (1995). *Minorities in Juvenile Justice.* Thousand Oaks, CA: Sage.

Krisberg, B. and J. Austin (1993). *Reinventing Juvenile Justice.* Thousand Oaks, CA: Sage.

Krisberg, B., I. Schwartz, G. Fishman, Z. Eisikovits, E. Guttman and K. Joe (1987). "The Incarceration of Minority Youth." *Crime & Delinquency* 33:173-205.

Klein, M.W. (1979). "Deinstitutionalization and Diversion of Juvenile Offenders: A Litany of Impediments." In: Michael Tonry and Norval Morris (eds.), *Crime and Justice: An Annual Review of Research,* vol. 1. Chicago, IL: University of Chicago.

Lab, S.P., and J.T. Whitehead (1988). "An Analysis of Juvenile Correctional Treatment." *Crime & Delinquency* 34:60-83.

Lemann, N. (1992). *The Promised Land: The Great Black Migration and How It Changed America*. New York, NY: Vintage Books.

Lipsey, M.W. (1992). "Juvenile Delinquent Treatment: A Meta-Analytic Inquiry into the Variability of Effects." In: T.D. Cook et al. (eds.), *Meta Analysis for Explanation: A Casebook*. New York, NY: Russell Sage Foundation.

Martinson, R.. (1974). "What Works? Questions and Answers About Prison Reform." *Public Interest* 35:22-54.

Massey, D.S. and N.A. Denton (1993). *American Apartheid: Segregation and the Making of the Underclass*. Cambridge, MA: Harvard University Press.

Matza, D. (1964). *Delinquency and Drift*. New York, NY: Wiley.

McCarthy, B. and B.L. Smith (1986). "The Conceptualization of Discrimination in the Juvenile Justice Process: The Impact of Administrative Factors and Screening Decisions on Juvenile Court Dispositions." *Criminology* 24:41-64.

Mehlbye, J. and L. Walgrave (1998). *Confronting Youth in Europe. Dealing with Juvenile Crime in most Countries of the European Union*. Copenhagen, DK: AKF.

Messner, S. and R. Rosenfeld (1994). *Crime and the American Dream*. Belmont, CA: Wadsworth.

National Research Council (1993). *Losing Generations: Adolescents in High-Risk Settings*. Washington, DC: National Academy Press.

Palmer, T. (1991). "The Effectiveness of Intervention: Recent Trends and Current Issues." *Crime & Delinquency* 37:330-350.

Platt, A. (1977). *The Child Savers: The Invention of Delinquency. 2nd ed.* Chicago, IL: University of Chicago Press.

Podkopacz, M.R. and B.C. Feld (1996). "The End of the Line: An Empirical Study of Judicial Waiver." *Journal of Criminal Law and Criminology* 86:449-492.

—— (1995). "Judicial Waiver Policy and Practice: Persistence, Seriousness and Race." *Law & Inequality Journal* 14:73-178.

Polk, K. (1984). "Juvenile Diversion: A Look at the Record." *Crime & Delinquency* 30:648-659.

Pope, C.E. and W.H. Feyerherm (1992). *Minorities and the Juvenile Justice System*. Washington DC: U.S. Office of Juvenile Justice and Delinquency Prevention.

Queloz, N. (1991). "Protection, Intervention and the Rights of Children and Young People." In: T. Booth (ed.), *Juvenile Justice in the New Europe*. Sheffield, UK: Social Services Monographs.

Roberts, A.R. and M.J. Comasso (1991). "The Effects of Juvenile Offender Treatment Programs on Recidivism: A Meta-Analysis of 46 Studies." *Notre Dame Journal of Law, Ethics and Public Policy* 5:421-442.

Rothman, D.J. (1978). "The State as Parent: Social Policy in the Progressive Era." In: W. Gaylin, I. Glasser, S. Marcus and D. Rothman (eds.), *Doing Good: The Limits of Benevolence*. New York, NY: Panetheon Books.

—— (1980). *Conscience and Convenience: The Asylum and Its Alternative in Progressive America*. Boston, MA: Little, Brown.

Rubin, H.T. (1985). *Juvenile Justice: Policy, Practice, and Law* (2nd ed.). New York, NY: Random House.

Ryerson, E. (1978). *The Best-Laid Plans: America's Juvenile Court Experiment*. New York, NY: Hill and Wang.

Schlossman, S. (1977). *Love and the American Delinquent: The Theory and Practice of "Progressive" Juvenile Justice*. Chicago, IL: University of Chicago Press.

Schwartz, I.M. (1989). *(In)Justice For Juveniles: Rethinking the Best Interests of the Child*. Lexington, MA: Lexington Books.

Scott, E.S. (1992). "Judgment and Reasoning in Adolescent Decisionmaking." *Villanova Law Review* 37:1607-1669.

—— N.D. Reppucci and J.L. Woolard. (1995). "Evaluating Adolescent Decision Making in Legal Contexts." *Law and Human Behavior* 19:221-244.

Sechrest, L.B. (1987). "Classification for Treatment." In: *Crime & Justice, vol. 9*. Chicago, IL: University of Chicago Press.

—— S.O. White and E.D. Brown (eds.) (1979). *The Rehabilitation of Criminal Offenders*. Washington, DC: National Academy of Sciences.

Sheffer, J.P. (1995). "Serious and Habitual Juvenile Offender Statutes: Reconciling Punishment and Rehabilitation within the Juvenile Justice System." *Vanderbilt Law Review* 48:479-512.

Snyder, H.N. and M. Sickmund (1995). *Juvenile Offenders and Victims: A National Report*. Washington, DC: U.S. Office of Juvenile Justice and Delinquency Prevention.

Steinberg, L. and E. Cauffman (1996). "Maturity of Judgment in Adolescence: Psychosocial Factors in Adolesecent Decision Making." *Law and Human Behavior* 20:249-272.

Tonry, M. (1996). *Sentencing Matters*. New York, NY: Oxford University Press.

—— and N. Morris (1992). *Intermediate Sanctions*. Chicago, IL: University of Chicago Press.

Torbet, P., R. Gable, H. Hurst IV, I. Montgomery, L. Szymanski and D. Thomas (1996). *State Responses to Serious and Violent Juvenile Crime: Research Report*.Washington, DC: U.S. Office of Juvenile Justice and Delinquency Prevention.

U.S. General Accounting Office (1995). *Juvenile Justice: Representation Rates Varied as Did Counsel's Impact on Court Outcomes*. Washington, DC: author.

Van de Kerchove, M. (1977). "Des Mesures Répressives aux Mesures de Sûreté et de Protection. Réflexions sur le Pouvoir Mystificateur de Language" (From Repressive Measures towards Safety and Protective Measures. Reflections on the Mystifying Power of Language.) *Revue de Droit Pénal et de Criminologie* 4:245-279.

Van Ness, D. and K.H. Strong (1997). *Restoring Justice*. Cincinnati, OH: Anderson.

Van Sloun, T. (1988). *De Schuldvraag in het Kinderstrafrecht* (The Question of Guilt in Juvenile Penal Law.) Deventer/Arnhem, NETH: Kluwer/Gouda Quint.

Von Hirsch, A. (1976). *Doing Justice*. New York, NY: Hill and Wang.

—— 1986). *Past vs. Future Crimes*. New Brunswick, NJ: Rutgers University Press.

—— (1993). *Censure and Sanctions*. New York, NY: Oxford University Press.

Walgrave, L. (1993). "The Making of Concepts on Juvenile Delinquency and its Treatment in the Recent History of Belgium and the Netherlands." In: A.G.Hess and P.F.Clement (eds.), *History of Juvenile Delinquency*, vol. 2. Aalen, GER: Scientia Verlag.

—— (1994). "Beyond Rehabilitation. In Search of a Constructive Alternative in the Judicial Response to Juvenile Crime." *European Journal on Criminal Policy and Research* 2(2):57-75.

—— (1995). "Restorative Justice for Juveniles: Just a Technique or a Fully-Fledged Alternative?" *Howard Journal of Criminal Justice* 34: 228-249.

—— and H. Geudens (1996). "The Restorative Proportionality of Community Service for Juveniles." *European Journal of Crime, Criminal Law and Criminal Justice* 4:361-380.

Wiles, P. (1993). "Ghettoization in Europe?" *European Journal on Criminal Policy and Research* 1(1):52-69.

Whitehead, J.T. and S.P. Lab (1989). "A Meta-Analysis of Juvenile Correctional Treatment." *Journal Research Crime & Delinquency* 26:276-295.

Wilson, W.J. (1987). *The Truly Disadvantaged*. Chicago, IL: University of Chicago Press.

—— (1996). *When Work Disappears: The World of the New Urban Poor*. New York, NY: Knopf.

Zimring, F. (1982). *The Changing Legal World of Adolescence*. New York, NY: Free Press.

2. Restorative Juvenile Justice: In Search of Fundamentals and an Outline for Systemic Reform

by

Gordon Bazemore

and

Lode Walgrave

INTRODUCTION

Support for restorative justice has grown in what appears to be a unique period of convergence between emerging justice philosophies and political, social and cultural movements. As the victim's movement became stronger and drew attention to the need to deal with the suffering caused by crime, crime victims began to claim an expanded role in the justice process and to demand that the outcome of this process become more focused on reparation (Young, 1995; Peters and Aertsen, 1995). Community-oriented policing advocates criticized the ritualistic and often counterproductive approaches of the professional model of law enforcement and advanced more problem-oriented interventions based on partnerships with community groups and citizens (Sparrow et al., 1990; Moore and Trajanowicz, 1988).

In a similar way, indigenous dispute resolution processes and the accompanying political movements to "devolve" justice (Griffiths and Hamilton, 1996; Melton, 1995) challenged the alienating and authoritarian modalities of criminal courts, and proposed that communities be given greater latitude over the sentencing process and the general response to crime. The women's movement gained influence and articulated a feminist critique of patriarchal justice that pleaded for a more caring and reconciling system (Harris, 1990; Bowman, 1994). Strong critical positions were also advanced with regard to individual treatment or social welfare models for juvenile justice, which were reproached for their neglect of legal rights and for an insular focus on the individual needs of offenders that took rehabilitation out of context and ignored the multiple needs of crime victims and communities (Walgrave, 1994; Feld, 1993; Bazemore and Terry, 1997). At the same time, just deserts (or rights-based) perspectives were subjected to a growing theoretical critique that emphasized their rigidity, obsession with punishment, retrospective orientation, and emphasis on an abstract moral balance based on uniformity rather than a concern with resolving genuine conflict and addressing underlying social and interpersonal problems (Braithwaite and Pettit, 1990; Bazemore and Umbreit, 1995). In many of these tendencies and movements, a basic heritage can also be traced to various themes and statements within critical criminology (i.e., van Swaaningen, 1997; Pepinsky and Quinney, 1991).[1]

Given these diverse influences, it should not be surprising that the field is not unanimous about core values and definitions.[2] In fact, there remains a great deal of controversy about almost every aspect of restorative justice today, to the extent that it may even be doubted whether any unified "restorative justice movement" exists. Adding to the confusion about defining and placing parameters on restorative justice is the fact that there appear to be a number of apparently similar, yet independent, "alternative justice" movements and philosophies. Although some seem to overlap to a great extent with restorative justice, their proponents prefer to use different names including transformative justice, peacemaking criminology, relational justice and community justice.

We will consider many of these controversies in this and other chapters, but we are unlikely to persuade those with strong positions on these topics or to develop definitive resolutions. It is only recently that practitioners and scientific researchers have become aware that there are important fundamental commonalities upon which to more fully develop what some regard as a new justice paradigm. When examined in this context, disagreements appear less extreme and can be viewed as healthy tensions that are essential in the process of developing a well-balanced and increasingly clear vision of what restorative justice is and how it can be implemented in a continually evolving domain.

The primary purpose, and challenge, of this chapter is to uncover and underscore this fundamental commonality, in order to outline some core principles for a restorative juvenile justice. As proposed in the introduction, the necessary condition for developing restorative justice as a "third way," or fully-fledged alternative for juvenile justice, is the ability of restorative justice advocates to meet three basic challenges. Hence, in each section of this chapter, we address a challenge to making restorative justice a fully-fledged alternative.

Part One addresses the first challenge, to develop a clear and explicit definition and vision for restorative justice. A coherent definition and vision should serve as a unifying focus for reflection and experimentation among practitioners and scientists, and should inform policy makers and the public about what restorative justice is and *is not*. Part Two has a more strategic focus that considers what is distinctive about youth crime and the social reaction to it that invites restorative justice adherents to focus on juvenile justice as a primary reform context. It also examines whether or not restorative justice principles may need adaptation by virtue of the different reparative needs of victims, offenders and communities when the crime is committed by a young person. Finally, turning to the future and issues of implementation, Part Three outlines the basic components of an agenda for systemic juvenile justice reform that we believe will be necessary to sustain and institutionalize a restorative response to youth crime.

DEFINING RESTORATIVE JUSTICE

In considering definitions, it is important to begin by acknowledging the controversy about what should and should not be included under the "restorative justice tent." Indeed, variation in definitions and attempts to expand, or more typically, *contract* the tent are apparent throughout the emerging literature and practice of restorative justice (e.g., Messmer and Otto, 1992; Hudson and Galaway, 1996; Umbreit, 1994).

For the time being, the concept of restorative justice has different definitions and interpretations (see McCold, 1998). Some authors would appear to limit restorative justice to a face-to-face process (see, e.g., Marshall 1996), involving victim, offender and (perhaps) other stakeholders. These authors tend to confine restorative justice to a form of diversion, because they accept that some crimes can only be responded to by the use of some degree of force, and because coercion is rejected as unthinkable in a restorative justice model. For advocates of this position, restorative justice is an opportunity for diverting as many cases as possible from the formal court-ordered process, thereby expanding a "restorative informalism" (Duenkel, 1996). Others are open to a variety of processes or procedures, including those that occur within the formal justice system, aimed at reaching an outcome focused on repair (Walgrave, 1995; Van Ness and Strong, 1997).

Restorative justice interventions should generally occur in informal settings as voluntary, negotiative encounters that include victim, offender and their relevant "communities" (McCold, 1996; Bazemore, 1996). But it is also possible to imagine a transformation of the formal system to make it operate in a more restorative manner as well. Moreover, restorative justice need not be limited to completely voluntary processes, but may also include a variety of more or less coerced restorative obligations such as restitution or community service imposed by more formal proceedings. What makes these obligations and processes "restorative," rather than retributive or rehabilitative, is the *intent* with which they are imposed and also the *outcome* sought by decision-makers (Packer, 1968).

In order to make our own vision clear, we contrast it with a recent widely discussed definition. Marshall's (1996:37) commendable effort to capture the spirit of restorative justice brought him to define it as a "process whereby the parties with a stake in a particular offense come together to resolve collectively how to deal with the aftermath of the offense and its implications for the future." No doubt this definition underscores the importance of a unique justice process that engages and involves stakeholders in an effort to deal with the problems crime causes. In contrast to retributive justice, restorative justice places great value on the meaningful participation of the victim, the offender and community members in the dispositional process (see, e.g., Zehr, 1990; Van Ness and Strong, 1997).

If the goal is a fully-fledged restorative alternative, however, Marshall's (1996) definition is at once too broad and too narrow. First, restorative justice cannot be limited to a process. Rather, the primary distinguishing feature of restorative justice is an effort to repair the harm crime causes. While this repair cannot be accomplished in a vacuum — and should therefore engage victims, victimized communities, and offenders in a process in which participants define the harm and develop a plan to repair it — such a process can occur without a "coming together," if this refers only to a *face-to-face* meeting between the parties with a stake in the particular offense. Therefore, we also include under the restorative justice tent, for example, a wide variety of services provided for victims, whether or not an offender is involved or even known to the system or the community. Even efforts to involve victims and other citizens in advisory boards to design and monitor restorative reforms or treatment programs that involve victims and community members could be considered as restorative interventions, as long as they are focused on the goal of repairing the harm crime causes. Finally, as we will argue later, sanctions should be included within the restorative justice definition, so long as their primary intent is to reinforce an obligation to make amends to the victim and the victimized community.

Second, a definition focused on a general process is also too broad. Restorative justice is primarily about restoration. Hence, the most fundamental critique of Marshall's (1996) definition is that it does not at all refer to repairing harm, and thus provides no specific boundaries on the kinds of processes included. Specifically, one may ask whether a process in which stakeholders in a crime come together to discuss feelings and share information is restorative if no effort to repair the harm occurs. Regardless of how empowering it may be for participants, is a process without outcomes or obligations objectively sufficient, and is a process in which stakeholders conclude with recommendations that are focused simply on treating and punishing the offender restorative?

Provisional Definitions

We begin our search for the essence of restorative justice with a very simple definition that contains what we think is the core element in the restorative response: restorative justice is every action that is primarily oriented toward doing justice by repairing the harm that has been caused by a crime. Whereas this definition may also seem too simple, it has the advantage of provoking the key theoretical and empirical questions and establishing major lines of discussion salient to restorative justice: (1) What do we mean by a "harm caused by a crime?" (2) Who (and what) shall we consider as suffering that harm? (3) How can that harm be repaired? (4) What is "justice" and how can it be achieved? The answers to these questions are interrelated.

The Harm

The focus on the harm provoked by the crime is the key to understanding restorative justice and to distinguishing it from both the traditional retributive and rehabilitative justice models. If we may speak of restorative justice as a new justice paradigm, it is because this framework offers a distinctive "lens," in Zehr's (1990) words, for defining the problem posed by crime and for solving this problem. Specifically, crime is defined by the harm it has caused to victims, and the primary function of the reaction against it is not to punish, nor even to rehabilitate, but to repair or compensate for the harm caused by the crime.

Retributivists primarily consider the harm to be of an abstract judicio-moral order, which creates an imbalance that must be corrected by an equal harm to the offender. All other possible elements of harm that might be considered are subsidiary to that principle. Proponents of treatment or rehabilitation models do not focus on harm, but, using these terms, it could be said that they try to redress harm to the offender caused by socio-psychological misfortunes that occurred before the offense was committed. The restorative justice approach considers in principle all kinds of harm, including material losses, physical injuries, psychological consequences, relational problems and social dysfunctions, insofar as they have been caused by the occurrence of an offense.

The Victim

Who should be considered as suffering the harm resulting from an offense is a matter of discussion among restorative justice adherents. It is evident that the kinds of harm to be restored will depend on the types of victims recognized. All agree that the injuries and losses inflicted on the individual victim and his or her intimates are most concrete and must be at the center of any restorative action. Most authors also include the victimized community, but it is more difficult then to define such communities and to concretize the kind of harm that has been suffered. Strong disagreement exists about the question of whether society should also be considered a victim, and even about the nature of society's interest or "stake" in conflicts between individuals that have been formally labeled as crimes (see, e.g., Christie, 1982). Some fear that recognizing society as a victim will bring about a return to the retributive focus, wherein the state has set itself up as the primary victim, thereby pushing the individual victim into a subordinate position. Others argue that because civil society inevitably has a role to play in the settlement of a crime, it is better to specify its interest accurately in order to avoid the feared dominance of the state.[3] Indeed, one of the most delicate challenges in the restorative justice undertaking is to sort out the role of the state (or government) in such a way that its norm-enforcing role does not impede or prohibit genuine restorative processes (Van Ness and Strong, 1997). In other words, it will become increasingly important, as Pranis (1997) has expressed it, to distinguish between and also harmonize the *legal authority* of the state and the *moral authority* of community.

The Restoration

How the restoration can be achieved is a question composed of two subquestions: what process must be utilized and what are the outcomes of that process? The reparation of the harm caused by a crime can be accomplished by a wide range of possible actions including, but not limited to, restitution, compensation, service to victims and apologies. These actions may be direct or indirect, concrete or symbolic. Depending on the nature of the victimization under consideration, and the wishes of the victimized parties, reparative interventions may be focused on the concrete victim, his or her intimates, a community or even a society. Several types of victim restitution or community service seem to have become prototypes for such interventions, but creative practitioners continue to invent and adapt alternative restorative practices to address emerging needs. Ultimately, what makes a *process* more or less restorative is the extent to which it is aimed at, and moving toward, repairing the harm. Moreover, the "restorativeness" of any process is best viewed along a continuum rather than as an absolute (Balanced and Restorative Justice Project, 1998; Umbreit, this volume).[4]

A wide variety of processes can be utilized to achieve restorative outcomes. One of the most important distinctions between them focuses on the extent to which participants become involved on a voluntary basis. On one side, there are processes of purely voluntary negotiation and consultation — direct or indirect — between offender and victim as individuals, or supported by their intimates or other community members (victim-offender-mediation, restorative group conferences and the like). On the other side, the possibility of restorative *sanctions* has led some restorative justice advocates to address the way in which juridical procedures and coercion may lead to restorative objectives and outcomes. Because it will be opposed by those who wish to limit restorative justice only to those processes where victims and offenders meet voluntarily and carry on face-to-face dialogue, this position needs additional justification.

First, a crucial pragmatic argument against limiting restorative justice to processes in which victims and offenders mutually agree to participate is that such a limitation would exclude from the opportunity for restoration many victims who chose not to become involved in such meetings (still a majority in most jurisdictions).[5] Such a restriction would also exclude those victims whose offender is unknown and who may simply want information and compensation. Does not restorative justice wish to address the needs for reparation and healing of all victims?

Second, acceptance of coercive restorative processes (or procedures) in our definition of restorative justice as "every action that is primarily oriented toward doing justice by restoring the harm that has been caused by a crime" is based on a reasoned, if not universal, view of formal criminal sanctions. Like any other sanctions — such as court-ordered treatment and restrictions imposed for punitive or risk management purposes — restitution, community service or other reparative obligations, when not completely voluntary, should be viewed for what they are: coercive measures taken to enforce community or societal standards (Packer, 1968). And like other sanctions, these restorative measures (and indeed, even restorative processes such as mediation) may be experienced by offenders as painful, even as punitive. Hence, as Packer (1968) noted, it is the *intent* to incapacitate, to punish, to deter, to rehabilitate or to restore that must be the key distinguishing characteristic in any effort to classify sanctions. Sanctions are "restorative" to the extent that they are carried out with the intent to repair harm, and in such a way that they maximize the likelihood of repair and satisfaction to victims and community. This requirement itself implies careful attention to process.

In our view, restorative justice implies that a distinctly *restorative process* would indeed be associated with every action carried out by both stakeholders and justice professionals. While this *way of doing justice* is no doubt often the most apparent and even the most important distinguishing feature of the practice of restorative justice, such a process need not always involve victim-offender mediation or other face-to-face encounters. A process that, for example, tries to ensure that community service actually repairs harm to a community (rather than simply serves as another punishment or treatment for the offender), by giving community members input into the nature and terms of a service obligation, is from this perspective a restorative process. Although many victims may chose not to participate in a meeting with their offenders, in a restorative justice system the victim would always be represented by surrogates and involved, at least symbolically, in any justice process concerned with determining an appropriate obligation or sanction for the offender. When so involved and represented, the process may thereby be viewed as restorative.[6] However, the objective of bringing about repair is critical in distinguishing a restorative process from what may be a more humane, user-friendly and inclusive process the aim of which is to carry out an action targeted at retribution, deterrence or some other nonrestorative objective. In a restorative process, decisions about the *nature* of the restoration are, of course, based on the input of victims, offenders and community members.[7]

Input from victims and communities affected by crime provided in face-to-face, non-adversarial, informal and voluntary meetings with offenders in safe settings will almost always provide the best process to determine restorative obligations. Research, theory, practice and a strong set of ethical principles also suggest that such processes *in and of themselves* provide benefits that go beyond those that can be derived from even the most creative court-ordered sanction — and that use of these process could be widely expanded (Umbreit, 1994; Wright, 1991; Stuart, 1995). Our own position is that advocacy and support is needed to encourage much greater efforts to facilitate face-to-face meetings between stakeholders, especially in informal settings, and we believe that greater "space" could also be allowed for such "coming together" encounters within the formal system as well as the community (Van Ness and Strong, 1997). But even victim-offender mediation may be "unrestorative" if it is, for example, carried out in such a way that victims do not feel empowered, do not feel satisfied that some progress toward healing has occurred, or feel that they have actually experienced secondary victimization (Umbreit, this volume). It may also be that the part of a restorative "process" that has the most satisfying effect for some victims might be getting some of their possessions back or seeing the offender make good on his or her commitment. While most victims and offenders derive a great deal of initial satisfaction from the mediation process itself (see, e.g., Umbreit, 1994), some may derive more benefit from the end result. Still others may later feel quite unsatisfied in the final analysis when an offender fails to complete a reparative obligation.

Ultimately, limiting restorative justice to informal and voluntary processes also seems to uncritically take pressure off courts, corrections and other parts of the justice system to undertake reforms that make these formal justice processes more responsive to the needs of those victims, offenders and other community members who do not chose to avail themselves of informal options (assuming they exist and are available). In this case, restorative justice would simply remain a form of diversion, the application of which may indeed be greatly expanded. However, such expansion would not affect the fundamentally punitive and unsatisfying manner in which societies now deal with most crime. And while their motivation would be to avoid coercion, restorative justice advocates who focus only on the informal side would have no impact on the coercion that is now used by the formal system to enforce punishment and treatment obligations. For this reason, an emphasis on both formal and informal justice processes seems necessary if the goal is to ensure that the "new paradigm" will become more than an ornament to the "hard core" criminal justice system.

The discussion of how to achieve restoration is in its infancy. Research and practice at this early stage of the emerging restorative justice paradigm needs to be open to the possibility that reparation and restoration is achieved in different ways in different circumstances, for different victims and different victimized communities. Research must also be open to the possibility that some programs labeled as restorative may cause even more harm in actual implementation, while some practices now on the margins of the mainstream discussion may have positive impacts. Because many highly restorative interventions probably have yet to be discovered, our definition therefore incorporates a diverse "menu" of practices that may initially seem outside the domain of what is now considered restorative justice.

Doing Justice

Restorative justice is not only about restoration; it is also about "justice" broadly defined. Justice has three meanings here. First, it refers to a feeling of *equity*, of being treated in a similar way as others in similar circumstances. Second, justice in a broader sense also means optimal *satisfaction* of all parties with a stake in the offense. Victims should feel that their victimization has been taken seriously, that they had the opportunity to express their anger and fear, that they have been supported by the community and that care has been taken to address their losses. Offenders should receive a clear message that they have transgressed the limits of social tolerance, and that they have an opportunity to make up for their lapse in a reasonable and constructive way. Communities should be strengthened by the restorative process and experience reduced fear and a greater sense of efficacy and social cohesion, as well as satisfaction that crime and offenders have been sanctioned, safety and security enhanced, and offenders reintegrated in an acceptable way. Third, justice also refers to *legal* protection of the individual against unwarranted intrusion by the state. Restorative justice would then mean that any restorative process and its outcomes must respect those legal safeguards to which all citizens are entitled. Even in voluntary settlements, victims and offenders have legal rights upon which mediation and similar processes must not encroach. Participation may in no way be imposed, exchanges must be open and free, and agreements must be fully accepted and reasonable in relation to the seriousness of the harm and the capacities of the parties. When a coercive procedure is entered, all legal guarantees such as due process and proportionate maximums for sanctions must be observed.

This third aspect of justice, of course, forces restorative proponents to consider the fundamental question of the role of the state and its justice system in the restorative justice process. We believe that the state has a crucial role to play as guardian of the individual legal rights of citizens, or, as Braithwaite and Pettit (1990) put it, of their "dominion". But concern with justice in this legal sense is not self-evident in the restorative justice movement. Many who have turned to restorative justice as a result of dissatisfaction with the way the formal justice system deals with crime may unreflexively exclude any notion of state intervention in what they regard as a purely consensual and communitarian process. For us, justified criticism of the existing formal system should not lead to a rejection of the judicial system as such. On the contrary, it should lead us to reformulate the function of the state and its original justice apparatus, in order to prevent restorative justice practices from deteriorating into unjust practices.

CORE PRINCIPLES

Our provisional effort to define restorative justice, and the considerations noted thus far, now brings us to the need for a standard and methodology to identify restorative justice in practice and to assess progress toward the restorative vision. Standard here refers more to a set of principles, and less to a set of practices or programs that are judged *a priori* to be "restorative." Such principles can in turn provide criteria that suggest various dimensions by which programs can be characterized as more or less restorative. For those concerned that the uninhibited growth in the number of practices admitted into a large and expanding "restorative justice tent" will begin to allow "leaks" that ultimately "water down" practice, we suggest that the principles will become the "gatekeeper" that ultimately determines entrance to the tent.

For example, there are a wide range of intervention practices that focus exclusively on treating and and/or punishing offenders, and would do so by methods that isolate offenders from victims and their community. Principles would exclude them, at least in their current form, from any likely list of restorative interventions. Sound criteria would allow for the possibility, however, that some of these intervention practices may be substantially modified — as when offender treatment programs begin to include attention to crime victims and the suffering they undergo — and can thereby be redefined as partly restorative. Principles also allow, as suggested earlier, for the possibility that a number of as-yet undiscovered practices may emerge that meet these criteria.

Given our definition of restorative justice, what core principles would then provide the framework for developing these criteria? Van Ness (1997:8) has proposed that the foundation of restorative justice can be built on three principles that flow from the common premise that "crime is more than lawbreaking; it also causes injuries to victims, communities and even to offenders." If crime is thought of as "peace breaking," the three principles can be stated as follows:

Principle 1: Justice requires that we work to heal victims, offenders and communities that have been injured by crime.

Principle 2: Victims, offenders and communities should have the opportunity for active involvement in the justice process as early and as fully as possible.

Principle 3: We must rethink the relative roles and responsibilities of the government and the community. In promoting justice, government is responsible for preserving a just order and the community for establishing peace. [Van Ness, 1997:8-9].

For us, these principles provide an adequate core foundation for a fully-fledged restorative juvenile justice. In essence, "doing justice" in the restorative sense is centered around the effort to heal the three parties that may be injured by crime. The word "healing" means that in an ideal situation more is aimed at than simple restitution, but that relational and emotional injury is also to be restored. The latter, of course, will be less often (if at all) achieved in a coercive procedure, but even an imposed restitution or community service sanction will, if meaningfully executed, more successfully address the healing criterion then a traditional punitive intervention.

Van Ness's (1997) second principle states that victims, offenders and communities should have the opportunity for active involvement. This does not mean that they must necessarily participate in person in the restorative justice process. Again, the degree of their willingness to cooperate may be different, and this will in fact determine the degree of possible healing or restorativeness of the process. Even if no participation can be realized, the judicial procedure should then be oriented toward the maximally achievable restoration of injuries to victims, communities and offenders, through imposed restitution or community service and/or other reparative obligations.

A different role for the system in promoting justice and supporting community efforts to establish peace, as stated in Van Ness's (1997) third principle, refers to the tension between community and government. According to Van Ness (1997), government is responsible for preserving a just order in society, and the community for establishing or keeping peace in its midst. This rightly distinguishes between what we may expect from both, given their specific capacities and powers. In another statement of principles (Declaration of Leuven, 1997), the role of public authorities has been defined as:

contributing to the conditions for restorative responses to crime,

safeguarding the correctness of procedures and the respect for individual legal rights,

imposing judicial coercion, if voluntary restorative actions do not succeed and a formal response to the crime is considered to be necessary,

organizing judicial procedures if the crime and the public reactions to it are of a nature that a purely informal voluntary regulation appears to be insufficient. [recommendation 3].

Here also, the priority of community-based responses is stressed, while the specific protective rights and law-enforcement role of the state is preserved and specified within clear limits.

In addition to his three foundational principles, Van Ness (1997) proposes ancillary principles that include the *encounter* (an emphasis on: making connections among stakeholders in each crime); *reparation* as a debt to victim and the victimized community rather than to the state in the abstract; *reintegration* of offenders and victims; and *participation* of all stakeholders (Van Ness, 1997; Van Ness and Strong, 1997).

Van Ness's (1997) inclusion of reintegration of both victims and offenders as part of the foundation of a restorative framework also looks to the future of all those affected by crime. Within this framework, restorative justice practitioners would not be content with a process that merely addresses the past (Van Ness and Strong, 1997). Rather, an emphasis on "transformation" provides an even stronger link to the needs of the future, and raises questions about the relationship between the restorative response and both the rehabilitative and preventative agendas. Because these agendas retain a high profile in the juvenile justice debate, which remains more future-oriented in its optimism about the prospects for offender reintegration and the possibility that early delinquent tendencies can be stifled, it is important to increase the compatibility and resonance between the emphasis on repairing prior harm and these more future-oriented transformative efforts. Indeed, an emerging critique of restorative justice has been that it is essentially conservative in its reactive and limited focus on past damage caused by crime (Morris, 1994), and that it does not include prevention (Maloney, 1997).

For us, although offender rehabilitation/reintegration is important, it cannot prevail over or be viewed as somehow independent of restorative concerns. Indeed, it must be incorporated within the restorative framework. Or as stated in the Declaration of Leuven (1997):

> Within the rules of due process and proportionality which have been designed and in so far it does not obstruct the restorative response itself, the action towards the young offender should maximally contribute to his competency building and his reintegration.

> The implementation of a restorative process, within or outside the judicial system, may not obstruct the possibility to offer in addition, but from outside the judicial system, voluntary treatment, assistance and support to the juvenile offender and and/or his family [recommendation 5].

Obviously, the reintegrative impact of the restorative action may help the offender avoid future reoffending. In addition, restorative actions that involve community and victim in addressing the aftermath of crime may themselves have more generalized preventive effects. As part of a process of community learning, one successful peace-making or restorative encounter thus informs and empowers community members and organizations to try another. As Judge Barry Stuart (1995) has described it:

> When citizens fail to assume responsibility for decisions effecting [sic] the community, community life will be characterized by the absence of a collective sense of caring, a lack of respect for diverse values, and ultimately a

lack of any sense of belonging. [On the other hand,] conflict, if resolved through a process that constructively engages the parties involved, can be a fundamental building ingredient in any relationship [p.8].

Crime, in Christie's (1977; 1982) framework, is an opportunity that provides social fuel for positive action to rebuild relationships and strengthen communities, and to (ultimately) address the conditions that cause crime. In essence, each successful community sanctioning or problem-solving process can also be viewed as a demonstration that builds confidence elsewhere in the community that citizens are capable of resolving conflict.

But restorative justice is primarily a method of reacting after a crime or harm has occurred. The rehabilitative focus must remain subordinate, because it would otherwise overrule the rights and needs of victims and victimized communities, and threaten the legal safeguards that protect offenders. Restorative justice then would be nothing more than old wine in new bottles, as some critics now already suggest (Feld, this volume). Similarly, prevention is not the primary purpose of restorative justice. Whether or not an action may be called "prevention" is dependent on its intention (Bailleau and Garioud, 1994), and prevention cannot be the primary intent of restorative justice intervention if the coherent focus on repair is to retained. Hence, although preventive outcomes may be probable "spin-offs" of restorative actions, the complete range of possible preventative strategies and actions should be provided by community agencies and socializing institutions, as well as by social welfare and police initiatives (see, e.g., Lab, 1997; Tonry and Farrington, 1995).[8]

Having assessed what are for us the basics of restorative justice, it is necessary to look more critically at what many now consider to be the most desirable milieu for experimentation. We therefore concentrate on restorative justice as it would be introduced as a response to youth crime within the juvenile justice context.

JUVENILE JUSTICE CONTEXT

An initial question one may ask is why there is a need to single out youth crime and juvenile justice. Could there not be a single "restorative justice" that applies regardless of the crime committed, age of the offender, or what court or community-based system is responsible for monitoring the terms of accountability? Or, put another way, even if the juvenile court and justice system is ultimately abolished, would there not remain a need for a restorative response that is then tailored to the needs of juvenile offenders and their victims?

A Principled Option For A Unique Restorative Justice System

These questions are fundamental. If we believe that one can find in the common principles sufficient guidelines for a restorative response to any crime, it would seem inconsistent to assert *a priori* that a general restorative justice system would provide a formal response to youth crime that would be significantly inferior to that provided by a specialized restorative juvenile court. Certainly, we could not defend the need for juvenile justice systems *as they currently exist* if confronted with the alternative prospect of one integrated restorative system.

The need for a unique response within a separate juvenile justice system has been attributed to the supposedly distinctive characteristics of young people. By itself, however, this is a dangerous principle. If it is accepted that the intrinsic qualities of a category of offenders may justify the maintenance of a separate system, there are no reasons not to establish a separate court system for female offenders, or for the elderly, for example. Members of these groups may claim that their own individual attributes, living conditions, social prospects and social networks are so unique that motivation for their crimes may be different enough to also justify a separate justice response.

The premise that young people are developmentally different from adults, and therefore are less culpable or accountable for the crimes they commit, is not a sufficient argument to justify a separation of the social reaction to crime into two distinct systems. Rather, this premise may just as easily support a case for one system that is flexible enough to allow adaptations in procedures and sentences. Moreover, the role of motivational development in accountability is posed differently in a restorative context than in a punitive one. All victims and victimized communities are in need of restoration, regardless of the age of the offender. The required effort of the offender in the restorative action, however, may be geared to his or her capacities, and age may play a role in such an adjustment.

At first glance, this position may seem close to Feld's (this volume) proposal to abolish the juvenile court in favor of the promise of more just dispositions in adult court — with consideration for age as a mitigating factor. There is, however, a major difference. Whereas Feld's abolitionist proposal would hand juveniles over to the criminal justice system as it currently exists, we foresee the possible reunification of the juvenile and the adult criminal justice systems as a vision for the future. Such reunification would *only* be desirable when a systemic restorative justice model is in place as an alternative for both young people and adults.

There are several reasons to reject an incorporation of juvenile justice under the regime of penal justice grounded in a just desert model. First, there is growing evidence that juveniles in criminal justice systems are not faring as well on most outcome measures as their counterparts who remain under the jurisdiction of juvenile justice agencies (see, e.g., Bishop et al., 1997). Second, criminal justice systems in much of the world find themselves in even greater crisis — and, in many ways, less effective — than juvenile justice systems. Third, and above all, there is no basis for assuming that any constructive contribution can result from any further expansion of a systematic punitive response to crime, especially juvenile crime. We have briefly outlined theoretical and empirical arguments against this position in the introduction, and will explore the punishment problem in greater depth in the concluding chapter.

In the current climate, however, the response to juvenile crime seems to be shifting more and more in the direction of greater punitiveness. In the U.S., for example, one can observe a growing number of transfers to adult court and more punitive sentencing in the juvenile courts (Feld, 1993; this volume). In most European countries, recent changes in statutes and in sentencing and dispositional practices appear to be moving in the same direction, supported by a public discourse that is asking for more "credible" and "tough" reactions against the "worrying increase in juvenile crime" (Walgrave and Mehlbye, 1998). With some exceptions — including many U.S. states, where the punitive trend is driven primarily by a general "crime control" or "get tough" political agenda — the shift in most of the world, with Canada and Europe providing the clearest examples, is grounded in the just deserts philosophy (Griffiths and Corrado, this volume). The rise of influence of the justice model is moreover supported by one legitimate rationale, namely, the awareness that juvenile justice systems provide insufficient legal guarantees and few clear limits on the scope of interventions aimed at young offenders. Whatever the motivation, from a strategic point of view, the concern to limit or redirect these punitive turns in the reaction to juvenile crime coincides with and supports the agenda for expanded implementation of the restorative approach.

A Strategic Choice For A Restorative Juvenile Justice

For restorative justice advocates, the best reasons for opposing any future merger of juvenile and adult systems in their current form is a practical one. Such a merger would in essence greatly reduce, if not eliminate, the chances for implementing restorative justice as a systemic alternative. Hence, despite our principled belief that the ultimate objective of restorative justice advocates should be one restorative system providing flexible and more satisfying responses to all crime, juvenile justice systems currently offer greater opportunities for credible and consistent implementation of restorative justice as the primary response to crime. It is even possible that successful implementation of restorative justice principles in juvenile justice could provide a pathway for strategic expansion within criminal justice systems.

But is juvenile justice really a promising laboratory for implementing restorative justice? Will restorative justice help to strengthen and provisionally preserve a juvenile court? No one can provide definitive answers to these questions at this time. Currently, the most obvious opportunity presented by juvenile justice for experimentation is the "open door" that these systems seem to be providing, at least to restorative ideas. However, restorative justice advocates must take care that this open door is not a trap, and that admission to the juvenile justice system is not contingent upon restorative justice interventions becoming indistinguishable from practices associated with currently dominant models.

In juvenile justice systems, restorative philosophy faces the added challenge of competing with two alternative paradigms rather than one (Bazemore, 1996). In the U.S., as in Europe, several adult corrections systems have moved with surprising speed to implement victim-focused restorative reforms (Seymour, 1997). Juvenile courts and juvenile justice systems interested in restorative justice, on the other hand, have had perhaps the greatest difficulty in providing even basic services to victims (Bazemore, 1994; Young, 1995). In part, juvenile justice initiatives to increase victim involvement and improve the quality of the juvenile justice response to victims are more likely to be viewed by staff as competing obligations that interfere with their "real duties" to provide offender services. This appears to be less the case in criminal justice systems, where the rehabilitative focus has been greatly weakened in the past two decades. Privacy and confidentiality also stand in the way of the flow of information about cases, which is still off limits to crime victims in juvenile courts in many jurisdictions. Perhaps most significantly, juvenile justice administrators today are often overwhelmed with responding to policy-maker demands that they get tough (while continuing to provide treatment), which too often means focusing attention and scarce resources on building and operating new secure facilities.

In the context of the juvenile justice crisis, the open-door to restorative justice may, on the one hand, be part of a desperate search for legitimacy, motivated more by survival instinct than by commitment to the values of restorative justice. Will restorative justice be viewed as another intervention approach that must compete with boot camps or whatever new surveillance and treatment programs are currently trendy? In an already very crowded field where a new "program of the month" and a new "crisis of the week" vie for the attention of juvenile justice administrators, it is questionable whether restorative justice practices and polices will break through as priorities. There are also no guarantees that such community-based restorative justice approaches will not simply widen the net of the juvenile justice system, without making any significant changes (Polk, 1994; Bazemore, 1997a).

On the other hand, opening up the closed setting of the juvenile court to citizen and victim input may begin to break down much of the distrust communities feel toward juvenile justice and their victims (Bazemore, 1997b), and may in individual cases increase understanding of and support for young offenders and their victims (Umbreit, 1994; Young, 1995). Moreover, the restorative approach to sanctioning and accountability may garner more credibility among citizens than the existing individual treatment approach, and could provide some challenge to the retributive juggernaut that is now sweeping through juvenile justice systems internationally. Hence, despite the above-mentioned caveats, there are a number of reasons to hypothesize that restorative justice may more easily gain a foothold as a viable alternative in juvenile justice systems.

First, the widely accepted premise that young people are at least somewhat less blameworthy than adults, and that they are therefore more malleable, leads to a generally greater acceptance of newer forms of intervention that may be less punitive. Many citizens would probably support the flexibility of restorative justice which, for example, allows for a number of new and creative public safety strategies and restorative rehabilitative alternatives to connect or reconnect young people to the community. Citizens might also more easily accept approaches (e.g., community service with a mentoring component) that would be less relevant as responses to adult crime. This could make broad implementation of restorative principles in the juvenile justice system politically more feasible than in criminal justice systems.

Second, the restorative justice model is, in some ways, compatible with the rehabilitative tradition of juvenile justice. Indeed, it is important to note that restorative justice shares with the treatment model a type of prospective focus. That is, the commitment to repair harm is not only to "make things right," but is more broadly aimed at preserving the future peace between victim and offender, and at facilitating the ultimate reintegration of both into more peaceful communities (Van Ness and Strong, 1997). But while restorative justice also shares with the treatment model a rebellion against the uniformity that in practice substitutes for fairness in justice models, the restorative concern with individualization in the response to each case is by no means equated with the clinical emphasis associated with correctional treatment. In restorative justice, the "case" encompasses more than a concern with the unique needs of the offender. Rather, restorative intervention varies based upon the unique and mutual needs of victim, offender, and community in the aftermath of a crime.[9]

Third, accountability for youth crime is more likely than adult crime to be viewed as spread among other entities. This perspective first creates greater opportunities for family and extended family involvement. While typically not a consideration in either sanctioning or reintegration of adult offenders, historically, the family has been a central consideration in juvenile court. Restorative justice also provides a role for parents, other relatives, and supportive adults in interventions like family group conferencing, and views the family as a resource in addressing reparative goals (see, e.g., Braithwaite and Mugford, 1994). In addition, sources of group support also extend to a variety of youth development and service organizations, as well as socializing institutions (especially schools and faith communities). Each of these non-justice entities can hence become informal contexts for repairing the initial harm caused by crime and promoting mediation and dispute resolution processes that can serve as an alternative to juvenile justice referral. In support of these community-focused responses to youth deviance and conflict, conventional adults, including some police officers (Bazemore and Senjo, 1997), are generally more inclined to accept responsibility for mentoring, and monitoring, delinquents than adult offenders. Restorative justice applications such as family group conferencing as a response to school crime, for example, hold great promise for cutting down on referrals to courts by developing ways to resolve or mediate disputes in the educational "community" (Moore, 1994; Riestenberg, 1997).

Fourth, the experiential accounts of crime victims, reports from victim advocates, and qualitative evidence from focus groups (Young, 1995; Bazemore et al., 1998) suggest that the victimization experience is different when the offender is a young person. Differences based on the offender's age may lead to different needs as victims begin to move toward healing, and may therefore require adaptations in reparative requirements. In addition, adult victims of juvenile crime appear to be more often focused on the needs of young offenders (especially when exposed to them in face-to-face meetings), and are often more concerned that they receive appropriate treatment than is the case when the offender is an adult (Umbreit, 1994; Bazemore, et al., 1998).

Finally, it may be possible to avoid simply subsuming restorative justice under the traditional juvenile court mission because its proponents also share many of the concerns that have led advocates of just deserts to oppose the treatment model (see, e.g, Walgrave, 1994). Hence, despite its general compatibility with a rehabilitative agenda and some fundamental disagreements with retributivists, the restorative justice model — like retributive justice — begins with an initial retrospective consideration of the harm that has been caused by the crime (Feld, 1993). This focus on past harm provides a yardstick for basing legal safeguards like due process and for developing proportionate maximums for sanctions, despite the rejection of uniformity of punishment as an absolute standard for fairness. This combination of flexibility and limits leaves space for negotiated and individualized agreements or sanctions and is less rule-driven, but it is also bounded by a legal framework.

To conclude, promising models and experiments, as well as some unique aspects of the structural and cultural context of the response to the deviance and crimes of young people, provide cause for some optimism about the prospects for implementing restorative models in juvenile justice systems. The increasingly bureaucratic nature of these systems and the surrounding service networks that support them, however, appear to be increasingly coalescing within a larger retributive framework. This trend raises questions about the extent to which change or even expanded experimentation is feasible. The hope of restorative justice is in the energy and human resources in communities that have thus far remained untapped. But tapping this energy will require more than a few diversion programs or alternative treatment opportunities within the existing system. As we argue in the next section, what is needed is a vision and strategy for promoting an expanded and empowered role for victims, communities and offenders in response to youth crime that is guided by restorative justice as an overarching philosophy.

THE LIMITS OF PAST REFORM AND PROSPECTS FOR SYSTEMIC CHANGE

Juvenile justice reform is nothing new. As "closed-system" initiatives, few if any modern reforms have been spurred by community input but have instead been system-driven, and often top-down and reactive, responses to crisis and abuse. Like the treatment and punishment paradigms on which they are based, modern reform efforts have been insular and one-dimensional, and while *system-driven*, no reform has been truly *systemic*. While many modern reforms have brought about well-intended improvements — whether focused on diversion, deinstitutionaliza-tion, case management, detention crowding, or due process concerns — these reforms have in common a piecemeal focus on one component or system function. Most juvenile justice reforms have sought to rationalize and improve the structure, process and techniques by which offenders are treated and punished, but have not questioned why or the nature of the intervention enterprise. At the end of most reform initiatives, paid professionals continue to administer treatment, punishment, and offender surveillance outside the context of the offender's and victim's community. As they fail to address other community concerns about crime surfacing, it is little wonder that these interventions often do not mean much to offenders, victims and other citizens.

Currently, systemic reform in juvenile justice is difficult because decisions about staff roles, as well as resource allocation and management approaches, are based primarily on tradition and the needs of juvenile justice bureaucracies (e.g., treatment providers, case workers), and on the current skills and role definitions of juvenile justice professionals. Innovation, when it occurs, is often based on the addition of specialized units or programs, and often seems to be driven by the need to be in step with the "program trend of the month." Any justice system can imple-ment specialized programs, including those concerned with restoring harm. How-ever, if only 10% of offenders are referred to a court's restitution or meditation program, for example, and similar small proportions complete meaningful commu-nity service or victim awareness programs with little increase in victim and commu-nity involvement in the justice process, the jurisdiction can hardly be said to be "restorative." The restorative justice framework has been developed based on innovative programs and processes such as restitution, community service, victim offender mediation and family group conferencing, rather than through a more deductive theoretical process (Zehr, 1990; Braithwaite and Mugford, 1994). Yet, programs are not ends in themselves, but simply a means to achieve outcomes that should flow from a clear understanding of community and other client needs (Goldstein, 1979; 1987).

If prior reform efforts provide any indication, there are certainly many ways restorative reforms could fail to deliver the kind of change hoped for by many advocates. Criminal and juvenile justice systems have proven capable of absorbing a variety of new concepts and policies. Too often, they have done so while making few real changes, and in some cases expanding the reach and responsibility of the dominant formal system. Most juvenile justice professionals now sense that some change is inevitable, and juvenile justice systems are currently quite open to change of a certain superficial kind.

Restorative justice could therefore become just another "buzzword" in jurisdictions that adopt new mission statements and slogans while taking few actions to disrupt the "business-as-usual" mentality. Restorative reforms could be limited to special programs, new alternatives to court processes such as victim-offender mediation, or new job descriptions such as "restorative justice coordinator." Restorative justice could also easily be pigeonholed in one component of the system, such as diversion or corrections, or could become associated with one function, such as disposition or one ancillary specialization such as victim services, while exerting little impact on the way courts work, or on mainstream public safety and rehabilitative initiatives.

To avoid such outcomes, we have insisted that restorative justice aim at becoming the leading principle guiding the justice response to youth crime, and have attempted to articulate a clear definition and statement of restorative justice principles. If restorative juvenile justice is to be understood as a fully-fledged alternative rather than a few programs around the margins of current systems, this definition and these principles must be clearly communicated. A fully-fledged restorative alternative will, in addition, require systemic reform of two basic types.

The first type refers to change at every *level* crime may be dealt with in the system, or in every place that crime is responded to in the community. Administrators, policy makers and the public must be able to identify a range of tangible, practical, restorative responses to crime of all varieties, wherever it occurs, and regardless of where the offender providing for repair of harm happens to be located in the justice system continuum. While these responses might differ greatly in the case of, say, a minor property crime by a first-time offender and a serious violent crime (based in part on the level of restrictiveness imposed on an offender according to the threat imposed to public safety or to individual victims), restorative interventions would be carried out according to what must become widely understood basic principles and familiar processes. Juvenile justice professionals, whether police, judges, or corrections workers, would share a set of basic restorative principles for intervention that would in turn be reflected in the policies and procedures governing community agencies and citizen involvement.

The second type of systemic reform is focused on mainstream justice functions, which, in a fully-fledged restorative justice system, would be carried out in a way that is clearly different from how these functions are fulfilled under a retributive, social welfare, or some type of blended system. Such reform requires that efforts to meet public expectations for ensuring safety, sanctioning crime and reintegrating offenders are based on the core principles and values of restorative justice.

Systemic Change in Juvenile Justice: Value-Driven Reform

What is most "new" and different about the restorative justice model that we propose is its three-part agenda for systemic reform in the context, content and structure of the response to youth crime. This agenda is based on a vision of a distinctive, holistic justice system that gives priority to repairing harm by involving victim, community and offender in the justice process, and by attempting to address the diverse justice needs communities experience in the aftermath of crime.

First, restorative justice advocates propose broad changes in the justice process itself, which ultimately shifts the focus more toward community solutions rather than criminal justice system reactions, and seeks to build capacity in communities to sanction crime, reintegrate offenders, repair harm to victims, and promote genuine public safety (see, e.g., Van Ness and Strong, 1997; Stuart, 1995). In this regard, genuine systemic reform begins with a questioning of prevailing values and assumptions about crime, and a challenge to examine common myths about the ends and means of the response to it. Unlike most past and current juvenile justice reforms, systemic reform initiatives therefore first raise questions about the *context* of intervention (see Figure 1, right column). What values, principals, and assumptions frame prevailing views of the essence of crime, and what should be done about it? Who should the system serve as its "clients," and what stakeholders should be involved in the response to crime and in making decisions about intervention? By what process should these decisions be made?

Second, as the right side of Figure 1 suggests, based on the answers to these questions and an effort to develop interventions aimed at meeting community needs and expectations, systemic reform would then seek change in the mission of juvenile justice. Such change in the *content* of intervention raises other questions. What goals and performance outcomes will be pursued as the justice system seeks to address the needs of its clients? What messages are to be communicated, and what changes in clients are to be brought about as a result of intervention? What methods will be used to accomplish these goals? While current policy and reform efforts are often *program-driven* (seldom addressing outcomes or questioning values), systemic reform would ensure that programs and intervention priorities are *value-driven* (established based on their capacity to accomplish mission objectives; see Figure 1, right column).

Finally, the choice of new intervention priorities should then provide the blueprint for transforming the *structure* of the juvenile justice system. These priorities, and the commitment to new and more active roles for victims, communities, and offenders, then determine what staffing patterns, resources, and professional roles

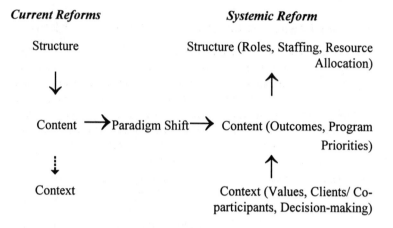

Figure 1: New Paradigms and Systemic Reform

and responsibilities are required to carry out these interventions and accomplish system goals. Current intervention models take existing structural arrangements for granted. Hence, while current policy and reform *begins* with existing bureaucracies and seeks to make top-down changes in procedures and programs, systemic reform from the "bottom up" *ends* with questions about structure, after holistic change in context and content has been addressed (see Figure 1).

As part of a new justice paradigm, restorative justice theory (Zehr, 1990; Van Ness, 1993) and practice (e.g., Pranis, 1997; Stuart, 1996) thus provides the basis for a new vision for a future systemic response to youth crime that can be clearly distinguished from both treatment/welfare and punishment-focused approaches.

Addressing the Justice Needs of the Communities: Achieving Resonance

Restorative justice advocates promote processes that run counter to adversarial procedures, and rarely talk about fear of crime and genuine citizen concerns about risks of victimization. While restorative principles will never completely resonate with traditional justice ideologies, and cannot be readily classified as punitive or lenient, basic community expectations about public safety, sanctions, and the reintegrative needs of offenders are real and relevant.

For those juvenile justice professionals and policy makers grounded in the one-dimensional punishment versus treatment debate, the goal of repairing harm must seem tangential to core concerns about how to respond to chronic and violent offenders. Indeed, advocating what appear by traditional standards to be low-impact, rather marginal practices such as mediation and community service as solutions to the youth crime problem would border on elitism that could easily relegate restorative justice to the status of a fringe movement. Restorative justice advocates have at times surely confused even those policy-makers who are generally supportive of restorative programs. Although a primary *strength* of the restorative justice paradigm is that it rises above the treatment/punishment debate and insular concerns with the needs and risks presented by offenders, the debate is a fact of life and these concerns are *not trivial*. Moreover, advocates of restorative justice are unlikely to significantly influence juvenile justice policy, or be viewed as relevant to the youth crime debate, if they continue to ignore or talk past basic public and policy maker questions about safety, rehabilitation, and clear norm enforcement (or sanctioning). If they are to be seen as something other than odd or Utopian zealots, restorative justice advocates must address these questions and link restorative principles to the legitimate expectations citizens have of their justice systems.

The reality is that restorative justice principles do have much to offer communities whose members feel overwhelmed by public safety concerns and fear of crime. Restorative justice also speaks to those citizens who believe that there is an absence of tolerance limits or sanctions for young people who misbehave and break laws, and to those who want guidance in how patterns of delinquent behavior can be corrected and known offenders habilitated and safely reintegrated. The focus on repairing harm *is* relevant to the concerns of these communities, and to the concerns of many juvenile justice professionals to develop a holistic alternative set of intervention principles and practices (Young, 1995; Bazemore and Umbreit, 1995b). But restorative justice reform must ensure that basic community expectations — that any justice system work to enhance public safety, sanction crime and promote reintegration of offenders — are directly addressed in a manner that is not inconsistent with the dominant goal of repairing harm.

More than this, we argue that there are explicitly restorative ways to address each of these expectations. For example, from a restorative perspective, sanctioning needs are best met when young offenders are held accountable and participate in community mediative processes with their victims and community members that lead to reparative agreements. Public safety needs are best addressed when communities increase their capacity to resolve conflict (Van Ness and Strong, 1997; Guarino and Klein, this volume). A systemic restorative justice model would also seek to ensure compatibility, or "resonance," among strategies to meet public safety, sanctioning, victim healing and offender reintegration objectives based on the common goal of repairing harm. This idea of resonance has two practical meanings for restorative interventions. First, programs, processes and strategies to accomplish one objective (e.g., to reintegrate an offender) should not detract from, and should ideally reinforce, efforts to accomplish other goals (e.g., to enhance public safety, or assist victims in their healing process). Second, from a restorative perspective, resonance ultimately implies that the best interventions will simultaneously give attention to the needs of victim, offender, and community — and to the common needs of all citizens for safety, tolerance limits on behavior, and practical ways to reclaim those who have defied these limits.

Hence, if it is to become a fully-fledged alternative, restorative justice cannot simply be limited to a few alternative practices and processes that allow victims and offenders to meet and discuss the crime. Showing policy makers and the public how restorative responses relate to their basic fears and concerns, while reframing the problem of crime, should be a primary project for restorative justice practice and theory. Indeed, in those rare parts of the world where restorative justice has become something more than a few alternative sanctioning processes — in New Zealand, for example —advocates have engaged decision-makers head-on in debates of real importance, such as overcrowding, the increasing drain on scarce resources as a result of spending on youth corrections, and the systemic overrepresentation of minorities in secure facilities. In doing so, they have used restorative justice principles to develop practical solutions to problems that have become the primary driving forces in juvenile justice policy (e.g., McElrae, 1993).

CONCLUSION

In this chapter, we have developed a practical working definition of restorative justice and have outlined a general strategy to implement restorative justice as a fully-fledged alternative to both the retributive and purely rehabilitative responses to youth crime in society. As a vision for the future, we believe that a systemic restorative response to crime in general could remove the rationale for a separate juvenile justice system. For strategic reasons, however, we focus on youth crime and on the community and systemic responses to it. Currently, the juvenile justice system seems to be the most suitable location to introduce restorative justice as a dominant response — in part because this system is now vulnerable to the threat of abolition, or to the dominance of a new retributivism. Juvenile justice has the most to lose if these trends continue, and the most to gain from restorative justice. These prospects make the development of a credible alternative both most urgent, and most feasible.

We are fully aware that some of our arguments are controversial among restorative justice adherents and other justice scholars. The idea of coercive restorative sanctions, the repeatedly underlined need for judicial safeguards, the insistence on an outcome focus on repair (as well as on restorative process), and the option of a fully-fledged alternative rather than a less holistic (e.g., programmatic) focus, for example, are likely to be matters of discussion and disagreement. It must even be said that the editors of this volume do not completely agree on several subquestions that are derived from these fundamental options. Regarding such disagreements, there may be some basic differences, for example, between the American and the European approaches. More specifically, American, Canadian, Australian and New Zealand proponents of restorative justice tend to display a stronger belief in the potential of local communities as the center of the justice response, and as a necessary ingredient — if not the driving force — in any restorative process (Braithwaite, 1994; Braithwaite and Mugford, 1994; Van Ness and Strong, 1997; Pranis, 1997; Bazemore, this volume; Griffiths and Corrado, this volume). European writers tend to more emphatically stress the importance of legal rights and see the state in a stronger position as a possible guardian of these rights, while viewing with some skepticism the confidence in communities (Walgrave and Guedens, 1996; van Swaaningen, 1997).

These and other divergences will become apparent in the chapters to come. Some will develop arguments and present research findings in support of the agenda we have presented here. Others will defend other points of view. At this time, most of these positions nevertheless remain complementary to each other because they stress primarily different sub-themes within the broader restorative justice model, and do so from within a common framework that, despite internal differences, is easily distinguishable from the two competing models. As stated earlier, the controversies should for the time being be seen as healthy tensions in the developmental process of the restorative justice paradigm.

★   ★   ★

REFERENCES

Bailleau, F. and G. Garioud (1994). "Social Strategies Aimed at Avoiding the Production of Criminalisable Behavior." In: Council of Europe (ed.), *New Social Strategies and the Criminal Justice System*. Nineteenth Criminological Research Conference. Strasbourg, FR: Council of Europe Press.

Balanced and Restorative Justice Project (1997). *A Framework for Juvenile Justice in the 21st Century*. Washington, DC: U.S. Office of Juvenile Justice and Delinquency Prevention.

Bazemore, G. (1994). "Understanding the Response to Reforms Limiting Discretion: Judges' Views of Restrictions on Detention Intake." *Justice Quarterly* 11(3):429-453.

—— (1996). "Three Paradigms for Juvenile Justice." In: J. Hudson and B. Galaway (eds.), *Restorative Justice: International Perspectives*. Monsey, NY: Criminal Justice Press.

—— (1997a) "The 'Community' in Community Justice: Issues, Themes and Questions for the New Neighborhood Sanctioning Models." *Justice System Journal*, 19(2):193-228.

—— (1997b) "Evaluating Community Youth Sanctioning Models: Neighborhood Dimensions and Beyond." In: *Crime and Place: Plenary Papers of the 1997 Conference on Criminal Justice Research and Evaluation, National Institute of Justice Forum.* Washington, DC: U.S. National Institute of Justice.

—— S. Day, A. Seymour and H.T. Rubin (1998). *Victims, Judges and Partnerships for Juvenile Court Reform. Final Report.* Washington, DC: U.S. Office for Victims of Crime.

—— and S. Senjo (1997). "Police Encounters with Juveniles Revisited: An Exploratory Study of Themes and Styles in Community Policing." *Policing: An International Journal of Police Strategies & Management* 20(1):60-82.

—— and C. Terry (1997). "Developing Delinquent Youth: A Reintegrative Model for Rehabilitation and a New Role for the Juvenile Justice System." *Child Welfare* 75(5):665-716.

—— and M. Umbreit. (1995). "Rethinking the Sanctioning Function in Juvenile Court: Retributive or Restorative Responses to Youth Crime." *Crime & Delinquency* 41(3):296-316.

Bishop, D., L. Wimmer, L. Lanroca-Kaduce and C. Frazier (1997). "The Transfer of Juveniles to Criminal Court: Re-Examining Recidivism Over the Long-Term." *Crime & Delinquency* 43(4):548-562.

Bowman, C.G. (1994). "The Arrest Experiments: A Feminist Critique." In: R. Monk (ed.), *Taking Sides: Clashing Views on Controversial Issues in Crime and Criminology.* Gilford, CT: Dushkin Publishing Group.

Braithwaite, J. (1994). "Thinking Harder About Democratizing Social Control." In: C. Alder and J. Wundersitz (eds.), *Family Group Conferencing and Juvenile Justice: The Way Forward or Misplaced Optimism?* Canberra, AUS: Australian Institute of Criminology.

—— and S. Mugford (1994). "Conditions of Successful Reintegration Ceremonies: Dealing with Juvenile Offenders." *British Journal of Criminology* 34(2):139-171.

—— and P. Petitt (1990). *Not Just Desert. A Republican Theory of Criminal Justice.* Oxford, UK: Clarendon.

Christie, N. (1982). *Limits to Pain.* Oxford, UK: Martin Robertson.

—— (1977). "Conflict as Property." *British Journal of Criminology* 1:1-14.

Duenkel, F. (1996). "Täter-Opfer-Ausgleich: German Experiences with Mediation in a European Perspective." *European Journal of Criminal Policy and Research* 4(4):44-66.

Feld, B. (1993). "Criminalizing the American Juvenile Court." In: M. Tonry (ed.), *Crime and Justice: A Review of Research*, vol. 17. Chicago, IL: University of Chicago Press.

Goldstein, H. (1979). "Improving Policing: A Problem-Oriented Approach." *Crime & Delinquency* 25:236-258.

—— (1987). "Toward Community-Oriented Policing: Potential, Basic Requirements and Threshold Questions." *Crime & Delinquency* 33:6-30.

Griffths, C.T. and R. Hamilton (1996). "Spiritual Renewal, Community Revitalization and Healing. Experience in Traditional Aboriginal Justice in Canada." *International Journal of Comparative and Applied Criminal Justice* 20(1):285-310.

Hahn, P. (1998) *Emerging Criminal Justice: Three Pillars for a Proactive Justice System.* Thousand Oaks, CA: Sage.

Harris, M.K., (1990). "Moving into the New Millennium: Toward a Feminist Vision of Justice." In: H. Pepinsky and R. Quinney (eds.), *Criminology as Peacemaking.* Bloomington, IN: Indiana University Press.

Hudson, J. and B. Galaway (1996). "Introduction." In: J. Hudson and B. Galaway (eds.), *Restorative Justice: International Perspectives.* Monsey, NY: Criminal Justice Press.

International Network for Research on Restorative Justice for Juveniles (1997). *Declaration of Leuven on the Advisability of a Restorative Approach to Juvenile Crime.* Leuven, BEL: author.

Lab, S. (1997). *Crime Prevention: Approaches, Practices and Evaluations (3rd ed.).* Cincinnati, OH: Anderson.

Marshall, T. (1996). "The Evolution of Restorative Justice in Britain." *European Journal of Criminal Policy and Research* 4(4):21-43.

Maloney, D. (1997), "Community and Balanced Juvenile Justice." Paper presented at the annual meeting of the Coalition of Juvenile Justice, Washington DC, February.

McCold, P. (1996). "Restorative Justice and the Role of Community." In: J. Hudson and B. Galaway (eds.), *Restorative Justice: International Perspectives.* Monsey, NY: Criminal Justice Press.

—— (1998). "Restorative Justice: Variations on the Theme." In: L. Walgrave (ed.), *Restorative Justice for Juveniles. Potentials, Risks and Problems.* Proceedings of the International Conference, Leuven May 1997. Leuven, BEL: Leuven University Press.

McElrae, F.W.M. (1993). "A New Model of Justice." In: B.J. Brown (ed.), *The Youth Court in New Zealand: A New Model of Justice.* Publication #34. Canberra, AUS: Legal Research Foundation.

Melton, A., (1995). "Indigenous Justice Systems and Tribal Society." *Judicature* 70(3):126-133.

Messmer, H. and H. Otto (Eds.) (1992). *Restorative Justice on Trial: Pitfalls and Potentials of Victim Offender Mediation: International Research Perspectives.* Norwell, MA: Kluwer.

Moore, D.B. (1994). *Illegal Action — Official Reaction.* Canberra, ACT, AUS: Australian Institute of Criminology.

Moore, M. and R. Trojanowicz (1988). "Policing and the Fear of Crime." *Perspectives on Policing.* Washington, DC and Cambridge, MA: National Institute of Justice, U.S. Department of Justice and Harvard University.

Morris, R. (1994). *A Practical Path to Transformative Justice.* Toronto, CAN: Rittenhouse.

Packer, H. (1968). *The Limits of the Criminal Sanction*. Palo Alto, CA: Stanford University Press.

Pepinsky, H.E. and R. Quinney (eds.) (1991). *Criminology as Peacemaking*. Bloomington, IN: Indiana University Press.

Peters, T. and I. Aertsen (1995). "Restorative Justice: In Search of New Avenues in Judicial Dealing with Crime." In: C. Fijnaut et al., (eds.), *Crime and Insecurity in the City. Changes in Society, Crime and Criminal Justice in Europe*, vol. 1. The Hague, NETH: Kluwer/Kluwer Law International.

Polk, K. (1994). "Family Conferencing: Theoretical and Evaluative Questions." In: C. Adler and J. Wundersitz (eds.), *Family Group Conferencing and Juvenile Justice: The Way Forward or Misplaced Optimism?* Canberra, AUS: Australian Institute of Criminology.

Pranis, K. (1997). "From Vision to Action: Some Principles of Restorative Justice." *Church & Society* 87(4):32-42.

Riestenberg, N. (1997). "Changing the Paradigm: Restorative Justice in Minnesota Schools." *ICCA Journal* 8(1):17-29.

Seymour, A. (1997), "Looking Back, Moving Forward — Crime Victims & Restorative Justice. " *ICCA Journal* 8(1):13-17.

Sparrow, M., M. Moore and D. Kennedy (1990). *Beyond 911: A New Era for Policing*. New York, NY: Basic Books.

Stuart, B. (1995). "Sentencing Circles — Making 'Real' Differences." Unpublished paper. Territorial Court of the Yukon.

—— (1996). "Circle Sentencing—Turning Swords Into Ploughshares." In: B. Galaway and J. Hudson (eds.), *Restorative Justice: International Perspectives*, Monsey, NY: Criminal Justice Press.

Tonry, M. and D. Farrington (eds.) (1995). *Building a Safer Society. Strategic Approaches to Crime Prevention*. Chicago, IL: University of Chicago Press.

Umbreit, M. (1994). *Victim Meets Offender: The Impact of Restorative Justice and Mediation*. Monsey, NY: Criminal Justice Press.

Van Ness, D. (1997). "Perspectives on Achieving Satisfying Justice: Values and Principles of Restorative Justice." *ICCA Journal on Community Corrections* 8 (1):7-12.

—— (1993) "New Wine and Old Wineskins: Four Challenges of Restorative Justice." *Criminal Law Forum* 4(2):251-276.

—— and K.H. Strong (1997). *Restoring Justice*. Cincinnati, OH: Anderson.

van Swaaningen, R. (1997). *Critical Criminology. Vision from Europe*. London, UK: Sage.

Walgrave, L. (1994). "Beyond Rehabilitation. In Search of a Constructive Alternative in the Judicial Response to Juvenile Crime." *European Journal of Criminal Policy and Research* 4(2):57-75.

—— (1995). "Restorative Justice for Juveniles: Just a Technique or a Fully-Fledged Alternative?" *Howard Journal of Criminal Justice* 34:228-249.

—— and H. Geudens (1996) "Community Service as a Sanction of Restorative Justice: A European Approach." Paper presented at the annual meeting of the American Society of Criminology, Chicago, November.

—— and J. Mehlbye (1998). *Confronting Youth in Europe*. Copenhagen, DEN: AKF.

Wright, Martin. (1991). *Justice for Victims and Offenders*. Buckingham, UK: Open University.

Young, M. (1995). "Restorative Community Justice: A Call to Action." Monograph for National Organization for Victim Assistance, Washington DC.

Zehr, H. (1990). *Changing Lenses: A New Focus for Crime and Justice*. Scottsdale, PA: Herald Press.

NOTES

1. While the relationship between these movements is not clear cut, the philosophy and rhetoric of community policing, for example, and restorative justice share many common themes. In fact, they seem compatible and potent enough that one writer, in a recent volume on criminal justice reform, identified each as two of three key pillars for a "proactive criminal justice system" (Hahn, 1998).

2. To list only a few examples of topics that remain unresolved among both researchers and practitioners, there are disagreements on the role and value of punishment, the role of victims and the relative priority given to victim needs, the importance attached to restorative processes versus outcomes, the role of the offender and of rehabilitation, and the role of the "community" vis-a-vis the "state." Indeed, we suspect that the issue that forms the very rationale for this book — the juvenile justice system as a primary context for implementing restorative reform — will continue to be one of the most strongly debated topics.

3. We are of the latter position, though we are aware of the problems that this may involve. Peaceful living and harmonious relations between citizens and collectives cannot be sustained without some degree of social organization. A society that does not articulate and enforce its norms will lose its authority and plunge communities into continuing conflict that also invites abuse of local power. We also recognize that societal norms are a matter of discussion and the means of enforcing them is rightly criticized, and we share the fear that state intrusion into the restorative process will decrease or even take away the human and relational quality of this process.

4. This is not, however, a matter of speed or efficiency in reaching a settlement for reparation. Overly routinized or scripted processes may undercut true restoration, and quite often the most satisfying end result or outcome of a restorative process is an unexpected reparative outcome based on the unique needs and wishes of the victim and/or victimized community (Umbreit, this volume).

5. Restorative justice advocates appear to be unanimous in the view that *victim* participation in restorative processes must always be completely voluntary. Hence, the discussion here of coercion, and the concomitant need for legal safeguards, is focused on the offender's role.

6. Restorative sanctions also require a different process for determining harm and the nature of the obligation that seeks input from the victim and the community. Completion of the reparative sanction is not only an outcome, but may also become a ceremonial process that brings closure for the victim, the offender and the community.

7. This allows for a wide range of flexibility in actions aimed at defining harm, planning for reparation, and carrying out and monitoring reparative obligations. However, it does not allow for choices such as simply punishing the offender or providing treatment — as might be permitted as an option when parties simply "come together to resolve how to deal with the aftermath of the offense" in the absence of a restorative agenda focus on repair as an outcome.

8. We recognize of course that distinctions among prevention, treatment, sanctioning and public safety are somewhat arbitrary constructs associated with Western retributive justice systems, and that these have a tendency to develop specialized bureaus and units for what should be closely related functions. In this regard, use of these terms in the context of a restorative vision could be viewed as temporary and strategic. Like traditional and many current indigenous societies, in which such distinctions tend to blur, a restorative justice vision would be most clearly distinguished by a problem-solving, planning and community-building focus that would have little need for such compartmentalization of functions (Melton, 1995; Stuart, 1995).

9. Moreover, individual offender characteristics are considered in restorative justice primarily as a yardstick to gauge personal accountability rather than simply to develop a treatment plan based on need.

3. The History of Restorative Justice

by

Elmar G.M. Weitekamp

INTRODUCTION

In reviewing the historical background of restorative justice, we must point out that the terms restitution, reparation, compensation, reconciliation, atonement, redress, community service, mediation and indemnification are used interchangeably in the literature, and that the term restorative justice is fairly new. All the above mentioned terms can be united under the umbrella of restorative justice. Restorative justice is a distinct and unique response to crime and has to be distinguished clearly from retributive and rehabilitative responses to crime. While the latter responses sometimes have nuances of restorative concerns, their purpose according to Walgrave (1994) is quite different: The retributive response to crime takes place in a societal context of state power, focuses on the offense, inflicts harm, seeks just desert, and ignores the victim. The rehabilitative response takes place in the societal context of a welfare state, focuses on the offender, provides treatment to him or her, seeks conforming behavior and ignores the victim as well. Conversely, the restorative justice response takes place in the societal context of empowering the state, focuses on losses, repairs the damage inflicted, seeks satisfied parties and views the victim as the central person of the whole process.

1. RESTORATIVE JUSTICE IN ACEPHALOUS SOCIETIES

According to Michalowski (1985), human societies can be broken down into two broad categories: acephalous (non-state) and state. Acephalous societies, the earliest type, did not have rulers and were the only type of human community for some 30,000 years. Acephalous societies can, according to Hartmann (1995), be distinguished as nomadic tribes and segmental societies. The former are constituted by gatherers and hunters, while segmental societies develop if the tribe changes from a food-gathering to a food-producing economy. These societies were small, economically cooperative, and relatively egalitarian, and used simple technology. Toennies' (1940) concept of *gemeinschaft* comes to mind in this regard. That these societal forms were very basic and stable did not preclude instances of deviance or trouble. As Michalowski (1985) pointed out, because of the acephalous society's diffuse structure, kin-based social organization and the concept of collective responsibility, individuals were bound very strongly to the group, thus reducing the likelihood of egoistic interests. These characteristics also minimized the potential for trouble while producing conformity and placing restraints on a potential deviant. If trouble did occur, the acephalous society resolved it without a formal legal system. After evaluating the harm, the society had to regain its lost balance by doing something either for the victim or to the offender. A state of unrest remained until the victim was satisfied; and because collective responsibility was combined with important social and economic ties between the offender's group and the victim, a resolution was important for facilitating a quick return to daily life. Resolutions were usually achieved through: (1) blood revenge, (2) retribution, (3) ritual satisfaction or (4) restitution.

1.1. Blood Revenge

Blood revenge normally applied only in cases of homicide, and, because of its link to collective responsibility, allowed the victim's clansmen to kill the offender or one of his clansmen. If a homicide occurred within a clan, blood revenge was impossible as the clan was both the victim and the offender simultaneously. Because blood feuds between kin groups were mutually destructive and potentially could cause more problems than they resolved, blood revenge was seldom used in acephalous societies to respond to homicides.

In some Eskimo villages in which blood revenge was accepted in cases of homicide but was used only rarely. As Hoebel (1954) describes, often there was no need for a community response because the murderer discharged the victim's immediate responsibilities: "Murder is followed quite regularly by the murderer taking over the widow and children of the victim. In many instances the desire to acquire the woman is the cause of the murder, but where this is not the motive, a social principle requiring provisions for the bereaved family places the responsibility directly upon the murderer" (p.83). Eskimo villages that were able to insure the well-being of the victim's wife and children without creating a burden on the village saw no further need to respond to the crime. Eglash (1958a, 1958b, 1959, 1975, 1977), who coined the term "creative restitution," would have been delighted by the creativity of these Eskimo communities.

Evans-Pritchard (1940) described the segmental order and the principles of cross-cutting ties as defined by Colson (1962) in his classical study of the Nuer tribe of the Sudan. If a Nuer is killed the reaction depends on whether the offender and victim belong to the same lineage, different lineages or different tribes. The smallest lineage segments of the Nuer are part of larger ones and several of these together form a segment of the tribe. If the victim and offender belong to a minimal lineage, no blood feud takes place. A minimal lineage is defined by the fact that inside this closely related group no blood feuds take place. The group can place a curse on the offender or expel him from the group, but no physical sanctions are imposed. However, if the offender and victim come from different lineages, a blood feud takes place and the men of the victim's clan will try to kill a man from the offenders lineage. The Nuer had a process of avoiding the blood feud and compensating the clan for the killing of the person. After a killing occurred, the offender usually fled to the tent of the leopard-skin chief, a professional mediator, where he was granted asylum, received ritual cleansing processes and was protected against taboo problems. The leopard-skin chief then began negotiations with the involved lineages. The lineage of the victim rejected, of course, the first offers of compensation out of honor and respect for the killed member. The cleverness of the leopard-skin chief, the knowledge about the destructiveness of blood feuds and the taboo problems — which did not allow the relatives of the victim to eat or drink before the mediation process was finished — usually ended in an appropriate compensation contract.

1.2. Retribution

Retribution requires returning to the offender something equivalent to the harm he or she has inflicted upon the victim. It does not require, as in the case of blood revenge, an identical harm. In this instance, the concept of "let the punishment fit the crime" would be applicable. Nevertheless, retribution in acephalous societies also meant that the injured kin group could attack the offender's clan to make it suffer in a comparable way. Like blood revenge, this could lead to continuous fights between clans.

As Michalowski (1985) points out, both forms had serious drawbacks in acephalous societies. These small, interdependent and economically cooperative communities could not afford to kill, expel or, in any other form, render unproductive those who caused trouble, because every member was valuable and often needed to guarantee the clan's survival. Furthermore, the community had to find a way to absorb that person back into the community quickly and harmoniously. Thus, ritual satisfaction and restitution became the favored forms for resolving criminal behavior in acephalous societies.

1.3. Ritual Satisfaction

The use of ritual satisfaction and restitution facilitated the return to normalcy with only minimal social disruption. According to Michalowski (1985), ritual satisfaction required some symbolic demonstration of the offender's guilt, a process in which the offender had to suffer public ridicule, a token harm or both. Although Michalowski (1985) distinguished restitution from ritual satisfaction, we think this distinction is unnecessary because both sanctions are aimed at restoring the balance between the offender and the victim, and giving the victim some sort of satisfaction. Both sanctions accomplish this task by using different forms of payment: public ridicule or a token harm in the case of ritual satisfaction, and the payment of goods in the case of restitution. An excellent example of ritual satisfaction is exemplified by the Tiwi of North Australia,:

> No Tiwi father, except in the most unusual cases, ever thought of bestowing an infant daughter upon any male below the age of twenty-five…This meant that a youth of twenty-five had his first wife betrothed to him at that age but had to wait another fourteen years or so before she was old enough to leave her father's household and take up residence and marriage duties with him…This did not necessarily lead to chastity among men under forty years old and most young wives continued to become pregnant with monotonous regularity, no matter how ancient and senile their husbands were. Since seduction constituted a serious crime the young offender and the old person faced each other in a "deadly" duel. The elder arrived with hunting spears and the younger man usually with no weapon. After a period of publicly humiliating the accused, the elder commenced to throw his spears at the offender who was expected not to retaliate. However, since he was much younger and hence almost invariably in better shape than the older man the offender could dodge the old man's spears indefinitely if he wanted to. However, rather than exacerbate the problem by publicly humiliating the older man, the young seducer having five or ten minutes demonstrated his physical ability to avoid being hit, then showed a proper moral attitude by allowing himself to be hit… A fairly deep cut on the arm or thigh that bled a lot but healed quickly was the most desirable wound to help the old man inflict, and when the blood gushed from such a wound the crowd yelled approval and the duel was over. The young man had behaved admirably, the old man vindicated his honor, the sanctity of marriage and the Tiwi institution had been upheld, and everyone went home satisfied and full of moral rectitude. Seduction did not pay. [Hart and Pilling, 1962:16]

This example shows that ritual satisfaction as a means of resolving trouble is a most appropriate sanction because it allows both the offender and the victim a degree of honor, and enables both parties to continue their normal daily activities. Of importance is the fact that the community's life is no longer disrupted, and that the offender avoids being relegated to a second-class citizen status with a negative label or stigma because of his or her crime.

1.4 Restitution

Restitution was probably the most common form of resolving a conflict in acephalous societies because it also allowed the disputing clans to resume normal relations expeditiously. Since both the offender's clan and the victim's clan were involved in the restitution negotiations, both were to a certain degree in control of the negotiations and their outcome, thus allowing a compromise that satisfied both parties. According to Nader and Combs-Schilling (1977:34-35), the restitution process in acephalous societies constituted six purposes and functions: (1) to prevent further, more serious, conflicts, particularly to avoid a feud; (2) to rehabilitate the offender back into society as quickly as possible and to avoid a negative stigma; (3) to provide for the victim's needs; (4) to restate the values of the society by addressing the needs of both the victim and the offender, thus indicating that the society desired some type of justice for all its members; (5) to socialize the members about its norms and values; and (6) to provide regulation as well as deterrence for its members. These functions clearly indicate that restitution as a form of sanction had multiple purposes in these societies and that these elements are clearly restorative justice-oriented.

One of the main reasons for the underlying pressure to come to an agreement in kinship networks was the implicit threat of a feud should no settlement be reached. After a crime was committed, a cooling-off period usually took place, during which some safety measures were provided for the offender and after which the case was evaluated. According to Nader and Combs-Schilling (1977), in some societies the offender fled to the household of a sacred leader who provided sanctuary until the conflict was resolved. The sacred leader was often chosen as the negotiator between the victim's and the offender's clans. In the absence of a sacred person, the offender and his clan often had to flee the area for safety reasons or break off communications with the other community groups until a negotiator with ties to both groups initiated the mediating process. This negotiator was frequently a member of the offender's clan who had married into the victim's group.

Using the example of the Ifuago of Northern Luzon, the Philippines, Barton (1919) noted: "The kin of each party are anxious for a peaceable settlement, if such can honorably be brought about Neighbors and co-villagers do not want to see their neighborhood torn apart by internal dissension Instead of feuding, claims and counterclaims are relayed by the monkalun (the go-between) until a settlement is achieved." (p.94; as cited in Michalowski, 1985:61) Once a monkalun had been chosen the two parties could not attack each other.

The monkalun was not a legal official, nor did he represent the delegated power of a centralized authority. However, he did serve as a quasi-legal functionary who lost his power after the conflict was resolved and was not necessarily chosen during a different conflict. As described by Hoebel (1954), the monkalum:

> ...explicitly expresses the general societal interest in the clearing up of tensions, the punishment of wrongs and the reestablishment of social equilibrium when the normal balance has been disturbed by an alleged illegitimate act...He is not a judge; for he makes no judgement. He is not an arbitrator;

for he hands down no decrees. He is merely a forceful go-between — an admonishing mediator of limited authority but of unusually persuasive effectiveness [p.21, as cited in Michalowski, 1985:62].

Typically the determination of damages involved the nature of the offense, the victim's relative class position, the solidarity and behavior of the kinship groups involved, the personal temperaments and reputations of the victim and the offender, and the geographical position of the two clans. Nader and Combs-Schilling report similarly (1977) that among the Kapauku of New Zealand, the Nuer, the Middle Atlas tribes, the Egyptian Bedouin, the Yourok Indians, and the Tonga tribe of Zambia, the nature of the offense and the victim's status — not the offender's economic status — were the main determinants of the amount of restitution or compensation to be granted.

Negotiated restitution or compensation culminating in some form of payment to the victim was an important mechanism for resolving criminal behavior in acephalous societies; there was no need for either supra-familial authority or state control. As this type of society is brought within a state legal system, it is apparent that severe conflicts will arise, one of which is often the absence of restitution or compensation in the state legal system. As Nader and Combs-Schilling illustrate (1977), this conflict can be observed in countries such as Zambia, Sardinia, Mexico, and Lebanon. Canter (1973) described this process among the Mongule tribe of Zambia as follows:

Prior to the imposition of state law, cattle-rustling cases were settled by restitution. With state law, people accused and convicted of cattle rustling were sent to jail. To make matters worse, jailing people did not decrease the incidence of cattle rustling. The Mungule measure the competence of the legal system by whether there is a decrease in recidivism, by which they would mean a decrease in cattle-rustling cases. Since they lost confidence in the State legal system, the consequences were "self-help" and rioting [n.p.; cited in Nader and Combs-Schilling, 1977:35].

Schneider (1988) described a similar process for the Aborigines in Australia. Originally they formed a peaceful, ecologically balanced, nomadic culture with strong familial and tribal orientations. Following the invasion of white settlers, however, their lifestyle was destroyed, and they were forcibly resettled into three reservations. By imposing upon the Aborigines a white Protestant culture, the Australians created a culture conflict that led to the destruction of the former's culture. Today welfare checks have replaced hunting and gathering. The Aborigines' high crime rate constitutes 1% of the total rate in Australia, yet this group represents 30% of the prison population. Since they view crime as a collapse of relationships rather than as an individual guilt phenomenon, the Aborigines reject the white criminal justice system because its formality makes reconciliation impossible. Imprisonment is not a deterrent; and once they are released on parole they cannot be supervised because of the difficult topographical conditions in which they live. Grabosky (1989) noted that the new approach of the Australian government is to let the Aborigines handle their own problems because all the programs — and there have been many —it has imposed have failed miserably.

As we pointed out earlier, the historical origin of restorative justice has existed since humans began forming communities. It is easy to assume from the literature that punishment is the most universal way of responding to norm violators. However, by expanding the analysis to acephalous societies, we find that restitution to victims and their kin frequently takes precedence over taking action against the offender, and that the reestablishment of peace in society or gemeinschaft was of utmost interest. While restitution or compensation takes something away from the offender, it is different in form, purpose and consequences from punishment in the form of revenge or retribution. Human societies seek to resolve problems, but that does not necessarily mean that something must be done to the offender out of a desire for revenge. As Michalowski (1985) concluded:

> It is ironic that modern state societies, with their elaborate institutions for law enforcement (often supported by an array of high-technology crime control devices such as cars, two-way radios, computers, etc.), cannot achieve the degree of social order and long term stability characteristic of simpler societies that have none of these tools. The reason for this seeming irony is that the degree of social peace a society enjoys depends upon the nature of its social organization, not upon its ability to capture and punish those defined as deviant. [p.65]

A number of characteristics contributed to order without a state government in acephalous societies. These societies were more egalitarian; and most of their members had nearly equal access to material consumption and opportunities to develop a sense of personal worth. This might explain why there was little basis for the development of property crimes in these societies. In addition, because every member was necessary for the life of the community, deviant members were neither devalued nor disgraced, nor did they receive a negative label or stigma for even a short period of time as these societies were interested in restoring the peace as quickly as possible. Because these communities were small, all relationships and interactions were personal, thus leading to strong bonds among the members and a reduction in deviant behavior. Usually viewed in these groups as a collective responsibility, deviant behavior constituted both a community problem and a community failure and thus provided motivation for all the members to resolve the conflict — most commonly by means of kin-based restitution and in a restorative justice manner.

Christie (1978) argued similarly for the establishment of community-based courts, with only laypeople involved, which would re-situate the ancient concept of restitution in acephalous societies into modern times. In addition, because deviance constitutes a community problem, the absence of a state authority requires that both the victim and the offender play an active role in the problem-solving process. This means that the offender must often confront those whom he or she had directly harmed rather than some abstract justice system — something Christie (1978) also advocated and singled out as a procedure most offenders try to avoid. In addition, such a practice might restrain a potential criminal because the consequences of his or her crime would be dealt with on a personal level.

All the material presented on restorative justice in acephalous societies is in direct contrast to Edelhertz's view (1977; as summarized in Galaway, 1977) that the offender's economic status is more important than the harm to his or her victim and thus the threat of punishment is traded away for money, with the victim becoming only an incidental party. We agree with Nader and Combs-Schilling (1977) that the nature of restitution and a restorative justice system in these societies contradicts these statements. Galaway (1977c) argued that restitution has been used historically as a mechanism for the offender's kin group to avoid more severe sanctions by the victim's kin group, which they could impose legitimately although it is questionable whether they would be able to.

As we demonstrated earlier, restitution and restorative justice mechanisms are used to restore order and peace as quickly as possible, and to avoid a feud (which would not be beneficial to the victim's family). However, satisfying the victim is the most important maxim of restitution. There is no doubt that this approach is beneficial to the offender and his or her clan. But to claim that it serves the offender primarily, with the victim as only an incidental party, is simply wrong and contradicts the restorative justice paradigm.

These few examples from an abundant literature on primitive and acephalous societies reflect the wide extent of restorative justice in some form, and indicate that "punishment" — in today's sense — was the exception rather than the norm. It is no surprise that Fry (1951:124) asked: "Have we not neglected overmuch the customs of our earlier ancestors in the matter of restitution? We have seen that in primitive societies this idea of "making up" for a wrong done has wide currency. Let us once more look into the ways of earlier men, which may still hold some wisdom for us." Tallack (1900:7)argued similarly in comparing ancient forms with more modern forms of punishment: "For injuries both to person or property, it enacted restitution, or reparation, in some form, as the chief, and often as the whole, element of punishment. And this was wiser in principle, more reformatory in its influence, more deterrent in its tendency and more economic to the community..." Barnes and Teeters (1959:401) suggested: "It is perhaps worth noting that our barbarian ancestors were wiser and more just than we are today, for they adopted the theory of restitution to the injured, whereas we have abandoned this practice, to the detriment of all concerned."

2. RESTITUTION IN EARLY STATE SOCIETIES

In examining the early literature on restitution and elements of restorative justice, we find that the scholars usually began with state societies rather then acephalous societies (Klein, 1978; Laster, 1975; Schafer, 1970a; Sutherland and Cressey, 1960; Wolfgang, 1965; to name but a few), thus taking for granted the existence of political power and state law. This might explain why, according to Schafer (1970a, many scholars have identified the historical origin of restitution as a key element of restorative justice in the Middle Ages. Schafer (1970a) also pointed out that earlier sources did not offer clear information, and thus he found only sporadic reference to restitution. As we have shown, that is not the case. Overlooking earlier historical facts means that if we change its basic elements, we have limited our ability to understand how a society changes in defining and dealing with trouble.

As in acephalous societies, the norms and laws of early Western cultures provided forms of restitution and elements of restorative justice for the parties involved in a dispute. The Code of Hammurabi (c.2380 BC) espoused the practice of individual compensation, which, according to Gillin (1935), was related primarily to property offenses and in general did not apply to personal injuries; however, in one case it served as a substitute for the death penalty. The Code of Hammurabi is the only source in the historical literature on restitution where the concept of restitution is restricted to property crimes. In all the other sources, this concept is applied to both property and personal crimes. Drapkin (1989) also identifies elements and/or true concepts of restorative justice for almost all societies in the ancient world that included property offenses as well as crimes against persons. Therefore, we have been unable to determine why the concept of restorative justice and restitution in today's literature is almost always limited to property offenses.

It is interesting to note that all the authors in the 1970s and 1980s have focused on restitution and restorative justice as a concept for property offenses without providing a reasonable explanation for the exclusion of personal crimes. They simply take for granted the exclusion of personal crimes, even though an examination of the history of restorative justice elements and forms clearly emphasizes the applicability of a restorative justice approach for personal crimes. In addition, most of the literature on acephalous societies deals with restorative justice elements and forms of personal crimes since property crimes played a minor role in those societies. The limitation of restitution and restorative justice to just property offenses has hampered the movement of restorative justice for the better part of the 1970s and 1980s and has no logical explanation.

The early Hebrews also used restitution and forms of restorative justice for personal crimes. Gillin (1935:198) described the case of two men involved in a fight that resulted in non-fatal injuries to one of the men. The one who inflicted the injury was required to pay for the employment time the other man lost due to the healing process. Similarly, if an ox was known to be dangerous but the owner did not take proper precautions and the ox gored a person to death, both the ox and its owner were to be killed unless the victim's family was willing to accept a reparation instead. Tyler (1889, as cited in Gillin, 1935) reported that the transition from blood vengeance to compensation could be observed in Arabia. While the nomad tribes outside the cities continued to enforce the blood feud rather strictly, the people living in the cities found it necessary to resolve violent conflicts through compensation in order to avoid the blood feud's devastating effects.

Homer, in the Ninth Book of the *Iliad*, referred to the case of Ajax, who reproached Achilles for not accepting Agamemnon's offer of reparation. Ajax reminded Achilles that even a brother's death may be compensated by the payment of money so that the murderer, having paid restitution, may remain free among his people. Tacitus (n.d., as cited in Michalowski, 1985) reported that among the ancient Germans: "Even homicide is atoned by a certain fine in cattle and sheep; and the whole family accepts the satisfaction to the advantage of the public weal, since quarrels are most dangerous in a free state."

Diamond's (1935) research on the sanctions imposed for homicide confirmed that monetary restitution was an accepted form throughout the Western world:

> Of fifty to one hundred scattered tribal communities as to which the information available is of undoubted reliability 73 percent called for a pecuniary sanction versus 14 percent [that] called for a certain number of persons to be handed over to the family of the victim as a sanction. This too is actually a fine, though not a monetary one. One hundred percent of the Early and Early Middle Codes, beginning with the Salic code (around 500-600 A.D.) and lasting through the Anglo-Saxon laws (900-1100 A.D.), called for pecuniary sanctions for homicide. It was not until the Late Middle and Late Codes that death was established as the exclusive sanction for intentional homicide [p.148; as cited in Barnett, 1977:352].

Schafer (1970a) noted that among Semitic nations the death fine was used and continued to prevail under the Turkish Empire. He also described the use of restitution and atonement among Indian Hindus under the theme of "he who atones is forgiven," where the offender was obliged to pay compensation to the king, the relatives of the deceased or both.

While each tribe had its own set of laws, the contents of these laws were quite similar. The first written laws were the Salic Law of the Franks (about 500 A.D.) and the Laws of Ethelbert of Kent (about 600 A.D.), whose main concern was to avoid the blood feud. Every crime was a crime against the family or clan, and the offender's clan was held responsible for crimes committed by its members. The Laws of Ethelbert invented a system of compensation involving the *wergild, bot* and *wite* (Jeffrey, 1957). The *wergild* was money paid to a family for the death of one of its members; the *bot* was money paid for injuries not leading to the death of a family member; and the *wite* was money paid to a mediator to cover the costs of overseeing the compensation plan. However, some crimes were considered *botless* crimes, that is, no bot or compensation could be paid, making it necessary for the victim's family to resort to the blood feud. An example of a *botless* crime was a secret murder. The *wergild* was to be paid by the offender, often with the help of friends and family, within 12 months. If the offender failed to pay the compensation, he or she was liable to bear the consequences of a vendetta.

These tribes developed extremely elaborate systems of accounting for the injuries suffered by their members. Under the Laws of Ethelbert, according to Pollock and Maitland (1968:460, as cited in Barnett, 1977:351): "...the four front teeth were worth 6 shillings each, the teeth next to them four, the others one; thumbs, thumbnails, forefingers, middle fingers, ringfingers, little fingers and their respective fingernails were all distinguished and a separate *bot* [italics added] was set for each..." Gillin (1935) reported that similarly, under the early Saxon Laws a man who knocked out the front tooth of another man had to pay eight shillings; if it was an eyetooth he had to pay four shillings, and if it was a molar the price was 15 shillings. In addition, the Saxons had a catalogue for almost all types of injuries. Similar provisions can be found in the Salic Laws of the Franks, where compensation rates were provided in detail for all types of crimes. It is interesting to note that compensation was determined by the rank of the injured person. Gillin (1935) further noted that compensation for the murder of a free Frank or a barbarian was 800 dinars, with half the restitution money paid to the sons of the slain father and the other half to the nearest relatives on both the mother's and father's sides. In the absence of relatives, the money went to the "fisc," or royal treasury. Private revenge by the victims or their clans was sanctioned in this tribal society. However, if offenders refused to pay the demanded compensation they were, according to Schafer (1968), stigmatized as outlaws, and any member of the community could kill them with impunity.

As these examples of early state societies demonstrate, restitution was an important tool for resolving conflicts. As in acephalous societies, the main reason was to avoid the devastating effects of the blood feud. The reported systems of compensation and restitution were applied mostly for crimes against the person rather than property offenses. As the form of the tribal organization advanced, the role of a recognized ruler or chief, with the authority to issue commands, increased. Michalowski (1985) describes these early forms of proto-states that were characterized by simple technology, simple division of labor, some form of control over the produced property and limited material inequality. The rulers and chiefs exercised a certain degree of power, but could control or exploit the labor of others by making them work for the former because the state lacked a class of rule enforcers. The rules were enforced by the rulers' kinship members, who had to work for the support of the kinship in the first place, thus limiting the rulers' power.

As centralized rulers emerged and took an increasingly interested and active role in the resolution of trouble, the needs of the victims, as Schafer noted (1968), were replaced progressively by the interests of the state as the basis for settling conflicts. Michalowski (1985) describes a Zulu tribe where people were said to belong to the king. As a result, restitution was no longer paid to the victim and his clan but rather to the king. The king collected monetary restitution from the offender for having killed one of his people, thus denying the victim and his clan compensation for the loss suffered. This decline in the victim's role in settling disputes signified an important change in the nature of social control. As the leader or the state became the central leader for settling disputes, he or it took this role away from the clans or kinship, thus making a restorative justice approach impossible. Responsibilities became increasingly individualized rather than collective, thus making more abstract the obligation to conform to social rules. As historian Maine (1905, as cited in Michalowski, 1985) observed, with the coming of the state power "the individual is steadily substituted for the family as the unit of which civil laws take account." Or, as Christie (1978:226) noted: "Individuals become less beautifully tied into a web of social relations where an unexpected move results in a magnitude of subtle counter-moves and where deviant behavior is not necessarily seen as deviance or called deviance, but is kept under control through daily interaction with a number of other persons who are of great importance..." In sum, Michalowski (1985:71)said, "as kinship and community are supplanted by state law as the basis of social control, the potential for trouble and conflict increase."

In the Anglo-Saxon hemisphere the increasing power of kingships as trans-local and trans-tribal institutions, uniting large areas containing various people, marked the beginning of a radical change in societal structure: the communitarian tribal society was supplanted by a hierarchical feudal system. After the division of the Frankish Empire by the treaty of Verdun in 843 A.D., restitution was replaced by a fine, assessed by a tribunal, which went to the state rather than to the victim and his kinship. Parallel with the rise of the feudal system was the increasing influence of Christianity on legal concepts. According to Barnett (1977), the rise of Christianity influenced ecclesiastical law leading to canon law and an attempt to influence tribal, local and feudal customs in Europe. Using this system as their model and their rival, the kings created their own legal systems that vested legal and political authority in themselves. Previously as Oppenheimer (1913:162, as cited in Barnett, 1977:353) noted, the state was concerned only with its own affairs and "did not include among its functions the repression of wrongs between individual and individual, between family and family, between clan and clan." The crown began to claim a share of the compensation payment, according to Oppenheimer (1913:162), as: "a commission for this trouble in bringing about a reconciliation between the parties, or, perhaps as the price payable to the malefactor either for the opportunity which the community secures for him of redeeming his wrong by a money payment, or for the protection which it affords him after he has satisfied the award, against further retaliation on the part of the man whom he has injured."

Tallack (1900) referred to the greedy feudal barons and ecclesiastical powers who exacted a double vengeance upon the offender by taking his property instead of giving it to the victim and his kinship, and by applying corporal punishment or imprisonment to the offender while ignoring the victim. By monopolizing the institution of dispute settlement, the kings increased their share of payments and eventually absorbed the entire amount (Schafer, 1975b). Jeffrey (1957) reported similarly that:

Early Germanic justice was based on a folkpeace, a peace of the community. This idea gave way to the *mund* [italics added]. A *mund* [italics added]was the right of the king or lord had [sic] to protect a person or area. At first the *mund* [italics added]was restricted to special persons and areas; gradually it was extended to include the king's court, army, servants, hundredcourt, and finally the four main highways in England. It was not referred to as the king's peace. The kings, lords, and bishops now received the compensation rather than the kinship group. They had a *mund* [italics added]which had to be protected [p.657]

Wolfgang (1965) pointed out that the state's claim to the exclusive right to inflict punishment was made in the interest of peace but not necessarily of justice. He noted further that:

It may be argued that an injury to any citizen is an injury to the social whole of which the citizen is a member, but under the feudal system (and as late as Louis XIV who dared to say, "L'etat c'est moi") the grand seigneurs disposed of the property and persons of the common people on the pretext of their criminality, almost at discretion. Using the principle of composition of public injuries to find offenders, they abused their power until the administration of justice became an act of confiscation, if not outright blackmail [p.9].

By the end of the 12th century the erosion of restorative justice elements and restitution in Europe was complete; but the system of compensation surrendered only after a struggle. The system was not voluntarily abandoned by the people; it was deliberately and forcibly co-opted by the crown and then discarded. The victim's right to receive compensation directly from the offender and his kinship was transferred to the collective society, where it remains to this day.

As Barnett (1977) pointed out rightly, that criminal punishment by the state emerged from a bloody Hobbesian jungle is pure myth. Monetary payments replaced violence as the means of dispute settlement and have functioned well for most of the time humans have lived together if we include acephalous societies. It was through the violent conquest of most of Europe that state criminal punishment was accepted reluctantly. Michalowski (1985) noted that formal law emerged as a means of controlling property relations in civilizations and that the concept of individual property and the history of law are inseparable or, in Jeremy Bentham's words (cited in Diamond, 1935:33), "Property and law are born together and die together."

Before turning our attention to more recent developments in the area of restorative justice, we must clarify a controversy about restitution as one form of restorative justice in the Middle Ages. As Klein (1978:383) noted, "If one is to believe Pollock and Maintland (1968), the state of affairs during what Schafer (1968) has termed the 'golden age of the victim' can only be described as brutal." Geis (1977:150-152) also called for the dismemberment that surrounds the history of restitution, while others (Jacob, 1970; Laster, 1975; Wolfgang, 1965; Schafer, 1968, to name but a few) have emphasized that restitution was used widely and well in the Middle Ages. While one side of this controversy praises the Middle Ages for its wise use of restorative justice as a humane penal sanction perceived as being beneficial to the offender and his kinship, the victim and his kinship, and society in general, the other side argues that that view is absolutely wrong, that restorative justice in its applied forms was abused by people in power, misused by the rich people as a cheap way out of trouble, and led to chaos in society. The restorative justice advocates argue in addition that restorative justice and restitution disappeared as a penal sanction after the state took over the criminal justice system, thus leading to an inhumane and brutal system of criminal justice where the victim had no place. The other side argues that the state moved in and took control of the criminal justice system because of the public outcry about the horrors of the existing system. While this controversy appears to be unsolvable, we suggest that by looking at the definition of the Middle Ages we might find a reasonable solution to this dilemma. *The Random House Dictionary of the English Language* (1968:906) defines the Middle Ages as: "...the time in European history between classical antiquity and the Italian Renaissance (from the late 5th century A.D. to about 1350): sometimes restricted to the later part of this period (after 1100) and sometimes extended to 1450 to 1500."

Because this definition indicates two time frames for the Middle Ages, we think it is worthwhile to examine both in connection with restorative justice and the controversy surrounding these periods. If we talk about the Middle Ages as occurring from 500 to 1350, the advocates of restorative justice and restitution are correct because, for the better part of that period, restorative justice was used in a humane way that benefited the victim, the offender and society in general. According to the advocates, the use of restorative justice declined at the beginning of the 12th century; and it is generally agreed that by the end of that century the erosion of restorative justice was complete. If, on the other hand, the critics of the historical use of restorative justice use the time frame from 1100 to 1500 — as their criticism indicates — they are right as well. Geis (1977) uses historical examples in his critique in which he clearly talks about a time during which kings established their power and took the conflict-solving process away from the parties involved by creating a firm, state-controlled, criminal justice system. Klein (1978:383-85) writes about the same time frame and the atrocities committed during the decline of restorative justice approaches and the establishment of a state-run criminal justice system.

All the evidence in this controversy indicates that the facts presented by both sides are correct and that the two definitions of the Middle Ages, which are both correct, led to the controversy. However, Geis (1977) and Klein (1978) were incorrect in their historical critiques of restorative justice and restitution because they ignored the "golden age of the victim," and began their reviews with the decline of the restorative justice approach and restitution as a penal sanction. Their critiques of the decline period were nevertheless correct because restorative justice approaches and elements had prevailed for about 600 years, and both periods took place in what is known as the Middle Ages.

3. RESTITUTION AT THE TURN OF THE CENTURY

By the end of the 12th century the erosion of restorative justice elements was complete, and the state had taken control of the criminal law. Harding (1982) noted that as the rights of the state gradually overshadowed and supplanted those of the victim, the link among restorative justice, restitution and punishment was severed. As Harding (1982) and Schafer (1970a) pointed out, restorative justice and restitution to the victim plays an insignificant role in the administration of criminal law and justice, and, with the disappearance of compensation, a crime was considered an offense against the state while a tort was an offense against individual rights only. The victim, in terms of his or her rights to pursue compensation or restitution for damages suffered, had to pursue his or her claim through the separate body of civil law. Because the victim could not always afford the expense in terms of time and money of bringing a civil action against the offender, Harding (1982) concluded that the civil remedy had not been a very effective measure for obtaining restitution on the victim's behalf, let alone the principles of restorative justice and their benefits for the victim, the offender, their extended families, the communities and society.

In some countries the criminal case was combined with civil action for purposes of procedural processing. In the 16th and 17th centuries the German legal system developed the "*Adhaesionsprozess*" in which the judge of a criminal process was allowed, at his discretion, to decide a victim's claim for restitution within the scope of the criminal proceeding. As Schafer (1970b) noted, the criminal trial still predominates in the German system and takes precedence over hearing the victim's claim. For reasons of convenience, the victim's claim for restitution is heard at the same time as the criminal charges; however, technically, the two hearings are independent of each other. This practice has been adopted by a number of other countries. However, as Schafer (1970a) pointed out, it was almost abandoned only a few years after its invention and was kept alive only by the force of tradition. In general, because victims are ignored by most criminal justice systems, they have been forced to resort to civil law procedures to obtain restitution or compensation.

Despite the increasing interest in reforming the offender, which has been matched by decreasing concern for the victim, some legal philosophers and reformers have reiterated the importance of restitution and compensation and, on a more general level, a restorative justice approach. Among them were Sir Thomas More who suggested in his 17th century *Utopia* that restitution should be made by offenders to their victims and that offenders should be required to work for the public to raise money for the restitution payments. Another philosopher, James Wilson (1985), discusses justice as the protection of rights through restorative justice: "Every crime, as we have seen, includes an injury: this I consider as a leading maxim in the doctrine of crimes. In the punishment of every crime, reparation for the included injury ought to be involved; this I consider a leading maxim in the doctrine of punishments." (as cited in McCloskey, 1984:626).

Other advocates of restorative justice and restitution have outlined similar plans of reparation. Despite the widespread adoption of retributive justice throughout Europe, Beccaria (1977) emerged as a brilliant criminal law reformer. Credited with having begun the classical school with its seemingly rigid approach, Beccaria was actually a humanitarian opposed to capital punishment and the often arbitrary and unfair way the law was applied, thus laying the groundwork for advocates of restorative justice. Bentham (1977:40), for instance, stressed the necessity of taking care of the crime victim by means of restorative justice: "[S]atisfaction is necessary in order to cause the evil . . . to cease, and reestablish everything in the condition it was before the offense; to replace the individual who has suffered in the lawful condition in which he would have been if the law had not been violated." He argued strongly for a restorative justice approach of punishment and complained that satisfaction is given with grudging parsimony while punishment is meted out with a lavish hand. One of the first advocates of a state compensation plan should the offender be unable to pay satisfaction, he considered satisfaction almost as necessary as punishment and beneficial to the public.

Bonneville de Marsangy proposed in 1847 a compensation plan that combined restitution and compensation:

> Now if it is true that there is no real social security without reparation, the conclusion is that this reparation must take place, cost what it will, and as one of the *sine qua non* [italics added] conditions of the social contract; and that, in consequence, society must rigorously impose it on the culprit, at the same time and under the same justification that it imposes punishment on him; however, by the same token, we must conclude that [if] there is no known culprit, society itself must assume the responsibility for reparation. . . . It would be easy to show, with arguments of an irresistible logic, that, when the authors of a crime are unknown or when the condemned persons are insolvent, the State should repair the harm done to the victim [Normandeau, 1973:133]

Ferri (1917) argued that the state was negligent in protecting its citizens and must be indemnified for the harm caused them by crimes; the state must take into account the victim's rights. Garofalo (1914) pointed out the benefits of restorative justice to society as a whole: "If offenders were persuaded that . . . they could in no wise evade the obligation to repair the damage [of] which they have been the cause, the ensuing discouragement to the criminal world ... would be far greater than that produced by temporary curtailment of their liberty" (p.419).

Advocacy for restorative justice, restitution and compensation was discussed at a number of International Prison Congress meetings between 1878 and 1900. At the 1878 Congress in Stockholm, it was proposed that all nations return to the ancient concept of restitution; Garofalo raised the same issue at the next Congress in Rome in 1885 (Jacob, 1970). Further Congresses in 1890 in Petersburg, Russia and in 1891 in Christiana, Norway led, according to Schafer (1970b:10) to the following conclusions:

1. modern law does not sufficiently consider the reparation to injured parties;
2. in the case of petty offenses, time should be given for indemnification; and
3. prisoner's earnings in prison might be used to this end.

At the following Congress in 1895 the question of restorative justice, restitution and compensation to the victim was dealt with intensively. As Schafer (1970b) pointed out, it was felt that (1) modern laws were weak on this point, and (2) in some countries the laws were harder on the victim than on the offender. The final resolutions of this Congress were similar to the conclusions of the Christiana meeting, and, in the absence of sufficient evidence, the problem was adjourned to the next meeting. At the Brussels Congress in 1900, restorative justice and restitution were discussed exhaustively, and, as Barrows (1903) reported, Prins (1895) proposed that restitution be considered a condition of suspension of sentence or of conditional release after imprisonment. The penalists tried to agree upon a resolution that was presented by Garofalo and described by Barrows (1903) in his summary report about the conference as follows:

> In the case of prisoners having property, steps should be taken to secure it, and to prevent illegal transfers. As to insolvent offenders, other methods of constraint must be sought. The minimum term of imprisonment being sufficiently high, its execution should be suspended in the case of offenders who beyond the costs of the process have paid a sum fixed by the judge as reparation for the injured party, exception being made in the case of professional criminals and recidivists. The State Treasury would gain, since it would not only be spared the expense of supporting the prisoner, but would be reimbursed for all other expenses. The delinquent would be punished and the injured party reimbursed. In the case of serious offenses in which imprisonment is deemed necessary, Garofalo would make parole after a certain time of imprisonment depend on the willingness of the prisoner to reimburse his victim from his earnings saved in prison. He favors a public fund to assure reparation for those who cannot obtain it in any other manner. [p.23-24]

Unfortunately, the members of the conference were unable to pass any specific proposal or resolution that would have required restorative justice and restitution in any of its various forms. The members did finally pass a resolution that merely readopted the recommendations of the previous Congress, and called for increasing the rights of the victim of a crime under civil law. As Geis (1977:160) noted, the Brussels Congress had the effect of "blatantly misstating both the ingredients and the spirit of the earlier resolutions and effectively managed to bury the subject of victim compensation as a significant agenda topic at international penological gatherings from hence forth to the present time." The resolution adopted buried not only the subject of victim compensation by the state but restitution by the offender to the victim, as well as any other restorative justice components. It took nearly 50 years after the Brussels conference, before Fry (1951:124) asked whether our ancestors were not wiser with reference to the extensive use of restorative approaches to solve conflicts. Tallack (1900:7) had already argued that "reparation as the chief, and often as the whole, element of punishment was wiser in principle, more reformatory in its influence, more deterrent in its tendency and more economic to the economy." Barnes and Teeters (1959:401) suggested in this context that our barbarian ancestors were wiser and more just than we are today. However, it was not until 1975 that Hudson and Galaway rediscovered the victim and the ideas of compensation, restitution, and other forms of handling and solving conflicts that are collectively known today as restorative justice.

4. OLD AND ANCIENT FORMS OF RESTORATIVE JUSTICE AS PACEMAKERS FOR THE NEW MILLENIUM

In looking at the latest developments in restorative justice, one finds that some of the newly implemented programs are in fact very old, and that ancient forms of restorative justice have been used in acephalous societies and by early forms of humankind. This is illustrated by the adoption of family group conferences, family conferences and circle hearings by indigenous people such as the Aboriginals, the Inuit, and the native Indians of North and South America. This astonishes at first glance, but makes sense if one takes into account that the European and American systems are, according to Walgrave and Geudens (1996:361), under severe pressure. Feld (1993:98) argues that "the child receives the worst of both worlds: he gets neither the protection accorded to adults nor the solicitous care...postulated for children." It is not surprising that authors write in this context about: youth justice — crisis or opportunity (Tutt, 1994); American juvenile justice — method and madness (Klein, 1994); the juvenile court — an endangered species (Doek, 1994); and the juvenile justice system — will it survive (Junger-Tas, 1994). Walgrave and Geudens (1996) rightly point out that: "many scholars believe that a way out of this dilemma could be found in developing the restorative justice paradigm as a full-fledged alternative to both the rehabilitative and retributive approaches to juvenile justice."

It is kind of ironic that we have at the approach of the year 2000 to go back to methods and forms of conflict resolution that were practiced some millennia ago by our ancestors who seemed to be much more successful than we are today. The rebuttal to the above-mentioned critique of current juvenile justice systems and their failures could indeed be a return to the ancient concepts of family group conferences and other forms of reintegration processes and ceremonies as described for instance by Braithwaite and Mugford (1994). Besides, these ancient forms of family or circle conferencing seem to be the most promising approaches today, as evidenced by victim-offender mediation programs practiced in many countries, and as Walgrave and Geudens (1996) rightly argue are (creative) forms of community service. All these forms of restorative justice have distinct advantages over the retributive and rehabilitative approaches. Their goal is not to give the state the power to inflict harm, seek just deserts, and ignore the victim, to focus the attention on the offender, try to rehabilitate him or her, and ignore the victim as well, but to focus on losses for all parties involved, repair the damages inflicted, restore peace within the communities and make the victim the centerpiece of the whole healing process. Weitekamp et al., (1996) point out in this context that even today in the areas of policing a great shift has taken place away from traditional forms of crime control and towards community- and problem-oriented policing that rely heavily on the restorative justice philosophy. Weitekamp (1997) further shows that this is true as well for newer forms of prevention programs such as the programs of "communities that care." All these developments indicate that the common forms of handling problems and conflicts these days are outdated, lead to dissatisfaction among citizens, do not make societies more secure, do not improve the quality of life of citizens, and are unable to restore peace in communities. Therefore, the very old and ancient forms of solving conflicts seem to be among today's most promising forms of restorative justice programs.

According to Hudson et al., (1996b), the family group conference encompasses the following ingredients:

- Children and families have a fundamental right and responsibility to participate in decisions that affect them.

- Families are competent to make decisions rather than the more traditional view that they are "pathological," "dysfunctional," or "deficient" in some way.

- Sensitivity and practical recognition of culture and cultural identity are crucial. Affirming the values of indigenous people and enabling these values to be reflected in the decision-making context are of great importance.

- A restorative and not a retributive approach is paramount, with concern for the broader relationships among offenders, victims and the communities. A crime in this context is considered more than a simple violation of a law, and the key of this approach is to focus on the damage and injury done to victims and communities.

In looking at the potentials and possibilities of the family group conference one has to distinguish between two major models: the welfare and the justice models. While the first form seems to work well in the area of protecting children (Fraser and Norton, 1996; Ban, 1996; Marsh and Crow, 1996), the latter is of greater importance and interest in the context of restorative justice. The "new form" of family group conference was first introduced by New Zealand in the Children, Young Persons and Their Families Act of 1989, and incorporated the above-mentioned forms. Hassall (1996) identifies four "philosophical strands" on which the act was based: family responsibility, children's rights including the right to due process, cultural acknowledgment, and partnership between the state and the community. Essentially, a family group conference is intended to be a relatively informal, loosely structured meeting in which the offender and his or her extended family, together with a legal advocate in some systems, get together with the victim, his or her supporters, and other relevant parties to discuss the offending and to negotiate appropriate responses (Alder and Wunderslitz, 1994a). Braithwaite (1994) suggests that a more appropriate term for the conferences is community accountability conferences.

The same or similar forms of family group conferences can be found in Australia, which in 1991 introduced family conferencing in Wagga Wagga as an Australian variation of the New Zealand family group conferencing (New South Wales Law Reform Commission, 1996). The program of Wagga Wagga was founded as a community policing project and placed into the context of the police cautioning program (Moore and O'Connell, 1994). Programs like this can also be found in Canada, the U.S., and England, and, as Morris et al., (1996) report, interest in this practice exists in such diverse countries as South Africa, the Philippines, Israel and Singapore. A quite similar form was, according to Yazzie and Zion (1996), established in 1982 in the Navajo Nation by introducing the Navajo Peacemaker Courts. In the peacemaker courts, respected community leaders preside over traditional Navajo processes to resolve disputes. This process is not confrontational, and the victims, perpetrators, and their families have to find a solution in order to end the dispute. The role of the peacemaker is to offer practical advice and to draw upon the traditions and stories of the culture of the Navajos. Similar procedures are reported by Nielsen (1996) for the native justice committees in Canada. In addition, a process of sanctioning and healing in this context is described by Griffith and Hamilton (1996) for the Canadian Aboriginal communities. Also in Canada, Stuart (1996) reports on circle sentencing in which the family together with the community discusses the circumstances underlying a crime. The circles involve offenders, victims, the friends and family of each, and community members.

T. Stewart (1996:65) points out that, with regard to youth justice, the New Zealand family group conference can use the following procedures: "increase the range of diversionary options through which young offenders can be made accountable for their offending; ensure a shift in philosophy from one of unilateral state intervention in the lives of children, young people and their families to one based on partnership with the state; enable culturally diverse processes and values to be reorganised and affirmed; and involve victims in the decisions about outcomes for the children and young people who have offended against them."

The key to this process is that the children and young offenders are held accountable and are encouraged to accept responsibility for their behavior. Further on, the youthful offender should be dealt with in a manner that acknowledges his or her needs, and that gives him or her an opportunity to develop in a responsible, beneficial and socially acceptable way. According to T. Stewart (1996) the following persons can participate in the conference: the child or young person; their parents or guardians; members of the family; *whanau* (extended family) or family group; a representative of an *iwi* (tribal groupings tracing their descent from the same ancestor) or cultural authority; the youth coordinator; a representative of the police;

any victims of the offense or a representative of the victim; a supporter of the victim; any barrister, solicitor, youth advocate, or lay advocate representing the offender; a social worker in certain cases; and any other person whom the family, *whanau*, or family group wishes to be present.

According to the literature, the family — particularly the extended family — plays a crucial role in the process. The relationship between the child or young person and his or her family, *whanau, hapu* (families linked by marriage and identified with a particular home ground, a subtribe), *iwi,* and family group should by all means be strengthened, improved or at least be maintained. Since the young people are supposed to take responsibility for their actions it is very important and even a postulate of restorative justice that the victim participates in the conference. Victims are also, in most forms, allowed to bring somebody who they trust and who supports them.

In New Zealand, the police are involved in the family group conference through the youth aid officer. The youth aid officer's cases are referred by frontline police officers, and his or her primary role in the conference is that of an informant who represents the police. In the absence of victims, he or she will represent their interests. In the conference itself, the youth aid officer will read the summary of facts, which may then be corrected by the offender or the victim. In addition, the youth aid officer can give advice on which areas of the juvenile's problem behavior, such as drug or alcohol problems, the conference should pay special attention to. T. Stewart (1996), reports that the introduction of the family group conference was seen by the frontline officers as a soft option and cuddling of juveniles and not punitive enough, but that this resistance and reluctance is diminishing, partly through the education of the frontline officers by the youth aid officers. In the Australian family conference in Wagga Wagga, the police play a much more important role, which is criticized heavily by Polk (1994a) who fears the negative effects of netwidening. It seems to be unclear what role the police should play and to what extent they should be involved in such processes, though their participation is necessary.

The actual conference is usually held at a neutral venue to ensure that the victim is not intimidated. According to T. Stewart (1996), in cases where it is feasible and appropriate, the meeting should be held on the offender's *marae* (tribal meeting ground, including a meeting house). In other cases, the neutral venue can be a local hall, community house, school or church. The participants usually sit in a circle during the conference. The conference itself consists, according to Wundersitz and Hetzel (1996:127), of three distinct stages: "the introductory stage, the second stage in which the impact of the offence is discussed, and the final stage in which the hoped-for resolution is reached." In the first stage, the coordinator introduces the participants and sometimes opens the conference with a prayer or customs of indigenous people. The second stage starts with the outline of the offense through the youth aid officer who asks at the end whether the juvenile agrees with the facts. The young person then usually tells the story of what happened. Wunderslitz and Hetzel (1996) point out that the involvement of the youngster in the beginning of the conference is done deliberately in order to engage the juvenile from the outset. The victim and his or her family or supporters then express their feelings. It is during the second stage where the groundwork for a successful and/or positive outcome is laid, and the quality of the interaction between the offender and the victim is the decisive factor for this. The final stage usually takes place after a break in which the families of the offender and victim can deliberate about the contract. The third stage determines what constitutes appropriate reparation through a proc ss of negotiations during which the offender and his or her family are ques-tior l as to the means by which they want to repair the damage. The views of the victim and his or her family and other participants are sought afterward. After the participants reach an agreement, the police representative is asked whether he or she agrees with the negotiated contract. The police often have the power to veto and send the case to the youth court, but according to Wundersitz and Hetzel (1996) this is rarely done. The goal is to find a fair outcome which takes the following points into ccount: (1) the victim's need for restitution and reparation; (2) the expecta-tior. of the community for accountability; and (3) the juvenile's needs and circum-stances

It is very important that the negotiation process involves not only the offender and the victim, but also their extended family members and other social networks that have been harmed through the crime. The ultimate goal of this form of restora-tive justice is according to Wundersitz and Hetzel (1996) one of healing and redressing of the harm done to the victim though restitution. By repairing the damage, the offender can be reconciled with the victim and reintegrated into their family and social networks. The reconciliation and reintegration restore the har-mony and peace in the community.

CONCLUSION

As we have shown, humans have used forms of restorative justice for the larger part of their existence. Penal law and the often destructive retributive answer to crime — or, more recently, the failed rehabilitative efforts — have been fairly new. The two latter approaches have led to systems of (in)justice that have to be considered as failures. Forms of restorative justice, as we could find them in acephalous societies and especially early state societies, seem to be the better answer to the crime problem of today's societies. It is interesting to note that at the approach of the year 2000, the most promising answers to the ills of society caused by crime are of a restorative justice nature. The family group conferences of New Zealand and other forms of conflict resolution as practiced by indigenous people seem to be in this context the most promising ones, and can look back to an extraordinarily long tradition. The advantage of such programs lie in their healing power for all involved people, and the participation of the enlarged family, social group and community.

★ ★ ★

REFERENCES

Alder, C. and J. Wundersitz (eds.) (1994a). *Family Conferencing and Juvenile Justice: The Way Forward or Misplaced Optimism?* Canberra, AUS: Australian Institute of Criminology.

—— and J. Wundersitz (1994b). "New Directions in Juvenile Justice Reform in Australia." In: C. Alder and J. Wundersitz (eds.), *Family Conferencing and Juvenile Justice*. Canberra, AUS: Australian Institute of Criminology.

Ban, P. (1996). "Implementing and Evaluating Family Group Conferences with Children and Families in Victoria Australia." In: J. Hudson, A. Morris, G. Maxwell and B. Galaway (eds.), *Family Group Conferences: Perspectives on Policy and Practice*. Leichhardt, AUS and Monsey, NY: Federation Press and Criminal Justice Press.

Barnes, H.E. and N.K. Teeters (1959). *New Horizons in Criminology 3rd ed.* New York, NY: Prentice Hall.

Barnett, R. (1977). "Restitution: A New Paradigm of Criminal Justice." In: R. Barnett and J. Hagel (eds.), *Assessing the Criminal*. Cambridge, MA: Ballinger.

Barrows, S. (1903). *"Report on the Sixth International Prison Congress, Brussels, 1900."* Washington, DC: U.S. Government Printing Office.

Barton, R.F. (1919). "Ifugao Law." In: *University of California Publications in American Archeology and Ethnology*, 15.

Beccaria, C. (1977). *On Crimes and Punishment (6th ed.)*. Indianapolis, IN: Bobbs-Merrill.

Bentham, J. (1977). *A Fragment on Government and an Introduction to the Principle of Morals and Legislation.* Oxford, UK: Basil Blackwell.

Braithwaite, J. (1994). "Thinking Harder About Democratising Social Control." In: C. Alder and J. Wunderlitz (eds.), *Family Conferencing and Juvenile Justice*. Canberra, AUS: Australian Institute of Criminology.

—— and S. Mugford. (1994). "Conditions of Successful Reintegration Ceremonies." *British Journal of Criminology* 34:139-171.

Canter, G. (1973). "Consequences of Legal Engineering: A Case from Zambia." Paper presented at the annual meeting of the American Anthropological Association, New Orleans.

Christie, N. (1978). "Conflicts as Property." *British Journal of Criminology* 17:1-15.

Colson, E. (1962). *The Plateau Tonga. Social and Religious Studies*. London, UK: Oxford University Press.

Diamond, A.S. (1935). *Primitive Law*. London, UK: Longmans, Green & Co.

Doek, J. (1994). "The Juvenile Court: An Endangered Species?" *European Journal of Criminal Policy and Research* 2:42-56.

Drapkin, I. (1989). *Crime and Punishment in the Ancient World*. Lexington, MA: Lexington Books.

Edelhertz, H. (1977). "Legal and Operational Issues in the Implementation of Restitution within the Criminal Justice System." In: J. Hudson and B. Galaway (eds.), *Restitution in Criminal Justice*. Lexington, MA: Lexington Books.

Eglash, A. (1958a). "Creative Restitution: A Broader Meaning for an Old Term." *Journal of Criminal Law, Criminology, and Police Sciences* 48:619-622.

—— (1958b). "Creative Restitution: Some Suggestions for Prison Rehabilitative Programs." *American Journal of Corrections* (November-December):20-34.

—— (1959). "Creative Justice: Its Roots in Psychology, Religion, and Law." *British Journal of Delinquency* 10:114-119.

—— (1975). "Creative Restitution." In: J. Hudson and B. Galaway (eds.), *Considering the Victim*. Springfield, IL: Charles C Thomas.

—— (1977). "Beyond Restitution: Creative Restitution." In: J. Hudson and B. Galaway (eds.), *Restitution in Criminal Justice*, Lexington, MA: Lexington Books.

Evans-Pritchard, E.E. (1940). *The Nuer*. London, UK: Oxford University Press.

Feld, B. (1993). "Criminalizing the American Juvenile Court." In: M. Tonry (ed.), *Crime and Justice: A Review of Research,* vol. 17. Chicago, IL: University of Chicago Press.

Ferri, E. (1917). *Criminal Sociology*. Boston, MA: Little, Brown.

Fraser, S. and J. Norton (1996). "Family Group Conferencing in New Zealand Child Protection Work." In: J. Hudson, A. Morris, G. Maxwell and B. Galaway (eds.), *Family Group Conferences: Perspectives on Policy and Practice*. Leichhardt, AUS and Monsey, NY: Federation Press and Criminal Justice Press.

Fry, M. (1951). *Arms of the Law*. London, UK: Victor Gollan.

Galaway, B. (1977). "Toward the Rational Development of Restitution Programming." In: J. Hudson and B. Galaway (eds.), *Restitution in Criminal Justice*. Lexington, MA: Lexington Books.

Garafalo, R. (1914). *Criminology*. Boston, MA: Little, Brown.

Geis, G. (1977). "Restitution by Criminal Offenders: A Summary and Overview." In: J. Hudson and B. Galaway (eds.), *Restitution in Criminal Justice*. Lexington, MA: Lexington Books.

Gillin, J.L. (1935). *Criminology and Penology* (rev. ed.). New York, NY: Appleton-Century.

Grabowski, P.N. (1989). Personal communication to the author .

Griffith, C.T. and R. Hamilton (1996). "Sanctioning and Healing: Restorative Justice in Canadian Aboriginal Communities." In: B. Galaway and J. Hudson (eds.), *Restorative Justice: International Perspectives*. Monsey, NY: Criminal Justice Press.

Harding, J. (1982). *Victims and Offenders: Needs and Responsibilities*. London, UK: Bedford Square Press.

Hart, C.M.W. and A.R. Pilling (1962). *The Tiwi of North Australia*. New York, NY: Holt, Rinehart, and Winston.

Hartmann, A. (1995). *Schlichten oder Richten. Der Täter-Opfer-Ausgleich und das (Jugend-) Strafrecht*. München, GER. Willem Fink Verlag.

Hassall, I. (1996). "Origin and Development of Family Group Conferences." In: J. Hudson, A. Morris, G. Maxwell and B. Galaway (eds.), *Family Group Conferences: Perspectives on Policy and Practice*. Leichhardt, AUS and Monsey, NY: Federation Press and Criminal Justice Press.

Hoebel, E.A. (1954). *The Law of Primitive Man*. Cambridge, MA: Harvard University Press.

Hudson, J. and B. Galaway (1975). *Considering the Victim*. Springfield, IL: Charles C Thomas.

—— A. Morris, G. Maxwell and B. Galaway (eds.) (1996a). *Family Group Conferences: Perspectives on Policy and Practice*. Leichhardt, AUS and Monsey, NY: Federation Press and Criminal Justice Press.

—— A. Morris, G. Maxwell and B. Galaway (1996b). "Introduction." In: J. Hudson, A. Morris, G. Maxwell and B. Galaway (eds.), *Family Group Conferences: Perspectives on Policy and Practice*. Leichhardt, AUS and Monsey, NY: Federation Press and Criminal Justice Press.

Jacob, B. (1970). "Reparation or Restitution by the Criminal Offender to His Victim: Applicability of an Ancient Concept in the Modern Correctional Process." *Journal of Criminal Law, Criminology, and Police Science* 61:152-167.

Jeffrey, C.R. (1957). "The Development of Crime in Early English Society." *Journal of Criminal Law, Criminology, and Police Sciences* 47:645-666.

Junger-Tas, J. (1994). "Will the Juvenile Justice System Survive?" *European Journal of Criminal Policy and Research* 2(2):76-91.

Klein, J.F. (1978). "Revitalizing Restitution: Flogging a Horse That May Have Been Killed for Just Course." *Criminal Law Quarterly* 20:383-408.

Klein, M. (1994). "American Juvenile Justice: Method and Madness." *European Journal of Criminal Policy and Research* 2(2):24-41.

Laster, P.E. (1975). "Criminal Restitution: A Survey of Its Past History." In: J. Hudson and B. Galaway (eds.), *Considering the Victim*. Springfield, IL: Charles C Thomas.

Maine, H. (1905). *Ancient Law*. London, UK: J. Murray.

McCloskey, H.J. (1984). "Respect for Moral Rights Versus Maximising Good." In: R. Frey (ed.), *Utility and Rights*. Oxford, UK: Blackwell.

Marsh, P. and G. Crow (1996). "Family Group Conferences in Child Welfare Services in England and Wales." In: J. Hudson, A. Morris, G. Maxwell and B. Galaway (eds.), *Family Group Conferences: Perspectives on Policy and Practice*. Leichhardt, AUS and Monsey, NY: Federation Press and Criminal Justice Press.

Michalowski, R.J. (1985). *Order, Law, and Crime*. New York, NY: Random House.

Moore, D. and T. O'Connell (1994). "Family Conferencing in Wagga Wagga: a Communitarian Model of Justice." In: C. Alder and J. Wundersitz (eds.), *Family Conferencing and Juvenile Justice*. Canberra, AUS: Australian Institute of Criminology.

Morris, A., G. Maxwell, J. Hudson and B. Galaway (1996). "Concluding Thoughts." In: J. Hudson, A. Morris, G. Maxwell and B. Galaway (eds.), *Family Group Conferences: Perspectives on Policy and Practice*. Leichhardt, AUS and Monsey, NY: Federation Press and Criminal Justice Press.

Nader, L. and E. Combs-Schilling (1977). "Restitution in Cross-Cultural Perspective." In: J. Hudson and B. Galaway (eds.), *Restitution in Criminal Justice*. Lexington, MA: Lexington Books.

New South Wales Law Reform Commission (1996) Sentencing Discussion Paper #33. Sydney, AUS: Author.

Nielsen, M.O. (1996). "A Comparison of Developmental Ideologies: Navajo Peacemaker Courts and Canadian Native Justice Committees." In: B. Galaway and J. Hudson (eds.), *Restorative Justice: International Perspectives*. Monsey, NY: Criminal Justice Press.

Normandeau, A. (1973). "Arbould Bonneville de Marsangy (1802-1894)." In: H. Mannheim (ed.), *Pioneers in Criminology*. Montclair, NJ: Patterson-Smith.

Oppenheimer, H. (1913). *The Rationale of Punishment*. London, UK: University of London Press.

Polk, K. (1994). "Family Conferencing: Theoretical and Evaluative Questions." In: C. Alder and J. Wundersitz (eds.), *Family Conferencing and Juvenile Justice*. Canberra, AUS: Australian Institute of Criminology.

Pollock, F. and F.W. Maitland (1968). *The History of English Law (2nd ed.)*. London, UK: Cambridge University Press.

Prins, A. (1895). "Paris Prison Congress Summary Report." London, UK.

Random House Dictionary of the English Language (abbrev. ed.). (1968). New York, NY: Random House.

Schafer, S. (1968). *The Victim and His Criminal*. New York, NY: Random House.

—— (1970a). *Compensation and Restitution to Victims of Crime*. Montclair, NJ: Patterson Smith.

—— (1970b). "Victim Compensation and Responsibility." In: *Southern California Law Review* 43:55-67.

Schneider, H.-J. (1988). "Leben im gesellschaftlichen Niemandsland: die Kriminalität der Aborigines in Zentralaustralien—Eine empirische Studie der vergleichenden Kriminologie." In: G. Kaiser, H. Kury and H.-J. Albrecht (eds.), *Kriminologische Forschung in den 80er Jahren*. Freiburg, GER: Max Planck Institute.

Stewart, T. (1996). "Family Group Conferences With Young Offenders in New Zealand." In: J. Hudson, A. Morris, G. Maxwell and B. Galaway (eds.), *Family Group Conferences: Perspectives on Policy and Practice*. Leichhardt, AUS and Monsey, NY: Federation Press and Criminal Justice Press.

Stuart, B. (1996). "Circle Sentencing: Turning Swords into Ploughshares." In: B. Galaway and J. Hudson (eds.), *Restorative Justice: International Perspectives*. Monsey, NY: Criminal Justice Press.

Sutherland, E.H. and D.R. Cressey. (1960). *Principles of Criminology (6th ed.)*. Chicago, IL: Lippincott.

Tallack, W. (1900). *Reparation to the Injured and the Rights of Victims of Crime Compensation*. London, UK: Wertheimer, Lea..

Toennies, F. (1940). *Fundamental Concepts of Sociology (Gemeinschaft und Gesellschaft)*. New York, NY: American Book Company.

Tutt, N. (1994). "Youth Justice — Crisis or Opportunity." *European Journal on Criminal Policy and Research* 2(2):9-23.

Tyler, E.B. (1889). *Anthropology*. New York, NY: .

Walgrave, L. (1994). "Beyond Rehabilitation: In Search of a Constructive Alternative in the Judicial Response to Juvenile Crime." *European Journal on Criminal Policy and Research* 2:57-75.

—— and H. Geudens (1996). "The Restorative Proportionality of Community Service for Juveniles." In: *European Journal of Crime, Criminal Law, and Criminal Justice* 4:361-380.

Weitekamp, E.G.M. (1997). "The Paradigm of Restorative Justice: Potentials, Possibilities, and Pitfalls." Keynote lecture at the 9th World Symposium on Victimology, Amsterdam.

—— H.-J. Kerner and U. Meier. (1996). "Problem Solving Policing: Views of Citizens and Citizens Expectations." Paper presented at the International Conference and Work-Shop on Problem-Solving Policing as Crime Prevention, Stockholm.

Wilson, J.Q. (1985). *Thinking about Crime*. New York, NY: Basic Books.

Wolfgang, M.E. (1965). "Victim Compensation in Crimes of Personal Violence." *Minnesota Law Review* 50:223-241.

Wundersitz, J. and S. Hetzel (1996). "Family Conferencing for Young Offenders: The South Australian Experience." In: J. Hudson, A. Morris, G. Maxwell and B. Galaway (eds.), *Family Group Conferences: Perspectives on Policy and Practice*. Leichhardt, AUS and Monsey, NY: Federation Press and Criminal Justice Press.

Yazzie, R. and J.W. Zion (1996). "Navajo Restorative Justice: The Law of Equality and Justice." In: B. Galaway and J. Hudson (eds.), *Restorative Justice: International Perspectives*. Monsey, NY: Criminal Justice Press.

4. Restorative Justice Is Republican Justice

by

John Braithwaite

and

Christine Parker

INTRODUCTION

This paper argues that restorative justice set in a context of a republican politics of non-domination can give us hope for a more decent future of juvenile justice. First, we will show how republican theory motivates a commitment to using restorative justice, and how family group conferences are one instantiation of this ideal. Second, we outline the dangers of a restorative justice that is too individualistic and insufficiently aware of the community context of power and inequality in which it occurs. Third, we argue that republican justice addresses these concerns by ensuring that specific restorative justice initiatives such as conferences are placed within the context of a wider republican politics of non-domination that weds political and face-to-face action. Finally, we show what implications this might have for doing justice to juvenile offenders and their victims, and for making their communities more just.

1. BASIC CONCEPTS

1.1. Republicanism in Brief

In our writings, we share with Philip Pettit a commitment to a conception of republican justice as the pursuit of freedom as non-domination (Braithwaite and Pettit, 1990; Parker, 1997; Pettit, 1997). In this previous work, freedom as non-interference is seen as the core of the liberal tradition, while freedom as non-domination is seen as the common strand of the civic republican tradition from Rome, to the early modern Northern Italian republics, to the English republican writing of the seventeenth century, to Montesquieu, Madison and Jefferson (who founded the Democratic Party in the U.S. as a republican party—with a small r!). The republicans wanted more than liberty in the impoverished sense favored by the liberals who increasingly dominated Western political discourse through the nineteenth century. Republican freedom required more than the accident of managing to escape interference; it required the assurance of not even being exposed to the possibility of arbitrary interference by an uncontrolled power. In practice, republicans equated being free with living under a rule of democratic law and civic norms that would make everyone secure against interference, without giving anyone cause for complaint that they were not being treated as equals.

The free individual was an equal member of a free community so that there was a solid basis for the connection the French made in 1789 among liberty, equality and fraternity (or sorority or community). Traditional republicans were excessively narrow in their conception of who could be citizens; they limited the citizenry to propertied, mainstream males. But there is no reason why we cannot exploit republican ideas under an inclusive conception of the community to which the republic has to answer. There is every reason why we should make contact with the writing of Mary Wollstonecraft (Tomaselli, 1995), who argued the case for women in essentially republican terms, and with the early socialists, who argued in republican vein that those bound to masters under contemporary contracts were nothing more or less than wage slaves. Our republicanism is an inclusive one.

Our argument, joining Pettit (1997), has been that the republican conception of freedom as non-domination is a rich and inspiring one, particularly in regard to the connection it makes between equality and community. What must a community achieve to make it possible for members to enjoy equally their freedom as non-domination? A constant struggle for greater equality is necessary for liberty as a subjective sense of assurance against domination by others, because one can never enjoy assurance against domination by others if one lives in poverty. Community is necessary for freedom as non-domination because assurance against domination must be moored in a strong community that will mobilize collective disapproval against the arbitrary exercise of power. Empirically, we argue that individualist, privatized societies do not have the capacity to mobilize community disapproval against violation of the rights that assure non-dominated freedom (Braithwaite, 1989).

1.2. Restorative Justice in Brief

Restorative justice, at least in the "balanced" form articulated by Bazemore and Umbreit (1995) and Bazemore and Maloney (1994), means restoring victims, offenders and community. The justice model, which reached its highwater mark around 1980, is offender-centered and oriented to proportionate punishment ther than restoration; it is the justice of liberal individualism. Its main alternative in the first 90 years of the twentieth century — the welfare model — was also offender-centered (Walgrave and Geudens, 1996). A republican theory of criminal justice (Braithwaite and Pettit, 1990) directs our attention to victims as much as offenders, because the criminal justice system should also be designed, by republican lights, to protect the liberty as non-domination (or dominion) of victims. We have noted above the republican emphasis on strengthening community: republicanism does require a balanced concern with correcting the impacts of crime on victims, offenders and community. Restoring individual victims and offenders is not enough. If racism in a school community is an underlying cause of bullying, then republican restorative justice requires the restoration of racial harmony in the school so that freedom from bullying is guaranteed (for racial minorities).

There is an earnest debate among restorative justice scholars and advocates as to whether it should also incorporate a concern with equality (see John Wilmerding's regular stirring of this pot on the restorative justice CERJ network: cerj@cerj.org). The republican rationale for restorative justice does require it to incorporate a concern for equality. Republicanism does not value formal equality for its own sake; rather, it only values those forms of equality that will increase freedom as non-domination. The formal equality of the liberal justice model — equal punishment for equal wrongs — unfortunately creates an oppressive punitive complex in which domination is rampant. In practice, the equal justice model delivers just deserts to the poor and impunity to the rich because of the way the dominations of punishment interact with the dominations of unequal wealth and power (Braithwaite and Pettit, 1990). In Australia, for example, more than 50% of Aboriginal young people experience a punitive encounter with the justice system (Gale et al., 1990; Morgan and Gardner, 1992); that system is quite a significant part of their oppression, not just another among many more important burdens. We also know, for example, that criminal convictions are an important cause of unemployment, not just for racial minorities (Hagan, 1991). The formal equality of the just deserts model therefore engenders both excessive dominations of punishment and poverty that crushes freedom as non-domination.

However, republicanism does share with the just deserts model an equitable concern to put upper limits on permissible punishment. Indeterminate sentences destroy the subjective security of citizens against unbridled state power (Braithwaite and Pettit, 1990). Citizens cannot enjoy dominion in a society where the limits on the punitive power of the state are not clearly specified. While the republican case for upper limits on permissible punishments for all types of crime is strong, there is no republican case for lower limits. Mercy and forgiveness are important values for republicans because of a requirement to search for the least dominating form of social control possible (Braithwaite and Pettit, 1990). In most cases, the least dominating form will involve no punishment at all. It will involve no more than dialogue about how members of a community might protect and care for one another.

2. DIMENSIONS OF RESTORATION

In previous writing, Braithwaite and Pettit (1990), Pettit and Braithwaite (1993) and Braithwaite (1996) have outlined in republican terms why a number of different dimensions of restoration are important. Consider the following list of dimensions of victim restoration (most of which are also relevant to restoring offenders and communities) from Braithwaite (1996):

2.1. What Does Restoring Victims Mean?

- Restore property loss
- Restore injury
- Restore sense of security
- Restore dignity
- Restore sense of empowerment
- Restore deliberative democracy
- Restore harmony based on a feeling that justice has been done
- Restore social support

Some of these are utterly uncontroversial from the perspective of mainstream legal doctrine (e.g., restore property loss, restore injury), while others accord with recent adaptations of that doctrine to partially accommodate the needs of victims (e.g., restore a sense of security). Others, like restoring deliberative democracy, have a strong foundation in the republican tradition (Sunstein, 1988, 1993) but not much in the criminal law tradition that crushed citizen deliberation over justice in favor of professional judgment in terms of the king's formal rules.

A question often asked about restorative justice is whether there is much concern with justice embedded within the palpable concern for restoration. The aim of *restoring harmony based on a feeling that justice has been done* is the key one here. Restoring harmony alone, while leaving an underlying injustice to fester unaddressed, is not enough. "Restoring balance" is only acceptable as a restorative justice ideal if the "balance" between offender and victim that prevailed before the crime was a morally decent balance. There is no virtue in restoring the balance by having a woman pay for a loaf of bread she has stolen from a rich man to feed her children. Restoring harmony between victim and offender is only likely to be possible in such a context on the basis of a discussion of why the children are hungry, and what should be done about the underlying injustice of their hunger. As we shall see below, the practical problem of ensuring that restorative justice does restore justice in a society full of dominations is difficult and is where most restorative justice institutions are vulnerable to criticism.

2.2. Restorative Justice Conferences

We find the above list of dimensions of restoration not only important in republican theory, but in the popular imaginations of citizens as manifested in restorative justice processes. The particular micro-institutions of restorative justice our research group is evaluating are what in Canberra are called diversionary conferences, and what elsewhere are called family group conferences or community accountability conferences, or, generically, restorative justice conferences (Alder and Wundersitz, 1994; Brown and McElrea, 1993; Burford et al., 1995; Hudson et al., 1996; LaPrairie, 1995; McDonald et al., 1995; Moore et al., 1995; O'Connell and Moore, 1992). After an admission of guilt to the police (or "declining to deny" in New Zealand), instead of going to court, a conference is convened. The victim(s) and supporters of the victim are invited, as are the offender(s) and supporters of the offender. For offenses where there is no victim, such as drunk driving, one or two community representatives attend. This group discusses what damage the crime has done and how justice might be restored. More than 90% of the time a consensus is reached about a plan of action to bring about the restoration of victims, offenders and community. The community of care and the police then monitor implementation of the plan and reconvene the conference if implementation fails. Preliminary evidence from the first 548 adult and juvenile cases to be randomly assigned to conferences versus court in Canberra suggest high levels of satisfaction among victims, offenders, supporters, police and community representatives with the justice, respect for rights and usefulness of conferences — higher levels of satisfaction than the juvenile and adult courts enjoy in Canberra (Sherman and Barnes, 1997; Sherman and Strang, 1997, Strang and Sherman, 1997).

3. THE DANGERS OF RESTORATIVE JUSTICE

Proponents see conferences as a way of restoring victims and communities, of giving victims and offenders a say in decision-making that intimately affects their lives (restoration of a sense of empowerment and deliberative democracy) and that ensures that popular concerns become a vital part of criminal justice. Yet restorative conferences can equally be seen as a naive, idealistic way of dealing with serious problems. They are in danger of doing too little justice with too little equity. Proponents sometimes fail to recognize the societal contexts of domination and structural inequality affecting victims and offenders (Stubbs, 1995). These criticisms have been directed at other means of informal justice, such as mediation and alternative dispute resolution (Abel 1981, 1982a, 1982b; Fitzgerald 1985; McEwen 1987, Nader, 1979, 1980).

Mediation in family law and domestic violence returns disputes to families already imbued with imbalances of power between men and women, gives unaccountable power to mediation professionals, and detours women away from enforceable decisions of courts (Astor, 1991; Cain, 1985). Consumer complaint programs in banks or telephone companies send pacified customers away, unaware that their problem confronts thousands of others who may or may not complain, and leave exploitative company policies untouched (Nader, 1979). Internal dispute resolution in a workplace changes issues of institutional bias and discrimination into individual management problems for particular work areas to deal with (Edelman et al., 1993).

Like informalism in civil cases, the communitarianism of restorative justice in criminal matters might drag domination into the justice process without an opportunity for accountability. Offenders, particularly if they are low in power and status like juvenile members of minority groups, may not have their rights adequately protected, and will certainly not get all the protections of a fully fledged criminal trial (Bargen, 1996; Warner, 1994).[1] At its worst, the philosophy of empowering victims and encouraging victim advocacy. can legitimate the "justice" of lynch mobs and the tyranny of the majority (Scheingold et al., 1994). Conferencing may hand even more power to police who already dominate suspects. If lawyers and the criminal process already fail adequately to supervise cultures of police violence and coercion of confessions (McConville and Mirsky, 1990), then surely they are even more likely to run rampant under a regime in which conferences appear to grant even more discretion to the police.

From the victim's point of view, mediators or facilitators may dominate conferences, failing to take violence or damage seriously enough (Braithwaite and Daly 1994; Maxwell and Morris, 1993; Morris and Maxwell, 1991). Thus critics argue that restorative justice might:

- fail to take violence seriously
- lack procedural accountability
- fail to deal with the unequal bargaining power of the parties
- give police or professional mediators too much unaccountable power over serious criminal problems
- empower the "victim advocacy" of the lynch mob

The underlying issue is that restorative justice is susceptible to perpetuating all the dominations of everyday community. To its critics, restorative justice "purports to restore a social peace that never existed" (Abel, 1982a:8). It neutralizes conflict by individualizing and privatizing grievances and offenses (Fitzgerald, 1985). Informal justice may stymie opportunities for conflict to be used creatively to achieve social change, to work toward a community based on equality and liberty rather than the tyranny of the majority.

It is true that restorative justice cannot resolve the deep structural injustices that cause problems like homelessness or hunger. Republicans look primarily to other institutions, especially economic institutions, for that challenge. But republicanism does require two things of restorative justice. First, it must not make structural injustice worse (in the way, for example, that the Australian criminal justice system does by being an important cause of the unemployment and oppression of Aboriginal people). Indeed, we should hope from restorative justice for micro-measures to ameliorate macro-injustice where this is possible (for example, finding a home for the homeless offender). Second, restorative justice should restore harmony with a remedy grounded in dialogue that takes account of underlying injustices. Restorative justice does not resolve the age-old questions of what should count as unjust outcomes; it is a more modest philosophy than that. It settles for the procedural requirement that the parties talk until they feel that harmony has been restored on the basis of a discussion of all the injustices they see as relevant to the case. Within that dialogue about justice, republicans will want to make the case that justice is what secures freedom as non-domination (with respect to both procedure and outcome).

4. REPUBLICAN SOLUTIONS TO THE DANGERS OF RESTORATIVE JUSTICE

In the remainder of this paper we suggest three strategies by which the justice of restorative justice can be maximized using the republican politics of non-domination. Three republican solutions are advanced to the dangers of restorative justice outlined in the last section:

(1) Contestability under the rule of law whereby legal formalism empowers informalism while checking the excesses of informalism.

(2) De-individualizing restorative justice, muddying imbalances of individual power by preferring community conferences over individual-on-individual mediation.

(3) Vibrant social movement politics that percolates into the deliberation of conferences, defends minorities against tyrannies of the majority and connects private concerns to campaigns for public transformation.

4.1. Contestability under Rule of Law

Critics of restorative justice sometimes implicitly put forward legalism as the only viable means of doing justice in individual cases that institutionalizes enough accountability. The proceduralism and publicity of the court system is certainly designed to protect alleged offenders against domination, although in practice only a small percentage of alleged offenders ever receive the benefit of a full criminal trial.[2] And, as we have seen, this does little for victims and restoration. A more practical model gives the rule of law the task of overseeing institutions of restorative justice. The proceduralism of law has a role in supervising the compromises of conferences, and functions as a last resort when restorative justice fails to do justice. Restorative justice should not replace rule-of-law considerations, but add to them and fill them with meaning and relevance to particular situations. We will see that out of this process of mutual influence formal justice might become more restorative (e.g., community service substituting for imprisonment in many cases; see the right hand arrow of Figure 2).

Thus, the preference is to use restorative justice first to achieve healing, and to use the rule of law to ensure that minimal procedural constraints that protect people from domination have been followed. Where restorative justice is dominating, either party has the right of recourse to the rule of law. Braithwaite and Daly (1994) argue that in those circumstances, the formalism of the rule of law has the capacity to empower the informalism of restorative justice conferences because contestability by reference to legalism encourages parties to ensure the justice of communitarian justice in the first place. Formalism empowers informalism when it gives offenders the right to a conference and requires that they be informed of their right to walk out of the conference (so that the matter can be heard in court).

4.2. De-Individualizing Restorative Justice

Private justice does risk rendering "the personal apolitical" in the dyadic form of offender and victim, mediated by a professional. Conferences are controversial when used for offences like domestic violence, rape, armed robbery, attempted murder and serious white-collar crime. This controversy is about the imbalance of power between offenders and victims for these kinds of offenses. There might also be an imbalance of power in the other direction, where the offender is a juvenile and the victim an adult. Yet there is no reason why Abel's (1982b: 288–289)criticism of informal justice must hold true of restorative justice conferences: "Although neighbourhood institutions constantly speak about community, what they actually require (and reproduce) is a collection of isolated individuals ... Informalism appropriates the socialist ideal of collectivity but robs it of its content. The individual grievant must appear alone before the informal institution, deprived of the support of such natural allies as family, friends, work mates, even neighbours."

Restorative conferencing in criminal justice can turn institutions of informal justice into fora where individuals are empowered through the presence and support of their most trusted friends to confront and receive an apology and compensation from those who have wronged them, even when the offender is much more powerful than themselves. The problem with dyadic victim-offender mediation is that there is an imbalance of power if the offender is the school bully and the victim is a nerd; if the offender is a child, the victim an adult; the offender a man, the victim a woman. What is different about a conference is that it is a meeting of two communities of care, both of which contain men and women, children and adults, the "cool" and the "uncool," the organized (like an Aboriginal Community Council) and the unorganized (like a demoralized Aboriginal adolescent [see Figure 1]). The conference by no means eliminates imbalances of power; one community of care might be consistently middle class, the other lower class. Yet the muddying of power imbalance, as illustrated in Figure 1, amounts to an improvement over individualized justice. While this is one of a number of theoretically important differences between a conference and a dyadic encounter, it would be a mistake to characterize mediation as always dyadic. With traditional victim-offender mediations, other supporters on the victim, or offender, side are often present.

4.3. Connecting Private Troubles to Public Issues through Republican Social Movements

Central to civic republicanism as a political ideology is the notion that active, organized citizenship in civil society is a bulwark against abuse of state power. Equally, it is a crucial protection against abuses of community power (Pettit, 1997). In combination, there is a vital role for social movement politics in checking the tyrannies of both state law and community. How might this be accomplished in the case of juvenile justice?

We see public funding for youth justice advocates as a primary mechanism. Already such publicly funded advocacy services exist in many countries, with a mandate to check abuses of police power by taking strategic cases against the police to the courts, conducting research on abuses of police power against young people and advocating changes to policing policies to remedy the structural problems. More infrequently, youth advocacy services have checked the power of juvenile courts by taking test cases to higher courts and exposing dominating practices toward young people in the courts.

The additional role for such advocacy services under a regime of restorative justice (which would require additional public funding) would be to check abuses of power in restorative conferences or victim-offender mediation programs. Cost would obviously ration the attendance of youth advocates at actual conferences or mediations in any jurisdiction where hundreds of these were occurring every month. However, as with legal aid, strategic attendance would be required at those cases where the advocacy group judged there to be risk of a serious breach of rights. This need not imply returning the control of citizens over the conference to the more dominating expert discourse of lawyers. There is a risk here with advocates who tend to be specialists in conflict rather than in peace. Youth advocates might be present at the conference as advisors only, not as principals to the conflict. This can mean that lawyers are not normally allowed to speak unless their principal asks and special permission to do so is granted by the facilitator. In practice, what happens under such a policy is that occasionally the advocate might whisper something in their client's ear, or, more rarely, ask for a momentary adjournment of the proceeding so they can have a chat outside. Mostly the advocate just sits, listens and monitors the justice of the proceeding.[3]

Figure 1: De-Individualizing Restorative Justice
ONE ON ONE
VICTIM-OFFENDER MEDIATION

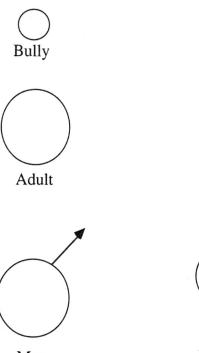

Bully

Nerd

Adult

Child

Man

Woman

CONFERENCE

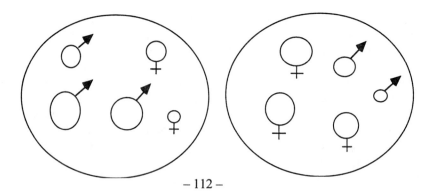

When youth justice advocates do not attend conferences, they should nevertheless receive on-line from the criminal justice system the results of all conferences. When the youth advocate notices that there has been a case where a sanction imposed by a conference exceeds that which would likely have been imposed by a court for the same offense, he or she can then call offenders and point this out to them. It may be, of course that the offender really wants to do more than the court would require. But if the offender wants to contest the conference outcome, he or she could use the resources of the youth advocate to walk away from the conference agreement and insist that the matter be adjudicated in a court of law.

The youth advocate is not the only kind of advocacy needed for juvenile crime. In the Australian context, where Aboriginal youths are a large part of the juvenile justice system's clientele and greatly discriminated against, there is a special need for Aboriginal advocacy services to keep an eye on what is happening under restorative justice programs. When women and girls are victims of rape, sexual assault and family violence, there is a need for monitoring of restorative justice cases (and attendance in special circumstances) to protect against the domination of victims' rights, even in cases where the offender is a juvenile. In our jurisdiction in Australia, we have a Victims of Crime Assistance League, which could also reasonably be publicly funded to play the same role on the victim side as the Youth Advocate would play on the side of the juvenile offender. If this sounds unrealistic in an era of contracting legal aid budgets, bear in mind that selective attendance of advocates at conferences for purposes of monitoring rights does not require the resources involved in mounting a defense for a criminal trial.

This is a general republican strategy. With corporate crimes against consumers, republicans want consumer advocacy groups to monitor the protection of consumer interests in restorative corporate justice; trade unions, to monitor occupational health and safety crimes against workers; and environmental advocacy groups to monitor environmental crimes (Ayres and Braithwaite, 1992; Fisse and Braithwaite, 1993). If these advocacy groups are doing their job, they will not be so lacking in strategic sense to allow all disputes to be privatized. Advocates for Aboriginal victims of a consumer fraud that raises the need for regulatory reform of an industry may ask that a press conference be held to communicate to the public and its political leaders the problem revealed by the crime, as happened in the Colonial Mutual insurance frauds against Aboriginal Australians (Fisse and Braithwaite, 1993).

With juvenile offenses, it is exceptionally rare for the communities of care around offenders and victims to decide that it is wise to go public with a conference outcome, though it has happened. That is not to say that well-resourced youth advocacy groups would not seek to connect narrow disputes over juvenile crime into wider advocacy campaigns. In the early 1990s, youth advocacy groups in Australia, networked with other community groups, lobbied for what became known as "the Job Compact." The Job Compact, which became government policy for a brief moment in Australian history, obligated the state to find a job, even if only temporary employment, for all long-term unemployed people, young or old. It also imposed obligations with respect to access to labor market training. Given that unemployment is so concentrated among the young, one might hope that the kinds of state obligations in the Job Compact would continue to be structural priorities for youth advocacy groups. Therefore, one would hope that in restorative justice conferences for young offenders who have been denied job opportunities or labor market training opportunities, youth advocates would seek to persuade participants to put demands on the table in conferences for state-funded training and job opportunities. If these demands were persistently denied, then youth advocates might want to persuade participants to go public with strategically selected cases to demonstrate the failures of the state to respond to its responsibilities for employment and training as solutions to crime, or simply to write as a group to members of parliament.

A similar situation concerns some of the appalling educational policies that have been major contributors to juvenile crime in Australia. We refer to educational policies that stigmatize children who perform badly, and then expel them from the school as soon as they misbehave in some serious way, or even in a less serious way such as smoking marijuana. We have already seen some wonderful conferences in Australia, where even without the support of youth advocacy groups, citizens from both the victim and offender sides have decided to join together to confront a school on the destructiveness of its policy of suspending the young offender involved in the case. We have seen conferences where citizens decided, following a sexual assault, to confront the culture of dominating masculinity in a school (see Braithwaite and Daly, 1994). We have seen conferences where Aboriginal peoples have asked that their traditions of how to transact justice in the future be more respected by the white justice system, a most important structural change for Aboriginal people. On the victim side, advocacy groups can watch for structural injustices for which there are large classes of additional victims whom the advocates should apprise of their access to a remedy. Publicly funded monitoring of restorative justice by advocacy groups is actually a potentially more efficient way of publicizing access to remedies than the haphazard publicity of the court.

Under a republican conception of restorative justice, advocacy groups thus have two crucial roles. First, they check abuses of power by community majorities in a conference by ganging up on the client group represented by their organization. serving in effect as a check on the tyranny of community. Second, advocacy groups connect individual grievances to structural ones, taking strategic actions to draw out the public dimensions of private disputes. They are a check on the tyranny of individualized privatism that is blind to underlying structural problems.

Yet advocacy groups themselves can be dominating. The Ku Klux Klan is an advocacy group of sorts. Some victims of crime advocacy groups in some parts of the world are closer to the Ku Klux Klan than to our republican ideal of freedom as non-domination (Scheingold et al., 1994). A world with stronger advocacy groups in civil society will be a stronger republic even though many of the advocacy groups will be anti-republican. Republicans believe in the theory of checks and balances, including checks and balances between citizen groups. When the Ku Klux Klan has reared its ugly head, it stirred up competing forces in civil society, such as black Christian churches in the South and white college students in the North, who succeeded in getting the U.S. to check its abuse of communitarian power. Moreover, the more deeply we can embed restorative justice institutions that deliver superior remedies only on condition that protagonists sit and listen to each others' point of view, then the more we nurture a civility that leaves less space for groups that endorse advocacy by dominating speech and action rather than by dialogue and persuasion. Republican institutions make political life less rewarding for anti-republican forces who support the politics of domination. At the same time, republican institutions leave a seat at the table for those very anti-republican voices. That is the paradox of democracy no less than the paradox of republicanism.

5. CHECKING AND BALANCING LAW AND COMMUNITY

Our solutions to the problem of unjust restorative justice would institutionalize a republican interplay among community concerns about restoration, the proceduralism of the rule of law and social movements motivated to check domination. The three strategies proposed for ensuring that restorative justice restores victims, offenders and communities on the basis of justice — ensuring the contestability of restorative justice under the rule of law, de-individualizing mediation and propagating social movements that transform private troubles raised in individual conferences into public issues — together comprise a republican theory of justice. Because the republican conception of freedom is a rich one, republican strategies for doing justice (i.e., for restoring freedom/non-domination where it has been damaged) are also rich and multi-dimensional. They rely on the rule of law and on the communitarianism of social bonds and the active citizenship of social movement politics. We argue that institutions of restorative justice, such as family group conferences, form a crucial axis for this republican interplay of mechanisms of justice in criminal cases, as illustrated in Figure 2.

At the base of the pyramid are the subjective and contextual justice concerns of individuals and communities with restoration and healing. Restorative justice conferences are attempts to empower and institutionalize these concerns through communitarian processes that restore social bonds. Yet we have also seen that micro-institutions of restorative justice can be criticized for being dominating. The need for restorative justice conferences to be made accountable to the procedural concerns of the rule of law is represented by the apex of the pyramid — the fact that victims and offenders should always have a right to walk out of a conference and go to court. As a result of the possibility and actuality (in some cases) of court intervention to strike down conference injustices, a rights/procedural justice discourse percolates down into restorative justice conferences and, eventually, even into the popular concerns that people bring to conferences at the base of the pyramid. Thus, the restorative justice of the people is shaped by the justice of a law that creates space for justice under the control of affected citizens. The informalism of restorative justice is also empowered by the formalism of state law, which gives everyone assurance that if a tyrannous family, tribal patriarch or police officer takes over, the state can step in to check that tyranny. Restorative justice theory, research and praxis show that justice needs many ante-rooms before one reaches the courtroom if he or she is to be given a chance to heal (Cragg, 1992; Galaway and Hudson, 1990; Marshall, 1985; Messmer and Otto, 1992; Van Ness, 1986). The pyramid leaves plenty of space for healing because it also makes a prudent space for the judge's hammer.

Yet the rule of law may also dominate conferences by ignoring the full dimensions of restoration and healing required in each particular situation. This does not mean law should be abandoned in favor of the domination of a community that fails to respect rights and procedural safeguards. We advocate a model for restorative justice conferences in which the justice of law and the restorative justice of the community interact and interplay. Indeed, in this model the prevalence of restorative justice conferences that institutionalize community concerns with restoration and healing institutionalize a critique of and alternative to traditional trial processes, which helps make the whole criminal justice system more responsive. Citizens' concerns have an avenue for bubbling up the pyramid into legal discourses and procedures through legal supervision of conferences, just as the discourse of the justice of law has a way of percolating down.

Habermas (1996) comes close to the model we propose in Figure 2. He speaks of the way rationality potential can be "set aflow" (Habermas, 1996:98) by both law affecting lifeworld from above and lifeworld affecting law from below. In this, he admittedly does have an overblown regard for the democratic potential and centrality of law: "...in complex societies, morality can become effective beyond the local level only by being translated into the legal code" (p.110). Nevertheless, Habermas (1996:176) is undoubtedly right that law can be a "power transformer" under conditions of high complexity, spreading local moral concerns more widely along the transmission lines of legal regulation. The public sphere generates the democratic impulses that the law both transmits and constitutionalizes through guaranteeing rights and fair procedures. Public reason is an emergent property set aflow by these impulses moving up and down Figure 2.

Figure 2: Checking of Law and Community to Make Restorative Justice Just

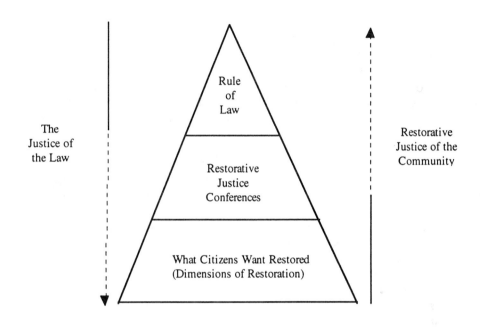

Individual encounters between victims and offenders (either in court or conferences) do not occur in a vacuum. Because crime is set in a context of structural problems and social inequalities, the pyramid is set in a context of political and social action to confront the realities of domination. The second and third strategies proposed earlier address this problem by changing conferences from dyadic, individualistic encounters into dialogues between communities of care (de-individualizing mediation), and by connecting private troubles in individual conferences to public issues and patterns of inequality through the involvement of social movement advocacy groups.

The involvement of advocacy/community groups in the conference process also helps solve the potential problem of legalism percolating down the pyramid in such a way that it overwhelms restorative justice and citizen concerns. Lawyers who are themselves captive to advocacy groups are less likely to capture restorative justice with legalism. Thus Parker (1994) suggested that a youth advocacy center was better at empowering clients than other community legal centers because the lawyer was just one worker among many.

For republicans, restorative justice institutions are a crucial link between desirable features of a criminal justice system. In our model, restorative justice institutions join the concerns and needs of citizens and community with the procedural safeguards of the rule of law and the social/political action of groups fighting the politics of non-domination in a way that transforms how criminal justice is done (to make it more just). There is no room for clear-cut distinctions between private and public justice, individual and community. Institutions of restorative justice in this model, far from segregating individual crimes to be dealt with behind closed doors as individualized problems of healing, become links to public struggles for justice. At the same time, they give enough space to individuals and communities to make their own justice in terms and under procedures meaningful to them. In both these respects courtroom justice generally fails. Justice is not confined to the procedural justice of lawyers that dominates criminal trials and the non-justice of pretrial plea negotiations. Nor is it defined purely according to the feelings of the individuals involved or the norms of a potentially tyrannous community. The formal justice of lawyers and the contextual justice of a community are rendered vulnerable to the struggle for social justice of social movements.

Perhaps this has all been too abstract. So let us illustrate how the rule of law might cascade down into restorative justice, and then how the restoration citizens want might bubble up into the rule of law.

5.1. Imagining a Rule of Law that Percolates Down into Restorative Justice

Case 1.

A young first offender admits putting graffiti on a shop window. A conference agrees to a demand from the shopkeeper for 200 hours of work at the shop by the offender. When the youth advocacy service sees the printout of the previous week's conference outcomes, this demand jumps out as a disproportionately onerous agreement for the young first offender. It contacts the offender and advises that should he or she choose to walk away from the agreement and have the offense adjudicated by a court, the penalty would probably be substantially reduced. The offender decides to go to court with the youth advocate, and the court strikes down the conference agreement, imposing a penalty of 40 hours of community work.

Case 2.

An adolescent female goes to a conference for a burglary she admits. At the conference, the police and victim seek to hold her responsible for another, more serious, burglary at the same house for which she denies responsibility. She walks out of the conference. The initial burglary goes to court. When the magistrate asks her why she walked out of the conference, she explains the attempt by the police to clear the second burglary. The magistrate reprimands the police sternly for the injustice of this action, a reprimand that is reported in the local newspaper.

Case 3.

A young First Nations woman in Canada takes to a healing circle (LaPrairie, 1995; Ross, 1996) a complaint of sexual abuse against her by the son of a powerful elder. The elders abuse this restorative justice process by closing ranks around the man. The upshot is that the young victim is vilified in her community for making the complaint.[4] A women's rights advocacy service takes up her case in the Canadian criminal and juvenile courts, which convict and punish the elder's son. The Canadian government sends in a First Nations lawyer from another community to negotiate with the local people on how procedures for healing circles in this community might be reformed. The new healing circle procedures are enthusiastically embraced by the community. Under them, the whole community participates in a series of healing circles in which they seek forgiveness as a community from the victim of the sexual assault.

5.2. Imagining a Restorative Justice that Percolates Up Into the Rule of Law

Case 1.

We do not really have to imagine how restorative justice can percolate up into the law because we can see how the Maori restorative justice ideas in the family group conference have penetrated New Zealand statute and case law. In a seminar on youth justice held in Australia six years ago, a New Zealand participant described a conference where a young first offender had agreed to give his own car to the victim of his joyriding offense. An Australian lawyer objected at the seminar that this was a breach of proportionality constraints on sentencing: a juvenile court would never impose something as heavy as what amounted to a $15,000 fine on a first offender for joyriding. But the circumstances of the case were such that the offender was from a wealthy family that had given him the car; the victim was unemployed and uninsured and desperately needed a car that was beyond repair as a result of the joyride. Handing over the offender's car fitted the sense of equity of all participants in the conference, including the offender. It was simply a different sense of equity than one finds in the proportionality metrics of criminal sentencing. Interestingly, however, the restorative equity of the conference was hardly at odds with the conception of equity in tort law.

Let us imagine a conference in Australia deciding a case in this way. The youth advocacy service advises the young offender to go to court to contest the disproportionality of the agreement. In a moment of weakness when he is missing the car, the offender agrees to the challenge. The Juvenile Court strikes down the agreement as a disproportionately severe sentence and orders return of the car. On appeal, the Juvenile Court decision is found to be an excessively narrow construction of the proportionality of criminal sentencing that leaves insufficient space for the sense of equity that emerges from participatory justice.

Case 2.

Another juvenile goes to a conference for stealing a car. At the conference, the offender's mother complains that the police used excessive force at the time of her son's arrest. Further, she complains that the police have branded her son as "a little crim." Whenever anything happens in the neighborhood, he is their automatic suspect. In this particular case, other children were involved in planning the car theft, but action was being taken only against her son. Of greater concern to the youth advocate present at the conference was that no action was being taken against a major car dealing and repairing company who provided the offender with a list of car models that it wanted young people to steal (largely for parts). It is decided that participants will assist the youth advocacy service to produce a report and call a press conference on police responses to the car theft problem in the city. The young offender puts in 150 hours of community work helping the youth advocacy service with photocopying and other work associated with the project. The report is critical of the police for its use of excessive force against young people, and for the discriminatory way in which it targets its vehicle theft enforcement efforts on young people in areas with high unemployment, totally neglecting the white collar criminals who are supplying these unemployed young people with illicit work. The report exposes the practice of motor vehicle traders in the city supplying desperate young people with lists of cars they would like to be stolen. The press conference shocks the community. In response, the police arrest two motor traders and a police officer who has taken bribes from them. It also initiates discussions with car manufacturers about the possibility of marking certain strategic parts with numerical identification at the point of manufacture, and initiates other preventive measures with insurers. Motor vehicle theft in the city drops by a third over the next two years.

Like the previous case, this one is imagined from some foundation in fact. The New South Wales Police dealt with escalating motor vehicle theft rates in Sydney in the early 1990s through the dialogic method of setting up a Motor Vehicle Theft forum with the Motor Traders Association, insurers, and manufacturers, among others. They found that one factor in the increase was white collar criminals in the car trade supplying juveniles with computerized lists of parts (or whole cars) that had been ordered by customers. The motor vehicle theft rate in Sydney dropped by a third in the two years following the work of the Motor Vehicle Theft Forum (Braithwaite, 1993:386).

Case 3.

A police officer in a remote part of Australia has strong grounds to suspect that a young Aboriginal person has committed a criminal offense. When the police officer questions him, he does not reply, staring angrily back at the officer. Being new to the area, the officer is puzzled by this response until an Aboriginal elder explains that direct interrogation is rude by the standards of their culture. The elder, who has had training in conferencing, offers to convene a meeting of appropriate indigenous people to discuss the matter with the young person. The elder starts the conference, not by asking questions, nor by making any statements about the young person's case. He starts by telling a story about how he got into trouble as a young person and what he did to put it right. Some other old people do the same. Eventually the young offender adds his story, expresses regret and seeks advice from the elders on how to put things right. The convening elder writes this out as a conference agreement that will have status under "white fella law" so that the matter might not go to court. While the police officer accepts this, the local prosecutor does not. He thinks the agreement is oppressive and was procedurally oppressive because the offender was not asked at the outset whether he admitted guilt. When he takes it to court, it becomes a *cause célèbre* for the Aboriginal Legal Service. The upshot is the government accepting a Law Reform Commission Report that concedes that indigenous justice based on truth-finding by sharing stories can be accommodated. The Australian test of an admission of guilt before a conference can proceed is abolished in favor of a New Zealand "declining to deny" test.

CONCLUSION

Nowhere in the world does the practice of restorative justice approach the imagined world of the preceding six cases. Nowhere does restorative justice satisfy the republican prescriptions of: (1) contestability under the rule of law, (2) de-individualizing restorative justice in a way that counterbalances the imbalances of power, and (3) vibrant social movement politics that connect private troubles to public issues, publicly deliberated and structurally reformed. Strategic steps suggested by our analysis might include: (1) Engaging restorative judges with the challenge of intervening to check abuses of power in restorative justice processes by developing a restorative justice case law. (2) Conducting empirical research on the effect on injustice and power imbalance of the size and plurality of conferences, and the development of strategies for a plurality that empowers what Nancy Fraser calls "subaltern publics."[5] (3) Evaluating innovations that publicly fund advocacy groups to connect conferenced private troubles to public issues and deliberation of structural change.

We do not despair in the least at the failure of any currently working model of restorative justice to live up to our republican ideals. Rome was not built in a day, nor has its Republic totally crumbled. Thanks to Emperor Justinian, the Roman Empire bequeathed to us the rule of law; it also bequeathed to us the ideas of freedom as non-domination, deliberative justice and the separation of powers. We are hopeful that restorative justice is being built one brick at a time. Like Rome, it will be deeply flawed, but perhaps better than what went before. Our objective in this paper is to inspire reformers to lay restorative justice bricks with a vision of how many rooms must be built, how much better we can make the structure through a process of progressive extension. Without the vision of a possible future, however, we risk building rooms that are sealed off from other rooms.

Many bricks are already in place in many nations. Most restorative justice programs already enable contestability by the rule of law by advising juvenile offenders of a right to walk out of the conference room and into the courtroom. Many countries are engaged in research and development with conferences, healing circles and restorative probation which might improve our capacities to counterbalance power imbalances by de-individualizing mediation (see, for example, the work of Pennell and Burford, 1995). Social movements — from youth advocacy, to the women's shelter movement, to civil liberties, worker, environment, consumer and Aboriginal rights groups — are all increasingly engaged with the possibilities of restorative justice. They are also increasingly vigilant about the possibilities for their constituents to be seduced into domination by its velvet glove. Most importantly, within the social movement for restorative justice itself, we can be important checks on one another through the self-critical discussion of our restorative innovations at meetings such as this in Leuven. Let us build an optimistic social movement, oblivious to despair at how pitifully small are the steps we take toward a more just society. But at the same time, let us be committed to a process of learning from where we have put our foot wrong, so that we might take bigger strides in the future.

★　　★　　★

REFERENCES

Abel, R. (1981). "Conservative Conflict and the Reproduction of Capitalism: The Role of Informal justice" *International Journal of the Sociology of Law* 9:245–267.

—— (1982a). "Introduction." In: R. Abel (ed.), *The Politics of Informal Justice: Volume One: The American Experience*. New York, NY: Academic Press.

—— (1982b). "The Contradictions of Informal Justice." In: R. Abel (ed.), *The Politics of Informal Justice: Volume One: The American Experience*. New York, NY: Academic Press.

Alder, C. and J. Wundersitz. (eds.) (1994). *Family Conferencing and Juvenile Justice: The Way Forward or Misplaced Optimism?* Canberra, AUS: Australian Institute of Criminology.

Astor, H. (1991). "Mediation and Violence against Women." Position paper on mediation. Prepared for the National Committee on Violence Against Women.

Ayres, I. and J. Braithwaite (1992). *Responsive Regulation: Transcending the Deregulation Debate*. New York, NY: Oxford University Press.

Baldwin, J. and M. McConville (1977). *Negotiated Justice: Pressures to Plead Guilty*. London, UK: Martin Robertson.

Bargen, J. (1996). "Kids, Cops, Courts, Conferencing and Children's Rights — A Note on Perspective." *Australian Journal of Human Rights* 2:209-228.

Bazemore, G. and D. Maloney (1994). "Rehabilitating Community Service: Toward Restorative Service in a Balanced Justice System." *Federal Probation* 58:24-35.

—— and M. Umbreit (1995). *Balanced and Restorative Justice: Program Summary.* Balanced and Restorative Justice Project. Washington, DC: U.S. Office of Juvenile Justice and Delinquency Prevention.

Braithwaite, J. (1989). *Crime, Shame and Reintegration*. Cambridge, UK: Cambridge University Press.

—— (1993). "Beyond Positivism: Learning from Contextual Integrated Strategies." *Journal of Research in Crime and Delinquency* 30(4):383-399.

—— (1996). "Restorative Justice and A Better Future." *Dalhousie Review* 76(1):9-32.

—— and K. Daly. (1994). "Masculinities, Violence and Communitarian Control." In: T. Newburn and E. Stanko (eds.) *Just Boys Doing Business? Men, Masculinities and Crime*. London, UK: Routledge.

—— and P. Pettit (1990). *Not Just Deserts: A Republican Theory of Criminal Justice*. Oxford, UK: Oxford University Press.

Brown, B.J. and F.W.M. McElrea (eds.) (1993). *The Youth Court in New Zealand: A New Model of Justice*. Auckland, NZ: Legal Research Foundation, University of Auckland.

Burford, G., J. Pennell and S. Macleod. (1995). *Family Group Decision Making: Manual For Coordinators and Communities: The Organization and Practice of Family Group Decision Making*. Newfoundland, CAN: Memorial University of Newfoundland.

Cain, M. (1985). "Beyond Informal Justice." *Contemporary Crises* 9:335–373.

Cragg, W. (1992). *The Practice of Punishment: Towards a Theory of Restorative Justice.* London, UK: Routledge.

Edelman, L., H. Erlanger and J. Lande (1993). "Internal Dispute Resolution: The Transformation of Civil Rights in the Workplace." *Law & Society Review* 27(3):497–534.

Fisse, B. and J. Braithwaite (1993). *Corporations, Crime and Accountability.* Cambridge, UK: Cambridge University Press.

Fitzgerald, J. (1985). "Thinking About Law and its Alternatives: Abel et al and the Debate Over Informal Justice." *American Bar Foundation Research Journal*:637–657.

Galaway, B. and J. Hudson (1990). *Criminal Justice, Restitution and Reconciliation.* Monsey, NY: Criminal Justice Press.

Gale, F., R. Bailey-Harris and J. Wundersitz (1990). *Aboriginal Youth and the Criminal Justice System: The Injustice of Justice.* Cambridge, UK: Cambridge University Press.

Habermas, Jurgen (1996). *Between Facts and Norms: Contributions to a Discourse Theory of Law and Democracy.* Cambridge, UK: Polity Press.

Hagan, J. (1991). "Destiny and Drift: Subcultural Preferences, Status Attainments, and the Risks and Rewards of Youth." *American Sociological Review* 56:567-582.

Hudson, J., A. Morris, G. Maxwell and B. Galaway (eds.) (1996). *Family Group Conferences: Perspectives on Policy and Practice.* Leichhardt, AUS and Monsey, NY: Federation Press and Criminal Justice Press.

LaPrairie, C. (1995). "Altering Course: New Directions in Criminal Justice and Corrections — Sentencing Circles and Family Group Conferences." *Australian and New Zealand Journal of Criminology* (Dec.):78-99.

Marshall, T.F. (1985). *Alternatives to Criminal Courts.* Aldershot, UK: Gower.

Maxwell, G.M. and A. Morris (1993). "Family Victims and Culture: Youth Justice in NZ." Wellington, NZ: Institute of Criminology, Victoria University of Wellington.

McConville, M. and C. Mirsky (1990). "Understanding Defense of the Poor in State Courts: The Sociolegal Context of Nonadversarial Advocacy." *Studies in Law, Politics & Society* 10:217–242.

McDonald, J., D. Moore, T. O'Connell and M. Thorsborne (1995). *Real Justice Training Manual: Coordinating Family Group Conferences.* Pipersville, PA: Pipers Press.

McEwen, C. (1987). "Differing Visions of Alternative Dispute Resolution and Formal Law." *Justice System Journal* 12(2):247–259.

Messmer, H. and H. Otto (1992). "Restorative Justice: Steps on the Way Toward a Good Idea." In: H. Messmer and H. Otto (eds.), *Restorative Justice on Trial.* Dordrecht, NETH: Kluwer.

Moore, D., L. Forsythe and T. O'Connell (1995). *A New Approach to Juvenile Justice: An Evaluation of Family Conferencing in Wagga Wagga.* Wagga Wagga, AUS: Charles Sturt University.

Morgan, F. and J. Gardner (1992). *Juvenile Justice I.* Adelaide, SA: Office of Crime Statistics, Attorney-General's Department.

Morris, A. and G.M. Maxwell (1991). "Juvenile Justice in New Zealand: A New Paradigm." *Australian and New Zealand Journal of Criminology* 26:72-90.

Nader, L. (1979). "Disputing Without the Force of Law." *Yale Law Journal* 88(5):998–1021.

—— (ed.) (1980). *No Access to Law: Alternatives to the American Judicial System.* New York, NY: Academic Press.

O'Connell, T., and D. Moore (1992). "A New Juvenile Cautioning Program." *Rural Society* 22(2):16-19.

Parker, C. (1994). "The Logic of Professionalism: Stages of Domination in Legal Service Delivery to the Disadvantaged." *International Journal of the Sociology of Law* 22:145-168.

—— (1997). Lawyers' Justice, Lawyers' Domination: Regulating the Legal Profession for Access to Justice. Doctoral dissertation, Australian National University, Canberra.

Pennell, J., and G. Burford (1995). "Family Group Decision Making: New Roles for 'Old' Partners in Resolving Family Violence." Implementation report, findings. St. Johns, CAN: Memorial University of Newfoundland.

Pettit, P. (1997). *Republicanism: A Theory of Freedom and Government.* Oxford, UK: Oxford University Press.

—— and J. Braithwaite (1993). "Not Just Deserts, Even in Sentencing." *Journal of the Institute of Criminology* 4(3):225-239.

Roach Anleu, S. and K. Mack (1995). "Balancing Principle and Pragmatism: Guilty Pleas." *Journal of Judicial Administration* 4:232–239.

Ross, R. (1996). *Returning to the Teaching: Exploring Aboriginal Justice.* Toronto, CAN: Penguin Books.

Scheingold, S., T. Olson and J. Pershing. (1994). "Sexual Violence, Victim Advocacy, and Republican Criminology: Washington State's Community Protection Act." *Law & Society Review* 28(4):729–763.

Sherman, L.W. and G. Barnes (1997). *Restorative Justice and Offenders' Respect for the Law.* Re-Integrative Shaming Experiment, working paper #3. Canberra, AUS: Law Program, Research School of Social Services, Australian National University.

—— and Strang, H. (1997a). *The Right Kind of Shame for Crime Prevention.* Re-Integrative Shaming Experiment, working paper #1. Canberra, AUS: Law Program, Research School of Social Services, Australian National University.

Strang, H. and L.W. Sherman (1997). *The Victim's Perspective.* Re-Integrative Shaming Experiment, working paper #2. Canberra, AUS: Law Program, Research School of Social Services, Australian National University.

Stubbs, J. (1995). "'Communitarian' Conferencing and Violence Against Women: A Cautionary Note." In: M. Valverde, L. MacLeod and K. Johnson (eds.), *Wife Assault and the Canadian Criminal Justice System.* Toronto, CAN: Centre of Criminology, University of Toronto.

Sunstein, C. (1988). "Beyond the Republican Revival." *Yale Law Journal* 97:1539–1590.

—— (1993). *Democracy and the Problem of Free Speech*. New York, NY: Free Press.

Tomaselli, S. (ed.) (1995). *A Vindication of the Rights of Men and a Vindication of the Rights of Woman*. Cambridge, UK: Cambridge University Press.

Van Ness, D.W. (1986). *Crime and Its Victims*. Downers Grove, IL: InterVarsity Press.

Walgrave, L. and H. Geudens (1996). "The Restorative Proportionality of Community Service for Juveniles." *European Journal of Crime, Criminal Law and Criminal Justice* 4:361-380.

Warner, K. (1994). "The Rights of the Offender in Family Conferences." In: C. Alder and J. Wundersitz (eds.) *Family Conferencing and Juvenile Justice: The Way Forward or Misplaced Optimism*? Canberra, AUS: Australian Institute of Criminology.

NOTES

1. However, most alleged offenders never see a fully fledged trial. Most plead guilty due to the insistence or domination of lawyers and other court personnel (Roach Anleu and Mack, 1995; Baldwin and McConville, 1977; McConville and Mirsky, 1990).

2. See footnote 1.

3. One of the authors has experience of such a policy with a rather restorative regime of regulating corporate crime under the *Trade Practices Act* (Cth) 1974. As a part-time commissioner of the Trade Practices Commission for a decade, Braithwaite would chair conferences of conflicting parties concerning alleged breaches of the act. Lawyers were allowed to attend (and normally did) but were not generally allowed to speak, a regime that engendered much more effective negotiated justice than other business regulatory regimes in Australia, where the lawyers were either excluded or allowed to take over.

4. Case 3 is based up to this point on a real Canadian restorative justice disaster somewhat like this.

5. "Until quite recently, feminists were in the minority in thinking that domestic violence against women was a matter of common concern and thus a legitimate topic of public discussion. The great majority of people considered this issue to be a private matter between what was assumed to be a fairly small number of heterosexual couples.... Then feminists formed a subaltern counterpublic from which we disseminated a view of domestic violence as a widespread systematic feature of male-dominated societies. Eventually, after sustained discursive contestation, we succeeded in *making* it a common concern" (Nancy Fraser cited in Habermas, 1996: 312).

PART TWO:
PROCESS, PROGRAMS AND PRACTICES

5. Community Service as a Cornerstone of a Systemic Restorative Response to (Juvenile) Crime

by

Lode Walgrave

In the literature, mediation and restorative justice are often implicitly presented as synonyms. However, reducing restorative justice to mediation in one form or another is far too narrow a conception of what the concept is and could be. Especially in view of the movement that aims at making restorative justice a fully-fledged alternative to both the rehabilitative and the retributive approaches to crime, the range of possible responses to crime should be more differentiated than an attempt to settle constructively the conflicts and disputes between victim and offender. Many authors understand that the community in which the offense has been committed is a concerned party too, and that it should at least partly be considered apart from the victim's losses. This is where community service can offer the necessary basic complement to the victim-focused steps in the restorative processing of a crime. However, introducing the community as a party concerned and community service as a sanction of restorative justice provokes specific problems and questions with regard to the definition and role of community, the position of the state and its legal procedures and the outcome of the intervention.

In this chapter, we develop the arguments to broaden the concept of restorative justice so that it can become a fully-fledged alternative to both the retributive and rehabilitative approaches of crime, and we examine the specific problems that arise from this broadening.

1. THE NEED FOR RESTORATIVE JUSTICE TO BE A FULLY-FLEDGED ALTERNATIVE

1.1. The Deadlock in the Discussions on Juvenile Justice

European and American systems of juvenile justice are under severe pressure (*European Journal on Criminal Policy and Research*, 1994; Feld, 1993).

Most critics find that the system's rehabilitative basis neglects the legal safeguards of young offenders and juvenile justice systems are generally ineffective and provide untrustworthy responses to some forms of juvenile crime. Commentators agree with the statement that "The child receives the worst of both worlds: he gets neither the protections accorded to adults nor the solicitous care ... postulated for children" (U.S. Supreme Court, as cited in Feld, 1993:198).

Some argue in favor of bringing the juvenile court back to criminal jurisprudence in order to provide better legal safeguards for juvenile offenders charged with crimes (Hirschi and Gottfredson, 1991; Feld, 1993; see also Feld, this volume). This option, however, would again hand minors charged with crimes over to a retributive system, that is itself heavily criticized for its negative social impact and poor instrumental performance.

The "retributivist" justifications of penal justice are based upon a naive classicist view of mankind and society, and they canalize revenge within the procedures of a constitutional state. This cannot be sufficient to govern a society. Moreover, if the point of retribution is to restore the moral balance, we should ask ourselves some questions, such as: What morality are we dealing with (geared to public order, personal security and property instead of, for example, solidarity or social and economic equity); Where lies the balance to be preserved, given the imbalance in the distribution of property and power (Braithwaite and Pettit, 1990)?

At least some instrumentalist arguments should be added to justify the punitive approach to crime. Empirical research has clearly shown that the instrumentalist ambitions of penal law are not met. Punitive prevention (or deterrence) is far less general than may be thought. Especially for juveniles, deterrence seems to yield hardly any significant effects (Schneider, 1990; Schuman and Kaulitzki, 1991). It would seem to be more the exception than the rule for an offender to be reformed by application of the conventional penalties of criminal law. To the contrary, in fact: various studies suggest that they have a 'marginalizing' and labeling effect, although the well known "nothing works" claim may be exaggerated (Lipton et. al., 1975). Moreover, the preservation of the victim's rights is certainly not central in the existing penal justice procedures. Therefore, many arguments in favor of the instrumentality of penal law would seem to be more cosmetic than based on established facts.

We therefore conclude that "the best reform of criminal law consists of its replacement, not by a better criminal law, but by something better" (Radbruch, as cited in Tulkens, 1993:489). A feasible alternative should be looked for that can drive back as much as possible the use of punitive responses to crime, but that at the same time safeguards the legal and social rights of victims, offenders and community.

1.2. Restorative Justice as a Fully-Fledged Way Out?

According to the restorative justice paradigm, the function of (juvenile) justice should not be to punish, not even to (re)educate, but to repair or to compensate for the harm caused by the offense. There is a growing body of empirical, theoretical and ethical literature supporting the idea that restorative justice could point to an alternative (Barnett, 1977; Galaway and Hudson, 1990, 1996; Messmer and Otto, 1992; Walgrave, 1994, 1995; Bazemore and Umbreit, 1995; Weitekamp, 1995; Wright, 1996). As the amount of empirical evidence increases, so do the positive expectations. This growing confidence is leading to the extension of restorative responses to more serious offenders.

But here, a point of discussion appears. Is restorative justice confined to being a form of diversion from the traditional systems or should it be developed as a fully-fledged systemic alternative intended to replace in the longer term both the rehabilitative and retributive juvenile justice systems?

Those who promote restorative justice as a form of diversion try to withdraw as many as possible cases from the criminal justice system, and do not believe that this system can constructively contribute to achieving real justice and peace in community. These advocates develop ways to resolve their own conflicts outside the system by empowering communities to resolve their own crime conflicts in a constructive way, and by doing convincing experiments that expand the range of restorative justice approaches. They also improve practical skills for achieving this kind of solutions, and train professionals and volunteers in these skills. They propagate to the public the knowledge and attitudes that are favorable to this kind of voluntary restorative response to crime and they plead for more reserve by the judiciary in using its interventionist power. On the other hand, restorative justice advocates exclude the justice system as such from their reflections and experiments, leaving in fact the cornerstone of the social response to crime to the traditional punitive or rehabilitative approaches.

This is not sufficient. Because of the unsatisfactory way in which both retributive and rehabilitative models respond to crime, a systemic alternative has to be looked for. If not, the restorative justice programs would simply be integrated into the existing systems. As long as restorative justice is presented as a model of voluntary settlement among victims, offenders and communities, based on free agreements between the parties concerned, it will be condemned to remain some kind of a "soft ornament" in the margin of "hard core" criminal justice. Successful settlements with heavy cases will continue to be interesting curiosities and anecdotal exceptions, without having any real impact on the fundamental options with regard to criminal justice. For "diversionists" the traditional criminal justice system cannot be replaced, because there is a need for a system that can use force, according to due process, to protect citizens from offenders and from abuse of authority as well (Marshall, 1996).

This is in fact the key question of this chapter: is a system that uses force according to due process doomed to be a punitive system, or can it also be restorative? As we will try to show, we believe it can. In the longer term, restorative justice programs should reform the criminal justice system into a restorative justice system. We therefore plead for an "ambitious," or "maximalist" version of restorative justice theory instead of a restricted one, which would confine itself to a marginal position within the existing systems of retributive or rehabilitative justice.

Presenting the restorative justice paradigm as a fully-fledged alternative to both the rehabilitative and the retributive responses to juvenile offending requires its advocates to clear out several topics: (1) Restorative justice should be able to deal with at least as many and as different types of crime as are presently dealt with by the traditional systems. (2) It should do this in a way that is more satisfying for the victims and more constructive for community. (3) Restorative justice should offer better legal guarantees and no worse educational results than the currently dominant rehabilitative systems of juvenile justice. (4) It should offer better educational results and no fewer legal guarantees than the retributive approach.

1.3. Restorative Justice Should be More Than Mediation

Of all restorative justice intervention schedules, mediation is the most common. The term "mediation" is used here as a generic concept. It covers all models of intervention that place emphasis on mostly informal but guided communication between the victim(s) of an offense and the offender(s), either directly or indirectly, face to face, or in the context of family or other group conferences implemented before, during and after judgement. Mediation as meant here can therefore lead to apologies, restitution, reparation, compensation, forgiveness, reconciliation and/or reintegration.

In mediation, the restorative aspect speaks for itself. The encounter in the mediating process itself is often considered as being part of the restoration, and it seems obvious that the outcome of such a successful process will be of a restorative kind (Van Ness and Strong, 1997). Most of the communication in the mediation process is about the harm and suffering incurred by the victim, which have a hard core, i.e., the individual victim's losses and injuries. They are often concrete and there are yardsticks to measure them. The restorative outcome aims at restitution, reparation and/or compensation of material damage, physical injury and/or psychological suffering. Sometimes, there is also involvement of the proximate community, where the anger, fear and other emotions caused by the offense can directly be observed and sensed. Mediation is about setting up and guiding exchanges and negotiations between victim (and local community) and the offender, in order to reach agreement on the type and extent of reparation and compensation and possibly to come to an emotional settlement. The mediation process is often followed by the monitoring of the implementation of that agreement. All these phenomena and processes can be observed and controlled.

Historically, this kind of regulation was the dominant mode of addressing the aftermath of the offense. It was only later that the state gradually assumed the role of firstly concerned victim, pushing aside the interests of the individual victims (Schafer, 1977; see also Weitekamp, this volume).

Maybe all this explains why, in the literature, restorative justice is often confined to these kinds of interventions, as is the case, e.g., in the recent reader *Restorative Justice: International Perspectives.* In their introduction, Galaway and Hudson (1996:5-8) describe the process of restorative justice as a "pre-mediation phase," "mediation phase" and "follow-up and outcomes." Most of the 31 contributions deal with actions focused on communication between the offender and the victim, wherein the role of community is to promote, frame and/or complete this communication. Often the communities play a marginal role. With the exception of two or three contributions, the concept of what a community is and how it should be delimited is vague. It is mostly unclear in how far communities' losses after the offense are considered separately from the victim's problems, complementary to them or only as an extension of them. The role of the state (or "the government") is mostly limited to that of scapegoat. Possible needs for a ruling power are sometimes mentioned, but not really elaborated. However, if we want to see the restorative justice paradigm evolve towards being the leading paradigm in dealing with crime in our society, such elaboration will be needed.

In a crime, there is more at stake than the relationship between the victim and his offender. This appears clearly through the existing difference between civil law and criminal law. Civil law aims at settling a conflict between two (groups of) citizens. Civil law is reactive, i.e., it acts only in response to a complaint. If no complaint is made about an alleged wrong suffered, civil justice will not be activated. Criminal law and the criminal justice system are different. In principle, criminal law is proactive. That means that it can initiate the proceedings itself. Even when, in practice, criminal justice acts proactively only to a small degree, the difference in basic intervention rules shows that other principles are at stake here. Not just the victim and offender, but also the broader social or societal group is concerned with the wrongdoing. There are, therefore, at least three parties involved. It is not just a matter of loss caused to an identifiable victim.

Some assume that focusing on the harm caused by an offense, instead of on the norm violation, could in fact shift the response from being ruled by public criminal law to being channeled by civil law of torts (Barnett and Hagel, 1977; see also Feld, this volume). We think, however, that a distinction must be preserved between dealing with conduct that results in torts to an individual person and an act that does more, by causing harm also to public life. In the latter cases, the harm done to the individual victim does not merge with the harm done to community. Community also is in need of restoration, and neither the victim nor the community necessarily speaks for each other in the process of settling the aftermath of an offense (Van Ness and Strong, 1997; Bussman, 1992).

Basically, a credible "ambitious" version of the restorative justice theory, aimed at replacing the existing criminal justice model, should therefore address such difficult questions on the core of crime treatment as: (1) Does the settlement of the consequences of a crime involve a third, more collective, party, besides the individual victim and the offender (and their immediate social environments), and, if so, how can this party be put into operation? (2) How can the losses and their restoration with regard to this third party be defined? (3) How can restorative justice be applied in cases where voluntary cooperation (from the victim and/or the offender) is not reached?

2. IN SEARCH OF THE THIRD PARTY, ITS DEFINITION AND ITS FUNCTIONING

Theoretically, the constitutional state itself sets up as being involved and it lays claims through the public prosecutor. For restorative justice advocates, this is in no way satisfactory. In their comments, they mostly include the "community," — and not the state — as a party in the restorative settlement of an offense.

2.1. What Is "Community"?

Community is a broad concept, which is defined very vaguely and often contradictorily in the various theories and is made concrete very differently in practice. However, if we want restorative justice to become a fully-fledged alternative, it is important to come to grips with the relation among the parties, agencies and processes of restorative justice, on the one hand, and the formal society and its institutions, on the other. Even if extensive discretionary power would be given to communities in dealing with offenses, it would have to be legally defined. The basic question is which groups of persons will legally be qualified for being considered as a community, when an offense occurred. The concept(s) of community(ies) will have to be defined in the legislation and put in operation in each jurisdiction. For the moment this is not at all the case.

One of the most difficult issues is that in modern, urbanized societies the local communities have lost much, if not all, of their power, and that we seem to be involved more and more in several networks of (often more superficial) relationships (Braithwaite, 1993; McCold, 1996). The community as a set of "dense networks of individual interdependencies with strong cultural commitments to mutuality of obligations" (Braithwaite, 1989:85) hardly still exists in our Western societies, and especially not in the cities (Crawford, 1996). We may deplore that. We may try to revitalize communities, though the outcome is not certain. In any case, building on communities for finding constructive responses to crime presupposes that a community really exists, and this is in many cases and situations not self-evident (Crawford, 1995). "How can we then thrust towards neighborhoods a task that presupposes they are highly alive?" (Christie, 1977:12). Christie himself admitted that he only had weak arguments against this skeptical question. There is no reason to believe that things have changed in the positive sense since then. Culture in general has evolved toward a growing individualism and fragmentation. In many neighborhoods, families live separated and isolated, hardly knowing each other, and certainly not sharing communal interests and values. Leaving the social reaction to crime to such "communities" would hand over the offender to local settlings of scores by locally powerful and maybe coincidental coalitions.

The offender as well as the victim is mostly involved in several networks of interdependencies, some of which surpass territorial boundaries: families, school, work, peers, sports clubs, political association, and many others (Braithwaite, 1993; McCold, 1996). The degree of their victimization and the way it is conceived can be very different. Employees who are temporarily incapable of working as a consequence of a violent assault, possibly entail secondary victims. There are emotional troubles and financial consequences in their families, economic losses for their employers, financial disbursements for the insurance company, recreational problems for their snooker peers, feelings of insecurity in their neighbors, and others. It is very unclear how a generic concept like "the community" can cover all this, and how it would be put into operation without formal rules. After all, the concept of community sometimes seems to be a kind of *fata morgana*, a mirage of what may exist somewhere far in our remembrances, but which we cannot really make concrete.

Even if the concept of community(ies) could be defined satisfactorily in some contexts, the next problem will be to decide who will be suitable for representing the community and how they will be appointed. What if the local gang sets itself up as the representative of the community of young people and deals with locally committed offenses? There is a need for identifying a power that will decide which persons and/or groups are acceptable to represent a community or the communities concerned. Criteria must be provided for and sound procedures designed. Will the mediator be a representative of the healing community, as is mostly the case in victim-offender mediation (Umbreit, 1994)? Will the family and other intimates of the victim and the offender play the role of the reintegrative shaming community (Braithwaite and Mugford, 1994)? Will a board of citizens represent the reparative sanctioning community (Bazemore, 1996)? Will that depend on the nature of the conflict (McCold, 1996)? Which characteristics of the conflict will be decisive on the kind of community to be involved in the restorative process?

The communitarian debate emerged especially forcefully after heavy criticism of judicial systems, followed by different forms of abolitionism (van Swaaningen, 1997). The problem is, however, that community has sometimes taken the form of a mythical belief, without attention for possible political, conservative moralizing lapses of its use. "Community that once had been rejected as a constraint can now not simply be hailed as the enabling capacity" (Bauman, as cited in van Swaaningen, 1997:207). Communities cannot be opposed only to formal societies. The tension that Habermas (as cited in van Swaaningen,1997), e.g., observes between systems and "life worlds" does not lead him to reject the (criminal justice) system. He rejects the degeneration of that system and advances "law as an institution of procedurally guaranteed dispute settlement..." (Habermas, as cited in van Swaaningen, 1997: 207). Also in restorative justice, one has to look for a constructive relation between a system and social life worlds, that promotes peace in these life worlds and justice in the broader society.

2.2. The Relation between Community and Society

As long as restorative justice initiatives take the form of local and provisional experiments, one can accept that some "artistic license" persists. But the ambition of the maximalist approach to restorative justice is that, in the longer term, the official way of dealing with juvenile crime would evolve towards a dominantly restorative system. At that moment, formalization and setting rules will be necessary.

That brings us inevitably to the question of the relationship between the community as the life world — the living social body — with its full richness of relationships, shared emotions, and commitments and bonds, on the one hand, and the society, the system(s), as the formal organization with its institutions, rules and powers, on the other hand. We cannot content ourselves with scapegoating all kinds of formalization by reproaching "the institutions," "the government," "the society," "the professionals" to be inhuman, ineffective, costly, alienating, conflict provoking and the like. There is more at stake than just "a shift from the state to the individual citizen and local communities" (Umbreit, 1994:162). Formalization is important in social life. The state is not just the Leviathan, using, and especially, abusing its power; it also is the protector of rights and legally defined guarantees.

In a democratic state, the government and the community(ies) are theoretically each other's extension. They differ in degree of formalization, in range and in power. The constitutional state and its government should be nothing else than the formalized institutionalization of the community or the community of communities. As Braithwaite and Pettit (1990) advance, the 'good' state and its government should safeguard the "dominion" of the citizens. By the concept of dominion, they refer to the whole range of societally guaranteed rights and freedom that all citizens enjoy. Governments have to set and enforce the rules that frame the dominion and that should form the foundation for developing prosperous communities. Both community and government have complementary missions in dealing with the aftermath of an offense. Community, aiming at peace in its midst, can offer healing to the victim and rehabilitation to the offender. The government, oriented toward order in society, brings support to redress the victim and guarantees fairness to the offender. Together, community's peace and society's order result in safety (Van Ness, 1996; Van Ness and Strong, 1997).

Of course, this is theory. The power of the state and its institutions has overruled the communities. Through its socioeconomic, urbanizational and criminal policies, the state has often even contributed to the decline of communities. What went wrong in the development of criminal justice policies is that the role of communities has been so neglected, that the attention to making or keeping peace has shrunk dramatically. Instead, governments have only paid attention to the necessity of public order in a way that has enhanced conflict in the communities — or even threatened community life itself.

This, however is no reason for excluding the formal state from dealing with crime, but it rather obliges us to rethink and re-examine the relation between the formal state and communities. In order to avoid this degeneration of the states' intervention, and to preserve the constructive capacities of communities, the role of governmental institutions should be redefined in a more limited way. The construction of restorative justice should involve four functions in the reaction to an offense.

(1) Promote restorative responses to crime in communities, with government leaving space to communities and empowering them to solve constructively the aftermath of offenses. In most cases, the criminal justice system should accept a subsidiary role, secondary to the responses given in the community. Communal initiatives to respond to local crime should be supported, if they meet certain conditions.

(2) Ensure that authorities warrant the respect for individual legal rights of the victim and the suspect or offender as well. Therefore, communities have to be submitted to a certain degree of control. That control is strictly focused on making sure that nobody is forced to cooperate in a restorative process at the communal level, that the process leaves space for free discussion and that the outcome of the process does not exceed a proportionate maximum.

(3) Recognize that judicial coercion is needed if voluntary restorative actions within a community do not succeed and a response to the crime is nevertheless considered to be necessary. In a constitutional state, public coercive intervention is only acceptable if it is carried out by a judicial authority, which is itself submitted to legal and procedural rules. In many cases, local communities are not very strong at all. One can suppose that the need for calling upon the judicial system will be prominent in many cases.

(4) Acknowledge that judicial coercion and procedures are also needed if the crime and public reactions to it are of a nature that a purely informal voluntary regulation appears to be insufficient. The community is in any case not given priority to deal with such crime, as its impact is considered to transcend the locality where it has been committed. A very important question here is whether this is the end of the restorative response to crime. We do not think so and shall deal with this question later.

3. RESTORING PUBLIC LOSSES

The harm caused by many offenses go beyond the concrete victim's suffering and losses. An offense damages the community, too. It is, however, difficult to make these losses more concrete. Are communities and/or societies victimized by the occurrence of an offense? What do they lose through the occurrence of an offense? How can we measure that?

3.1. What Are "Public Losses"?

The definition of "public losses" is difficult; the literature on this subject is not very concrete. Some vaguely quote "the impact of the offence on the rights of citizens or on society in general" (Thorvaldson, 1990:27). Others point to the "loss of public safety, damage to community values and the disruption, caused by crime" (Van Ness, 1990:9) or "physical, emotional or economic harm" (Gehm, 1992:548). Public losses can be material and concrete, e.g., when public goods have been stolen or vandalized or when the occurrence of many crimes has negative influences on economy. Most public losses, however, are indirect and more abstract. One cannot deny that the "collectivity" is suffering harm by the occurrence of a crime, but it is difficult to make the suffering concrete.

Maybe we can partly resolve the problem by reversing the question: what would happen if the community and/or society did not intervene after the occurrence of an offense? Besides the possible material damages, the community would probably suffer from a loss of peace in its midst. The victim and his supporters (family, peers) would not accept what has been done to them, and they would try to "make things even." Acts of revenge would risk escalating into a kind of vendetta, dragging down the community as a whole. The community would lose peace and be dominated by fear of crime. This would affect the general quality of life through losses of solidarity and mutual respect. Common values may fade away. What is at stake here is more than just the individual victim's losses: an offense is a threat to the peace and quality of life in a community, which it will lose if nothing happens.

But the state has a lot to lose too. If institutionalized society did not intervene adequately against crime, the public would lose its belief in public rules and in the authorities' power to preserve order and justice in social life. People would not feel assured of their dominion and would see each other as rivals and the government as a threat. Society would collapse or deteriorate into a tyranny. Such societies "would lose their freedom" (Braithwaite, 1989: 186). What is at stake for all citizens in a crime is their dominion as a set of rights and freedoms, which is guaranteed by the state and its institutions. Consequently, public losses from a crime are threats to the peace and general quality of social life and to the dominion of all citizens. They have to be considered apart from the injuries to the individual victim, but they may not compete with them.[1]

3.2. Restoring Public Losses through Community Service?

Considering the accountability of the offender, the question is what the offender can do in order to diminish or remove the threat to peace in community and to the dominion of all citizens. The offender can do acts of restoration. He or she can show repentance and express a willingness to respect the rules and peace in the community. He or she also can make the restoration more concrete and agree to make restitution to the concrete victim or do a community service. Community service is defined as unpaid work done by the offender for the benefit of a community or its institutions meant as a compensation for the harm caused by an offence to that community. The community has been victimized by the loss of peace and quality of life, and citizens are threatened in their dominion and can demand compensation for it through community service. The compensation may only have a symbolic aspect, but it is no less important for that. The community itself is restored through the material results of the service rendered and through the peace-restoring gesture of the offender. Dominions are restored by the fact that the response to the intrusion into the dominion has been supported and possibly even organized by government. Government has taken the dominions seriously, which is reassuring for citizens. A problem arises when the offender does not accept voluntarily to do a community service, which we shall discuss shortly.

The option for including community service in the responses of restorative justice to an offense is not without problems. They include:

(1) Some fear that accepting community service as a restorative response toward community and even society will again result in too much attention for the restorative claims from societal institutions. They think it would be to the detriment of the concrete victim's needs, especially because the collective damages are difficult to indicate and measure (Harland and Rosen, 1990). Though these fears may seem justified, they do not lead us to exclude community service for principled reasons. On the contrary, excluding community and society from being addressed in the restorative response would be catastrophic for the potentials of the maximalist approach, which we defend. The mentioned dangers are, however, reasons to clarify accurately "the nature and extent of the harm done to society at large, as well as the most appropriate means for the offender to repair that harm" (Van Ness and Strong, 1997:55). We get back to that later in this chapter.

(2) More important still is that, because the notion of community service has been used in so many contexts, it is often unclear how it fits into the restorative model. Much of the resistance against including community service in the restorative frame is based on the use of it in non-restorative contexts, as illustrated in Table 1.

Some practices use community service as a punishment. The objective is not to restore a harm by fulfilling a compensating service, but to inflict suffering by imposing an unpleasant and even degrading task. The offender must feel pain, in order to be deterred from reoffending and to satisfy the victim's feelings of revenge. Instead of a restorative response, this is a form of retributive forced labor. In most countries, where rehabilitation is predominant in juvenile justice systems, community service is mostly used as a method for re-education (Geudens and Walgrave, 1994). The kind and the duration of the service are then dependent on the offender's specific treatment needs. Community service is primarily intended to influence the offender's attitudes, competencies and social network. This is in fact a form of treatment, but it is not focused on restoring harm to victims nor to community or society. On the contrary, the victim's or community's losses are often used as tools in the re-education program. Quite understandably, many restorative justice advocates are hesitant or even reluctant to incorporate such responses into the restorative concept.

However, community service can also be used in a restorative sense, if it is meant to compensate for harm, restore peace in the community and contribute to safety feelings in society. The explicit motivation for the service, the content and duration of the service and the way its compliance is coached will be different. Attention will now be turned to the harm and the restoration of it, including the reintegration of the offender, as this is an important item in restoring peace in the community.

Table 1: Community Service in Different Judicial Settings

	Punitive	Rehabilitative	Restorative
Objective	Deterrence	Adequate treatment	Reasonable restoration
Content	Painful for offenders	Adapted to needs of offenders	Symbolic for harm to community
Duration depends on	Seriousness of crime	Treatment needs	Seriousness of harm
Evaluation according to	Just desert	Conform behavior	Peace in community

Skeptics will point to the misuses of community service, as mentioned before. This, however, is not a reason to reject it, but rather to be very accurate in describing how restorative community service could and should be carried out, very strict in setting the conditions for restorative community service in practice, and very sensitive for possible non-restorative implementations of community service. After all, the potentials of restorative justice to become a fully-fledged systemic alternative are dependent on the possible inclusion of finding ways to restore the harm to community and society.

This brings us to the conclusion that in a fully-fledged restorative paradigm for responding to crime, community service is the necessary counterpart with regard to community of what the restitution is with regard to the concrete victim. Both have in common:

(1) A definition of crime as an injury to victims (concrete and societal). This is a quite different definition from the retributive definition of crime, which considers it as a transgression of a general juridical-ethical rule.

(2) The intervention is primarily oriented toward restoration of that injury, which is unlike the "constitutionalized revenge" to which the retributive response is oriented and also different from the treatment aims of the rehabilitative approach.

(3) Both community service and restitution start from the accountability of the offender and involve him or her actively and directly in the restorative action. The retributive or rehabilitative responses reduce the offender to being a passive object of retribution or treatment.

(4) Finally, we also advance the judicial framework as a common characteristic of both intervention models. The latter may be surprising in reference to the principle of subsidiarity, which gives priority to voluntary

settlements of crime in the community and without judicial intervention. But even in cases of victim-offender mediation, the judicial background is necessary; it offers the frame for designing and guaranteeing the legal rights of the victim and the offender. Moreover, the very fact that the judicial response is an option leads to more certainty that the non-judicial agreements are based on truly voluntary commitments by the parties involved. If this judicial warrant is not available, the restorative responses may go off the rails toward outcomes that are not 'just' at all (see functions 2 and 3 for public authorities, indicated in the subheading 2.2.The Relation between Community and Society.).

4. RESTORATIVE COERCION?

When thinking about restorative justice, we have to make a distinction between the reaching of an agreement or decision on the one hand, and the concrete restorative action that is carried out after the agreement or decision is reached on the other hand. The concrete restorative action may consist of offering apologies, restitution, community service and the like. The process that leads to such action may be a victim-offender mediation, a group conference, or another form of voluntary deliberation and negotiation between parties with a stake in the offense. However, restitutive or compensatory actions may also be imposed. In such cases, such actions become restorative sanctions and the process preceding these sanctions is mostly a judicial procedure.

For restorative justice advocates, this is not self-evident. Most of the literature on restorative justice is on voluntary deliberations, reintegrative shaming, exchanging gestures of re-acceptance, respect, and willingness to reenter the community in a constructive way, leading to reparation, reconciliation, and/or reintegration. Often, hardly any distinction is made between process and action, suggesting that the process itself is part of the restoration.

There must not be any doubt that voluntary deliberation with all parties concerned is the best way of dealing with the aftermath of an offense and that it should be granted many more opportunities than is actually the case. The only task of the public institutions here is to create the conditions to promote all of this (see functions 1 and 2 for public authorities, indicated in subheading 2.2.). The situation is different, however, if the offense cannot be settled informally. This can happen for several reasons, e.g., because agreement on the informal level is not reached, or because the crime is of such a nature that public proceedings are deemed to be necessary (see functions 3 and 4 for public authorities, indicated in subheading 2.2.). This is the case with many offenses, and coercion may have to be exercised.

The questions here are: (1) whether coercive procedures in the response to a crime can be included in the restorative justice frame; (2) how the legal safeguards can be implemented in such cases; and (3) how to make sure that the content of the actions imposed are really restorative and not punitive. These are the most essential questions for the possible extending of restorative justice toward being the dominant paradigm in dealing with crime in society.

4.1. Can Restorative Actions Be Enforced?

Even if the voluntary restorative response to crime will broaden its range of applicability, it will continue to have its limits. Would this then also be the limit to the restorative approach? Several situations are possible wherein the voluntary settlement appears to be impossible. However, the fact that a restorative process appears not to be feasible does not mean that restorative sanctions cannot be imposed, as illustrated in the following situations.

(1) The victim and/or the local community may not be prepared to conclude a reasonable restorative settlement of the offence, while the offender him or herself is willing to do so. In such cases, it seems unfair to subject the offender to the traditional retributive system. He or she should be offered the opportunity to accomplish a restorative action. Because the victim or the community is lacking in the negotiation, a settlement should be made with a judicial authority. Real mediation cannot be forced, but the restorative action can consist in making formal restitution, doing work for the benefit of a victim's fund or in doing community service.

(2) The offender him or herself may refuse to accept a reasonable restorative action after the offense. The victim and the community are not capable of imposing coercive interventions, so that only the judicial institution is left, possibly to impose a sanction. These sanctions can be of a restorative kind: the offender can be forced to make restitution, work for the benefit of a victim's fund or complete community service.

(3) Some offenses are serious to that extent that they surpass the impact on local communities. A coercive public intervention and sanction by the formal justice system may be considered to be necessary, possibly even on top of the settlement with the concrete victims and the community. Here also the restorative aspect of public judicial intervention is not entirely lost. One of these aspects could lie in the fact that it would try not to hamper the tentative agreements for restorative settlements with the individual victims and with the community, but would leave space for it. A second aspect may lie in the content of the imposed sanction. As in the earlier two situations, the sanction can be to make restitution, do work for the benefit of a victim fund and/or do a community service. If concerns

for security would necessitate it, the offender could be incapacitated through a forced stay in a closed facility, but restorative actions should be tried from within that facility.

Of course, such a forced intervention does not involve the complete potentialities of the restorative paradigm, nor does it achieve its most constructive purposes. Referring to Van Ness and Strong's (1997) statements, one could say that in coercive restorative sanctions, there is no encounter, participation is very reduced, reintegration is unsure and reparation is only elementary. However, coercive restorative sanctions are still preferable to the forced retributive or forced rehabilitative interventions, for several reasons.

- There is, first of all, the material benefit. The mere fact that something is actually done for the victims and for the community is certainly more beneficial than the retributive response, criticized by Wright (1992:5) as: "Balancing the harm done by the offender with further harm inflicted on the offender. That only adds to the total amount of harm in the world."

- Secondly, there is a reintegrative advantage. Even if the offender does not freely accept to accomplish a restorative action, he or she may in the longer term understand the sanction in a constructive way and the chances for him to be reaccepted by the community are greater than after a retributive action. This seems also to be true in comparison with the rehabilitative measures, as appears through the results of research on the impact of restorative sanctions on the offender (Geudens, 1997; Walgrave and Geudens, 1996; see also Schiff, this volume). Moreover, the carrying out of restorative sanctions within the community is also educational for the community itself. It has the opportunity to observe young offenders doing constructive services, which may contribute to the deconstruction of stereotyped images.

- Finally, coerced restorative sanctions give more coherence in principle, and the option for restorative justice is consequentially extended. Even if individuals (victims or offenders) or communities do not adhere to the constructive character of the restorative response, the state should have the mission to stick to the principle and to act, as much as possible, logically with it.

4.2. Coercive Restorative Sanctions and Legal Rules

The acceptance of force in the imposition of restorative actions entails the necessity for legal safeguards. There is no longer any question of an agreed compensation arrangement as the result of mediation or another form of deliberation. Imposed restitution or community service can involve a restriction of freedom imposed as the result of an offense. The accountability for the offense and the extent of the restriction of freedom must, therefore, be determined. In our legal system this can only be done according to legal safeguards. This creates the need for a more formal procedure, which is also public. Formal rules must be established and their observation must be controlled carefully. This is truer still in community service, because the direct reparation element has been removed, making the link between the offense and the sanctions for it more tenuous and difficult to perceive. Moreover, whereas community service is seen as a restorative act toward community or society, any other agency but the court could seem to be the judge in its own case in deciding upon the amount and kind of community service to be imposed.

In general, the literature concerning restorative experiments in a judicial context pays little attention to this issue. Out of a review of 28 published and analyzed experiments, it appears that few reports comment explicitly on the question of legal safeguards for offenders.[2] The context of all experiments is educational. In 11 projects, the aim of restoration is also mentioned, although subordinated to the educational purposes. Very often, victim-offender mediation or community service is imposed in informal stages of the procedure, in an investigative context. The rights of the accused or defendant are not mentioned, and no attention is given to any form of proportionality between an imposed community service and the sanctioned offense(s). We also found neglect of legal safeguards in the application of community service by the Belgian youth courts (Walgrave and Geudens, 1996). The minimal attention given to the legal status of the restorative sanctions and to the rights of the defense seems to be symptomatic of the rehabilitative *parens patriae* climate in which most restorative projects operate, and this leads to inadequate concern or even neglect of this topic.

The discussion of the judicial handling of offenses in a restorative perspective can be based on the republican theory of criminal justice put forward by Braithwaite and Pettit (1990). According to this theory, the main aim of criminal justice is the protection and promotion of the dominion (the range of societally guaranteed rights and freedoms for all citizens) of all the parties involved (victims, offenders and other citizens). Every theoretical statement and every practical decision must be evaluated in terms of its consequences for the dominions of all citizens.

The restorative orientation creates an opportunity to contribute to the fundamental purpose of the republican criminal justice theory, to protect and to promote the dominion of all citizens. Material and psychological reparation following apologies, restitution or compensation to the victim and symbolic or (partly) material reparation through community service, contribute to the recognition and restoration of the other individual's dominion. If the organized society plays a role in this, it confirms at the same time the society as an ordered community, secure in its rights. Braithwaite and Pettit (1990:127) expressly prefer "punishments" which means a restorative option. "The reprobation and reintegration presumptions lead us to favor restitution as a form of punishment; it symbolizes the harm, connoting through its content the wrong that was done." Both the direct restitution to victims and community service are indicated as the most preferable sanctions.

There are some problems with the term "punishment." A punishment strictly means a willful infliction of suffering as a reaction to an undesirable behavior. In an imposed restorative action the painfulness is not deliberately inflicted but may be a consequence of the restriction of freedom (Wright, 1992). Therefore, an imposed restorative action is no punishment in the strict sense of the word. In using the term punishment, Braithwaite and Pettit (1990) probably mean restriction of freedom as a response to an offense, which will mostly be unpleasant.

In the republican theory of criminal justice, no restriction of freedom is self-evident, but must be positively justified by the demonstrable gains in terms of dominion for those involved. This leads to the principle of "parsimony in punishment": "The state should use those legislative, enforcement and sentencing options which are minimally interventionist until the evidence is clear that more intrusive practices are required to increase dominion. More than that, the state should actively search for alternative ways of promoting dominion to such interventionist policies as criminal punishment" (Braithwaite and Pettit, 1990:79-80). Accordingly, restorative justice gives priority to extra-judicial solutions to crime conflicts and is seeking for "alternative ways of promoting dominion." Parsimony does not mean exclusion. The theory therefore also accepts that sanctions can be imposed.

The public proceedings in relation to an offense are highly formalized. And rightly so, since the coercion that is exercised constitutes an infringement of the citizen's dominion, and that must only take place under strict and controllable conditions. The judicial authorities are bound by "the recognition of uncontroversial criminal justice rights" and must demonstrate that they "take the rights seriously" (Braithwaite and Pettit, 1990:75). Formalizing the proceedings is the most important way of achieving this.

One important aspect of criminal justice is its public character. "Denunciation is a central justification for the criminal justice system," and this must be done publicly so that it can send "an important reprobative message to the community" (Braithwaite and Pettit, 1990:177). Public response to the infringement of a norm makes clear to the public that the defense of the dominion is being taken seriously, which may promote the restoration of feelings of security and the belief that the authorities guarantee this. Moreover, the public character of the judicial proceedings offers opportunities for controlling the judicial procedure. It submits the social controllers themselves to public control, which is necessary for counterbalancing the power.

An essential condition for a good criminal justice system is that it is "satiable." The principles of criminal justice must also comprise clearly defined upper limits of intervention. This requirement is met by a principle of proportionality, which places emphasis on the relationship between the seriousness of the crime and the upper limit of permissible state intervention. Because this seems to be one of the most difficult points in formalizing the restorative justice approach, we will delve deeper into this point in the next section.

4.3. Restorative Proportionality as the Indication of an Upper Limit

The problem of proportionality in restorative justice is presented here as an example of how formalizing the restorative response to crime entails its own difficulties and possibilities. Traditionally, the principle of proportionality is seen in the context of retribution, where the rule of "just desert" is a leading consideration (von Hirsch, 1976). Proportionality is based on the Kantian principle that the social-moral balance must be restored by punishing the culpable offense with an equal amount of harm. In this context, "just desert" would mean that the culpable offense must be answered in law by an appropriate punishment that matches the amount of harm done by the offender — no more, no less. In the retributive approach, a minimum sentence is also necessary in order to apply at least some retribution for the harm done. The criminal law system is given little scope to define its own policy, so that it cannot, for example, renounce a minimum sentence. Instead, it safeguards an abstract juridical-moral code the credibility of which is served by a systematic application.

Braithwaite and Pettit (1990:157) rightly reject this interpretation, based on their principle of parsimony in punishment: "we should be parsimonious in punishment, not going beyond the lowest level which will certainly promote dominion." Punishment or another form of restriction of freedom is only permissible if it can serve a social goal that is more important than the loss of democratic rights occasioned by a restriction of freedom. There is no longer any need for a minimum punishment. The penal law system is forced to conduct a policy in which a consideration of the consequences for the "dominion" of citizens is essential. From such a perspective, forgiveness and clemency have a place, informal processes are preferable and the eventuality of criminal prosecution is only a subsidiary consideration. On the other side, neglect of a proportionate upper limit in the restorative justice response would lead to an erosion of democracy, since it would give the state an unlimited opportunity to restrict an offender's freedoms or even dismantle them altogether. Since every citizen commits some offence at some time in his or her life, this would make "intrusion in the dominion" of each citizen too easy. This is in fact one of the main reasons why the rehabilitative model in the treatment of juvenile offenders is so strongly criticized.

In the retributive approach, proportionality between the seriousness of an offense and the severity of the restriction in freedom is a sociolegal construction. It is not naturally given. There is no natural relationship between, for example, burglary and a prison sentence, or between a traffic violation and a fine. These are social conventions, based on tradition and endorsed in penal law. "The amount of disapproval conveyed by penal sanctions is a convention" (von Hirsch, 1993:40). Striking differences exist among the industrialized nations, which demonstrates that the intrinsic value of proportionality in ordinary criminal law should not be overestimated.

To determine proportionality, it is essential that the judicial response be chosen retrospectively, as happens in criminal law. "Punishment is retrospective and imposes unpleasant consequences for past offences..." (Feld, 1993:234). Due to the fact that the offence has already been committed, the authority imposing the punishment has a verifiable yardstick against which to determine the chosen punishment. The degree of accountability must be established first and only then can the proportionate punishment be determined. This is why the criminal law preserves the legal rights of citizens more than the rehabilitative approach, since in the latter "treatment is prospective and seeks to improve the offender's future welfare" (Feld, 1993:234). There is consequently no verifiable yardstick available at the moment when the measures are imposed, so that they are awarded disproportionally, without a clearly fixed upper limit.

In a proper system of restorative law, it is theoretically possible to construct such proportionality, since in principle restorative law also works retrospectively in that it focuses on the need to put right the harm that has already been done. The degree of sanctioning can thus be weighed against an available, verifiable and specifiable yardstick. However, restorative proportionality deviates significantly from retributive proportionality in that the two restorative variables, which must be related to each other, differ fundamentally from the retributive variables. There is no point in determining a "just desert" on the basis of a link between the moral-juridical severity of the offence and the degree of punishment that would restore the moral balance. Instead, a "correct restoration" is required here, to be determined on the basis of a link between the severity of the material, relational, and social harm caused by the offence and the degree of restorative effort required by the offender. There is as yet no tradition in which restorative sanctions have been compared, weighed against each other and commented on in terms of their relationship to the harm caused by the offense.

One can presume that the agreement itself, after an informal settlement is reached, means that the agreeing parties consider the result of their negotiation to be a reasonable (proportionate) compensation for the harm at stake. But we are confronted here with the question of coercively imposed sanctions, intended to be restorative. Useful indications may be available to decide upon the amount of restitution or compensation to be requested for the concrete victim. Especially difficult, however, is the search for a reasonable relation between the "public losses" and their compensation through some kind of service to the community. As described earlier, the definition of "public losses" is difficult.

Another question is how to measure the gravity of public losses. Whereas the retributive rank order refers to an abstract judicial-moral weighing of the offenses, the restorative yardstick would refer to an estimation of abstract social losses, which we have defined as a threat to peace, to the general quality of social life and to the dominions of citizens. The difference is that the restorative gravity estimation is based on social morality, inspired by concern for peaceful life in the community and safety in the society, rather than on a totalitarian morality, using absolutist categories of "right" and "wrong" (Pires, 1991). But, in fact, this could be a theoretical distinction without essential consequences in practice. If worked out, the restorative gravity evaluations would probably not deviate so much from the existing retributivist gravity scales (Weitekamp, 1995).[3]

How can accountability for damage be measured? Criminal law points to the guilt that can be attached to the person of the offender. This leads to a system of sanctions resulting in stigmatization and social exclusion. Restorative law will in all probability need to place more emphasis on accountability, with the question of personal guilt left out of the equation. The approach would be "consequence vs. guilt, harm vs. intent" (Fattah, 1993). The offender has caused harm, culpably or otherwise, and as such he or she is (partly) responsible for putting things right. The degree of accountability has to include the degree of capacity to bear it. Persons judged incompetent cannot be held accountable. In juvenile justice, minors who are juridically not competent cannot be considered completely accountable either. But their personal competencies and the circumstances of the offense also have to be taken into account in the definition of the degree of accountability of an actor for the harm he or she has caused by the offense.

How should the relationship be established between the gravity of the damage and the degree of accountability on the one hand, and the severity of the community service imposed on the other hand? The link between both variables is indirect and almost always symbolic. As mentioned earlier, the retributive link between crime and punishment is a construction based on a long tradition, which is lacking with regard to the restorative link. Therefore, experience, comparison and reflection must result in a framework in which the gravity of public losses can be estimated, and reasonable forms and amounts of compensation could be indicated. The aim is not to find a rigid rating scale of restorative sanctions but a frame for achieving "reasonable" restoration. The accepted reasonableness is the guarantee for the settlement of the conflict, and for the chances for reintegration of the offender. Reasonableness also takes into account the psychological, social and economic capacities of the person from whom the restoration is being demanded. Accepting these capacities as elements in sentencing is no return to individualized arbitrariness, as is criticized in the rehabilitative responses. Whereas in the latter the capacities are used to define the needs for treatment in the future, the capacities in restorative justice serve as elements to define the amount of accountability for the existing harm and to decide upon the amount of restorative effort that can reasonably be demanded.

5. CONCLUSION

In the development of a restorative justice approach, the problem is that restorative techniques are mostly used in connection with rehabilitative or retributive systems. Paradoxically, one could even say that the most serious threat to restorative justice is the enthusiasm with which police officers, magistrates and social workers insert mediation and community service as simple techniques into their traditional punitive or rehabilitative approaches. That is why further research on restorative principles and conscious implementation strategies is badly needed. Reflection on socio-ethical, philosophical and legal theory must be further developed in order to construct a coherent normative theory based on the paradigm of restorative justice, which can serve as a frame of reference to ensure correct application in practice and to guide experimentation with appropriate methods and techniques.

The fundamental choice to be made is the one between a restorative justice meant as (1) a form of diversion from the existing systems, and as (2) a path toward a fully-fledged systemic alternative that should, in the longer term, replace both the retributive and the rehabilitative systems of official responding to crime.

The first option would restrict restorative justice, relegating it to a marginal status in dealing with crime in society. Only cases that the formal system would be willing to cede would be eligible for being dealt with in a restorative way. Restorative justice would not become more than some kind of an "addendum" or footnote to the system, not dealing with the essential part of criminality, but with the benign cases or those that are not interesting anymore for the criminal justice system. Moreover, the very fact that such selected cases would be handed over to the non-judicial circuit would lead to the reinforcement of the punitive responses against those who are kept within the criminal justice system. The diversionary option would primarily lead restorative justice to be diverted from its potential to become a fundamental reform of the way society deals with its criminality.

We therefore opt for the maximalist interpretation of restorative justice, i.e., aiming at reforming the criminal justice system and transforming it into a restorative justice system. This option inevitably confronts its advocates with a number of questions on the hard core of dealing with crime that could remain unanswered by the diversionist approach. Maximalist restorative justice proponents pretend to have primarily restorative responses to serious crimes too, and that obliges them to face questions with regard to public safety and coercion. Considering coercion immediately brings about the necessity of integrating the use of force into the fundamental rules of a constitutional democratic state.

In this chapter, we have asked ourselves whether the maximalist pretensions might be justified, by examining if the just-mentioned hard core problems could find a satisfying solution. The results are not negative. Many problems are unresolved, but there are many arguments to support the belief that solutions can be found. Community service will have to be included in the restorative justice frame, and a vast effort of socio-ethical and juridical normative reflection will be needed, together with empirical and theoretical work based on careful experimentation and evaluation. These efforts are worthwhile, because they serve as the litmus test for restorative justice as a fundamentally renovating appeal.

Acknowledgement: This research was supported by the Fund for Scientific Research-Flanders, and by the Special Research Fund of the Katholicke Universiteit Leuven.

REFERENCES

Barnett, R. (1977). "Restitution: A New Paradigm of Criminal Justice." In: R. Barnett and J. Hagel (eds.), *Assessing the Criminal.* Cambridge, MA: Ballinger.

—— and J. Hagel (eds.) (1977). *Assessing the Criminal.* Cambridge, MA: Ballinger.

Bazemore, G. (1997). "The 'Community' in Community Justice." *Justice System Journal* 19(2):193-228.

—— and D. Maloney (1994). "Rehabilitating Community Service: Sanctions in a Balanced Justice System." *Federal Probation* (Mar):24-35.

—— and M. Umbreit (1995). "Rethinking the Sanctioning Function in Juvenile Court: Retributive or Restorative Responses to Youth Crime." *Crime & Delinquency* 41(3):296-316.

—— (1996). "Three Paradigms for Juvenile Justice." In: J. Hudson and B. Galaway (eds.), *Restorative Justice: International Perspectives.* Monsey, NY: Criminal Justice Press.

Braithwaite, J. (1989). *Crime, Shame and Reintegration*. Cambridge, UK: University Press.

—— (1993). "Shame and Modernity." *British Journal of Criminology* 33(1):1-18.

—— and S. Mugford (1994). "Conditions of Successful Reintegration Ceremonies." *British Journal of Criminology* 34(2):139-171.

—— and Ph. Pettit (1990). *Not Just Desert. A Republican Theory of Criminal Justice*. Oxford, UK: Oxford University Press.

Bussman, K. (1992). "Morality Symbolism and Criminal Law: Chances and Limits of Mediation Programs." In: H. Messmer and H.U. Otto (eds.), *Restorative Justice on Trial*. Dordrecht, NETH and Boston, MA: Kluwer.

Christie, N. (1977). "Conflict as Property." *British Journal of Criminology* 1:1-14.

Crawford, A. (1995). "Appeals to Community and Crime Prevention." *Crime, Law and Social Change* 22:97-126.

—— (1996). "The Spirit of Community: Rights, Responsibilities and the Communitarian Agenda." *Journal of Law and Society* 23:247-262.

European Journal on Criminal Policy and Research (1994). "The Juvenile Justice System." Special issue 2(2):5-90.

Fattah, E. (1993). "From a Guilt Orientation to a Consequence Orientation. A Proposed New Paradigm for the Criminal Law in the 21st Century." In: W. Küper and J. Welp (eds.), *Beiträge zur Rechtswissenschaften*. Heidelberg, GER: Müller.

Feld, B. (1993). "Criminalizing the American Juvenile Court." In: M. Tonry (ed.), *Crime and Justice: A Review of Research*, vol. 17. Chicago, IL: University of Chicago Press.

Galaway, B. and J. Hudson (1990). "Towards Restorative Justice." In: B. Galaway and J. Hudson (eds.), *Criminal Justice, Restitution and Reconciliation*. Monsey, NY: Criminal Justice Press.

—— and J. Hudson (1996). "Introduction." In: B. Galaway and J. Hudson, (eds.), *Restorative Justice: International Perspectives*. Monsey, NY: Criminal Justice Press.

Gehm, J. (1992). "The Function of Forgiveness in the Criminal Justice System." In: H. Messmer and H.-U. Otto (eds.), *Restorative Justice on Trial*. Dordrecht, NETH and Boston. MA: Kluwer.

Geudens, H. (1997). "The Recidivism Scores of Juvenile Offenders after a Community Service, Compared with the Scores after a Traditional Sanction." Paper presented at the First International Conference on Restorative Justice for Juveniles, Leuven, Belgium, May.

—— and L. Walgrave (1994). "Community Service as a Sanction of Restorative Juvenile Justice. A European Approach." Paper presented at the annual meeting of the American Society of Criminology, Miami, November.

Harland, A. and C. Rosen (1990). "Impediments to the Recovery of Restitution by Crime Victims." *Violence and Victims* 5(2):127-132.

Hirschi, T. and M. Gottfredson (1991). "Rethinking the Juvenile Justice System." In: T. Booth (ed.), *Juvenile Justice in the New Europe*. Sheffield, UK: Social Services Monographs.

Lipton, D., R. Martinson and J. Wilkes (19975). *The Effectiviness of Corrections Treatment: A Survey of Treatment Evaluation Studies*. New York, NY: Praeger.

Marshall, T. (1996). "The Evolution of Restorative Justice in Britain." *European Journal on Criminal Policy and Research* 4:21-43.

McCold, P. (1996). "Restorative Justice and the Role of Community." In: B. Galaway and J. Hudson (eds.), *Restorative Justice: International Perspectives*. Monsey, NY: Criminal Justice Press.

Messmer, H. and H.U. Otto (eds.) (1992). *Restorative Justice on Trial*. Dordrecht, NETH and Boston, MA: Kluwer.

Pires, A. (1991). "Ethiques et Réforme du Droit Pénal: au delà des Philosophies de la Peine." (Ethics and the Reform of Penal Law: Beyond Philosophies of Punishment.) *Ethica* 3(2):47-78.

Schafer, S. (1977). *Victimology. The Victim and His Criminal*. Reston, VA: Prentice Hall.

Schneider, A. (1986). "Restitution and Recidivism Rates of Juvenile Offenders: Results from Four Experimental Studies." *Criminology* 24(3):533-552.

—— (1990). *Deterrence and Juvenile Crime*. New York, NY: Springer.

Schuman, K. and R. Kaulitzki (1991). "Limits of General Deterrence: The Case of Juvenile Delinquency." In: K. Sessar and H.J. Kerner (eds.), *Developments in Crime and Crime Control Research. German Studies on Victims, Offenders and the Public*. New York, NY: Springer.

Thorvaldson, S. (1990). "Restitution and Victim Participation in Sentencing." In: B. Galaway and J. Hudson (eds.), *Criminal Justice, Restitution and Reconciliation*. Monsey, NY: Criminal Justice Press.

Tulkens, F. (1993). "Les Transformations du Droit Pénal aux Etats Unis. Pour un autre Modèle de Justice." In: *Nouveaux Itinéraires en droit*. Bruxelles, Belgium: Bruylandt.

Umbreit, M. (1994). *Victim Meets Offender: The Impact of Restorative Justice and Mediation*. Monsey, NY: Criminal Justice Press.

Van Kerckvoorde, J., L. Walgrave, H. Malewska and V. Peyre (1985). "Evaluation by Professionals of the Seriousness of Juvenile Delinquency, with a Belgian-French-Polish Comparison." *Annales de Vaucresson* 22(1):109-125.

Van Ness, D. (1990). "Restorative Justice." In: B. Galaway and J. Hudson (eds.), *Criminal Justice, Restitution and Reconciliation*. Monsey, NY: Criminal Justice Press.

—— (1996). "Restorative Justice and International Human Rights." In: B. Galaway and J. Hudson (eds.), *Restorative Justice: International Perspectives*. Monsey, NY: Criminal Justice Press.

—— and K.H. Strong (1997). *Restoring Justice*. Cincinnati, OH: Anderson.

van Swaaningen, R. (1997). *Critical Criminology. Vision from Europe*. London, UK: Sage.

von Hirsch, A. (1976). *Doing Justice: the Choice of Punishment*. New York, NY: Hill and Wang.

—— (1993). *Censure and Sanctions*. Oxford, UK: Clarendon.

Walgrave, L. (1994). "Beyond Rehabilitation: In Search of a Constructive Alternative in the Judicial Response to Juvenile Crime." *European Journal on Criminal Policy and Research* 4(2):57-75.

—— (1995). "Restorative Justice for Juveniles: Just a Technique or a Fully-fledged Alternative?" *Howard Journal of Criminal Justice* 34(3):228-249.

—— and H. Geudens (1996). "The Restorative Proportionality of Community Service for Juveniles." *European Journal of Crime, Criminal Law and Criminal Justice* 4:361-380.

Weitekamp, E. (1995). "From 'Instant' Justice till Restorative Justice: In Search of New Avenues in Judicial Dealing with Crime." In: C. Fijnaut et al. (eds.), *Changes in Society, Crime and Criminal Justice in Europe, (vol. 1)*. Antwerpen, BEL and the Hague, NETH: Kluwer Rechtsweten-schappen/Kluwer Law International.

Wright, M. (1992). "Victim-offender Mediation as a Step Towards a Restorative System of Justice." In: H. Messmer and H.-U. Otto (eds.), *Restorative Justice on Trial*. Dordrecht, NETH and Boston, MA: Kluwer.

—— (1996). *Justice for Victims and Offenders: A Restorative Approach to Crime* (2nd ed.). Winchester, UK: Waterside.

NOTES

1. For certain presently criminalized conducts, their damage to society can be doubted. From the restorative point of view, this would be the reason to withdraw them from the criminal justice system.

2. Of the publications, seven deal with experiments in the U.S., five in England and Wales, four in Belgium, three in the Netherlands, two in Canada, France, and Germany and one in New-Zealand, Scotland and Switzerland (see H. Geudens and L. Walgrave, 1994).

3. In earlier research, we found that groups of professionals in juvenile justice and welfare work (judges, police officers, social workers, streetworkers, educators) used different criteria in estimating the seriousness of juvenile delinquency, but that they finally constructed a very comparable rank order in the offenses (J. Van Kerckvoorde et al., 1985).

6. After Shaming, Whither Reintegration: Restorative Justice and Relational Rehabilitation

by

Gordon Bazemore

INTRODUCTION

Should offender rehabilitation be a concern of restorative justice? If so, would a restorative model of rehabilitative intervention be clearly different than current approaches to juvenile offender treatment? Objections to addressing rehabilitation or reintegration within a restorative framework are based on concerns that doing so: may diminish the focus on involving and meeting the needs of crime victims (e.g., Wright, 1991; Umbreit, 1994); [1] opens the door to the danger of making juvenile justice more intrusive because juvenile justice professionals will be invited to add dispositional requirements without concern for proportionality (see Walgrave, 1993; Feld, 1993); and places responsibilities on the justice system that are more appropriately assigned to social services, education, or youth development systems (e.g., Feld, 1993).[2] Moreover, there is a danger that in bringing rehabilitation to the forefront, we tend to diminish the primary focus of restorative justice, which is to neither punish nor rehabilitate offenders, but to repair the harm caused by crime (e.g., Zehr, 1990).

But restorative justice is more than a jurisprudential model. Focused on informal as well as formal justice processes, and community intervention as well as system responses to crime, a restorative perspective would insist that justice is much more than what *justice systems* do (see, e.g., Van Ness et al., 1989). Hence, a premise of this paper is that as a holistic model, restorative justice also has significant implications for efforts to change and reintegrate offenders (see Zehr, 1990, 1994). The primary purpose of this paper is to explore the implications of restorative justice principles and assumptions for what I will describe and refer to as a *relational* approach to rehabilitation. Such an approach links crime to a breakdown in social relationships and hence prescribes a reintegrative response to crime focused on attempts to repair, rebuild and enhance bonds or ties between young offenders and their communities.

FROM NOTHING WORKS TO "WHAT WORKS": THE DECLINING SIGNIFICANCE OF TREATMENT PROGRAMS AND TREATMENT RESEARCH

Worse still, we fear that even when something does work, it is seen to do so only in the eyes of certain professionals, while 'outside' the system ordinary citizens are left without a role or voice in the criminal justice process [Braithwaite and Mugford, 1994:34].

The problem of crime can no longer be simplified to the problem of the criminal [Wilkins, 1991:312].

Offender-based control strategies are incomplete, since they take a closed system view of correctional interventions: *change the offender and not the community* [Byrne, 1989:472].

Some funny things happened to ideas about treatment and rehabilitation on the way to the current crisis in juvenile justice. First, in the 1970s, criminologists and policy makers initiated a provocative critique of the individual treatment model, or social welfare model as it is known in Europe. Motivated by concerns with the overreach of the juvenile justice system into the lives of young people, specific criticisms of the treatment model included its potential for: violating due process rights; net widening; labeling and stigmatization; inequities and disparities resulting from unchecked clinical judgements and paternalism; lack of concern with evaluation and performance objectives; and what could be argued in some cases to be a criminogenic effect (see, e.g., Schur, 1972; Kittrie, 1973; Mitford, 1973). Unfortunately, in rightly questioning the treatment enterprise, these critics may have unwittingly reinforced the position of policy-makers who wanted to undermine the juvenile court and its emphasis on rehabilitation and prevention in favor of an expanded adult-like court and justice system (see, e.g., Regnery, 1985). These "get tough" policy makers made use of what became known, following the meta-analyses of Martinson (1974) and others (see, e.g., Sechrest et al., 1979), as the "nothing works" view as an implicit endorsement of punishment. According to this view, if treatment doesn't work, the answer is to add more punishment and give up on the idea that offenders can be rehabilitated.

Second, in the 1980s, in the process of repairing the damage caused by the nothing works perspective, some criminologists and their followers in administrative and policy-making positions adopted a rather uncritical and overly optimistic perspective on the effectiveness and viability of treatment programs as a rehabilitative tool. Inspired by several eloquent defenses aimed at challenging the nothing works view and "revitalizing rehabilitation" (see, e.g., Cullen and Gilbert, 1982) and by findings from meta-analyses suggesting that under some conditions (proper staff training and expertise, proper implementation and assessment) some things *do* work (Greenwood, 1996; Lipsey, 1992; Palmer, 1992; Cullen and Gendreau, 1988), many juvenile justice administrators and professionals set off on a quest to expand popular treatment programs and modalities and develop new ones.

This group of researchers, who have become proponents of what may be called a "what-works" perspective are to be commended for challenging the nothing-works view — and questioning the political push toward an ever-more punitive response to youth crime. Perhaps the greatest value of the serious meta-analyses of juvenile justice intervention, however, is that the studies most clearly demonstrate what does *not* work.[3] Unfortunately, this negative part of the message of "some things work" was not heard as clearly as the positive part. Ironically, many of the least successful programs are the very interventions most commonly seen in juvenile justice, and even those that have been most unequivocally debunked empirically, such as Scared Straight, are often those favored intuitively by judges and other decision makers. In the meantime, many treatment models and programs that have been shown to be of questionable benefit, costly, demonstrably ineffective and even harmful to offenders got a reprieve in the form of an increasingly popular folk belief that has become accepted in many juvenile justice circles as scientific fact. The problem, in the view of many defenders of the treatment model, was not that things didn't work but that there was often a mismatch between interventions and the specific needs and risks presented by offenders (see, e.g., Palmer, 1992; Andrews et al., 1990). If programs weren't working, the answer was not to shut them down, but rather to improve assessment.[4]

Debate continues among meta-analysts about the extent to which there is a cause for real optimism about treatment programs in juvenile justice (Garrett, 1985; Lab and Whitehead, 1988; Feld, 1993). Most of these questions of validity and reliability of treatment research are beyond the scope of this paper.[5] I do not wish to revive the nothing works view, or to reinforce the nihilism of those who wish to question the very possibility of rehabilitation and/or promote the value of more punishment either as a deterrent or just consequence for youth crime. In fact, libertarians and generic skeptics who express serious concerns about the rehabilitative enterprise will be critical of a key premise of this chapter: that rehabilitation is indeed possible and does occur; it simply has little to do with what currently goes on in most juvenile justice treatment programs.

While it is difficult to challenge the *science* of the "what-works" research or the credibility of the researchers, it is important to question the conceptualization of rehabilitation underlying the evaluation of treatment program impact. The what-works proponents oversimplify the rehabilitative/reintegrative process, while at the same time mystifying it by exaggerating the importance of clinical or therapeutic methods. Hence, my contention that the rehabilitative potential of delinquency treatment programs have been oversold is based on the claims of meta-analyses about what are in fact interventions of very limited scope. Like empirical research that is divorced from the thoughts, actions and environment of the respondents it wishes to describe (Braithwaite, 1993), treatment program interventions have been effectively decontextualized because they are based on a "closed-system" paradigm (Reiss, 1986) that is both *insular* and *one-dimensional*. Specifically, I wish to challenge the what works perspective on two grounds: the first, theoretical and empirical; and the second, political.

Theoretically and empirically, the treatment model is insular in several respects. First, grounded in individualistic assumptions about delinquent behavior, intervention techniques focus almost exclusively on the offender. At best, treatment programs may seek to influence family dynamics — but often with little or no theoretical guidance about how and why the family intervention effort is in any way related to the offender's behavior (Bazemore and Day, 1995). For the most part, treatment programs are isolated attempts to address the offender's thinking and behavior. Second, targeting individual youth — rather than adults and adult institutions — for change, the treatment model fails to address the role of relationships, group conflict, and the institutional and community context of crime causation (Reiss and Tonry, 1986). More importantly, it fails to address how these factors may either encourage or discourage rehabilitation. By implicitly promoting a view of habilitation and rehabilitation as something that happens *in treatment programs*, the treatment model also fails to build on naturally occurring supports that may enhance positive relationships and bonds with conventional community adults (Pittman and Fleming, 1991; Brown and Horowitz, 1993; Melton and Pagliocca, 1992). Third, the insular focus on offender deficits and disturbances supports a closed system of intervention outcomes that are effectively limited to successful adjustment and accommodation to the regime of treatment programs. It thus promotes a means-over-ends outlook that defines success almost exclusively in terms of process measures (e.g., number of clients served, number of program graduates, successful program completion), rather than outcomes relevant to reintegration (Scott, 1987; Bazemore and Umbreit, 1995). Finally, perhaps the most unfortunate result of the overselling of treatment by the followers of the what-works view is that treatment programs have increasingly taken responsibility away from communities and the socializing institutions (e.g., schools and work) that serve them. In reinforcing the value of treatment "experts" and highly specialized services, while downplaying the role of non-professionals, treatment programs divorce the rehabilitative enterprise from communities and the real people in them.

But while treatment programs take rehabilitation out of context by focusing on individual delinquents in isolated environments, the most viable theories of crime and the most credible empirical evidence about maturation and desistance from crime (as well as common sense) point to community factors and institutional dynamics — school failure, peer and family interaction, the absence of work and service experiences, and the lack of meaningful adult interaction.[6] Longitudinal studies suggest that most delinquents grow out of their offending (Bazemore, 1985; Elliott, 1994), and studies of "resiliency" indicate that many of the most "high-risk" young people grow up normally despite their environments (e.g., Rutter, 1985; Werner, 1982). If reconceptualized, rehabilitation programs could *enhance or even speed up these processes* (and I will suggest some strategies for accomplishing this). But this assumes a linkage to the community and an appreciation for maturational processes that is currently missing in the conceptualization and practices of most isolated and expert-driven juvenile justice treatment programs.

The individual treatment agenda has also taken rehabilitation out of the context of other essential functions of juvenile justice. This form of decontextualization points to the second problem with the what-works perspective: political viability. As Feld (1993) observes:

> The critique of the juvenile court does not rest on the premise that "nothing works" or can ever work. Even if some model programs produce positive changes for some youth under some conditions, after a century of unfulfilled promises, a continuing societal unwillingness to commit scarce resources to rehabilitative endeavors, and treatment strategies of dubious efficacy, the possibility of effective treatment is inadequate to justify an entire separate system [p. 6].

The political issue goes beyond the concern with treatment effectiveness in that it challenges the fundamental *one-dimensionality* of the delinquency treatment program enterprise. Although, according to recent surveys, communities and most citizens support a rehabilitative agenda for juvenile justice (e.g., Schwartz et al., 1992), they also expect "justice" systems and agencies to do more than treat offenders. At minimum, the viability of a juvenile justice system will depend upon its ability to articulate new, community-driven strategies for achieving public safety, sanctioning, and victim restoration goals, and to effectively integrate these functions with rehabilitative initiatives. Treatment programs artificially separate treatment and services from sanctioning and efforts to enhance public safety. While professionals speak in great detail about the treatment needs of offenders and programs that allegedly meet these needs, they are seldom clear about what sanctions are being imposed on the offender and what is being done to protect the community. Should communities be expected to support interventions that appear to provide only a *benefit* to the offender, especially when sanctions and public safety issues seem to be ignored (Bazemore and Umbreit, 1995)? As this section's opening comment from Braithwaite and Mugford suggests, even if we could demonstrate that some things do "work," would anyone care?

TOWARD RELATIONAL REHABILITATION

"Government is responsible for preserving order, but the community is responsible for establishing peace" [Van Ness et al., 1989:20].

"Children grow up in communities, not programs. Development is most strongly influenced by those with the most intensive, long-term contact with children and youth -- family, informal networks, community organizations, churches, synagogues, temples, mosques and schools. Development is not achieved only through services, but also through supports, networks and opportunities" [Halperin et al., 1995:6].

- In inner-city Pittsburgh, PA, young offenders in an intensive day treatment program solicit input from community organizations about service projects the organizations would like to see completed in the neighborhood. The offenders then work with community residents on projects that include home repair and gardening for the elderly, voter registration drives, painting homes and public buildings, and planting and cultivating community gardens.

- In South Florida, youthful offenders, sponsored by the Florida Department of Juvenile Justice and supervised by The 100 Black Men of Palm Beach County, Inc., plan and execute projects that include providing landscaping services to a shelter for the care and treatment of abused, abandoned, and HIV-positive/AIDS infected infants and children.

- In cities and towns in Pennsylvania, Montana and Minnesota — as well as in Australia, New Zealand and Pennsylvania —family members and other citizens acquainted with an offender or victim of a juvenile crime gather to determine what should be done in response to the offense. Often held in schools, churches or other community-based facilities, these family group conferences are facilitated by a community justice coordinator or police officer, and are aimed at ensuring that offenders are made to hear community disapproval of their behavior, that an agreement for repairing the damage to the victim and community is developed, and that a plan for reintegrating the offender is designed and executed.

- In Minnesota, Department of Corrections staff collaborate with local police and citizens groups to establish family group conferencing programs and ways to inform the community about and involve them in offender monitoring and victim support. In Dakota County, a Minneapolis suburb, local retailers and senior citizens whose businesses and homes have been damaged by burglary or vandalism call a crime repair hotline to request a work crew of probationers to repair the damage.

– 160 –

- In Deschutes County, OR, juvenile offender work crews cut and deliver firewood to senior citizens, and recently worked with a local contractor to build a homeless shelter.
- In several Montana cities, college students and other young adult "core members" in the Montana Conservation Corps supervise juvenile offenders on environmental restoration, trail building and other community service projects, and also serve as mentors to one or more of the young offenders.

What do these examples have to do with rehabilitation? Very little, if the reference is to most treatment programs in most juvenile justice systems. While it is possible to find similar activities in various locations around the world, those interventions are viewed by many juvenile justice professionals — and most treatment program staff — as "side shows." They are clearly not viewed as part of the rehabilitative agenda of most juvenile courts.

Yet, these case studies contain at least some of the seeds of a new way of thinking about rehabilitation that is focused less on treating delinquents than on building communities; less on new delinquency treatment programs and more on institutional reform to promote youth development; less on counseling to improve self-image and more on changing the *public* image of young people in trouble; less on juvenile justice experts and more on building connections between young offenders and community residents.

Relationships and Crime

Crime, fear, withdrawal, isolation, weakened community bonds and more crime. This familiar cycle provides an important key to thinking about patterns of crime and communities (e.g., Reiss and Tonry, 1986) and about the capacity of community norms and tolerance limits to control harmful behavior and reinforce conventional, law-abiding behavior. The more connected community members are, the more likely they are to restrain criminal impulses. As community bonds are weakened, the power of community disapproval as a force for restraining crime is reduced (Pranis, 1997).

Crime harms victims, communities, offenders and other citizens, and, in essence, damages the social fabric and peace of communities. While it is impossible to say which comes first, citizens, crime victims, and offenders are caught up in a cycle in which crime is both a cause of breakdowns in individual and community relationships and a result of these breakdowns. One of the most basic themes in restorative justice is the need to strengthen social and community relationships (Van Ness et al., 1989; Stuart, 1995b; Pranis, 1997). Restorative justice responses to crime attempt to break into the cycle of crime, fear and weakened relationships, and in so doing offer a holistic approach to addressing sanctioning, safety, preventative, peace-making, and rehabilitative needs. Based on these principles and the foregoing critique of the individual treatment paradigm as a closed system, it is possible to outline key themes and components of a relational approach to reintegrating or rehabilitating delinquents.

At the community level, a restorative response to crime seeks first to build and strengthen relationships by increasing the nature and quality of participation in problem solving and the response to crime and conflict. The general health of a community — and its crime rate — is directly related to the extent to which citizens participate in the community:

> When citizens fail to assume responsibility for decisions effecting the community, community life will be characterized by the absence of a collective sense of caring, a lack of respect for diverse values, and ultimately a lack of any sense of belonging. Conflict, if resolved through a process that constructively engages the parties involved, can be a fundamental building ingredient in any relationship [Stuart, 1995a:8].

Since the root of crime is community conflict and disharmony, "justice" cannot be achieved by a government "war on crime" but rather by *peacemaking, dispute resolution, and rebuilding right relationships* (Christie, 1977; Van Ness et al., 1989).

Similarly, if communities can learn how to resolve conflict, they can also learn how to reintegrate offenders. Like conflict resolution, a restorative approach to rehabilitation is based on the general idea of relationship building. At the individual level, if crime can be viewed as the result of weak bonds, relational rehabilitation must be focused primarily on strengthening the offender's ties or bonds to the community, changing the community's view of the offender, changing the offender's view of the community, and increasing the willingness and capacity of residents to take responsibility for what happens in their communities. In the case of delinquent young people, the intervention approach would have the primary objective of increasing bonds to conventional adults. Delinquent rehabilitation, integration and habilitation, like the conventional maturation process, is about developing relationships.

It goes almost without saying that the juvenile justice system was not set up to create opportunities for this kind of relationship building. Treatment programs are designed to "cure" psychological problems or remediate offenders with presumed deficits rather than strengthen their bonds to community adults and institutions. In moving beyond the closed-system approach to rehabilitation, a relational approach would need to challenge the insularity and one-dimensionality of the individual treatment/social welfare model. Specifically, building — or rebuilding — youth/adult relationships requires attention to three principles that flow rather naturally from the relationship-building focus of restorative justice. These principles present a direct challenge to the treatment model and form the basic components of a new approach to reintegration.[7]

First, the three-dimensional focus on crime in terms of the needs of victims, offenders and the community and the need to involve each of these co-participants in the response to crime (see, e.g., Zehr, 1990, Van Ness, 1993) challenges reha-bilitative efforts that focus on offenders in isolation from the community and the victim. In addition, practically speaking, citizens are less likely to support the idea of reintegration and rehabilitation until sanctioning needs (e.g., providing conse-quences for crime, setting tolerance limits, reparation) and public safety concerns have been addressed. Hence, justice systems can no longer compartmentalize interventions designed to address sanctioning, public safety and rehabilitative needs, and they must give attention to the compatibility between efforts to reintegrate offenders and these other justice functions.

Second, to effectively meet the needs of the three stakeholders in crime and give them a voice and role in the response to crime, restorative justice encourages an intentional shift away from government (represented by the formal justice system) and toward a more informal, "naturalistic" response that emphasizes the role of citizens, community groups and socializing institutions (Van Ness and Strong, 1997; Stuart, 1995b; Brown and Polk, 1996). A relational approach to rehabilitation cannot be clinical in its focus, but rather must emphasize community socialization networks and naturally occurring processes in its analysis of how most delinquents grow up to be normal, productive adults. Policy and intervention strategy must then build upon and seek to enhance the capability of such networks and processes to support reintegration.

Third, based on this community outlook, an intentional focus on the broader context or "social ecology" of reintegration also requires an institutional framework and an approach to offender intervention consistent with that framework. Unlike the more insular treatment model, the aim of relational rehabilitation would be to provide young people with the experiences and capacities needed to create bonds to the community and to educate and train community adults in how to facilitate bonding on a continuing basis. At the *micro* level, the concept of *competency* as "the capacity to do something well that others value" (Polk and Kobrin, 1972) is also suggestive of intervention outcomes for young offenders that increase the likelihood that they will be able to develop meaningful relationships with adults and conventional peers, and ultimately gain community acceptance. At the *macro* level, policy and advocacy based on a relational approach would promote institutional change and community engagement to ensure the wide availability of new roles for young people in work, education and civic life that provide such capacities and experiences.

Sanctioning, Safety, and Rehabilitation: The "Resonance" of Juvenile Justice Functions

> ...the problem of crime cannot be simplified to the problem of the criminal. The majority of the public find it difficult to believe that deterrence does not work...It may seem more difficult to accept that even if rehabilitation of offenders worked far more effectively than the wildest claims on its behalf, the amount of crime would not be much reduced [Wilkins, 1991:312].

> Since punishment is reproaching, the best punishment is that which puts the blame...in the most expressive and least expensive way possible...It is not a matter of making him suffer...or as if the essential thing were to intimidate and terrorize. Rather, it is a matter of reaffirming the obligation....to strengthen the sense of duty, both for the guilty party and those witnessing the offense [Durkheim, 1961:178].

Rehabilitation can never be the only thing. Restorative justice recognizes the fact that the justice-related needs of communities can never be reduced to "just punishment," "individualized treatment" or even "crime control." Neither treating nor punishing offenders will make communities safe. Nor can these offender-focused interventions meet public demands to censure crime, affirm and enforce tolerance limits, provide consequences for crime, and effectively reintegrate law-breakers. Treatment and punishment fail to recognize that justice systems must be responsive to the needs and perspectives of crime victims and communities, as well as offenders, as "clients" or "customers" of the justice process (e.g., Bazemore and Washington, 1995). In addition, these interventions attempt to remove rehabilitation strategies from the context of the juvenile justice responsibility to also address public safety, sanctioning and victim reparation needs.

If there is to be a restorative justice "theory" of reintegration, it must therefore include a concern with the extent to which community and victim are meaningfully engaged in a more integrated justice process, and the extent to which key community needs other than the need for offender rehabilitation are addressed. An underlying premise of restorative justice is the idea that offenders are not well-served when the needs of victims and the community are neglected and, when these two stakeholders are not in some way involved in the process. The reason for this is that when justice is viewed as repairing the harm, and rebuilding damaged relationships, the response to crime must attend to all of those damaged by the crime. When these community needs for assistance in accomplishing sanctioning, safety, and victim restoration functions are not addressed, neither rehabilitation nor reparative needs can be effectively met. When they are, efforts to sanction crime, manage risks and reintegrate offenders become mutually interdependent, and they may be viewed as means toward the ends of repairing harm to victims, offenders, and communities and hopefully facilitating transformative changes in each (Van Ness, 1993; Morris, 1995). For example, when offenders are sanctioned by repairing harm to victims, they stand a better chance of preserving and enhancing their own human dignity, a necessary prerequisite for rehabilitation. Sanctions that degrade and isolate the offender, on the other hand, weaken bonds that foster reintegration and ultimately heighten risks to public safety. Similarly, efforts to reintegrate or sanction offenders that do not explicitly attend to public safety concerns of the community can never win public support or create a climate in which victim needs can be meaningfully addressed.

While justice professionals often think in terms of developing distinct agencies and programs to address sanctioning, reintegration and public safety needs, victims, offenders, and other citizens do not often consciously distinguish between these different functions of intervention. Logically and practically, then, the best overall response to crime from a restorative perspective involves each of the three justice co-participants in an effort to carry out interventions that *together* address each need and attempt to restore each co-participant as well as rebuild — or *build* — relationships. At a minimum, in an "open-systems" approach based on restorative justice principles, there should be compatibility or "resonance" between sometimes disparate efforts to address these primary justice needs of communities.[8]

There are three practical concerns in addressing this need for resonance between rehabilitative efforts and sanctioning and public safety functions, as well as between efforts to respond to the needs of each of the three justice clients. First, it is at minimum essential to articulate public safety strategies and sanctioning approaches that do not *detract* from the rehabilitative goal. In a relational approach to rehabilitation, one would never attempt to design and evaluate rehabilitative strategies that do not consider whether or not sanctions required of the offender and risk management measures help or hinder these efforts. Second, it is also possible to envision interventions whose primary objective is to enhance public safety or sanction offenders that are themselves potentially reintegrative. Teaching delinquent youths to be conflict mediators in schools and/or residential programs, and then using these youth to train others, comes to mind as an example of an intervention that is aimed ultimately at making schools and facilities safer but that also increases prospects for long-term rehabilitation by building offender competencies to resolve disputes before they lead to violence.[9] Third, in a relational approach, rehabilitative efforts must not be segregated from the community and from crime victims. It may be somewhat counterintuitive for overworked juvenile justice practitioners to accept the premise that they can enhance the potential of rehabilitative interventions by also devoting scarce time and resources to engaging crime victims and other citizens. There are, however, a variety of indirect, as well as direct, ways to bring the victim and her/his concerns into the reintegrative process (Umbreit, 1995).

Because sanctioning offenders has so commonly been thought of only in terms of the narrow objectives of "just punishment" — or as Christie (1982) suggests, to cause pain to the offender — it is especially important to think about the resonance, or lack of it, between sanctioning and rehabilitative interventions. Hence, while resonance between public safety and rehabilitative efforts is especially important, I will focus here on the need in relational rehabilitation for compatibility between reintegrative and sanctioning functions.

Rethinking Sanctioning

Punitive sanctions may detract from the accomplishment of both reparative and rehabilitative goals. Punishment, by stigmatizing, humiliating and isolating the offender, may have a counter-deterrent effect by minimizing prospects that the offender may gain or regain self-respect and the respect of the community (Makkai and Braithwaite, 1994; Bazemore and Umbreit, 1995). Ironically, punishment often encourages lawbreakers to focus on themselves rather than the person they harmed as the victim (Wright, 1991), and it may undermine self-restraint by attenuating natural feelings of shame and a sense of morality (Durkheim, 1961; Garland, 1990) while weakening community bonds by damaging family, peer, and other adult relationships (Zhang and Messmer, 1994). The current mood in most of the world (and certainly in the U.S.) seems to be to move more in the direction of punitive sanctions that maximize harm to the offender and hence limit the effectiveness of any reintegrative effort (not to mention giving low priority to victim reparation; see, e.g., Bazemore and Umbreit, 1995).

However, it is possible to think about sanctioning as having many potential objectives other than to deliver punishment for its own sake. Packer's (1968) classic discussion of the critical importance of *intent* in the sanctioning process, for example, lists compensation, deterrence, regulation, rehabilitation, and retributive punishment as among the many possible goals of sanctioning. Indeed, the continuum of possible sanctions ranges from punitive approaches, which generally emphasize incarceration, to healing, reparative and settlement approaches that may build community solidarity and commitment. Such sanctions may, as Durkheim (1961) and modern communitarians point out, provide an understanding of the suffering caused to other individuals that resulted from an offender's crime and a sense of obligation which can strengthen bonds between offenders and other community members and reinforce a sense of justice (e.g., Etzioni, 1993; see Schneider, 1990).

As intrusive and coercive measures taken to enforce societal standards (see, e.g., Packer, 1968), sanctions should not be disguised as another "treatment" provided in the interests of juvenile offenders. From a restorative perspective, sanctioning should be focused first on repairing the harm to victims and the community, and in so doing, allowing communities an outlet for symbolic, collective denunciation of crime, as well as the affirmation of tolerance limits (Braithwaite, 1989; Garland, 1990; Wilkins, 1991). The sanctioning process, however, has important implications for any rehabilitative approach, and when carried out based on restorative principles, sanctions can themselves have rehabilitative impact.

A growing body of empirical research is supportive of the rehabilitative value of reparative restitution, community service and other restorative sanctions and processes (Butts and Snyder, 1991; Schneider, 1986; Walgrave and Guedens, 1996; Schiff, this volume). Some studies suggest that the rehabilitative impact is increased when reparative sanctions are viewed by the offender as fair and when they are truly victim-focused (Schneider, 1990; Umbreit and Coates, 1993). Restitution, community service, and related reparative requirements such as victim awareness training — especially when reinforced with victim offender-mediation — can be high on the educative scale (see, e.g., Umbreit, 1994).[10] According to one study, completing restitution and community service was found to be associated with enhanced feelings of citizenship and community commitment (Schneider, 1990). At the top of the continuum of least-to-most educative sanctioning responses are settlement or dispute resolution processes, in which the offender also learns important competencies that are transferable to a variety of settings. Such learning is heightened and the rehabilitative power of sanctions enhanced, according to "affect" theorists (see, e.g. Tomkins, 1992) in processes that allow for emotional content and expression. Though too infrequently utilized in Western societies, such processes may enhance offender relationships in employment and other roles, while also providing essential competencies needed to prevent violent resolution of future conflicts (Stuart, 1995b; Griffiths and Hamilton, 1996).

The Rehabilitative Potential of Sanctions

Unfortunately, reparative sanctions have often been criticized unfairly by some meta-analysts, who have for the most part ignored, misread, or misinterpreted the positive — or at least encouraging — findings from experimental and other empirical studies of the impact of restitution and community service, as well as promising results on victim-offender mediation, victim impact panels, family group conferences and related interventions (see Schiff, this volume). In this regard, a major distortion on the part of some proponents of the what works perspective has been a tendency to portray all sanctions as negative and as detracting from the reintegrative process (see, e.g., Gendreau and Ross, 1994). The distortion also springs from the failure to distinguish theoretically and empirically between sanctions with reparative focus and aim such as victim restitution and restorative community service, and sanctions with solely punitive or deterrent intent.

In their list of programs that do *not* work, for example, Krisberg et al., (1995) reinforce this tendency by including restitution and community service — along with shock incarceration, Scared Straight and boot camps — in a category of interventions they conclude are ineffective, and possibly harmful. But sanctions that reinforce and affirm values about obligations to others and that provide benefit to the community do not detract from rehabilitative goals, and it seems foolish at best not to consider the possibility that such sanctions could have rehabilitative impact.

Are we to believe that meeting with one's victim, paying restitution or completing community service is as demeaning, stigmatizing and humiliating as being forced to clean toilets in a boot camp? Does community service in which youths work with adults to build a community shelter for abused women (Bazemore and Maloney, 1994) provide the same experience as a chain gang?

In lumping such dramatically different sanctions as boot camps and restitution together and discounting the contextual importance of the sanctioning function, some treatment advocates reinforce the one-dimensional approach to rehabilitation. Most important, politically, they strengthen the hands of those policy makers promoting truly harmful, retributive sanctions. Such policy makers seem determined to further "sort out" and limit the group of offenders viewed as worthy of *any* type of treatment from the ever-expanding group viewed as eligible for retributive punishment only. While the best of treatment programs being championed by the "what works" researchers might well reinforce the positive impact of restorative sanctions, they are, in the absence of an alternative sanctioning model (see, e.g., Bazemore and Umbreit, 1995), most likely to be used as add-ons to destructive punishments whose impact is likely to counter any possible positive effects of treatment.

Unfortunately, those who take the conclusions of some meta-analysts at face value may well give up on the idea that *any sanction* can be beneficial. Despite the unfounded dismissal of the idea of sanctions as potentially rehabilitative, however, a number of restorative sanctions are gaining popularity precisely because they are viewed as good for the offender, and, increasingly, this assumption is being supported by emerging theory and research. In addition to Schneider's (1990) work on equity theory and processes, which establishes a link between completion of reparative sanctions and reduced recidivism, there are recent promising findings and theory on the rehabilitative impact of community service (Walgrave, 1993; Bazemore and Maloney, 1994). Victim-offender mediation is being subjected to more rigorous tests. Thus far, results have shown a positive impact on offenders, supplementing clearly documented positive victim effects (Umbreit and Coates, 1993). The various affect theories and related perspectives underlying the reintegrative shaming process in family group conferencing (Tomkins, 1992; Retzinger and Scheff, 1996; Moore and O'Connell, 1994) provide further impetus for expansion of sanctioning processes aimed at reintegration as well as at holding offenders accountable (Maxwell and Morris, 1993; Hudson et al., 1996). Finally, an underlying assumption of restorative justice now being more frequently discussed is that sanctioning processes are more likely to enhance rehabilitation/reintegration when they involve family, victims and key members of the offender's community directly in the process (Braithwaite and Mugford, 1994; Stuart, 1995a). In this regard, perhaps the most promising potential bridge between sanctioning and rehabilitation in restorative justice practice has been the proliferation of new community decision-making models such as family group conferencing, circle sentencing, citizen panels, and various extensions of victim-offender mediation (Bazemore, 1997; Umbreit and Stacy, 1996). The excitement around such interventions is that in bringing citizens and victims into the process, much more than sanctioning or "shaming" may be accomplished. Among other things, conferences or circles contain some basic elements of a true offender support group (Stuart, 1995a).

Yet, the impact of spending two hours in a family group conference should not be expected to produce remarkable reductions in recidivism and should in no way be viewed as a complete model of rehabilitation (Alder and Wundersitz, 1994). Moreover, if not carried out with a thorough grounding in restorative goals and values, such conferences and other processes may even exacerbate the reintegration problem (Polk, 1994; Umbreit and Stacy, 1995). Advocates of restorative justice do not claim that reparative sanctions or processes are rehabilitative panaceas. And because too often many of the most promising restorative sanctioning programs have been poorly implemented (Bazemore and Maloney, 1994; Bazemore and Umbreit 1995), a more deliberate effort to differentiate reparative sanctions according to whether or not they are aimed at, and likely to accomplish, restorative versus retributive objectives should also help to inform more meaningful research on the rehabilitative impact of those sanctions (Van Ness, 1993; Bazemore and Umbreit, 1995; Bazemore and Maloney, 1994; Umbreit, 1995). More research is needed on the subtleties of this impact and on the potential for *enhanced* effects of reparative sanctions, especially when these interventions are combined with other relationship-building efforts to be discussed in this chapter.

There are, in addition, empirical questions one may ask to determine if a specific sanctioning approach or process is likely to be helpful or harmful. Braithwaite and Mugford's (1994) "conditions of successful reintegration ceremonies" provide a useful set of criteria in making this assessment. When these conditions are met, sanctions can also be a natural first step in a reintegrative process that begins with an acknowledgment of harm to victims, actively involves community members in sanctioning aimed at holding the offender accountable to the victim, and then engages a support group to reintegrate the offender following this process (e.g., Braithwaite and Mugford, 1994; Stuart, 1995). However, restorative approaches to sanctioning and public safety will not be enough without an intentional strategy for reintegrating offenders who have paid, or are currently paying, their dept to victims and the community, and whose risk to public safety is being effectively managed.

Devolving Rehabilitation: Offenders, Experts, Real People and "Naturalistic" Reform

Most people in communities who are familiar with former delinquent offenders such as "Johnny," a young gang member who "settled down" at age 25, know rehabilitation is often not the result of any complex therapeutic process. Johnny was not "rehabilitated" because he suddenly stopped using drugs or gained some new insights through counseling, but because an employer, his wife, his uncle, and other adults eventually provided him with a job, family ties, and a network of support. Those who know Johnny best also know that there was most likely a time when his criminal activities began to pose a risk to these emerging adult relationships. While they thought of Johnny as worthless as a kid and of little use to anyone, most neighbors acknowledge that today he has skills, works and pays taxes; they may also sense that should Johnny get into a little trouble today, they and others might intervene on his behalf.

Johnny, like many other delinquents, "aged out" of crime or experienced "maturational reform" (Bazemore, 1985; Polk et al., 1981; Elliott, 1993). This didn't happen magically nor did Johnny do it alone. But his success had nothing to do with treatment programs. The "community" — in this case clearly defined as a small group of neighborhood adults and key institutions, especially work and family — was primarily responsible for this metamorphosis. What average citizens understand about Johnny's rehabilitation also builds, somewhat ironically, on the insights of professional youth workers and service providers themselves, when they remind us that it is often not so much the nature of the treatment strategy or program but the *staff and the relationships they build with delinquent youths.* Unfortunately, such relationships, even when positive, are necessarily short-lived, and thus what is missed is the far greater significance of relationships youth build with other adults in their own communities. Hence, effective strategies for long-term rehabilitation must maximize neighborhood ties and seek to enhance those non-professional adult relationships.

Although it is increasingly discouraged by treatment professionals and by the restrictions imposed on use of non-professionals in response to the litigious nature of the current juvenile justice environment (especially in the U.S.), naturalistic rehabilitation is something some juvenile justice professionals intuitively try to support and encourage. It is what occurred when Florida Judge Frank Orlando, frustrated with the ineffectiveness and irrelevance of clinically focused treatment programs, asked a friend with a boat to spend a few hours with a delinquent and let him work on it (ironically, this experience was the beginning of what became the Associated Marine Institutes, a *non-clinical* rehabilitation program). Similarly, some of the most meaningful community service projects have been initiated because a group of citizens or a civic organization needed something done — restoring a historic black cemetery, registering voters, building a homeless shelter

(Bazemore and Maloney, 1994; Bazemore and Day, 1996) — and by chance encountered a juvenile justice worker who saw value for some delinquent youths (as well as for the community) in such an effort. Such workers do not do more of this because, as noted earlier, relationship building is not part of the mainstream treatment agenda in juvenile justice systems.

Doing Less Harm

When the role of the justice system is not defined in concert with the community's role, justice and youth service programs are likely to overextend their reach and contribute to the isolation rather than reintegration of young people in trouble. The reasons for this state of affairs are complex. One is that despite their unique professional niche, what social service systems have in common is a deficit focus emphasizing identification of needs and risks and the provision of services intended to correct presumed deficits and dysfunctions. Unfortunately, those who end up in the programs of social service systems often find it difficult, as McKnight (1995) suggests, to transition back to the mainstream of conventional socialization networks (e.g., in school, work, etc.):

> A preliminary hypothesis is that services that are heavily focused on deficiency tend to be pathways out of community and into the exclusion of serviced life. We need a rigorous examination of public investments so that we can distinguish between services that lead people *out of community and into dependency* and those that support people in community life [McKnight, 1995:20 (emphasis added)].

A second reason such systems can inadvertently cause harm is that, as David Moore (1994:10) has observed, government systems that "take sole responsibility for authoritarian control" may themselves be criminogenic because they "perpetuate the illusion that the state, rather than civil society, is ultimately responsible for social order." Hence, the very structures we have created to manage (not solve) the youth crime problem, despite our best efforts and intentions, may themselves be part of the problem.

Most "baby boomers" and older generations often recall a time when adults in their neighborhoods or small towns took responsibility for "looking after" neighborhood children other than their own. In effect, community members, with the encouragement and support of police, schools, and other institutions, often "took care of" problems that now end up in juvenile courts. While we can simply write these actions off as nostalgic memories of a different era, we can also examine ways in which juvenile justice intervention has reinforced a process by which community adults, and adult institutions, have become helpless and hapless in socializing young people.

Numerous case examples and research studies illustrate how efforts to centralize, professionalize, and expand criminal justice and social services have sent messages to communities to "leave it to the experts," thereby undercutting the role and responsibility of citizens, institutions, and community groups in socializing young people. Three decades of experience with diversion programs, for example, can teach important lessons about the intrusiveness, expansiveness and counterproductive impacts of some well intended social service interventions (Polk, 1984). [11] But while diversion is generally viewed as a failure because of net-widening (or the failure to *really* "leave kids alone") (Schur, 1972), another critique would point not to net-widening *per se* as the problem. Rather by widening *government* nets and ignoring the need to "strengthen community nets" (Braithwaite, 1994; Moore and O'Connell, 1994), diversion policy makers uncritically expanded juvenile justice intervention by failing to distinguish between interventions that build or enhance youth commitments and youth-adult relationships, and those that further stigmatize and exclude young people, isolate youths from conventional adults, and usurp the community's responsibility and its role.

A nagging and sensitive unanswered question in this regard is whether or not many of the treatment interventions being promoted for use with delinquent offenders and studied in "what works" research, are not themselves iatrogenic (Brown and Horowitz, 1993). The fact that meta-analyses show significant differences in recidivism between an incarcerated population receiving Treatment A and one receiving Treatment B (or a control group receiving the standard intervention for this population), for example, is not an indication that *both groups* would not have had lower recidivism, and improved at a faster rate if there had been no intervention. This is not to suggest that treatment providers lack skill and commitment, or that some treatments are not better than others, given the choices corrections administrators must make. Rather, the problem of avoiding "doing harm," like the obstacles to promoting positive youth development, is more systemic. As Pittman and Fleming (1991) observe, a dual system in youth policy tracks young people along two paths. One path provides custody and out-of-home placement, therapeutic services and remedial assistance to at-risk and delinquent youths, who are primarily poor and minority. The other path, which is increasingly reserved for the children of the upper middle class, provides for enhanced education, music lessons, Boy and Girl Scouts, meaningful work experience, travel, and eventually college and career.

Unfortunately, as Pittman and Fleming (1991) note, once set in motion treatment bureaucracies may be self-perpetuating — not to mention highly invested in diagnosing the kinds of disturbances they are trained to treat:

we have created a bloated, vastly overextended system of treatment/intervention (or secondary supports) while ignoring, to the detriment of all youth, primary supports that build competencies and prepare adolescents for adulthood. (Rather)... the best way to help at risk youth is to provide them with the same types of supports and services other adolescents need [p.8].

A relational approach must at some point confront social service bureaucracies that focus primarily on deficiency and exclusion and which, in the attempt to provide help, actually minimize the prospects for bonding and relationship building. In place of this youth service and individual treatment model, a new intervention paradigm is needed that seeks to rediscover and, if necessary, reinvent ways for communities to begin to take back the responsibility for youth socialization and offender rehabilitation.

Building on Community and Institutional Supports

What Johnny's neighbors and residents of communities around the world know about crime is that rehabilitation does not occur in a vacuum. They also know, as the quote at the beginning of this section suggests, that few of those who were delinquent stopped their offending because of treatment programs. As argued earlier, the "bad news" is that service bureaucracies functioning on clinical assumptions do not encourage naturalistic solutions — and even work against them. The "good news," however, is that some 90% of delinquent youths will "outgrow" their offense behavior, and there are known institutional and social ecological factors — notably a job, family ties (both family of origin and family of choice), access to higher education and community supports — that predict which of these young people will continue their offense patterns into adulthood (Elliott, 1993). In addition, the growing body of resiliency research suggests that most youths in high-risk neighborhoods grow up to be normal adults due to one relatively simple factor: the continuing presence of one or more caring adults (not necessarily parents) who are able to provide them with ongoing support and access to roles that allow them to develop legitimate identities (e.g., Rutter, 1985). A naturalistic approach would attempt to learn from these findings and tap into those maturation processes by enhancing, or creating, contexts which encourage the development of meaningful intergenerational relationships. Rather than focus on creating new treatment programs, however, it would attempt to build upon existing community and institutional networks to create "normalizing" rather than isolating experiences.[12]

What citizens and some professionals know about why Johnny "outgrew" his delinquency is also consistent with a growing body of theory that asks a different question about delinquency and maturational reform. Rather than beginning with the question of what makes youths delinquent, or what factors are linked to recidivism, to understand how Johnny grew out of his delinquency, the most meaningful focus is an examination of conventional adulthood. Such an examination would ask what is it about conventional adults that makes them "conventional," and what protects or "insulates" most adults from the temptation to commit crimes (e.g.,

Hirschi, 1969). A theory concerned with explaining how adults acquire legitimate identities in various communities would suggest that the roles they fill in basic institutions (work, family, community organizations) provide them with a self-image of usefulness and belonging, and a public image as a contributing member of the community (Erickson, 1968; Polk et al., 1981; Pittman and Fleming, 1991). By virtue of these roles, adults gain a commitment to those institutions and groups that make them feel that they belong and can do something that others value. They do not commit crimes because they are engaged in activities that provide them with a "stake in conformity" or "side bets," which ensures that they have much to lose by being caught in illegal activities (Becker, 1960; Briar and Piliavin, 1965; Hirschi, 1969).

Changing the Context of Rehabilitative Intervention: Restorative Justice, Reintegration and Youth Development

Unlike conventional adults, most youths lack this sense of "connectedness." They do not hold positions of responsibility in work, community or family groups that allow them to make meaningful contributions. For example, in contrast to 50 or even 30 years ago, few adolescents today are given the opportunity to experience meaningful work roles, and thus fail to develop the sense of "belonging and contributing that sustains us even when work is difficult or dull; youth are progressively denied the opportunity to participate in work that is important to others" (Howe, 1986:11). Hence, they become marginal commodities or even liabilities in a society where status is largely determined by one's productive participation in the economy. In addition, young people are viewed by businesses as consumers, and they are often manipulated in this role in ways that are harmful and destructive. At best, youths are for all practical purposes restricted to one rather limited conventional role, that of student. As Erickson (1968) has suggested, this reality puts a great deal of pressure on educational institutions to forge a link between the "moratorium" experience of adolescence and productive adult life in order to allow youths "to identify with *new roles of competency and invention*" (p.138, emphasis added).

For those youths who lack the clear promise of *future* access to meaningful adult roles that success in school may provide, there is little to lose by delinquent and other forms of deviant behavior, and the "stake" in conventional behavior is low. Further, youths who fail in school may develop a sense of incompetence in the legitimate world and a negative public image as a result of being stigmatized by the school (Polk and Schafer, 1972), further weakening their "bond" to conventional social groups (Hirschi, 1969; Hawkins and Catalano, 1992). The vast majority of youths under juvenile court supervision fit this description, and for those youths chronically in trouble, problems of isolation and lack of commitment are exacerbated. If it is assumed that all youths have a basic need to be viewed as competent, to feel useful, and to acquire meaningful affiliation with groups, it is easy to understand why those who are not doing well in the student role and are at the same time denied access to legitimate alternative roles seek out delinquent and other nonconventional groups.

The risk when community adults and institutions — employers, church leaders, educators — do not provide access to such roles, is that *other* naturalistic socialization processes are allowed to come into play. One of the most common these days in some communities is the process by which drug dealers recruit young people into what is for many of them becoming an alternative family and work environment. Communities and juvenile justice professionals can learn a lot from the informal dynamics and structure of these environments, which provide youths with many of the things they are not getting from law-abiding adults in their communities. The things youths need and receive from gangs, because we do not provide them elsewhere, include many of the basic requirements for adult life: earnings, status, belonging, a sense of competency and a sense of usefulness (Polk and Kobrin, 1972).

Treatment, Relationships and Institutional Capital

Completing treatment programs is not a ticket of admission to the community. While treatment programs may have been helpful for Johnny in addressing his drug problem, completing a treatment program would not have provided the skills to make Johnny a resource to his family and others in the community, nor would it have helped Johnny get a job. The *wrong* treatment program may also have exacerbated Johnny's problems and decreased the likelihood that he would grow out of his delinquency (Brown and Horowitz, 1993). Hence, in a relational rehabilitation, outcomes would not be stated as the absence of crime, drug use, or disturbances, but as capacities that have "currency" as social capital in legitimate adult institutions. At the micro level, a relational approach to rehabilitation has two primary concerns: increasing the capacity of young offenders to develop positive relationships with conventional adults by increasing competencies in a variety of domains, and increasing the capacity of adults and adult organizations to allow youths to demonstrate competency by creating new roles in which they can contribute productively to their communities (Polk and Kobrin, 1972; National Commission on Resources for Youth, 1974; Pittman and Flemming, 1991). Increasing vocational, educational, social, interpersonal and decision-making competency, for example, is best accomplished through an effort to place youths in institutional roles that engage them in productive activities including work, community service, dispute resolution, etc. This experiential approach is aimed at changing both behavior and cognitive decision-making, as well as the public image of the offender (Bazemore, 1991; Polk and Kobrin, 1972; Lofquist, 1983; Bazemore and Terry, 1997).

Table 1: "Lenses" of Intervention: Individual Treatment, Retribution and Relational Rehabilitation

(Victim Lens) Individual Treatment	(Villain Lens) Retributive Punishment	(Resource Lens) Relational Rehabilitation
Delinquency as a symptom of underlying disturbance	Delinquency motivated by evil impulses or lack of restraint due to permissiveness and absence of punishment	Delinquency viewed as a relatively normal response to the need for status and belonging
Delinquents fundamentally different from other adolescents in psychological and emotional makeup	Delinquents different in motivation and impulse for deviant behavior	Delinquents viewed as similar to other adolescents
Delinquents viewed as incapable of productive, rational action without therapeutic intervention	Delinquents incapable of conventional behavior without threat of punishment and strict discipline	Delinquents viewed as capable of productive contributions
Most offenders need individual treatment and benefit from therapeutic interventions	Treatment and service inappropriate and ineffective in the absence of punishment	Some offenders need individual treatment; others may be unnecessarily stigmatized or otherwise harmed by therapeutic interventions

While complete discussion of the various components of this difference are beyond the scope of this paper (see Polk and Kobrin, 1972; Bazemore and Cruise, 1995; Bazemore and Terry, 1997), Tables 1 through 4 describe three critical contexts in which a relational model of rehabilitation focused on competency development outcomes can be distinguished from the treatment model. Based on a different social ecology of intervention than the individual treatment/social welfare model, the relationship-building agenda would differentiate a restorative approach to reintegration from the treatment model in three separate contexts: the policy context, the outcome or evaluative context, and the program or practice context. Specifically, the two models differ in assumptions about delinquency that inform the "policy lens," which defines the targets of intervention and approaches viewed as appropriate for delinquent populations (see Schneider and Ingram, 1992) (see Table 1). The models also differ in intermediate outcomes expected to result from intervention (Table 2), in program contexts that define the roles of key participants including youths, community members, and professionals; and in a range of issues concerning the learning assumptions of intervention (Tables 3 and 4). In addition, the two models differ in content — specifically, the preferred programs and practices of rehabilitative intervention and the messages relayed by the intervention to the offender and the public (Table 5).

Table 2: Intermediate Outcomes of Intervention: Individual Treatment and Relational Rehabilitation

Individual Treatment	Relational Rehabilitation
Avoid negative influence of designated people, places and activities	Begin new, positive relationships and positive behavior in conventional roles; avoid placement of youths in stigmatizing treatments
Follow rules of supervision (e.g., curfew, school attendance)	Practice competent, conventional behavior
Attend and participate in treatment activities (e.g., counseling)	Actively demonstrate competency through completion of productive activity (service and/or work with community benefit)
Complete all required treatment and terminate supervision	Significantly increase measurable competencies (academic, social, occupational, etc.)
Improvements in attitude and self-concept; improved family interaction; psychological adjustment	Improve self-image and public image (community acceptance), and increase bonding and community integration

Identifying and Engaging Community

But naturalistic does not mean "naturally occurring." There is nothing accidental about relational reintegration, and it is not a libertarian or "radical nonintervention" (Schur, 1972) approach. Moreover, there is nothing magical about "the community," and identifying and mobilizing citizens to allow for a greater community role in rehabilitation will require a very intentional strategy which redefines, rather than seeks to eliminate the government role.

Perhaps the most overwhelming aspect of this new agenda is the initial task of *identifying* community. The magnitude of this challenge is exemplified by the fact that the dispersed, transient and disconnected residential enclaves of the modern urban metroplex often bear little resemblance to any standard notion of community in which residents naturally experience any sense of "connectedness" to others (van Gelder, 1993). In such "communities," the prospect that at-risk adolescents and young people will be able to develop bonds to conventional adults is even less likely. In fact, if one were to design a prototypical criminogenic community, one could do no better than to look to current urban neighborhoods which separate large numbers of people, especially the young, from the kind of work that could include them securely in community life (Currie, 1994).

Table 3: Learning Assumptions, Focus and Targets of Intervention: Treatment and Relational Rehabilitation

Individual Treatment	Relational Rehabilitation
Primary and initial focus on identifying deficits and ameliorative approaches to correct problems; youths defined as in need of services	Primary and initial focus on identifying strengths and building the positive; youths viewed as resources
For purposes of intervention it is best to assume incompetence and disturbance	For purposes of intervention it is best to assume competence and capacity for positive action
Remedial and reactive	Preventive and proactive
Emphasis on change in individual youth behavior	Emphasis on change in youth and community institutions and adult behavior
Offenders learn best through counseling and remedial training	Offenders learn best by doing
Counseling as a primary modality	Counseling as support for active engagement

Table 4: The Content of Intervention: Individual Treatment and Relational Rehabilitation

Individual Treatment	Relational Rehabilitation
Community is uninvolved; responsibility for offender rehabilitation is left to professionals	Community develops new opportunities for youths to make productive contributions, build competency and a sense of belonging
Role of offender as passive recipient of treatment or services	Role of offender as active, productive resource for positive action
Role of juvenile justice professional as "counselor" or "broker of services"	Role of juvenile justice professional as developing new roles for young offenders that allow for demonstration of competency

But while "community" can be an amorphous term, it is possible to break down communities into component parts such as schools, churches, mosques, synagogues, tribes, extended families and so on. In restorative justice sanctioning practice, this is being done increasingly by identifying "communities of concern" consisting of those closest to the offender and victim in a crime. In a restructured juvenile justice system, professionals would seek to ensure that sanctioning processes include victims, their family and supporters. Processes would also seek to involve those adults whose opinions are most important to young offenders, and who can hold them accountable while reinforcing rather than diminishing prospects for reintegration (Braithwaite and Mugford, 1994). Although engaging community in this way may certainly be viewed as a micro step which does not confront larger social justice issues of racism and oppression, it is a one component of a larger effort to connect the juvenile justice process to communities and their needs (Braithwaite and Parker, this volume).

Restorative justice advocates don't have all the answers for offender rehabilitation. Further, the importance of effective treatment programs for those offenders who, based on careful assessment, are determined to have mental health, substance abuse, and other needs that may be linked to criminal behavior is beyond dispute. However, in moving from one to three dimensions of concern, and attempting break down the insularity that characterizes much of the current treatment enterprise, restorative justice would first attempt to place rehabilitation in the context of the community. But given our knowledge of community dynamics, institutional roles, and maturational reform, how could juvenile justice intervention enhance or speed up those naturally occurring processes which helped Johnny and many like him grew out of their delinquency? How would they build or strengthen both formal and informal community relationships, and help to ensure that such young people had opportunities for work and other activities that would allow them to demonstrate that they had something to offer to the legitimate community?

In a different and restructured juvenile justice system, professionals would seek to ensure that sanctioning processes include and involve those whose opinions are most important to young offenders, and who can hold them accountable while reinforcing rather than diminishing the prospects for reintegration (Braithwaite and Mugford, 1994). In doing so, juvenile justice staff would work with adults as much as juveniles to ensure that citizens and community groups also begin to take responsibility for reintegration and *integration*. Such a strategy would redirect juvenile justice resources toward the difficult task of community building and would begin to redefine the role of the juvenile justice professional. In a naturalistic rehabilitation such professionals would no longer view themselves, or be viewed by their communities as "experts" providing service or treatment to change offender attitudes and behavior. Nor would their role be defined as "case manager" responsible for monitoring offenders on community supervision, making referrals for service, and completing paperwork. Such case-driven functions limit the potential for astute professionals to enhance naturalistic reintegrative processes. Rather than direct

Table 5: The Content of Intervention: Individual Treatment and Relational Rehabilitation

Individual Treatment	Relational Rehabilitation
(Best Practices)	
Drug therapy and drug education	Youths as drug educators, drug researchers
Recreational activities	Youths as recreational aides, recreational planners
Individual and family counseling, Group therapy (insight-based)	Peer counseling, leadership development, community service projects, family living skills, cognitive restructuring, anger management
Job readiness and job counseling	Work experience, service crews, employment, job preparation and career exploration
Cultural sensitivity training	Youths develop cultural education projects
Youth and family crisis information	Conflict resolution training, youths as school conflict mediators
Outdoor challenge programs	Conservation projects, community development projects, recycling and community beautification projects
Mentoring and "Big Brother" programs	Work with adult mentors on community projects, intergenerational projects with the elderly
Remedial education	Cross-age tutoring (juvenile offenders teach younger children), educational action teams, decision-making skills training
(Messages)	
To offender: "You have problems and need help."	To offender: "You are capable and needed in your community."
To the juvenile justice professional: "The best we can do is to enforce the rules of supervision."	To the juvenile justice professional: "We can work with the community to develop new roles for youths to practice and demonstrate competent behavior."
To the community: "Delinquent youths need services and treatment."	To the community: "Delinquent youths are a resource we cannot afford to waste. We need your help to give them opportunities to demonstrate this."

service, monitoring, and casework functions, juvenile justice workers would focus on creative problem-solving, community development, and relationship building. The professional role in relational rehabilitation would thus be more one of catalyst for building connections between young people and adults and adult institutions and facilitating change in the role of offenders from liability to resource.[13]

There will be, of course, always be a need for a different relational response to more chronic and violent offenders. But relational rehabilitation is by no means limited to prevention or first offender intervention. Indeed, while the intensity of surveillance and incapacitation will differ significantly for higher risk offenders, the principles of relationship rehabilitation and restorative justice will be the same. Building community and adult relationships — as well as meeting the needs of victims of serious and chronic offenders and requiring that these offenders hear about the consequences of their crime — is, if anything, even more important in intervention with serious offenders. Engaging citizens, especially when offenders are incapacitated in secure facilities, is more difficult, but not impossible (Immarigeon, this volume), and some neighborhood-based intensive day treatment programs for serious delinquent offenders have actually demonstrated greater capacity to involve community members than most traditional probation and diversion programs (Guarino-Ghezzi and Klein, this volume; Kinder and Speight, 1997).

At a more macro level, these tasks demand an advocacy and institutional change focus for "juvenile justice" (or whatever name is given to agencies and systems charged with responding to youth crime). New and positive roles that bond young people to adult institutions and allow them to contribute as productive resources will not emerge from informal relationships between youths and adults alone. Rather, they imply structural change in the socializing institutions of school, work and family (Polk and Kobrin, 1972; Polk, 1994). The third critical dimension of a relational approach to rehabilitation would hence broaden the focus beyond youth, families, victims and peers to include strategies to restructure education and work.

CONCLUSION

Although the country of New Zealand and a few states, provinces, and local jurisdictions constitute notable exceptions, the impact of restorative justice on juvenile justice policy has to date been minimal.[14] Valid reasons for this lack of policy impact include the fact that restorative justice does not fit well with the swing toward retribution and incapacitation in juvenile justice (Feld, 1990; Bazemore and Umbreit, 1995), and it is not easily reduced to a political slogan or identified as another in the array of treatment or trendy intervention programs like boot camps. Restorative justice is also not easily injected into what is often a vapid and insular, bureaucratic and procedural debate about which offenders will remain in the juvenile justice system and how this is to be decided. It can never be made relevant to an agenda that is solely offender-driven, and focused on treatment or punishment in isolated settings administered by "experts" who have little relationship to or concern for crime victims and the community.

The failure of restorative justice advocates to address the legitimate questions policy-makers and administrators pose about violent crime, system overload, and other practical concerns facing juvenile courts and juvenile justice agencies, however, is *not* a valid reason for lack of policy impact. One such concern is the need for a viable and effective correctional or rehabilitative model for reintegrating young offenders. Yet, while some writers have made important contributions to the development of a theory of restorative sanctioning (Braithwaite and Mugford, 1994; Moore and O'Connell, 1995), there is no complete model of reintegration or rehabilitation based on restorative justice principles.

While only a beginning, this paper has outlined three components of a relational model of offender reintegration grounded in restorative justice principles. Based on the central theme of the need to build or rebuild relationships, a relational rehabilitation would confront the insularity and one-dimensionality of the treatment/social welfare model of rehabilitation by insisting on: (1) an integration and resonance between rehabilitative interventions and efforts to address sanctioning and public safety needs, and an integration of efforts to serve and involve victims, communities and offenders in juvenile justice; (2) a "naturalistic" focus on community maturational and reintegrative processes rather than formal treatment programs; and (3) an institutional focus on the broader social ecology of reintegration and a policy agenda to develop new roles for young people.

Should there be a restorative model of reintegration/rehabilitation? My colleague, and co-author of this book, has raised perhaps the best argument against the effort to develop such a model and a number of concerns about whether an emphasis on offender rehabilitation could "fit" within a restorative frame. In other words, would any extensive focus on rehabilitation in an offender-driven environment not diminish the concern with repairing the harm?[15] The question itself raises the equally important counter-question (explored briefly in the "Principles" chapter) about whether a fully-fledged restorative alternative for juvenile justice could be developed by focusing only on mediation, restitution, and community service. From another perspective, would it not be possible that a compatible model of reintegration might reinforce the overall reparative project, and indeed itself become part of a larger effort to repair the harm (Van Ness and Strong, 1997)? Historically, the treatment and punishment agendas have left little room for restorative justice. Restorative justice seems even less likely in the current climate to have much influence unless advocates develop restorative alternatives to meet the very real reintegrative and sanctioning needs these agendas have attempted, most often unsuccessfully, to address.

The complex issue of coercion (Walgrave and Guedens, this volume), is also an important concern for those who may wish to promote a rehabilitative agenda, given the history in juvenile courts of forced treatment in the "best interests of the child" (e.g., Mitford, 1973; Schur, 1972). Yet, the issue of coercion is a relative one which must also be viewed along a continuum *and* in relation to current practice, not some abstract ideal. I would therefore challenge advocates of purely voluntary treatment to find an example of it in juvenile justice systems today. The first "test" for restorative interventions aimed at reintegrating the offender might then be that they be no more coercive than court-ordered counseling or other treatment programs. While the latter are seldom questioned and unlikely to be discontinued any time soon, a relational approach of the type described here could certainly be less intrusive, if no less coercive, than clinical interventions.

There are, in addition, several reasons to work harder to develop a restorative approaches for offender reintegration. First, with regard to juvenile justice policy on a practical level, without a rehabilitative model restorative justice may be viewed as simply an extension of the victims' rights movement (Young, 1995), and restorative interventions are in danger of being equated with victim service programs.[16] Second, in the absence of a restorative model of rehabilitation, we are in the intellectually unsatisfying and limited position of examining the effects of individual programs such as restitution and community service, or processes such as mediation or family group conferencing. Because we know that restorative justice cannot be reduced to one program or process, a coherent intervention theory is needed. Such a theory would help to define the "independent variable" in a restorative approach to rehabilitation as a coherent and integrated set of processes and supports aimed at achieving offender reintegration. Third, despite the acknowledged need for separate youth development systems to attend to youth socialization and integration (Polk, 1994), delinquent and at-risk young people are currently often excluded from such systems (Pittman and Flemming, 1991). They are instead tracked into treatment and service networks linked to, or part of, the juvenile justice court. These consume significant proportions of scarce intervention resources and often respond to youths with narrowly focused, clinical interventions that may be inappropriate if not counterproductive. Reallocating juvenile justice resources and refocusing intervention directed at those young people caught up in this system must therefore be a priority of a restorative juvenile justice which would also focus on advocacy for broader institutional change.

Unfortunately, the expansion of treatment-service bureaucracies and programs, and the obsession with the what works debate, has stifled discussion of this broader context of reintegration and of how youth workers could enhance the naturalistic rehabilitation process. Similarly, the tendency toward unlimited expansion of treatment-service bureaucracies must be viewed as a competing priority for those concerned to elevate the role of victims and communities as "clients" of juvenile justice.

But the best rationale for a relational rehabilitation is that the current individual treatment/social welfare focus is both politically and practically under-conceptualized. On the one hand, the treatment/social welfare model cannot sustain a separate and distinct juvenile justice system. On the other hand, juvenile justice makes much less sense without the hope of offender rehabilitation. If the juvenile court can no longer function as a "substitute parent," perhaps a restorative approach can help it function as a catalyst for building relationships and community.

★   ★   ★

Acknowledgement: The author wishes to thank Kay Pranis for helpful comments on an earlier version of this manuscript.

REFERENCES

Adler, C. and J. Wundersitz (eds.) (1994). *Family Group Conferencing and Juvenile Justice: The Way Forward or Misplaced Optimism?* Canberra, AUS: Australian Institute of Criminology.

Andrews, D.A., J. Bonta and R.D. Hoge (1990). "Classification for Effective Rehabilitation: Rediscovering Psychology." *Criminal Justice and Behavior* 17(1):19-52.

Armstrong, T., D. Maloney, and D. Romig. (1990). "The Balanced Approach in Juvenile Probation: Principles, Issues and Application." *APPA Perspectives* (Winter):8-13.

Bazemore, G. (1985). "Delinquent Reform and the Labeling Perspective." *Criminal Justice and Behavior* 12(2):131-169.

—— (1991). "New Concepts and Alternative Practice in Community Supervision of Juvenile Offenders: Rediscovering Work Experience and Competency Development." *Journal of Crime and Justice* 14(2):27-52.

—— (1996). "Three Paradigms for Juvenile Justice." In: J. Hudson and B. Galaway (eds.), *Restorative Justice: International Perspectives*. Monsey, NY: Criminal Justice Press.

—— (1997a). "What's New About the Balanced Approach?" *Juvenile and Family Court Journal* 48(1):1-23.

—— (1997b). "The 'Community' in Community Justice: Issues, Themes and Questions for the New Neighborhood Sanctioning Models." *Justice System Journal* 19(2):193-228.

—— and P. Cruise (1993). "Resident Adaptations in an AA-Based Residential Program for the Urban Homeless." *Social Service Review* 67:599-616.

—— and P. Cruise (1995). "Reinventing Rehabilitation: Exploring a Competency Development Model for Juvenile Justice Intervention." *APPA Perspectives* 19(4):12-21.

—— and S. Day (1995). "The Return to Family Interventions in Youth Service: A Juvenile Justice Study in Policy Implementation." *Journal of Sociology and Social Welfare* 22(3):25-50.

—— and S. Day (1996) "Restoring the Balance: Juvenile and Community Justice." *Juvenile Justice Journal* (December):3-14.

—— S. Day, A. Seymour and H.T. Rubin (1998). *Victims, Judges and Partnerships for Juvenile Court Reform. Final Report.* Washington, DC: U.S. Office for Victims of Crime.

—— and D. Maloney (1994). "Rehabilitating Community Service: Toward Restorative Service in a Balanced Justice System." *Federal Probation* 58:24-35.

—— and S. Senjo (1997). "Cops, Kids, and Police Reform: An Exploratory Study of Officer/Juvenile Interaction in Community Policing." *American Journal of Police* 20(1):60-82.

—— and C. Terry (1997). "Developing Delinquent Youth: A Reintegrative Model for Rehabilitation and a New Role for the Juvenile Justice System." *Child Welfare* 76(5):665-716.

—— and M. Umbreit (1995). "Rethinking the Sanctioning Function in Juvenile Court: Retributive or Restorative Responses to Youth Crime." *Crime & Delinquency* 41(3):296-316.

—— and C. Washington (1995). "Charting the Future of the Juvenile Justice System: Reinventing Mission and Management." *Spectrum: The Journal of State Government* 68(2):51-66.

Becker, H. (1960). *Studies in Sociology of Deviance.* New York, NY: Free Press.

Braithwaite, J. (1989). *Crime, Shame, and Reintegration.* New York, NY: Cambridge University Press.

—— (1993). "Beyond Positivism: Learning from Contexual Integrated Strategies." *Journal of Research in Crime and Delinquency* 30(4):383-399.

—— and S. Mugford (1994). "Conditions of Successful Reintegration Ceremonies: Dealing with Juvenile Offenders." *British Journal of Criminology* 34(2):139-171.

Briar, S. and I. Piliavin (1965). "Delinquency, Situational Inducements, and Commitments to Conformity." *Social Problems* 13(1):35-45.

Brown J.H., and J.E. Horowitz (1993). "Why Adolescent Substance Abuse Prevention Programs Do Not Work." *Evaluation Review* (Oct) 17:5.

Brown, M. and K. Polk (1996). "Taking Fear of Crime Seriously: The Tasmanian Approach to Community Crime Prevention." *Crime & Delinquency* 42(3):398-420.

Butts, J. and H. Snyder (1991) *Restitution and Juvenile Recidivism.* Monograph series. Pittsburgh, PA: National Center for Juvenile Justice.

Christie, N. (1977). "Conflict as Property." *British Journal of Criminology* 17(1):1-15.

—— (1982). *Limits to Pain*. Oxford, UK: Martin Robertson.

Cullen, F.T. and K.E. Gilbert (1982). *Reaffirming Rehabilitation*. Cincinnati, OH: Anderson.

Cullen, F.T., and P. Gendreau (1988). "The Effectiveness of Correctional Rehabilitation: Reconsidering the 'Nothing Works' Debate." In: L. Goodstein and D. McKenzie (eds.), *The American Prison: Issues in Research and Policy*. New York, NY: Plenum.

Durkheim, E. (1961). *Moral Education: A Study in the Theory and Application of the Sociology of Education*. New York, NY: Free Press.

Elliott, D. (1994). "Serious Violent Offenders: Onset, Developmental Course, and Termination." 1993 Presidential Address to the American Society of Criminology. *Criminology* 32(1):1-22.

Erickson, E. (1968). *Identity, Youth, and Crime*. New York, NY: W. E. Norton.

Etzioni, A. (1993). *The Spirit of Community: Rights, Responsibilities and the Communitarian Agenda*. New York, NY: Crown.

Ezell, M. (1992). "Juvenile Arbitration: Net Widening or Other Unintended Consequences." *Journal of Research in Crime and Delinquency* 26(1):358-77.

Feld, B. (1990). "The Punitive Juvenile Court and the Quality of Procedural Justice: Distinctions Between Rhetoric and Reality." *Crime & Delinquency* 36:443-464.

—— (1993). "The Criminal Court Alternative to Perpetuating Juvenile in Justice." In: F. Orlando (ed.), *The Juvenile Court: Dynamic, Dysfunctional, or Dead?* Philadelphia, PA: Center for the Study of Youth Policy, School of Social Work, University of Pennsylvania.

Finckenauer, J.O. (1982). *Scared Straight! And the Panacea Phenomena*. Englewood Cliffs, NJ: Prentice-Hall.

Garland, D. (1990). *Punishment and Modern Society: A Study in Social Theory*. Chicago, IL: University of Chicago Press.

Garrett, C. (1985). "Effects of Residential Treatment on Adjudicated Delinquents: A Meta-Analysis." *Crime & Delinquency* 22(4):287-308.

Gendreau, P., F. Cullen and J. Bonta (1994). "Up to Speed-Intensive Rehabilitation Supervision: The Next Generation in Community Corrections." *Federal Probation* 58(1):72-79.

—— and R.R. Ross (1987). "Revivification of Rehabilitation: Evidence from the 1980's." *Justice Quarterly* 4:349-407.

Griffiths, C.T. and R. Hamilton (1996). "Sanctioning and Healing: Restorative Justice in Canadian Aboriginal Communities." In: B. Galaway and J. Hudson (eds.), *Restorative Justice: International Perspectives*. Monsey, NY: Criminal Justice Press.

Halperin, S., J. Cusack, R. O'Brien, G. Raley and J. Wills (eds.) (1995). "Introduction." In: *Contract with America's Youth: Toward a National Youth Development Agenda*. Washington, DC: American Youth Policy Forum.

Hawkins, J.D. and R.F. Catalano (1992). *Communities That Care: Action for Drug Abuse Prevention*. San Francisco, CA: Jossey-Bass.

Hirschi, T. (1969). *Causes of Delinquency*. Berkeley, CA: University of California Press.

Howe, I. (1990). Cited in C. Rolzinski, *The Adventure of Adolescence: Middle School Students and Community Service*. Washington, DC: Youth Service America, p.4.

J. Hudson, B. Galaway, A. Morris and G. Maxwell (1996). *Family Group Conferences: Perspectives on Policy and Practice*. Leichhardt, AUS and Monsey, NY: Federation Press and Criminal Justice Press.

Jacobs. M.D. (1990). *Screwing the System and Making it Work: Juvenile Justice in the No-fault Society*. Chicago, IL: University of Chicago Press.

Kinder, G. and C. Speight (1994). "Community Intensive Supervision Project; 1993 Review." Allegheny County Juvenile Court (mimeo), February.

Kittrie, N.S. (1973) *The Right to be Different: Deviance and Enforced Therapy*. Baltimore: Penguin.

Krisberg, B., E. Currie and D. Onek (1995). "What Works with Juvenile Offenders: A Review of Graduated Sanction Programs." *Criminal Justice* (Sept) 20:35.

Lab, S.P. and J.T. Whitehead. (1988). "An Analysis of Juvenile Correctional Treatment." *Crime & Delinquency* 33:173-205.

Lipsey, M.W. (1992). "The Effects of Treatment on Juvenile Delinquents: Results from Meta-Analysis." Paper presented at the National Institute of Mental Health Meeting on Research to Prevent Violence. Bethesda, MD.

Lofquist, W.A. (1983). *Discovering the Meaning of Prevention: A Practical Approach to Positive Change*. Tucson, AZ: Ayd Publications.

Makkai, T. and J. Braithwaite (1994) "Reintegrative Shaming and Compliance with Regulatory Standards." *Criminology* 31:361-85.

Martinson, R. (1974). "What Works — Questions and Answers About Prison Reform." *Public Interest* 32:22-54.

Maxwell, G. and A. Morris (1993). *Family Participation, Cultural Diversity and Victim Involvement in Youth Justice: A New Zealand Experiment*. Wellington, NZ: Victoria University.

McKnight, J. (1995). *The Careless Society: Community and Its Counterfeits*. New York, NY: Basic Books.

Melton, G. and P.M. Pagliocca (1992). "Treatment in the Juvenile Justice System: Directions for Policy and Practice." In: J.J. Cocozza (ed.) *Responding to the Mental Health Needs of Youth in Juvenile Justice*. Seattle, WA: National Coalition for the Mentally Ill in the Criminal Justice System.

Mitford, J. (1973). *Kind and Usual Punishment: The Prison Business*. New York, NY: Knopf.

Moore, D.B. (1994). "Illegal Action - Official Reaction" Unpublished paper, March.

—— and T. O'Connell (1994). "Family Conferencing in Wagga Wagga: A Communitarian Model of Justice." In: C. Adler and J. Wundersitz (eds.). *Family Group Conferencing and Juvenile Justice: The Way Forward or Misplaced Optimism?* Canberra, AUS: Australian Institute of Criminology

Morris, R. (1994). *A Practical Path to Transformative Justice.* Toronto, CAN: Rittenhouse.

National Commission on Resources for Youth (1974). *New Roles for Youth in the School and in the Community.* New York, NY: Citation Press.

Packer, H. (1968). *The Limits of the Criminal Sanction.* Palo Alto, CA: Stanford University Press.

Palmer, T. (1992). *The Re-Emergence of Correctional Intervention.* Beverly Hills, CA: Sage.

Pittman, K. and Fleming, W. (1991). "A New Vision: Promoting Youth Development." Testimony to House Select Committee on Children, Youth and Families. Washington, DC: Academy for Education Development.

Polk, K. (1974). *"Rules for Institutional Reform."* Monograph, Marion County Youth Study. Eugene, OR: University of Oregon.

—— (1984). "When Less Means More." *Crime & Delinquency* 30:462-480.

—— (1994). "Family Conferencing: Theoretical and Evaluative Questions." In: C. Adler and J. Wundersitz (eds.). *Family Group Conferencing and Juvenile Justice: The Way Forward or Misplaced Optimism?* Canberra, AUS: Australian Institute of Criminology.

—— and S. Kobrin (1972). *Delinquency Prevention Through Youth Development.* Washington, DC: U.S. Office of Youth Development.

—— C. Adler, G. Bazemore, G. Blake, S. Cordray, G. Coventry, J. Galvin and M. Temple (1981). *Becoming Adult: An Analysis of Maturational Development from Age 16 to 30 of a Cohort of Young Men.* Final Report of Marion County Youth Study. Eugene, OR: Department of Sociology, University of Oregon.

—— and W.E. Schafer (1972). *Schools and Delinquency.* Englewood Cliffs, NJ: Prentice-Hall.

Pranis, K. (1997). "From Vision to Action: Some Principles of Restorative Justice." *Church and Society* 87(4):32-42.

Regnery, A. (1985). "Getting Away with Murder: Why the Juvenile Justice System Needs An Overhaul." *Policy Review* 34:65-8.

Reiss, A. (1986). "Why Are Communities Important in Understanding Crime?" In: A.J. Reiss and M. Tonry (eds.) *Communities and Crime.* Chicago, IL: University of Chicago Press.

Reiss, A. and M. Tonry (eds.) (1986). *Communities and Crime.* Chicago, IL: University of Chicago Press.

Retzinger, S. and T. Scheff (1996). "Strategy for Community Conferences: Emotions and Social Bonds." In: B. Galaway and J. Hudson (eds.), *Restorative Justice: International Perspectives.* Monsey, NY: Criminal Justice Press.

Roesch, R. (1988). "Community Psychology and the Law." *American Journal of Community Psychology* 1(4):451-463.

Rolzinski, C. (1990). *The Adventure of Adolescence: Middle School Students and Community Service.* Washington, DC: Youth Service America.

Rutter, M. (1985). "Resilience in the Face of Adversity: Protective Factors and Resistance to Psychiatric Disorder." *British Journal of Psychiatry* 147:598-611.

Schneider, A., (1986). "Restitution and Recidivism Rates of Juvenile Offenders: Results From Four Experimental Studies." *Criminology* 24:533-552.

—— (1990). *Deterrence and Juvenile Crime: Results from a National Policy Experiment.* New York, NY: Springer-Verlag.

—— and H. Ingram (1992). "The Social Construction of Target Populations." *Administration and Society* (23)3:333-351.

Schur, E. (1972). *Radical Nonintervention.* Berkeley, CA: University of California Press.

Schwartz, I., S. Guo and J. Kerbs (1992). *Public Attitudes Toward Juvenile Crime and Juvenile Justice: Implications for Public Policy.* Ann Arbor, MI: Center for the Study of Youth Policy.

Scott, R.W. (1987). *Organizations: Rational, National, and Open Systems.* Englewood Cliffs, NJ: Prentice-Hall.

Sechrest, L, S.G. West, M.A. Phillips, R. Redners and W. Yeaton (1979). *Evaluation Studies Annual Review.* Beverly Hills, CA: Sage.

Seymour, A. (1997), "Looking Back, Moving Forward — Crime Victims and Restorative Justice." *ICCA Journal* 8(1):13-17.

Solar, M. (1992). "Interagency Services in Juvenile Justice Systems." In: I.M. Schwartz (ed.), *Juvenile Justice and Public Policy.* New York, NY: Lexington.

Stuart, B. (1995a). "Circle Sentencing. Mediation and Consensus — Turning Swords into Ploughshares." Unpublished paper. Territorial Court of the Yukon.

—— (1995b). "Sentencing Circles — Making 'Real' Differences." Unpublished paper. Territorial Court of the Yukon.

Tomkins, S. (1992). *Affect/Imagery/Consciousness.* New York, NY: Springer.

Umbreit, M. (1995). "Holding Juvenile Offenders Accountable: A Restorative Justice Perspective." *Juvenile and Family Court Journal* 46(2):29-38.

—— (1994). *Victim Meets Offender: The Impact of Restorative Justice and Mediation.* Monsey: NY: Criminal Justice Press.

—— and R. Coates (1993). "Cross-Site Analysis of Victim-Offender Conflict: An Analysis of Programs in These Three States." *Juvenile and Family Court Journal* 43(1)21-28.

—— and S. Stacy (1996). "Family Group Conferencing Comes to the U.S.: A Comparison with Victim Offender Mediation." *Juvenile and Family Court Journal* 47(1):29-39.

Van Gelder, S. (1994). "The Ecology of Justice." *In Context* 38:1-14.

Van Ness, D. (1993). "New Wine and Old Wineskins: Four Challenges of Restorative Justice." *Criminal Law Forum* 4(2):251-276.

—— D. Carlson, T. Crawford and R. Strong (1989). *"Restorative Justice Practice."* Monograph. Washington, DC: Justice Fellowship

Walgrave, L. (1993). "Beyond Retribution and Rehabilitation: Restoration as the Dominant Paradigm in Judicial Intervention Against Juvenile Crime." Paper presented at the International Congress on Criminology, Budapest, Hungary.

—— and H. Geudens (1996) "The Restorative Proportionality of Community Service for Juveniles." *European Journal of Crime, Criminal Law and Criminal Justice* 4:361-380.

Werner, E. (1982). "Resilient Offspring of Alcoholics: A Longitudinal Study from Birth to 18." *Journal of Studies on Alcohol* 47:34-40.

Whitehead, J. and S. Lab (1990). *Juvenile Justice: An Introduction.* Cincinnati. OH: Anderson.

Wilkins, L.T. (1991). *Punishment, Crime and Market Forces.* Brookfield, VT: Dartmouth.

Wilson, J. (1967). *Varieties of Police Behavior: The Management of Law and Order in Eight Communities.* Cambridge, MA: Harvard University Press.

Wright, M. (1991). *Justice for Victims and Offenders* (2nd ed.). Winchester, UK: Waterside Press.

Young, M. (1995). *Restorative Community Justice: A Call to Action.* Monograph. Washington DC: National Organization for Victim Assistance.

Zehr, H. (1990). *Changing Lenses: A New Focus for Crime and Justice.* Scottsdale, PA: Herald Press.

—— (1994). "Justice That Heals: The Vision and The Practice." *Stimulus* 2(3):5-11.

Zhang, L. and S.F. Messner (1994). "The Severity of Official Punishment for Delinquency and Change in Interpersonal Relations in Chinese Society." *Journal of Research in Crime and Delinquency* 31:416-433.

NOTES

1. Because the current status of victims in the juvenile justice process is so low and because most juvenile justice systems are more resistant to victims' involvement than any other aspect of restorative justice (Bazemore and Umbreit, 1995), elevating the role of victims must remain a first priority. Moreover — as I will discuss in more detail here — we must continue to insist that a restorative perspective involving victims is not unrelated to and may even enhance other juvenile justice functions, including sanctioning and rehabilitation. Indeed, while restorative justice is no miracle cure for juvenile violence, it may offer more innovative and potentially effective, theoretically grounded responses to violence prevention (Schiff and Retzinger, 1996; Umbreit, 1995).

2. Polk, for example, has in several places expressed this view (e.g. 1994) and, in addition, has argued that it makes no sense to talk about "reintegration" when most Western societies in fact, lack a model of "integration" for young people. I use the terms "rehabilitation" and "reintegration" somewhat interchangeably in this essay because of their widespread familiar-

ity, while acknowledging that terms such as "habilitation" and "integration" may more aptly describe the goals of the model I will outline. The term "treatment" is used in this paper to refer to a specific type of rehabilitative intervention administered by social work or clinical professionals that is based loosely on the assumptions of the individual treatment or "medical" model. The terms "rehabilitation" or "reintegration" are used more broadly to refer to a process that may occur independent of any such treatment intervention.

3. What does not work are interventions based primarily on punishment and threats of punishment, both in the form of traditional institutional facilities and short-term detention, as well as shock incarceration programs such as the "scared straight" program and boot camps (Finckenauer, 1982; Gendreau et al., 1994). In addition to these and other studies that clearly debunk the deterrent value of punishment (e.g., Schneider, 1990), other findings of meta-analysts and other researchers also demonstrate that many commonly used forms of treatment — notably, insight-based individual and group counseling, self-esteem enhancement, and most probation and parole enhancements — clearly do *not* work (Elliott, 1993; Romig, 1982; Lab and Whitehead, 1988).

4. This claim of inappropriate referrals is one that can easily be verified anecdotally by anyone familiar with the "slot-driven" environment of most juvenile justice systems (see Jacobs, 1990). But such claims do not justify the inference that most treatment programs would be successful with the "right clients." While careers were advanced by a new emphasis in the 1980s on the search for more appropriate assessment tools, there is little evidence of much improvement in the quality of the programs to which delinquent youth are now referred, albeit accompanied by more comprehensive social histories. And in the U.S., increased funding is available in many states for what has now become a cottage industry of often-dubious private-sector treatment programs and treatment entrepreneurs.

5. Problems in meta-analytic and other treatment studies are well documented (Whitehead and Lab, 1990) and have to do with small samples, inadequate follow-up, and the lack of adequate control or comparison groups. The most promising findings show relatively positive treatment effects, some of which seem to be rather short-lived (e.g., Lab and Whitehead, 1988; Garrett, 1985) . However, these positive treatment effects are often gained at rather great expense, and efforts to replicate programs that may appear to work in one setting may fail in others because of extreme dependence on local leadership. Finally, no-treatment control groups are rare, making it difficult to answer the age-old question about the criminogenic impact of intervention: would the results have been better if nothing had been done? (Few seem as concerned about this question today than in the past — although it seems even more relevant in a climate that has encouraged an explosion in treatment and "early intervention," or prevention programs).

6. It is ironic then that a discipline such as criminology, so grounded in theories about the complex and community-oriented causes of crime, at times appears atheoretical and willing to beg the basic question of whether anyone should *expect* young offenders to be rehabilitated — habilitated and reintegrated — in settings that involve limited and relatively short-term individually focused treatment by experts detached from communities. This basic

suspension of doubt is not apparently shared by average citizens (and some juvenile justice professionals) when they remind us that young offenders — even in the most successful treatment programs — will go back to the same neighborhoods they came from.

7. The relational approach to rehabilitation presented here is not a theory of delinquency but rather an intervention model distinct from the treatment/social welfare paradigm. Building on general insights from the restorative justice literature, it is shaped by several philosophical, theoretical and policy influences that will only be mentioned in passing in this paper. These include: control or containment theory (Hirschi, 1969; Polk and Kobrin, 1972); labeling (Becker, 1960; Schur, 1973); new thinking in community psychology and the social ecology of crime (Reiss, 1986; Roesch, 1988); and research and theory on youth resiliency (Rutter, 1985) and developmental psychology (Erickson, 1968). Philosophically and politically, a restorative approach to rehabilitation builds upon insights from the new communitarianism (e.g., Etzioni, 1993; Moore and O'Connell, 1994), both in its demand for active involvement of citizens in community problem solving and skepticism about the ability of government to resolve problems.

8. While Aboriginal and many non-Western communities blur the distinction between sanctioning, public safety and reintegrative interventions (e.g., Griffiths and Hamilton, 1996), the current lack of integration and consistency across functions in the Western industrialized world may well be a factor in the alienation and confusion many citizens feel about the compartmentalization of justice systems into law enforcement, court, and correctional bureaucracies (and ever more narrow specialties within these domains). It appears, in turn, to be part of the impetus behind the support for processes such as family group conferencing and circle sentencing which effectively blur the distinction between these functions while breaking down barriers to active victim, offender and citizen involvement. When these processes are working well, they allow citizens to, almost simultaneously: express disapproval and even outrage about the crime and have input into the sanction, to hear and respond to the victim's needs, to address safety issues, and to explore ways to reintegrate the offender (Bazemore, 1997b). This concept of "resonance" in the balanced approach was first articulated by Troy Armstrong (see, Armstrong et al., 1990). Some have also previously argued that it is possible to think and speak of a restorative approach to rehabilitation and a restorative approach to public safety (Van Ness, 1993; Bazemore, 1996).

9. Similarly, because fear of youth crime is often more significant than the actual risks presented, Brown and Polk (1996) have discussed the importance of attention to fear reduction in any strategy to reduce juvenile crime and promote community safety. In their intervention strategy, developed in response to concern about the growing threat of youth crime in Tasmania, Brown and Polk (1996) addressed the fear problem through what could best be described as reintegrative, competency building projects in which youth and community adults work together in planning teams to address public safety issues.

10. Even when used in isolation and with little information about quality of implementation and "integrity of treatment" — two factors viewed as critical in treatment research by meta-analysts — (e.g., Andrews et al.,1990) — such programs do not do badly compared with other interventions, and in fact show great promise relative to other sanctioning approaches that often appear to exert a counter-deterrent effect (Gendreau, Cullen and Bonta, 1994). Neither experimental nor descriptive research on restitution (Schneider, 1990; Butts and Snyder, 1991) for example, has been able to control for such factors as whether offenders completed restitution or were provided with other supports such as employment. No known research has been conducted on community service implemented in a manner consistent with a restorative theory or restorative principles (Bazemore and Maloney, 1994).

11. James Q. Wilson's classic study of "Eastern and Western City" police departments (1967) was in this regard a harbinger for what soon became more intrusive, centralized juvenile justice systems with broader mandates, and for a concomitant decline in community capacity to respond to youth crime. In this 1960s comparison of these two departments, Wilson showed that the more professional dispassionate "by the book" responses to delin-quent and troublesome young people in Western City resulted in much higher rates of processing at a centralized intake facility than was the case in the less professional and less formal approach of Eastern City officers. Today, an increasing number of U.S. states appear to be establishing, or reestablishing, centralized juvenile court intake (now labeled assess-ment centers), and are thereby encouraging police to bring youth in for diagnosis, classifica-tion, screening and possible referral, rather than adjust their cases informally at the neigh-borhood level (Bazemore and Senjo, 1997). As they do so, the implications of Wilson's (1967) study for an expanded role for government and a diminished role for community and local social control agents such as community-oriented police, as well as residents them-selves, are becoming even more apparent.

12. The naturalistic focus borrows from the logic of "social model" approaches to drug and alcohol addiction based on mutual support, experiential learning and positive peer networks (Bazemore and Cruise, 1993). The important difference here, however, is that the peer and support networks must not be limited to ex-offenders and offenders (as they are limited to substance abusers in social model programs). Also, participants cannot be isolated in self-help monasteries in the way 12-step groups sometimes are. In addition, mutual support is unlikely to emerge on its own, and currently the technology of professional treatment works against those who seek to recruit community mentors and instead attempts to fill what has been characterized as a job for "experts" with paid professionals. The value of naturalistic supports is less likely to be questioned in Aboriginal and indigenous communities, because there are few if any paid staff despite increasingly chronic problems with youth crime (e.g., Griffiths and Hamilton, 1996).

13. While it is important not to diminish the role of professionals in rehabilitation, this new role should not be confused with "service brokerage" or other expert-driven strategies for improving system collaboration, in which the "usual suspects" (paid professionals) meet to develop ever-more complex treatment plans for offenders.

14. This is nowhere more true than in the U.S. where in the second half of the 1990s most states are busy dismantling juvenile justice systems. As they do so, they turn for guidance to just deserts and deterrence-based approaches while youth advocates struggle to retain some semblance of a treatment focus. There is little mention of restorative justice and much less understanding of it. Notable exceptions to this trend include several U.S. states and local jurisdictions that have adopted statutes or policies pronouncing the Balanced Approach or the Balanced and Restorative Justice model (Bazemore and Umbreit, 1995) as the mission for juvenile justice.

15. It might well diminish the growing commitment of the victims movement to restorative justice in the context of remaining suspicions among some victim advocates about the seriousness of the commitment of criminal justice professionals to victim needs (Seymour, 1997). Interestingly, however, many within the victims' movement are leading the way in breaking down the very forced categorization (challenged by restorative justice principles) between those who are "for the victim" and those who are "for the offender." Crime victims and advocates have also developed and promoted creative treatment programs for offenders (e.g., victim impact panels) (Young, 1995; Seymour, 1997; Bazemore et. al., 1998).

16. But, on the other hand, any genuine restorative juvenile justice would strongly collaborate in the implementation of comprehensive victim services (and victim services are indeed included within the array of interventions encompassed in the definition of restorative justice used in this text). Regarding the need for a restorative rehabilitation, it is precisely in those parts of the world where advocates have drawn explicit attention to its potential juvenile offender reintegration that restorative justice is now high on the juvenile justice policy agenda. The rise of international interest in the experiments with family group conferencing (Maxwell and Morris 1993; Alder and Wundersitz, 1994; Hudson and Galaway, 1997) and related community decision-making processes such as circle sentencing and community sanctioning panels (Stuart, 1995b; Griffiths and Hamilton, 1996; Bazemore, 1997) in the past few years has been primarily responsible for this policy impact and for refocusing attention on the rehabilitative potential of restorative justice practices and processes.

7. Protecting Community: The Public Safety Role in a Restorative Juvenile Justice

by

Susan Guarino-Ghezzi

and

Andrew Klein

I. BACKGROUND – THEORY AND RESEARCH

The focus of this chapter is on agencies in the criminal justice system — police, probation, and corrections — that purport to protect communities and provide a safe environment for residents. What role should these agencies play in a restorative juvenile justice? What is the relationship between the *restoration* of harms caused by crimes and the *protection* of communities? Stated differently, do existing criminal justice policies that are *not* grounded in restorative principles exacerbate *unsafe* environments?

Research on communities and crime suggests that high-crime neighborhoods experience deterioration of community institutions and social integration, leading to further erosion of neighborhood safety (Garbarino et al., 1992; Skogan, 1990). Communities that are vulnerable to disorder and crime lack "protective guardians" and safety rituals that perform effective crime prevention and response functions. Communities lacking resources are the most vulnerable to crime and social deterioration, and are the most adversely affected by juvenile justice policies that disrupt what little social cohesion does exist.

Criminal justice agencies contribute to the vulnerability of low-resource neighborhoods in two ways. First, they fail to implement problem-solving intervention models that encourage victims, witnesses, community residents, and offenders to participate in a productive process. Without such models, police, for example, inevitably err on the side of mechanistic coercion rather than negotiation with community residents, fueling long-term resentment and alienation (Skogan, 1990). Some evidence suggests that the distancing of community residents from the process of solving community problems is a primary cause of fear of crime, regardless of actual risk (Brown and Polk, 1996).

A second way that criminal justice agencies affect communities adversely is by weakening community bonds through aggressive attacks on neighborhood crime, particularly in inner cities. The destructive ramifications of neighborhood drug wars are numerous: Police undercover operations produce a decline of community residents' trust in police and throughout the community as residents grow suspicious of one another (Marx, 1988). Openly aggressive sweeps produce violations of civil rights, furthering community residents' alienation from the criminal justice system (Ogletree et al., 1995). The disproportionate incarceration of minorities imposes a particularly adverse impact on black and Latino communities, including the "exportation" of violent prison subcultures as ex-inmates return home (LeClair and Guarino-Ghezzi, 1991; Miller, 1996). Incarceration of offenders generally deprives communities and victims from direct involvement in holding offenders accountable. Finally, the increasing use of incarceration without prison reintegration programs increases the statistical probability of recidivism in the community (LeClair and Guarino-Ghezzi, 1991).

Interview data from a study of Boston juvenile offenders (Guarino-Ghezzi, 1993) suggest that "stop and frisk" policies used by police in high crime neighborhoods to confiscate weapons increased defiance and frustration, weakening police-youth relations. Not coincidentally, juvenile offenders in the study tended to be proficient at "self-help" behaviors — namely, retaliation against their enemies. Not only did they distrust the criminal justice system to protect them from crime, choosing to leave town if their lives were in danger rather than contact police, but they perceived police as dangerous threats.

When intervening with juvenile offenders, the three components of the juvenile justice system — police, courts and corrections — are rarely in communication. Probation and correctional agencies generally fail to provide a presence in neighborhoods as offenders return home. Police generally lack knowledge about juveniles in general, or about particular juvenile offenders. They incorrectly tend to treat juveniles as they would adults, ignoring developmental differences (Kelling, 1987). Worse, police develop unrealistic expectations that youths should respond to them with deference and respect, regardless of youths' past negative experiences with police. In urban areas, police expectations generally ignore youth perceptions of inconsistent enforcement of laws, police harassment, and police failure to protect youths from violent crime (Godfrey et al., 1997).

It is increasing recognized that many criminal justice policies are organizationally self-interested and contribute, with indifference, to the problem of community violence. For example, while police enforcement of drug activity has become especially aggressive in inner-city neighborhoods, the clearance rates for murder and other violent crimes have declined steadily (Godfrey et al., 1997).

Meanwhile, probation and correctional agencies have distanced themselves farther and farther from the communities in which juvenile offenders reside, with probation assuming more bureaucratic roles and corrections expanding toward institutional settings.

The linkage between crime and communities leads us to the following propositions:

(1) An effective juvenile justice system, which minimizes the harm caused by the juvenile justice system to communities, is a necessary condition for a cohesive community.

(2) An effective juvenile justice system, which reduces crime and fear and increases trust, is a necessary condition for a cohesive community.

(3) A cohesive community is a necessary condition for an effective juvenile justice system.

Most urban communities have juvenile justice systems that are perceived as ineffective and lacking integrity; at the same time, *and not coincidentally,* community cohesiveness is similarly insufficient and in decline. Since effective juvenile justice systems and cohesive communities are interdependent, we argue that a rational approach would purposefully design strategies to develop both simultaneously. That is, in some communities we have observed the reinvention of community cohesion through juvenile justice policies that are protective of communities and restorative of past harms. A protective paradigm can mobilize and entrench important community processes and rituals by increasing opportunities for cooperative interaction among residents. A primary community-focused goal of restorative juvenile justice strategies is to create or re-create community cohesion, including informal social controls and a culture of safety that encourages residents (victims, witnesses, offenders, and others) to participate in the justice process. We are calling this type of effort "protective restoration," and argue that it is a cornerstone of restorative justice.

"Protective restoration" means that juvenile justice agencies have, as a primary purpose, the goal of building capacity for repair and protection in communities. This is a shift for most agencies that are offender-directed, rather than community-directed. The prevailing community-relations strategy in most agencies is to attract community stakeholders that defend the juvenile justice organization's protection of the juvenile offender. This is organizationally self-serving and may enhance the resources and image of the organization, but have little positive impact on communities and crime. The protective restoration model, on the other hand, redirects efforts away from organizational enhancement through offender-focused programs and toward the communities they serve. With the focus of all agencies on the community, rather than in competition with one another, it becomes more natural for agencies to develop partnerships together, as shown in Figure 1 below:

Figure 1: Stakeholder versus Protective Restoration Models of Juvenile Justice Agencies and Communities

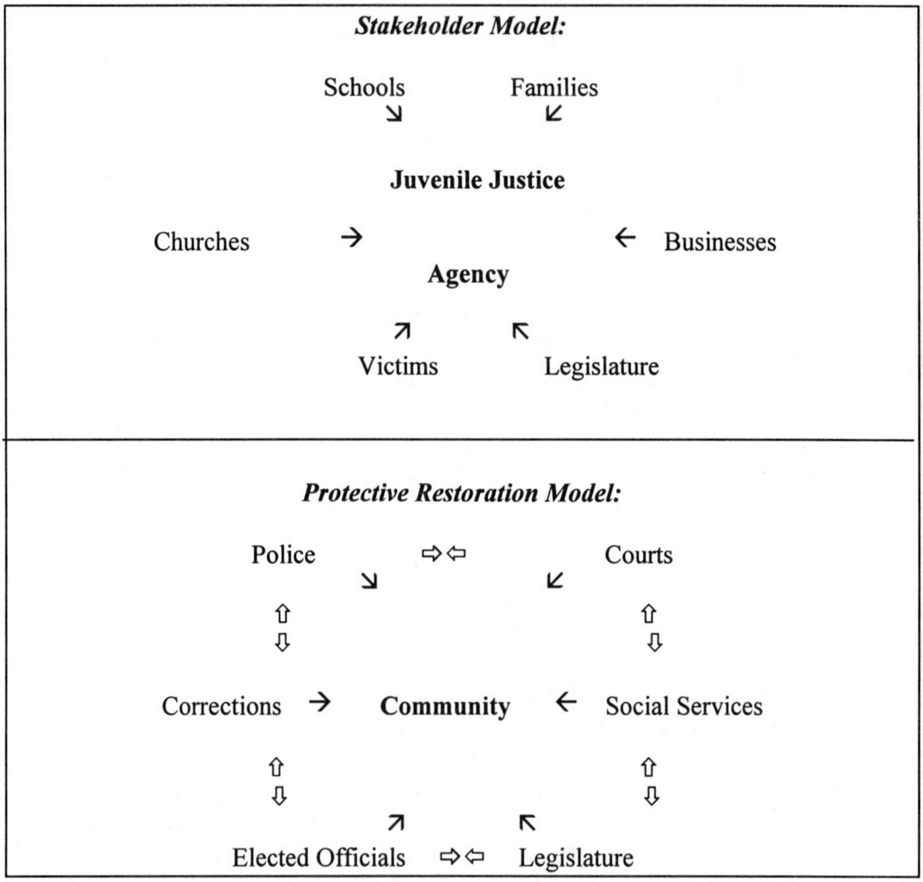

Stakeholder Model:

    Schools   Families
       ↘   ↙

Juvenile Justice

Churches   →   ←   Businesses
         Agency

          ↗   ↖
       Victims   Legislature

Protective Restoration Model:

    Police   ⇨⇦   Courts
       ↘   ↙
    ⇧   ⇧
    ⇩   ⇩

Corrections → **Community** ← Social Services

    ⇧   ⇧
    ⇩   ⇩
          ↗   ↖
Elected Officials ⇨⇦ Legislature

II. CONCEPTUAL PARADIGM

This chapter examines a theoretical role of agencies that purport to protect the public safety, given a restorative justice framework. A restorative justice framework would include the following basic principles:

- repairing harm
- building relationships
- building community capacity.

One approach is to pose the questions: How can the existing components of the juvenile justice system begin to partner more with the community in working toward restorative principles? What are the challenges of establishing partnerships, and can those challenges be overcome?

Popular public safety measures tend to lack a theoretical basis, and are therefore vulnerable to organizational co-optation. Popular "get-tough" measures that are followed by a particular juvenile justice organization to control an individual offender tend to elevate the organization's control vis-à-vis the community, and therefore have only a short-term impact. When the organization's control is removed, the community is once again vulnerable. We argue that the existing organizationally-based concept of public safety should be replaced by measures to strengthen communities' capacity for community crime prevention and self-protection based on social ecology theories (Bazemore and Schiff, 1996) and theories of juvenile behavior and development. Although many juvenile justice policies and programs are narrowly self-focused (Guarino-Ghezzi and Loughran, 1996), we will analyze the potential for programs that support community interests above organizational and political interests. The program and policy illustrations below demonstrate how roles that are protective and restorative are being created for communities, victims, offenders, and juvenile justice agencies.

III. PROGRAM AND POLICY ILLUSTRATIONS

A. Building Community through Protective Surveillance

Not all restorative justice programs address the problem of community vulnerability to crime, nor do all community protection programs apply restorative principles. In the traditional public safety model, the focus is on the offender. In a restorative justice model, the focus expands to the victim and community. The community and the victim become two of the juvenile justice system's legitimate clients (Klein, 1996). In a protective restorative justice model, the focus on *community* incorporates the long-term goal of community safety. As such, new roles and standards for public safety agencies are considered.

A restorative juvenile justice demands that police adopt practices toward juvenile offenders that reinforce good behavior in the community. Police practices that increase defiance and misbehavior of juvenile offenders, such as erratic responses to disorderly conduct, "habitual violent offender" policies, and police sweeps, need to be thoughtfully re-examined in light of a protective restoration model, as does the prevailing police theory that juveniles who cross the line into the correctional system are virtually guaranteed to embark on adult criminal careers (Jefferies, 1995; U.S. Federal Bureau of Investigation, 1995; Millar, 1995). For example, an FBI report titled "Youth Violence: Present and Future Law Enforcement Concerns" (1995) contains numerous examples of anti-rehabilitation rhetoric and support for stepped-up arrest and prosecution of juvenile offenders as "habitual offenders."

It is of concern that juvenile justice agencies rarely take advantage of one another's perspective to develop a more comprehensive source of knowledge about offenders' motivations and crime patterns. Police ordinarily draw their conclusions about human behavior from the volatile and desperate setting of the street. Probation officers and correctional staff, on the other hand, tend to have little direct knowledge of youths' behavior in their home environment. Many court and correctional employees fear to enter high-crime neighborhoods.

Yet new partnerships are providing a bridge to communities. For example, organizational and philosophical innovations in juvenile court probation have been cited as primary factors in the recent reduction of Boston gang homicides to almost zero in 1996-97, down from an annual high of 15 several years ago. In a partnership between local court probation departments and the Boston Police gang unit, gang members on probation became the focus of police and probation officers working together on the streets. Under the partnership, called Operation Night Light, judges impose 10:00 p.m. curfews on juvenile probationers. Probation officers, equipped with laptop computers, join police cruisers at night and conduct street surveillance and home visits. If any juvenile probationer is found on the street, the probation department requests that police arrest him or her for violation of probation. The juvenile is then detained until the next court session (Lupo, 1997; Mass Inc., 1996).

When the program first started, up to 50 youths were arrested each night. After several years of work, it is rare to find even the most committed youth gang member on probation out and about at night. The program's focused and consistent personal surveillance provides positive reinforcement for youths who abide by conditions and firm warnings to youths who do not. For parents who have lost control of their children and fear their presence on the streets at night, the effort provides a structure that supports parental discipline. Parents who have been neglectful are directly confronted on their home turf. The program gives juveniles, pressured by local gangs to be active members, an excuse to stay indoors. The project was recently honored by local ministers who work with police, probation, youth workers and community centers to bring peace to Boston's inner-city neighborhoods (Lupo, 1997). Replication of the Operation Night Light program is under way in the city of Brockton, MA, one of the most under-resourced and crime-producing communities in the state.

Another initiative involving the Boston Police Department is a partnership with the Massachusetts Department of Youth Services (DYS), the state agency responsible for youthful offenders committed by the courts, to improve reintegration programs for inner-city youths. The partnership focused in particular on youths whom police tend to categorize as "hopeless" — the youths returning back to communities following confinement in a DYS facility. One of the program's goals was to devise a role for police to invest in the rehabilitation of youths. A theoretical model of "reintegrative policing" was developed with input from DYS, police, and evaluations of pilot communication sessions between police and youths at a DYS secure treatment program (Guarino-Ghezzi, 1994). Subsequently, further sessions were held and a planning process created to specify the objectives of the program, which were to: increase interaction between youths and police in non-incident encounters; enhance mutual understanding by probing into the sources of negative perceptions and stereotypes on both sides; resolve role conflicts by teaching youths about police work and helping police to define their role with respect to youths who are reintegrating out of DYS programs; and reduce fear in the communities. Neighbors who saw young people misbehaving in the community needed to feel unafraid to call police or contact parents. Parents who saw older youths recruit younger children into criminal behavior needed to take action with fear of retribution. Thus the program was directed at high-risk youths not as isolated individuals, but as members of communities where the level of community reintegration reduced their risk of recidivism.

Police who participated in structured sessions with youths found the experience rewarding, and said that it allowed them to see that juvenile offenders are really "just kids" (Godfrey et al., 1997). Such partnerships between the police, who typically view themselves as representing victims of crime, and correction agencies, which advocate for offenders, are one approach to balancing the needs of victims, offenders, and the community so that police do not work at cross-purposes with correctional rehabilitation efforts. In a city where alienation is high and at least one young suicide victim connected his despair with negative police encounters (MacQuarrie, 1997), police and others are beginning to see positive results of incorporating restorative standards into their policies toward juvenile offenders.

Several aspects of the theory of reintegrative shaming (Braithwaite, 1989) are applicable to the relationship between public safety agencies and juvenile offenders, and underscore the need to redefine roles in interpersonal contact. First, the greater the social distance between the ex-offender and other individuals, the higher the probability of a stigmatic reaction impeding reform (see

Erickson, 1977). Second, evidence suggests that when police know and can communicate with neighborhood residents, they are more effective in defusing violent confrontations (Fridell and Binder, 1992). Third, in theory, all criminal justice professionals have a vested interest (albeit generally unacknowledged) in assisting with the moral education of youths. This requires a developmental understanding of adolescent behavior. The goal of protective restoration encourages understanding and interaction, which are necessary steps toward community cohesion.

B. Protective Restoration: Community Service and Restitution Programs

Reinforced by politicians, there exists a bias that any correctional program that is *not* centered around incarceration is automatically soft on crime and endangers the public. In juvenile corrections, this bias has resulted in several national and international trends. First, almost every state has taken measures to reduce the jurisdiction of juveniles covered by the juvenile court. State laws are automatically requiring that more and more juveniles charged with felonies are tried as adults. Second, within juvenile corrections, states are increasing the proportion of juveniles locked in institutions. In Massachusetts, the state which led the U.S. in the 1970s in closing its locked institutions, DYS regulations now mandate that all committed juveniles be confined for a minimum of 30 days. Many of these same offenders, if tried as adults, would never receive any period of incarceration.

Because public safety goals are paramount and the image of the juvenile justice system is weak, a balanced restorative justice approach is critical for creating the kind of correctional programs that significantly enhance public safety and are the antithesis of being soft on crime. (For a more detailed discussion, see Klein, 1991). Restitution is an important strategy that illustrates the balanced approach. Requiring juveniles to pay back their crime victims does more than restore victim's finances; it has a constructive impact on the offenders as well. It can increase empathy with the victim by providing the juvenile with a reality-based understanding of the victim's losses. When the juvenile has to go to work to earn the money to repay the victim, that juvenile may begin to appreciate the value of the victim's loss for the first time. This can be augmented with close victim/offender contact, described elsewhere in this book in more detail.

Bazemore (1991) has described a model of intensive aftercare that combines work experience with restitution, which he calls a "productive engagement" model of supervision. Employment is found for youths not primarily as a rehabilitation tool, but instead as a "tool to accomplish the primary goal of intensive supervision — public protection through 'incapacitation in the community'" (Bazemore 1991:124). For high-risk offenders, the performance of community service or payment of restitution earned through work represents an "opportunity cost." That is, the time spent working and learning job skills and self-discipline precludes time spent in other higher risk behaviors.

In serving their clients, probation departments can use their unique resources to strengthen community responses to crime. It is increasingly common that juvenile offenders are placed in the community to clean up public ways, remove crime inspiring graffiti as well as provide public services. Juvenile work crews in Deschutes, OR, for example, worked side-by-side with local community volunteers in constructing shelters for homeless families.

Brown and Polk's (1996) plan for offender/community restorative programs in the small Australian island state of Tasmania is based on Bazemore and Umbreit's (1994) expanded model of restorative justice, which includes victims, offenders and communities. The Tasmanian plan recommends the formation of community work teams consisting primarily of community residents in addition to pre- and post-adjudicated youths. The teams would perform various community service projects, such as restoring historic buildings of interest to the community. In addition, the Tasmanian proposal addressed residents' fear of youth disorder and crime in public walkways, malls and bus shelters. The proposal suggested that problem-oriented teams be established by local governments to study the problem and make recommendations. The teams would consist of community residents, including representatives of both young and elderly people who are on either side of the fear problem.

The Allegheny County Juvenile Probation Department, the jurisdiction centered in Pittsburgh, PA, developed the Community Intensive Supervision Program (CISP) in 1987 to hold offenders accountable to communities and victims without the use of incarceration. CISP operates out of half a dozen centers located in the area's most crime-prone urban neighborhoods. Post-adjudicated juveniles are referred from court in lieu of an institutional placement. Most are gang members and almost all are minority adolescents.

From a restorative justice perspective, a major problem of institutionalization is that it tends to foreclose opportunities for communities and victims to participate in holding juvenile offenders accountable for their crimes. Other problems of institutionalization are more widely recognized, including overrepresentation of minority youths (Schwartz, 1989) and insufficient treatment (Parent, 1993). Factors that precipitated the creation of CISP included a significant increase in African-American referrals to the Allegheny County Juvenile Court, the disproportionate residential placement of minority youths, the underrepresentation of minority youths in drug and alcohol treatment, and the rising costs of institutional placements. The court had to convince local government officials that the program would be cost-effective and would decrease institutionalization, and the court also needed to confront zoning issues and community opposition.

– 203 –

The community initially viewed the program from a traditional public safety perspective — as a threat, not an opportunity.

Each CISP center engages in significant community service work and employment projects that are consistent with restorative justice principles, in addition to providing traditional services and supervision. The community service projects include neighborhood cleanups, food bank volunteer service and painting the homes of elderly persons. One center cleared an abandoned city block and planted a victory garden with the help of area horticulturists. Participants donated the fresh vegetables to neighbors, the elderly, and food pantries and sold the rest. Another center obtained a contract to collect old telephone books for recycling, while still another received a contract to register area residents to vote. Local unions worked with one center to provide select juveniles with part-time jobs in house construction. Money from all these activities go to pay juvenile restitution orders. These programs integrate neighborhood residents and build community protection while restoring past harms.

When the program began ten years ago, neighborhood groups fought the establishment of the centers, fearing increased crime and lowered property values. Ironically, as the initial lawsuits are finally reaching the courts, the same groups now support the centers. Not only does the program lower offender recidivism (Kinder and Speight, 1994), but the centers' presence insures that surrounding buildings and businesses are graffiti and litter free through the daily work of community service crews. CISP centers keep the juveniles under constant supervision safeguarding the community, and their work actually strengthens these communities through community-building projects. To ensure a quick police response to any juveniles who violate program rules, miss curfew, or otherwise abscond, area police (often from community police substations, one of which is located in a CISP center) are immediately notified. The police have prewritten warrants for each juvenile, accompanied by photographs. Apprehension is usually swift, which increases community confidence. A more empowered community is, ultimately, a safer community. Due to the restorative focus of the program, juveniles that were once written off as drains on the community are now transformed into community assets.

Community integration is also evident in staffing decisions. To staff CISP centers, the Allegheny Probation Department hired residents of the communities in which each center is located. While the probation staff is predominantly white, and few live in the target neighborhoods, CISP staff are mostly minority. While the former expressed concern about venturing in the neighborhoods where the centers are located, CISP staff live there. To encourage neighborhood hiring, the department waived standard policies that precluded hiring probation staff with prior criminal convictions. The success of CISP as a community capacity builder as well as a juvenile correctional effort is perhaps revealed by the fact that its last center, created in Wilkensburg, a lower-class high-crime city abutting Pittsburgh, was requested by the city's mayor. Except for high-unemployment communities that site prisons where they would provide correctional jobs to community residents, when is the last time a community invited in a non-secure correctional program for high risk, minority youths who would otherwise be incarcerated?

Although most community service programs are run by probation or correctional agencies, there are important roles for police as agents of restorative justice. For example, the Police Citizens Youth Clubs in New South Wales, AUS, evolved in the late 1980s as a crime prevention program. One aspect of the program is that police provide transportation to youths under court order to attend substance abuse counseling, and they supervise court-referred youths who perform community service work at the youth clubs. Court-involved youths become familiar with youth club activities and learn from the positive involvement of other youths (Carter, 1989). The model seems to be a significant improvement over other community-service sentencing programs supervised by police, such as the Newark, NJ program, which was lacking in positive alternative activities for youths or the provision of role models (Skolnick and Bayley, 1986). It is another example of how public safety is enhanced through restorative efforts.

C. Protective Restoration: Providing Structural Alternatives to Violence

The school as a microcosm of the community allows us to examine the use of protective restoration strategies that increase public safety by strengthening community (school) protective structures. Several states have provided funding for local schools to develop training programs in conflict resolution. A program known as "SCORE" (Student Conflict Resolution Experts) illustrates the use of protective restoration principles. It is overseen by the Massachusetts Attorney General's Office in 25 high schools and middle schools throughout the state. The SCORE programs are testing safer alternatives for offenders, victims and witnesses of crime that are consistent with principles of restorative justice.

SCORE trains student mediators to resolve violent and potentially violent conflict among their peers. The Massachusetts Attorney General's office provides grants of $15,000 to $20,000 per school, on the condition that matching funds be raised. The funds pay for a full-time coordinator who works in a targeted school to develop and run a mediation program staffed by trained students and teachers. Rumors are the most common type of disputes, closely followed by physical fights and threats. The parties in dispute are generally acquaintances or friends. Many of the disputes concern sensitive racial issues with large groups of students on each side. Trained student mediators hear each side and help the parties to work out an agreement. Based on over 1,000 disputes mediated by SCORE members, 98% resulted in an agreement and fewer than 5% of the agreements were broken (Massachusetts Office of the Attorney General, n.d.). The program, which began with two high schools in 1990, grew to 20 high schools and five middle schools by 1996.

The following case studies from two Massachusetts high schools illustrate the types of conflict that are handled through student mediation. Although neither case involves violence, they reflect the types of disputes that tend to escalate into violent behavior, which are increasingly neglected in over-loaded courts. By handling such cases at the school level, the process is taught at an earlier, more resolvable stage of conflict, and students learn that a similar process can be applied to more serious types of disputes.

An ongoing conflict between two students in a freshman history class was resolved in mediation. "John," an African-American student, would get upset when the issue of slavery was brought up in history class. "Sandra," a white student, would become annoyed with him, roll her eyes and make "mouth noises." She felt that John was stuck on the race issue. John felt he had to bring up the race issue because no one else would. The situation deteriorated to the point where John was threatening to hurt Sandra. The teacher gave John the choice of mediation or the assistant principal. He "agreed" to try mediation. Sandra also agreed, reluctantly, to come to mediation. The teacher felt that each of these students was a leader of factions in the class, and that it was crucial to resolve this conflict so that open discussions could take place without hostility. Two white females conducted the mediation due to the fact that there were no African-American mediators available at the time the mediation was scheduled who felt comfortable with the issue. These two mediators felt slightly uncomfortable but felt that they could remain neutral. John at first kept making reference to the fact that everyone in the mediation room was white. But as the mediation went on, and the mediators listened and seemed to understand his concerns and did not take sides, he became less defensive and more cooperative. Sandra seemed stressed at first and concerned with being labeled a racist. When she was allowed to vent her frustrations with John, and his behavior and its effects on the class, she became more comfortable and was able to understand his feelings. Both wanted the other to respect their right to their own opinions and perspective on historical issues. John and Sandra agreed to the following: When they have a difference of opinion on a subject, they will state their opinion and not put each other down. Both agreed that the problem is behind them. If they have a problem in the future, they agreed to bring it to mediation. Follow-up interviews with both parties and the history teacher confirmed that the matter was resolved.

Two students, a male and female, had dated each other for eight months. The female student initiated a breakup. She heard that he called her a "whore" and asked him to stop on two occasions. He heard that she was telling people that she had used him, that she had not liked him for a while, but that he gave her lots of nice presents. Both were furious. These students had two confrontations with each other that almost resulted in a physical fight. Some of the students who saw these confrontations came to the school's mediation office and asked the coordinator to intervene. All of the components of the case were mediated or put into check through agreements.

The second case illustrates a critical dimension of the SCORE program: the willingness of witnesses to initiate referrals. Referrals to SCORE mediation tend to be made by administrators, teachers or counselors, but students are increasingly likely to make referrals either as parties in conflict or as witnesses. Data from the first three years of the program, drawn from three high schools, revealed that only 15% of early referrals were generated by students. By 1994-1996, however, student-initiated referrals doubled to 30%, suggesting that students were increasingly willing to use the program to anticipate or mitigate conflict.

The SCORE program thereby provides an empirical basis for discussion of the concept of protective restoration as a community-focused initiative. Although the state versus the individual offender has been a prime underpinning for U.S. conservative just-deserts policies, the successfully resolved case studies from the SCORE program demonstrate how victims and witnesses can be enlisted to de-escalate conflict, and how the community (represented by the school) can provide safe alternatives to violence. Violence is a less attractive choice when restorative alternatives are encouraged by both school administration and student peer culture.

IV. CONCLUSION

Protective restoration equals reexamining public safety measures and evaluating those measures based on their restorative capacity. A successful restorative public safety initiative should accomplish the following:

- restore communities to a less vulnerable state, in which victims are more likely to choose restorative structures to resolve conflict, versus retaliation, escalation of conflict, or vengeance
- create community guardians that protect routine activities
- improve the capacity of communities to resolve disputes through local restorative structures

- reduce fear of crime
- reduce crime.

What are the competing factors that might provide resistance to a protective restoration approach? Two primary competing factors are organizational and political self-interest. Organizational self-interest refers to the loss of authority of criminal justice agencies, as responsibilities for restoration are passed on to community members. It may not be in a criminal justice agency's self-interest to empower the community at the expense of the agency. For example, the SCORE program may reduce the mystique of the attorney general's office even as it teaches students how to develop their own protective skills. Similarly, the "thin blue line" of policing that separates offenders from victims may validate police in their law-enforcement role, despite the fact that victims and offenders can benefit from meeting together.

Political self-interest refers to the connection among politicians, voters and criminal justice policy. Canadian political scientist Anthony King (1997) recently observed that in the U.S., several factors converge to create a uniquely vulnerable environment for politicians: many elected officials have short terms of office compared to other democratic nations; office-seekers must first win primary elections, which is a practice that is unique in the democratic world; party unity and protection of individual candidates is less evident than in other countries; and politicians bear the individual burden of continually raising large sums of money to finance their campaigns. American politicians are more likely than those in other countries to mount symbolic campaigns in such areas as crime control, replacing the societal interest with self-interested rhetoric.

Decarceration advocate Jerome Miller estimates that 90% of young, urban, black males will enter the U.S. criminal justice system at some point in their lives (Miller, 1996). The cynicism and powerlessness with which many members of minority groups view the criminal justice system is but a symptom of the organizational and political decisions that are made at their expense. Protective restoration strategies suggest that there may be viable alternatives to popular just-deserts and incapacitation-based policies that would partner the existing criminal justice infrastructure with community protection innovations.

Without restorative correctional programming, the imposition of a "calculus" of punishment on offenders occurs essentially in a vacuum, without considering how to use the community structure as a tool in the process. As Young and Matthews (1992:9) contend:

> The commonplace distinction between social structure and the administration of criminal justice is important, yet confusing in that it grants too great and almost a symmetrical importance to the justice system, and suggests a temporal sequence: first the propellant, social structure and then the consequence, judicial reaction.

A protective restoration model does not sidestep the responsibility of communities to provide protective structures, of victims and witnesses to access those structures, nor of offenders to respond productively. The protective restoration model more accurately corresponds to a complex view of juvenile offending than the organizationally self-serving reactive models that are popular among opportunistic politicians. The protective restoration model supports strategies aimed at communities, victims, and offenders and thereby attempts to neutralize multiple sources of criminalistic tendencies.

★   ★   ★

REFERENCES

Bazemore, G. (1991). "Work Experience and Employment Programming for Serious Juvenile Offenders: Prospects For a 'Productive Engagement' Model of Intensive Supervision." In: T. L. Armstrong (ed.), *Intensive Interventions with High-Risk Youths.* Monsey, NY: Criminal Justice Press.

—— and M. Schiff (1996). "Community Justice/Restorative Justice: Prospects for a New Social Ecology for Community Corrections." *International Journal of Comparative and Applied Criminal Justice* 20(2):311-335.

—— and M.S. Umbreit (1994). *Balanced and Restorative Justice.* Washington, DC: U.S. Office of Juvenile Justice and Delinquency Prevention.

Braithwaite, J. (1989). *Crime, Shame and Reintegration.* Cambridge, UK: Cambridge University Press.

Brown, M. and K. Polk (1966). "Taking Fear of Crime Seriously: The Tasmanian Approach to Community Crime Prevention." *Crime & Delinquency* 42(3):398-420.

Carter, P. (1989). "The New-Look Police Club." In: J. Vernon and S. McKillop (eds.), *Preventing Juvenile Crime.* Canberra, AUS: Australian Institute of Criminology.

Erickson, R.V. (1977). "Social Distance and Reaction to Criminality." *British Journal of Criminology* 17:16-29.

Fridell, L.A. and A. Binder (1992). "Police Officer Decisionmaking in Potentially Violent Confrontations." *Journal of Criminal Justice* 20:385-399.

Garbarino, J., N. Dubrow, K. Kostelny, and C. Pardo (1992). *Children in Danger: Coping With the Consequences of Community Violence.* San Francisco, CA: Jossey-Bass.

Godfrey, K., S. Guarino-Ghezzi and P. Bankowski (1997). *Myths and Rituals: Juvenile Offenders and Police.* Final report. Boston, MA: Boston Police Department.

Guarino-Ghezzi, S. (1993). *Project Reinforcement: Program Description and Findings.* Boston, MA. (mimeo).

—— (1994). "Reintegrative Police Surveillance of Juvenile Offenders: Forging an Urban Model." *Crime & Delinquency* 40(2):131-153.

—— and E.J. Loughran (1996). *Balancing Juvenile Justice.* New Brunswick, NJ: Transaction.

Jefferies, M. (1995). "Positive Impact Programs for Violent Juvenile Offenders: A Mandate for Change." In: *Youth Violence: Present and Future Law Enforcement Concerns.* Washington, DC: U.S. Federal Bureau of Investigation.

Kelling, G.L. (1987). "Juveniles and Police: the End of the Nightstick." In: F. Hartmann (ed.), *From Children to Citizens, Volume II, The Role of the Juvenile Court.* New York, NY: Springer-Verlag.

Kinder, G. and C. Speight (1994). "Community Intensive Supervision Project; 1993 Review." Allegheny County Juvenile Court (mimeo), February.

King, A. (1997). "Running Scared." *The Atlantic Monthly* 279(1):41-61.

Klein, A. (1991). "Restitution and Community Work Service: Promising Core Ingredients for Effective Intensive Supervision Programming." In: T. L. Armstrong (ed.) *Intensive Interventions with High Risk Youths,* Monsey, NY: Criminal Justice Press.

—— (1996). "Community Probation: Acknowledging Probation's Multiple Clients." In: *Community Justice: Striving for Safe, Secure, and Just Communities.* Longmont, CO: LIS, Inc.

LeClair, D.P. and S. Guarino-Ghezzi (1991). "Does Incapacitation Guarantee Public Safety? Lessons from Massachusetts' Furlough and Prerelease Programs." *Justice Quarterly* 8(1):8-36.

Lupo, A. (1997). "Keeping the Night Light On." *Boston Globe,* Sunday, January 26, City Weekly Section, p.1.

MacQuarrie, B. (1997). "Hardship Grips a Development." *Boston Globe,* Sunday, May 4, pp.A1-A30.

Marx, G.T. (1988). *Undercover.* Berkeley: University of California Press.

Mass Inc. (1996). *Criminal Justice in Massachusetts: Putting Crime Control First.* Boston, MA: The Massachusetts Institute for a New Commonwealth.

Massachusetts Office of the Attorney General (n.d.). *SCORE: Student Conflict Resolution Experts.* Boston, MA: author.

Millar, B. (1995). "The Evolution, Analysis, and Suggested Reform of the American Juvenile Justice System." In: *Youth Violence: Present and Future Law Enforcement Concerns.* Washington, DC: U.S. Federal Bureau of Investigation.

Miller, J. (1996). *Search and Destroy.* London, UK: Oxford University Press.

Ogletree, C.J., M. Prosser, A. Smith and W. Talley (1995). *Beyond the Rodney King Story: An Investigation of Police Conduct in Minority Communities.* Boston, MA: Northeastern University Press.

Parent, D. (1993). "Conditions of Confinement." *Juvenile Justice* 1(1):2-23.

Schwartz, I.M. (1989). *(In)Justice for Juveniles.* Lexington, MA: D.C. Heath.

Skogan, W. (1990). *Disorder and Decline: Crime and the Spiral of Decay in American Neighborhoods.* New York, NY: Free Press.

Skolnick, J.H. and D.H. Bayley (1986). *The New Blue Line.* New York, NY: Free Press.

U.S. Federal Bureau of Investigation (1995). *Youth Violence: Present and Future Law Enforcement Concerns.* Washington, DC: author.

Young, J. and R. Matthews (eds.) (1992). *Rethinking Criminology: The Realist Debate.* Newbury Park, CA: Sage.

8. Avoiding The Marginalization and "McDonaldization" of Victim-Offender Mediation: A Case Study in Moving Toward the Mainstream

by

Mark S. Umbreit

INTRODUCTION

Restorative justice provides a very different framework for understanding and responding to crime (Galaway and Hudson, 1990; Umbreit, 1994a; Zehr, 1990). Crime is understood as harm to individuals and communities, rather than simply a violation of abstract laws against the state. Those most directly affected by crime — victims, community members and offenders — are therefore encouraged to play an active role in the justice process. Rather than the current focus on offender punishment, restoration of the emotional and material losses resulting from crime is far more important.

The practice of restorative justice can take many forms (Bazemore and Umbreit, 1995; Bazemore and Maloney, 1994). One of the most well-established and widely practiced expressions of the core principles of restorative justice is to be found in the growing practice of a mediated dialogue between crime victims and offenders (most often juveniles), which focuses on how the crime influenced those affected, usually resulting in a plan for compensating the victim.

The field of victim-offender mediation (VOM) has grown extensively in North America and Europe. In the late 1970s there were only a small number of programs in Canada and the U.S. Today, according to recent surveys, there are more than 1,000 mediation programs throughout North America (N=318) and Europe (N=712), nearly twice the number previously believed to exist (Umbreit and Greenwood, 1997; Wright, 1996). While many VOM programs continue to be administered by private community-based agencies, an increasing number of probation departments are developing initiatives, usually in conjunction with trained community volunteers who serve as mediators. A growing number of victim service providers and advocates are becoming actively involved in the development and operation of VOM programs.

Perhaps the clearest expression of how the field has continually developed and received greater recognition by the formal justice system is seen in the 1994 endorsement of VOM by the American Bar Association. After many years of supporting civil court mediation, with limited interest in criminal mediation, the ABA now endorses the process and recommends the use of "victim-offender mediation and dialogue" in courts throughout the U.S. Some programs are still quite small, with a very limited number of case referrals. Many other programs are receiving several hundred referrals a year. A few North American programs in recent years have been requested to divert a thousand or more cases a year from the court system, and local governments have provided hundreds of thousands of dollars to fund these mediation programs.

The movement of VOM from the margins toward the mainstream of juvenile justice systems is generally positive, in that a far larger number of crime victims and offenders will have the opportunity to experience the increasingly well-documented benefits of the mediation and dialogue process. A number of potential dangers, however, are also present in this trend. As any reform moves from its early stage of development and attempts to become accepted and institutionalized, the probability of it "losing its soul" is increased. As the primary focus of the process shifts from offering an experience of healing and closure for those most affected by the crime to serving justice system goals, the initial passion and creativity of the movement can be quickly lost. Helping solve the problems of an overcrowded juvenile court (e.g., by creating more diversion or dispositional options) can become a higher priority than offering a truly restorative community-based peacemaking process that is driven by the needs of those most affected by the reality of crime. In the rush to set up new VOM services, there will be a tremendous temptation for agencies to de-emphasize the restorative values on which mediation is based, while emphasizing the values of efficiency and moving cases quickly in the interest of relieving the overcrowded court system.

Having said this, it is very important to keep these issues in perspective. With many thousands of cases now participating in the VOM process each year, the number of cases that experienced the process in a negative way would appear to be small. That is no excuse, however, to ignore or minimize the stories of those victims and offenders who essentially felt revictimized by the mediation process. Trends such as eliminating pre-mediation individual meetings with the victim and offender, and focusing exclusively on restitution agreements rather than creating a safe place to facilitate a genuine conversation or dialogue about what happened and how things can be made right, could lead to the "McDonaldization of mediation." On the one hand, if not critically examined, this "fast food" version seems likely to strip the process of its most important restorative elements. On the other hand, if openly considered in a non-defensive manner, these negative cases can be a powerful learning experience that can lead to important program modifications. Such cases can serve as a challenge to program staff to continually examine the degree to which they are "walking the walk" as well as "talking the talk" of restorative justice.

As the oldest and most developed restorative justice intervention, VOM provides a rich case example of the challenges of moving from the margins toward the mainstream of juvenile justice (Umbreit and Niemeyer, 1996). Hence, many of the lessons learned and challenges currently being faced by mediation professionals will also apply to other, newer restorative policies and practices. Proponents of the various forms of community conferencing (Maxwell and Morris, 1994; Bazemore, 1997), for example, will no doubt also soon face the temptation to speed up or otherwise alter the victim-offender dialogue process to serve ends that may limit the achievement of restorative objectives.

This chapter will first address the linkage between restorative justice and VOM, including an overview of how the mediation process works. The manner in which the field has continued to expand internationally will be presented, along with a review of what has been learned from a growing number of studies of VOM. Finally, opportunities facing the mediation field as programs seek to overcome their marginalized status will be highlighted and potential dangers presented. The chapter concludes with a set of criteria that can help to gauge the extent to which any mediation/dialogue process is operating based on restorative justice principles.

OVERVIEW OF VICTIM-OFFENDER MEDIATION

The VOM process differs markedly across programs on the basis of referral source, diversion versus post-adjudication referral, use of volunteer mediators and so on. Nearly all VOM and reconciliation programs focus upon providing a conflict resolution process that is perceived as fair by the victim and the offender. The mediator facilitates this process, first by allowing time to address informational and emotional needs, followed by a discussion of losses and the possibility of developing a mutually agreeable reparative obligation (including money, work for the victim and work for the victim's choice of a charity). Despite diversity, most VOM programs in the U.S., Canada and Europe utilize a basic case management process that involves four phases: case referral and intake, preparation for mediation, conducting the mediation session, and follow-up.

The first phase begins when an offender, often convicted of such crimes as theft and burglary, is referred to the program by the court. Most programs (particularly in North America) accept cases that are referred, once the juvenile has admitted guilt, as part of a diversion effort. Many other programs accept referrals after a finding of guilt during a formal disposition and adjudication hearing. Each case is then assigned to either a staff or volunteer mediator.

Table 1: International Development of VOM Programs

Country	Number of VOM Programs
Australia	5
Austria	17
Belgium	31
Canada	26
Denmark	5
England	43
Finland	130
France	73
Germany	348
Italy	4
New Zealand	Available in all jurisdictions
Norway	44
South Africa	1
Scotland	2
Sweden	10
United States	292

Note: Data are taken from *Victim Meets Offender: The Impact of Restorative Justice and Mediation* (Umbreit, 1994a); *Justice for Victims and Offenders* (Wright, 1996); and the *National Survey of Victim Offender Mediation Programs in the U.S.* (Umbreit and Greenwood, 1997).

During the second phase of preparing for the mediation, the mediator typically meets with the offender and victim separately before the mediation session is scheduled. During this individual session, the mediator listens to the story of each party, explains the program and encourages their participation. Usually mediators meet first with the offender and then the victim, to determine if he or she is willing to proceed with the mediation process. The preliminary separate meetings with victims and offenders require effective listening and communication skills on the part of the mediator. Victim participation can be lost at the first phone call. Experienced mediators have found that the initial process of building rapport and trust through separate meetings with the victim and offender, as well as gaining valuable information, is essential to the quality of the later joint meeting with both individuals. While less desirable, a few programs conduct this pre-mediation interview over the phone rather than in person. When granted permission from the offender, the mediator often shares information about the offender with the victim during the separate pre-mediation meeting. Information about the offender is helpful to many victims in deciding to proceed with mediation.

Every effort should be made to insure, despite good intentions, that victims are not revictimized by the mediation process. For many in the field, this represents the strongest ethical principle of the VOM process. They stress that a victim should never be coerced into participating in the victim offender mediation and reconciliation process. While coercion is clearly inappropriate, mediators do encourage victims to consider participation by emphasizing both the potential benefits and risks of a meeting with the offender. Many programs have found that it is the voluntary exercise of choices, including the choice of participation, that leads to victims and offenders feeling empowered. Willingness to participate in mediation is directly related to the extent to which victim and offender feel safe with the process and the mediator.

A review of the literature in the field would imply that offender participation in the mediation process is also voluntary; actual practice would suggest that it is less than truly voluntary. When offenders are ordered by the court, via probation, or are diverted from prosecution if they complete the program, a rather significant amount of state coercion is exercised. Many programs attempt to temper this by allowing those offenders who are strongly opposed to participating, or who are determined to be inappropriate for mediation by the program staff, to opt out of the program.

The mediation session itself is conducted during the third phase. The mediator schedules a face-to-face meeting after the parties have agreed to participate during the initial separate meetings. This phase requires the completion of six tasks. These tasks are:

(1) Introductory/opening statement by mediator

(2) Storytelling by victim and offender

(3) Clarification of facts and sharing of feelings

(4) Reviewing victim losses and options for compensation

(5) Developing a written restitution agreement

(6) Closing statement by mediator

A typical mediation session between a crime victim and an offender begins with an opening statement by the mediator, usually a trained volunteer, that includes:

(1) introducing everyone and arranging seating

(2) explaining the role of a mediator: "I am here to help both of you to talk about what happened and to work out a restitution agreement, if possible... I am not a court official and will not be requiring you to agree to anything, nor will I be taking sides with either of you."

(3) explaining ground rules

(4) identifying the agenda:

- reviewing facts and feelings related to the crime
- discussing losses and beginning to negotiate restitution

(5) emphasizing fairness and balance: "Any restitution agreement that is reached must feel fair to both of you."

(6) Initiating direct communication between victim and offender, who are sitting across from each other: "Mrs. Smith (victim), could you tell John (offender) what happened from your perspective and how you felt about the burglary?"

Following the opening statement, each party has some uninterrupted time to tell their story, usually beginning with the victim. The first part of the meeting focuses upon a discussion of the facts and feelings related to the crime. Victims are given the opportunity to express their feelings directly to the person who violated them, as well as to receive answers to many lingering questions such as, "Why me?" How did you get into our house? Were you stalking us and planning on coming back?" Victims are often relieved to see the offender, who usually bears little resemblance to the frightening character they may have envisioned.

Offenders are rarely put in the uncomfortable position of having to face the person they violated. In mediation, they are given the equally rare opportunity to display a more human dimension to their character, and to express remorse in a personal fashion. Through open discussion of their feelings, victim and offender have the opportunity to deal with each other as people rather than stereotypes and objects.

After the victim and offender have discussed the crime and expressed their concerns, the second part of the meeting is initiated. It focuses upon discussion of losses and negotiation of a mutually acceptable restitution or other reparative agreement. The agreement is a tangible symbol of the conflict resolution that has occurred and a focal point for accountability. It is important that the mediator in no way imposes a restitution agreement. The written restitution agreement is negotiated between the parties, written up by the mediator, and signed at the end of the meeting by the victim, offender and mediator. Joint victim-offender meetings usually last from one to two hours.

Completion of restitution agreements is monitored during the follow-up phase, usually by a probation officer or staff person from the referring agency. Completion rates are generally believed to be higher when staff or volunteers from the mediation program do follow-up calls and convene a follow-up mediation session, if problems have emerged and the parties are willing to meet again.

WHAT WE HAVE LEARNED FROM RESEARCH

A growing number of studies in North America and Europe have provided increasing insight into how the VOM and dialogue process works, and the impact it is having on its participants and the larger justice system. The most essential findings that have emerged are as follows:

(1) Victims of property crime have been found to be quite willing to participate in a mediation session with their offender, when given the opportunity. Although there are no hard figures on the percentage of victims offered mediation who refused to participate, programs have reported participation rates as high as 90% and as low as 32%. Lower rates may result from involving unwilling offenders in the mediation process. Practitioners over a period of years have estimated that participation rates in well-run programs may average around 60% of those victims given the choice to mediate. (Coates and Gehm, 1989; Gehm, 1990; Galaway, 1988; Marshall and Merry, 1990; Umbreit, 1985,1989a,1991a; Umbreit and Coates, 1992).

(2) Research studies suggest that mediation is perceived to be voluntary by the vast majority of victims and juvenile offenders who have participated in it (Umbreit, 1993a, 1994b).

(3) VOM results in high levels of client satisfaction and perceptions of fairness with the mediation process for both victims and offenders (Coates and Gehm, 1989; Dignan, 1990; Marshall and Merry, 1990; Umbreit, 1988,1990,1991b, 1993b, 1994a, 1995a, 1995b, 1996; Umbreit and Coates, 1992, 1993).

(4) While the possibility of receiving restitution appears to motivate victims to enter the mediation process, following their participation they report that meeting the offender and being able to talk about what happened was the most satisfying aspect of the program (Coates and Gehm, 1989; Umbreit, 1991a, 1994a).

(5) Offenders involved in mediation programs, while anxious about a confrontation with their victim, report feeling at ease once the mediation is underway (Coates and Gehm, 1989; Umbreit, 1991a), and pre/post studies of VOM suggest a significant reduction in fear and anxiety among victims of juvenile crime (Umbreit, 1991a, 1994a, 1994b).

(6) Juvenile offenders seem to not perceive VOM to be a significantly less demanding response to their criminal behavior than other options available to the court. The use of mediation is consistent with the concern to hold young offenders accountable for their criminal behavior (Umbreit, 1994a).

(7) About 40 to 60% of cases referred to programs result in a face-to-face mediation session (Coates and Gehm, 1989; Galaway, 1988, 1989; Gehm,

1990; Marshal and Merry, 1990; Umbreit, 1988, 1989a, 1991a; Wright and Galaway, 1989).

(8) In 9 out of 10 cases that enter mediation (Coates and Gehm, 1989; Galaway, 1988, 1989; Gehm, 1990; Umbreit, 1986a, 1988, 1991a, 1994a), both parties perceive negotiated restitution agreements to be fair.

(9) A number of programs report successful completion of restitution agreements in the range of 79 to 98% (Coates and Gehm, 1989; Galaway, 1988,1989; Gehm, 1990; Umbreit, 1986b, 1988, 1991a, 1994a). According to one quasi-experimental study, VOM has a significant impact on the likelihood of offenders successfully completing their restitution obligation to victims (81 vs. 58%), when compared to similar offenders who complete their restitution in a court-administered program without mediation (Umbreit, 1993b, 1994a, 1994b; Umbreit and Coates, 1992, 1993).

(10) Considerably fewer and less serious additional crimes are committed within a one-year period by juvenile offenders in VOM programs, when compared to similar offenders who did not participate in mediation (Umbreit, 1993b, 1994a, 1994b; Umbreit and Coates, 1993). Although this finding was based on a limited sample, it is consistent with two recent English studies (Marshall and Merry, 1990; Dignan, 1990).

(11) Contrary to popular assumptions, there is some evidence that a larger number of victims of violent crime than initially believed are interested in confronting their offenders in a mediation process (Gustafson and Smidstra, 1989; Umbreit, 1989b, 1995c).

In addition to these findings, initial results from the first cross-national assessment (Umbreit et al., 1997) of VOM programs in 4 U.S. states, four Canadian provinces, and two cities in England suggest fairly consistent outcomes. Specific outcome measures examined include: victim and offender satisfaction with the criminal justice system response to their case by referring it to mediation; victim and offender satisfaction with the outcome of mediation; victim and offender perception of fairness in the criminal justice system response to their case through mediation; and victim fear of revictimization by the same offender following mediation.

In general, these findings are encouraging. As a whole, they also indicate that the VOM process has a strong effect in humanizing the justice system response to crime, for both victims and juvenile offenders (Coates and Gehm,1989; Marshall and Merry, 1990; Umbreit, 1991a, 1994a, 1995a, 1995b, 1996; Umbreit and Coates, 1993). Although a plausible interpretation of this finding is that better com-

Table 2: Comparison of English, Canadian and U.S. Studies of Victims and Offenders Participating in Mediation

	Combined English Sites (2)	Combined Canadian Sites (4)	Combined U.S. Sites (4)
Victim satisfaction with criminal justice system response to their case: referral to mediation	62%	78%	79%
Offender satisfaction with criminal justice system response to their case: referral to mediation	79%	74%	87%
Victim satisfaction with mediation outcome	84%	89%	90%
Offender satisfaction with mediation outcome	100%	91%	91%
Victim fear of re-victimization by same offender, following mediation	16% (50% less than victims who were not in mediation)	11% (64% less than victims who were not in mediation)	10% (56% less than prior to mediation for same victims)
Victim perceptions of fairness in criminal justice system response to their case: referral to mediation	59%	80%	83%
Offender perceptions of fairness of criminal justice system response to their case: referral to mediation	89%	80%	89%

pletion rates resulted from a more realistic negotiation of restitution amounts and more personal buy-in and ownership on the part of offenders who must face individual victims (Umbreit, 1994a), it is possible that the greater amount of attention and resources devoted to monitoring of restitution by VOM programs compared to that by probation departments was a primary factor. Second, while victims report meeting with and talking to offenders to be the most satisfying part of the mediation process, more research is needed on the extent to which satisfaction is diminished when reparative agreements are *not* fulfilled. That is, how important is the mediation process in producing victim satisfaction relative to the effect of the agreement being completed (see Schiff, this volume)? Issues that remain for further research on mediation include the actual *causes* of apparently greater restitution completion rates in VOM programs

Limitations on inferences that can be made from the otherwise strong body of mediation research are based on: (1) the inability to assess the strength and durability of positive outcomes over time due to the absence of longitudinal studies; the inability to rule out many threats to the validity of current findings, such as selection bias, in the absence of random assignment of cases into experimental and control groups (i.e., are participants who are predisposed to a restorative intervention self-selecting into the process?); and (3) a lack of information on which types of offenders or victims are most likely to experience the most positive outcomes as a result of mediation and the relationship between offense type and various impacts).

OPPORTUNITIES FACING THE FIELD: FROM THE MARGINS TO THE MAINSTREAM

With the increasing recognition of the value of VOM and restorative justice, the movement is faced with a number of important opportunities. In the 20-year history of VOM and reconciliation programs, there has never been a greater opportunity for significant impact on juvenile justice in the U.S. and certain parts of Europe. Although it is likely that smaller programs continue to exert minimal impact on local juvenile justice systems, other programs — including several in North America that receive nearly 1,000 or more referrals a year — are having an increasingly important influence. As more probation departments in the U.S. begin to sponsor VOM programs, and mainstream professional organizations such as the American Bar Association endorse the practice and recommend its use in all courts throughout the country, the VOM movement is likely to grow considerably. Recent changes in German law, which also allow for greater use of victim offender mediation, have resulted in a number of new programs, and related developments in other countries bode well for continued growth internationally.

However, despite its growth and increasing acceptance, the practice of mediating conflict between crime victims and their offenders as part of the larger vision of restorative justice continues to operate as a kind of side show to the main event of how justice is pursued in modern industrialized Western democracies. The basic principles of restorative justice require a fundamental shift in power related to who controls and "owns" crime in society — a shift from the state to the individual citizen and local communities. While restorative justice has significant popular appeal (Sessar, this volume; Pranis and Umbreit, 1992), the principles of retributive justice continue to drive juvenile and criminal justice systems. Moving the principles of restorative justice theory and the practice of VOM from the margins to the mainstream of how we do justice in our society represents a major opportunity, and presents several challenges.

The first challenge, as noted in the introduction to this chapter, is avoiding the threat to the integrity of the process itself. The second is overcoming the stereotypical view that mediation is only applicable to low-level cases that would otherwise never have entered the system, while providing wider public access to the VOM process. The third challenge is to confront media glorification of the current retributive justice process with successful examples of alternative responses based on restorative principles. The remainder of this paper focuses primarily on the first challenge. Challenges two and three are addressed briefly below.

Working with Severely Violent Cases

Many programs have worked with simple assault cases from their inception, even while focusing their main effort on nonviolent property crime. The small but growing trend to apply the VOM process in more serious, violent cases represents a major opportunity to expand the impact and credibility of restorative justice (Gustafson and Smidstra, 1989; Umbreit, 1989b). This trend has been brought about by requests from individuals victimized by such crimes as aggravated assault, armed robbery, sexual assault and attempted homicide. Mediation has also been requested by family members of homicide victims.

Mediation in cases of severely violent criminal behavior has a number of distinguishing characteristics, including: emotional intensity; an extreme need for a non-judgmental attitude; longer case preparation by mediator (8 to 12 months); multiple separate meetings prior to joint session; multiple phone conversations; negotiation with correctional officials to secure access to inmates and to conduct mediation in prison; coaching of participants in the communication of intense feelings; and boundary clarification (mediation versus therapy).

The field is only beginning to come to grips with how the basic mediation model must be adapted to serve the more intense needs of parties involved in serious and violent criminal conflict. Far more extensive advanced training of mediators is required, as is an entire new generation of written and audiovisual training resources. For example, mediators will need special knowledge and skills related to working with severely violent crimes, in addition to the normal mediation skills. From the *victim's* perspective, it will be important for the mediator to have the following: an understanding of the victimization experience/phases; knowledge of how to deal with grief and loss (our own and others); an understanding of post traumatic stress and its impact; and the ability to collaborate with psychotherapists. From the *offender's* perspective, mediators will need the following: an understanding of the criminal justice and corrections system; understanding of the offender and prisoner experience; the ability to relate to offenders convicted of heinous crimes in a non-judgmental manner; and the ability to negotiate with high-level correctional officials in order to gain access to the offender.

Most encouraging is the recognition by a growing number of representatives of major victim advocacy organizations in the U.S. of the value of mediation for those victims of violence who express a need for it (Lord, 1995). As they directly confront the very source of terror in their lives through mediation, some victims of violence are able to obtain a greater sense of healing and closure. The field of VOM is faced with an exciting opportunity to stretch its original vision, and significantly alter its original model to appropriately address the needs of parties affected by severely violent criminal conflict. This can only happen with: a serious commitment to reexamine the basic model and to understanding its limitations; an increased awareness of the victimization experience, including posttraumatic stress and grieving; and a willingness to apply tighter boundaries to when mediation is appropriate, what kind of advanced training is required, and who should serve as mediator(s). Far more extensive networking and coalition building with victim advocacy groups is also required.

Working with the Media

From the moment of birth, most of us are socialized in the belief that criminal conflict is, in the words of Christie (1981), the property of the state. We are, from a very early age through adulthood, bombarded with media images of cops and robbers. Many children's cartoons have themes of crime, violence and good conquering evil. Each year the prime-time television schedule includes police shows with intense action, adventure and violence. More recently, there has developed a series of television programs based on realistic recreations of actual crime incidents. These shows further project an adversarial perspective on crime and victimization, and reinforce commonly held stereotypes and images of criminals.

Restorative justice is based on very different principles than those that drive our current criminal justice systems. In fact, restorative justice values run counter to dominant legal culture, which rests upon the foundation of an adversarial process and the need for professional dispute resolvers (i.e., lawyers). In order for the VOM process to move beyond marginalization, it must become better-known and more accurately understood in the world of popular culture. The mass media in general, and television in particular, are critical to the development of such a strategy. Although care must be taken to avoid allowing the media to exploit victims and offenders — for example, by conducting live mediations on television entertainment shows in front of an audience — collaborating with credible television documentaries or newsmagazine shows that respect the needs of mediation participants, including the private filming of mediation sessions if the parties approve, can be an effective educational tool. Mediation programs must negotiate with the media so that their underlying interests and needs are met as much as possible. For example, programs must coach journalists in a clear and credible manner so that the message of the program comes across effectively to the general public, and programs must always assume an active rather than passive role in working with the media.

Increasing Access

While working with the media is a critical strategy in moving mediation beyond its current marginalization, other long-term policy initiatives and strategies that yield immediate short-term impact in expanding access also need to be considered. The most obvious need is to address the fact that many VOM programs receive only a small number of referrals. Even those programs that receive 300 to 500 cases or more per year often have a small impact on local juvenile justice systems, when compared to the total number of cases in that jurisdiction.

For the VOM process to be taken seriously, it must be able to demonstrate that it can work with a substantial volume and range of cases in a cost-effective manner through the use of trained community volunteers. Far more cases need to be referred to mediation as a true diversion from prosecution. In addition, more post-adjudication cases need to be referred as either a condition of probation or a sole sanction alternative to traditional probation supervision. In the short term, a presumptive referral-to-mediation strategy could be developed in most jurisdictions. Such a referral procedure would assume, for example, that all property offenses involving a restitution requirement would first be given the opportunity to participate in VOM, rather than selecting out only certain cases for referral.

Another short-term strategy already taking place in the U.S. is including mediation in victim rights legislation. Because such an approach tends to link mediation with only one side of the conflict, this strategy would not be preferable. While mediation is meant to serve both parties in a fair and impartial manner, promoting wider access in this manner would seem to be biased toward victims' concerns alone. Given the reality of criminal justice policy and public attitudes in most North American and European communities, however, no other strategy is more likely to greatly expand access to the mediation process for both crime victims and offenders. A recently passed victim bill of rights in Indiana became the first act of public policy to include these provisions. While strategies that lead to these short-run advancements must be weighed carefully against the aforementioned disadvantages, a more long-term alternative solution might ultimately involve systematic advocacy for mediation as a basic *right* of any crime victim in any community, conditioned upon the availability of a competent mediator, the willingness of the parties, the absence of any major mental health issues, and so on.

DISTURBING TRENDS AND POTENTIAL DANGERS: "FAST FOOD" MEDIATION

Thus far, I have discussed numerous challenges facing mediation advocates from juvenile justice systems and the larger societies themselves. As the field of VOM continues to develop in North America and Europe, it also faces a number of potential dangers from within. As the oldest and most widely implemented restorative justice practice, recent trends — as well as the course of the evolution of mediation in the near future — offer an important case study in threats to restorative justice and the ability of practice to overcome these threats.

Not unlike many other reform movements, the greatest threat to restorative justice is that of loss of vision. Programs developed to implement reforms often become preoccupied with securing more stable funding sources and developing more routine day-to-day operating procedures. As mediation professionals seek to collaborate with system professionals, it becomes easy to lose sight of the underlying values and principles that motivated the individuals who initiated the program, and that serve as the foundation for the program's existence. The importance of providing opportunities for addressing the emotional issues surrounding crime and victimization, including the possibility of genuine forgiveness and reconciliation for those interested, is a core principle of mediation. The data that have emerged from a growing number of studies continues to document high levels of victim and offender satisfaction with the mediation process and outcome. There is no evidence that large numbers of mediation programs have veered from this principle. However, a few developments suggest that maintaining the vision may require increasing diligence.

In some parts of the U.S. (and perhaps in other parts of the world), the term "victim-offender mediation" is used quite loosely to describe quickly arranged and executed negotiations between victims and offenders, often not face-to-face, held for the sole purpose of negotiating a restitution agreement to include in a diversion or dispositional order. A probation department in a large urban jurisdiction, for example, conducts its mediations in the probation officer's office, with no prior separate meeting with victim and offender. These sessions are said to be approximately 15-20 minutes in length, and focus exclusively on developing a restitution plan. Inadequate follow-up on cases and monitoring the offender's completion of restitution have also been common complaints heard from a number of victims in this and other similar programs.

In one mediation program, a victim reported feeling coerced to participate in the program, as if he or she had to do it in order to get restitution. Some victims in another mediation program reported feeling revictimized by the process, primarily because of the attitude of offenders and the inability of some mediators to effectively facilitate sessions. In yet another program in which offenders and their parents were required to participate in mediation, they were quite resistant and displayed a hostile attitude in the session, which predictably adversely affected the victim and his parent. Finally, perhaps the most disturbing story involves a program in which a mediator reportedly shouted at a victim, who later filed a complaint with the local victim services agency. While these are isolated anecdotal stories, a recent evaluation of a probation-based initiative found a lower level of victim satisfaction with the mediation process than previous studies, which have almost always found significantly higher victim satisfaction. The most distinguishing characteristic of this otherwise well-developed and thoughtful program is that offenders have no voluntary choice about participating in mediation.

Elimination of Separate Pre-Mediation Meetings

A small but growing trend among some VOM programs, that of bypassing individual meetings with victim and offender prior to the session, is disturbing to many restorative justice advocates. Although originally a major element of the initial VOM and reconciliation model (Zehr, 1980), a recent national survey conducted in the U.S. (Umbreit and Greenwood, 1997) found that 37% of programs do not require mediators to meet with the parties separately before the mediation session. Mediation by itself, with little preparation of the parties, is far less likely to tap into the major empirically validated restorative benefit of VOM, that of humanizing the process for both victim and offender so that they feel safe enough to engage in a genuine conversation or dialogue about what happened and how it affected each person.

Agreement-Driven Mediation

Another consequence of losing sight of the restorative vision could be a utilitarian and exclusive focus on restitution determination and payment. Allowing little time for the sharing of facts and feelings related to the crime, the mediation session could become "agreement driven," rather than "dialogue driven." While this is not to say that such mediation is of no value, healing and true peace making require more time and patience. The temptation to focus the mediation process primarily upon securing a mutually satisfactory restitution agreement is great, and it is understandable. As courts seek more options for handling cases in a more "efficient" manner, and mediation programs seek to justify their existence with large numbers of case referrals, program staff may be tempted to downplay the dialogue phase of the mediation encounter. If efficiency (rather than creating a safe place for the victim and offender to talk with each other about the full impact of the crime) becomes the primary value driving the program, it is quite possible that actual mediation sessions may be as short as 15-20 minutes. As noted earlier, a program in a large, urban jurisdiction in the U.S. that is operated by the probation department is known to conduct such "mediations" in little more than 20 minutes. Rather than facilitating a restorative process of dialogue, mutual aid and healing, the "mediator" in this "fast food version" of VOM is serving more as an arbitrator who directs the process toward an agreement, while the victim and offender have very little input. While reparative agreements nearly always occur in dialogue-driven mediation sessions, these agreements are secondary to the opportunity to first talk about what happened and how it affected the victim, the offender, and any support people or parents that are present. Many practitioners would even maintain that far more realistic and creative restitution agreements are likely to emerge following a dialogue about what actually happened and how people felt about the incident.

Taking Fewer Risks

As programs become preoccupied with acceptance into the mainstream of court services, there is often a tendency to take fewer risks, particularly related to the types of cases being referred to the program. In an eagerness to negotiate new referral arrangements, programs may be too quick to accept those cases that prosecutors' offices might refer due simply to lack of sufficient evidence for a court petition. The likelihood that mediation will be taken seriously is decreased if the process is identified with only the "easy" cases, those that the system would have otherwise dismissed.

Programs that place sole emphasis on the efficient negotiation of restitution agreements often are also likely to take few risks in regard to the type of cases they will handle. To effectively meet the needs of those most directly affected by the crime — the victim and offender — rather than system interests only, the key issue is one of balance between so-called easy cases and more serious cases (based upon the needs of victims). Programs must also strike a balance between facilitating a process of meaningful dialogue between the victim and offender and development of feasible restitution agreements as an outcome.

Lack of Victim Sensitivity and Involvement

Finally, as a growing number of probation departments in the U.S. and related agencies in other countries sponsor VOM programs, there is a clear danger that these historically offender-driven criminal justice agencies will lose sight of the central role of crime victims in any restorative process. A few probation-based programs in the U.S., for example, frequently ask probation officers to represent the views of victims rather than having the actual victim present. Such a practice is, at best, a weak alternative that undercuts the fundamental goal of giving the crime victim the opportunity to confront and enter into a dialogue with the person who violated them, including the development of a plan to compensate them for their losses. For offenders, hearing about the harm their crimes have caused from the mouth of a probation officer rather than actual victims may be expected to do little to reinforce accountability and empathy.

Another danger is that probation-based programs operating in isolation will be unlikely to develop the basic sensitivity in staff to effectively involve victims and address their needs. Victim service providers can help to remedy this and other program problems by providing training for mediators and other juvenile justice staff on the victimization experience and the range of needs victims face. Yet, a recent national survey of VOM programs in the U.S. (Umbreit and Greenwood, 1997) found that 61% of mediation programs do not take advantage of this resource and opportunity to increase staff sensitivity and effectiveness. From a broader restorative justice perspective, the concern for victim sensitivity should go far beyond just focusing upon mediators. Many would maintain that all correctional staff should receive victim awareness training in order to be far more prepared to understand the needs of crime victims and to invite their participation in the justice process (Bazemore, 1994).

GUIDELINES FOR RESTORATIVE VICTIM-OFFENDER MEDIATION AND DIALOGUE

No process or practice is perfect in real-world application. Indeed, if the standard of comparison is the current court and probation system, even agreement-driven mediation that results in reparation for victims and some degree of accountability for offenders is a superior alternative to current court processes in which even a mention of the victim is unlikely and restitution is a rare occurrence. Moreover, as long as the process is as sensitive as possible to victim needs, mediation — even with the absence of pre-mediation meetings — may be preferable to no victim-offender meeting at all. Indeed, as Table 3 suggests, restorative justice principles as applied to VOM may be viewed for practical purposes along a continuum.

In order to maximize the likelihood that VOM will be carried out according to truly restorative principles, and will avoid becoming another impersonal and mechanistic social service, the following guidelines for practice are offered:

(1) The mediation process and the training of mediators should be clearly and explicitly grounded in restorative justice values.

(2) If public agencies such as police or probation are initiating VOM programs, trained community volunteers should serve as the mediators or co-mediators. This insures active citizen and community involvement in the program and the larger justice system, and will also result in a far more cost-effective program.

(3) If a local victim services agency exists in the community, a new VOM program should be developed as a collaborative effort, including the use

of victim services staff as trainers to present a section on the victimization experience and the needs of crime victims.

(4) Victim-offender mediators should be trained in a humanistic/transformative model of mediation (Umbreit, 1997) that emphasizes a non-directive style of mediation, with the focus on facilitating a genuine dialogue between the parties rather than the more common highly directive and settlement-driven style of mediation used in civil courts and certain other areas of mediation.

(5) Mediators should be trained in understanding the experience and needs of crime victims and offenders.

(6) The VOM process should be conducted in the most victim-sensitive manner possible, including providing victims with a choice of when and where to meet, and allowing them to present their story first if they so desire. In approaching victims to consider the process, they should be informed of both the potential benefits and risks, and should not be pressured into a mediation session.

(7) In-person preparation of the primary participants in a mediation session (victim, victim's immediate family, offender, offender's immediate family) should occur in order to connect with the parties, build rapport and trust, provide information, encourage participation, and — should they chose to participate — prepare them for the mediation session so that they will feel safe enough to participate in a genuine dialogue with each other, with the mediator being as non-directive as possible.

(8) Mediators should be trained in cultural and ethical issues that are likely to affect the mediation process and participants.

CONCLUDING REMARKS

In addition to the aforementioned opportunities facing the field of VOM, several others also exist as mediation moves from the margins to the mainstream of juvenile justice practice. With its many years of experience, the field can now take the lead in: developing standards of practice grounded in restorative justice principles; developing new mechanisms for strengthening quality control in the field; greater networking among victim services and other justice system/correctional colleagues in North America and Europe; initiating longitudinal studies to assess the long-term impact of mediation upon victims, communities, and offenders; and conducting cross-national studies to gain a greater understanding of the development of the VOM process in differing national and cultural contexts.

Table 3: Victim Offender Mediation Continuum: From Least to Most Restorative Impact

LEAST RESTORATIVE IMPACT *Agreement-Driven: Offender Focus*	MOST RESTORATIVE IMPACT *Dialogue-Driven: Victim Sensitive*
• Entire focus is upon determining the amount of financial restitution to be paid, with no opportunity to talk directly about the full impact of the crime upon the victim and the community, as well as the offender	• Primary focus is upon providing an opportunity for victims and offenders to directly talk to each other, to allow victims to express the full impact of the crime upon their life and to receive answers to important questions they have, to allow offenders to learn the real human impact of their behavior and take direct responsibility for making things right • Restitution is important, but secondary to talking about the impact of the crime
• No separate preparation meetings with the victim and offender prior to bringing the parties together	• Separate preparation meetings with the victim and offender prior to bringing them together, with emphasis upon *listening* to how the crime has affected them, *identifying* their needs and *preparing* them for the mediation or conference session
• Victims not given choice of where they would feel the most comfortable and safe to meet, or whom they would like to be present • Victims given only written notice to appear for mediation session at pre-set time, with no preparation	• Victims are continually given choices throughout the process: where to meet, who they would like to be present, etc.
• Mediator or facilitator describes the offense and offender then speaks, with the victim simply asking a few questions or simply responding to questions of the mediator • Highly directive style of mediation or facilitation, with the mediator talking most of the time, continually asking both the victim and offender questions, but with little if any direct dialogue between the involved parties • Low tolerance of moments of silence or expression of feelings	• Non-directive style of mediation or facilitation with mediator not talking most of the time, high tolerance of silence, and use of a humanistic or transformative mediation model • Trained community volunteers serve as mediators or co-mediators, along with agency staff • High tolerance for expression of feelings and full impact of crime
• Voluntary for victim but required of offender whether or not they even take responsibility	• Voluntary for victim and offender
• Settlement driven and very brief (10-15 minutes)	• Dialogue driven and typically about an hour (or longer) in length

By viewing certain types of criminal behavior as conflicts between individuals within community settings, rather than exclusively focusing upon state interests, the VOM movement in North America and Europe represents a challenging new vision of how communities can understand and respond to crime and victimization. Such a strong emphasis upon restoration and healing rather than retribution and revenge may seem too radical for some. However, the vision of restorative justice — particularly as applied through the practice of VOM — is not a radical new concept. Rather, this vision of doing justice in contemporary society is deeply rooted in many of the religious and secular traditions that are part of our collective heritage, and is deeply rooted in the traditional practices of many indigenous peoples throughout the world, such as Native American, Pacific Island, Maori in New Zealand, and First Nations in Canada. Throughout the centuries, these traditions have emphasized the importance of viewing criminal behavior as conflict between individuals within the context of community, while stressing the values of direct accountability, restoration of losses, and even reconciliation or forgiveness whenever this can occur in a genuine manner. Connecting with these roots, and remaining true to the principles inherent in the restorative justice vision, provides the greatest hope that mediation can overcome the threats of both marginalization and McDonaldization.

REFERENCES

Bazemore, G. (1994). "Developing A Victim Orientation for Community Corrections: A Restorative Justice Paradigm and a Balanced Mission." *APPA Perspectives* 18(3):19-24.

—— (1997). "The 'Community' in Community Justice: Issues, Themes and Questions for the New Neighborhood Sanctioning Models." *Justice System Journal* 19(2):193-228.

—— and D. Maloney (1994). "Rehabilitating Community Service: Toward Restorative Service in a Balanced Justice System." *Federal Probation* 58(1):24-34.

—— and M.S. Umbreit (1995). "Rethinking the Sanctioning Function in Juvenile Court: Retributive or Restorative Responses to Youth Crime." *Crime & Delinquency* 41(3):296-316.

Christie, N. (1981). *Limits to Pain*. New York, NY: Columbia University Press.

Coates, R.B. and J. Gehm (1989). "An Empirical Assessment." In: M. Wright and B. Galaway (eds.), *Mediation and Criminal Justice*. London, UK: Sage.

Dignan, J. (1990). *Repairing the Damage*. Sheffield, UK: Centre for Criminological and Legal Research, University of Sheffield.

Galaway, B. (1988). "Crime Victim and Offender Mediation as a Social Work Strategy." *Social Service Review* 62:668-683.

—— (1989). "Informal Justice: Mediation Between Offenders and Victims." In: P.A. Albrecht and O. Backes (eds.), *Crime Prevention and Intervention: Legal and Ethical Problems*. Berlin, GER: Walter de Gruyter.

—— and J. Hudson (1990). *Criminal Justice, Restitution, and Reconciliation*. Monsey, NY: Criminal Justice Press.

Gehm, J. (1990). "Mediated Victim-Offender Restitution Agreements: An Exploratory Analysis of Factors Related to Victim Participation." In: B. Galaway and J. Hudson (eds.), *Criminal Justice, Restitution and Reconciliation*. Monsey, NY: Criminal Justice Press.

Gustafson, D.L. and H. Smidstra (1989). *Victim Offender Reconciliation in Serious Crime: A Report on the Feasibility Study Undertaken for The Ministry of the Solicitor General (Canada)*. Langley, CAN: Fraser Region Community Justice Initiatives Association.

Marshall, T.F. and S. Merry (1990). *Crime and Accountability*. London, UK: Home Office.

Maxwell, G. and A. Morris (1994). "The New Zealand Model of Family Group Conferences." In: C. Alder and J. Wundersitz (eds.), *Family Conferencing and Juvenile Justice: The Way Forward to Misplaced Optimism?* Canberra, AUS: Australian Institute of Criminology.

Pranis K. and M. Umbreit (1992). *Public Opinion Research Challenges Perception of Widespread Public Demand for Harsher Punishment*. Minneapolis, MN: Citizens Council.

Umbreit, M.S. (1985). *Crime and Reconciliation: Creative Options for Victims and Offenders*. Nashville, TN: Abingdon Press.

—— (1986a). "Victim Offender Mediation: A National Survey." *Federal Probation* (Dec.) 50(4):53-56.

—— (1986b). "Victim Offender Mediation and Judicial Leadership." *Judicature* (Dec.) 69:202-204.

—— (1988). "Mediation of Victim Offender Conflict." *Journal of Dispute Resolution* 31:85-105.

—— (1989a). "Victims Seeking Fairness, Not Revenge: Toward Restorative Justice." *Federal Probation* (Sept.) 53(3):52-57.

—— (1989b). "Violent Offenders and Their Victims." In: M. Wright and B. Galaway (eds.), *Mediation and Criminal Justice*. London, UK: SAGE.

—— (1991a). "Minnesota Mediation Center Gets Positive Results." *Corrections Today* (Aug):194-197.

—— (1991b). "Mediation of Youth Conflict: A Multi-System Perspective." *Child and Adolescent Social Work.* 8(2):141-153.

—— (1993a). "Crime Victims and Offenders in Mediation: An Emerging Area of Social Work Practice." *Social Work* 38(1):69-73.

—— (1993b). "Juvenile Offenders Meet Their Victims: The Impact of Mediation in Albuquerque, New Mexico." *Family and Conciliation Courts Review* 31(1):90-100.

—— (1994a). *Victim Meets Offender: The Impact of Restorative Justice and Mediation.* Monsey, NY: Criminal Justice Press.

—— (1994b). "Crime Victims Confront Their Offenders: The Impact of a Minneapolis Mediation Program." *Journal of Research on Social Work Practice* 4(4):436-447.

—— (1995a). *Mediation of Criminal Conflict: An Assessment of Programs in Four Canadian Provinces.* St. Paul, MN: Center for Restorative Justice and Mediation, University of Minnesota.

—— (1995b). "The Development and Impact of Victim-Offender Mediation in the United States." *Mediation Quarterly* 12(3):263-276.

—— (1995c). *Mediating Interpersonal Conflicts: A Pathway to Peace.* West Concord, MN: CPI Publishing.

—— (1996). "Restorative Justice Through Mediation: The Impact of Offenders Facing Their Victims in Oakland." *Law and Social Work* 5(1):1-13.

—— (1997). "Humanistic Mediation: A Transformative Journal of Peacemaking." *Mediation Quarterly* 14(3):201-213.

—— and R.B. Coates (1992). "The Impact of Mediating Victim Offender Conflict: An Analysis of Programs in Three States." *Juvenile & Family Court Journal* 43(1):21-28.

—— and R.B. Coates (1993). "Cross-Site Analysis of Victim Offender Mediation in Four States." *Crime & Delinquency* 39(4):565-585.

—— R. Coates and A.W. Roberts (1997). "Cross-National Impact of Restorative Justice Through Mediation and Dialogue." *ICCA Journal on Community Corrections* 8(2):46-50.

—— and G. Greenwood (1997). *National Survey of Victim Offender Mediation Programs in the United States.* St. Paul, MN: Center for Restorative Justice and Mediation, University of Minnesota.

—— and M. Neimeyer (1996). "Victim Offender Mediation: From the Margins Toward the Mainstream." *Perspectives* 20(1):28-30.

Wright, M. (1996). *Justice for Victims and Offenders.* Philadelphia, PA: Open University Press.

—— and B. Galaway (1989). *Mediation and Criminal Justice.* London, UK: Sage.

Young, M. (1995). *Restorative Community Justice Monograph; A Call to Action.* Washington, DC: National Organization for Victim Assistance.

Zehr, H. (1980). *Mediating the Victim-Offender Conflict.* Akron, PA: Mennonite Central Committee.

—— (1990). *Changing Lenses, A New Focus for Crime and Justice.* Scottsdale, PA: Herald Press.

PART THREE:
IMPLEMENTATION ISSUES

9. Implementing Restorative Youth Justice: A Case Study in Community Justice and the Dynamics of Reform

by

Curt Taylor Griffiths

and

Ray Corrado

INTRODUCTION

Among the nations of the world, Canada has long assumed a lead role in the development and implementation of alternative justice policies and programs, including a number of innovative initiatives that place Canadian communities and jurisdictions at the forefront of the community and restorative justice movement (Church Council on Justice and Corrections, 1996). For example, the first modern-day victim-offender reconciliation project was established in Elmira, Ontario in 1974, and, since that time, numerous jurisdictions worldwide have adopted and expanded on this practice. As of 1996, while there were 26 victim-offender mediation programs operating across Canada, there were nearly 300 in Germany and 130 in Finland.

More recently, Aboriginal peoples and communities have served as the catalysts for the development of a wide range of innovative, community-based restorative justice practices, including circle sentencing, originally developed in Yukon (Stuart, 1996); the community holistic healing program on Hollow Water First Nation, Manitoba (Lajeunesse and Associates, 1996); the community-based sex offender treatment program at Canim Lake, British Columbia (Griffiths, 1996); and youth justice committees in many jurisdictions.

Despite widespread public concern with what are perceived to be increasing rates of serious youth crime, and a number of legislative initiatives that reflect a hardening in the response to young offenders, there is among both Aboriginal and non-Aboriginal communities a growing interest and involvement in the development of community-based, restorative justice programs.

In the following discussion, we consider the trends and issues that surround restorative youth justice in Canada, considering these topics against the larger political/legislative backdrop as well as within the community context in which restorative justice initiatives are being undertaken. The discussion will consider the potential as well as the limitations of restorative justice practices for young offenders, while at the same time identifying critical issues that must be addressed if such strategies are going to become more effective than traditional alternatives to criminal justice practice, such as diversion.. The potential for substantial community involvement in the disposition and sanctioning of young offenders will also be examined.

A fundamental premise of this paper is that, despite political and legislative obstacles, the unique demographic, cultural, and jurisdictional attributes of Canada provide the framework within which there is unlimited potential for the development of restorative justice initiatives for young offenders. These initiatives have the potential to more effectively address the needs of victims, offenders, and the community, while at the same time assisting to mitigate the escalating costs of youth justice. Nevertheless, there are a number of potential obstacles to the development and expansion of community-based restorative justice initiatives. Among these are legislative and political control by justice authorities, which may function to hinder and/or discourage innovative community practices; the lack of a developed evaluative framework within which to assess the efficacy of restorative justice practices; and a myriad of issues related to the role and impact of community dynamics on restorative justice initiatives.

THE LEGISLATIVE, POLICY AND PUBLIC CONTEXTS OF CANADIAN YOUTH JUSTICE

Within the context of a cross-national consideration of restorative youth justice, it is useful to consider key elements of Canadian youth justice policy and practice and the political environment that currently exists in the country. These present serious, but not insurmountable, challenges for restorative youth justice, if restorative practices are going to involve communities as partners in the design and delivery of programs and services.

At the political and senior policy levels in Canada, debate and discussion about youth justice practice and the response to young offenders has centered almost exclusively on the Young Offenders Act (YOA). A federal law, the YOA, was passed in 1984 and represented a sharp departure from the traditional, "social welfare" approach to youth crime and young offenders under the Juvenile Delinquent's Act that it replaced. Under the YOA, youth were to be held more accountable for their behavior, while being provided with legal rights similar to those of adult accused. In addition to the philosophical changes, the YOA standardized the ages of young offenders in all jurisdictions, from 12 to 17 inclusive;

set out criteria and procedures for diversion from youth court; mandated the increased involvement of legal counsel; permitted the youth court to impose only determinate sanctions; and eliminated status offenses.

An additional provision of the YOA involves alternative measures (AM) programs that allow the young offender to avoid the formal youth court process, while facilitating victim-offender reconciliation and/or the payment of compensation through performance of general community service or specific tasks for the victim. However, in Canada the establishment of systems for the administration of justice, including youth courts and programs and services for young offenders, are the exclusive responsibility of the provincial and territorial governments, and there is considerable variation across the country in terms of the specific programs and services that are available. A review of AM (Griffiths and Verdun-Jones, 1994) has revealed numerous difficulties that have seriously undermined their potential efficacy. These include a lack of community awareness of and involvement in AM programs, organizational problems, the tendency of AM programs to "widen the net," and the lack of evaluative research on the efficacy of these initiatives.

The extent to which the YOA could serve as a catalyst and framework for the development of restorative justice initiatives has been seriously compromised by the continuing controversy that has surrounded the legislation since its enactment in 1984. Dominating the debate at the political and policy levels is the issue as to whether the apparent increase in violent youth crime since 1986 can be attributed to problems with the YOA. Crime control-oriented citizen and criminal justice professional interest groups have been adamant in asserting that this law protects the rights of youth criminals to such an excess, and that sentencing is so lenient that the public is left unprotected from these violent predators. There have been several crime control-oriented reforms of the YOA that, while preserving its essential philosophy, make it easier to transfer violent young offenders to adult criminal court and to impose longer sentences of incarceration for those disposed of by the youth court. As part of the continuing dialogue about youth crime and young offenders, two task forces — one involving federal, provincial and territorial youth justice officials, and the other consisting of a federal parliamentary committee — have recently completed an extensive review of the YOA and youth justice.

Illustrative of the controversies that continue to surround the provisions for responding to youth crime is the debate over violent youth crime and the role of the YOA as a contributor to what many perceive to be an increase in the rates and severity of youth crime. This debate has consumed a disproportionate amount of the attention and resources of federal and provincial/territorial officials, while at the same time hindering dialogue on the potential use of restorative justice strategies in responding to young offenders.

The Controversy Over Trends in Youth Violence

There has been a continuing debate among research scholars, senior government officials and criminal justice interest groups as to whether violent youth crime has increased over the past decade. This debate, while important, has consumed an inordinate amount of attention and continues to be a major distraction and obstacle to creating a dialogue on the potential for restorative justice strategies for young offenders. On one side are research scholars (Carrington and Moyer, 1994) and officials from federal agencies responsible for youth justice policy and statistics, such as the Ministry of Justice and the Centre for Criminal Justice Statistics, who have argued forcefully that the public is being misled by media distortions of the extent and threat of youth violence. In contrast, scholars such as Corrado and Markwart (1994) have maintained that youth violence, as measured by police charges, has increased substantially between 1986 and 1992 (see Table 1) . More recent data from the Province of British Columbia reveals that the rate continued to increase. In contrast, youth murder rates have remained stable (see Table 2). Nonetheless, public perceptions of youth murders and youth crime, in general, are that they have risen dramatically (Roberts, 1994).

By 1993, youth violence and the YOA had become a major political issue, and, for the first time in Canadian politics, youth justice played a critical role in a federal election. While all of the national political parties included proposals to reform the YOA in their electoral platforms, the newly emergent, populist Reform Party made it a prominent issue, arguing for measures that would facilitate the incarceration of violent and repeat young offenders. Among the fundamental changes to the YOA proposed by the Reform Party were a lowering of the minimum age for criminal responsibility to at least 10, and lowering the age limit of the jurisdiction of the youth court from 17 to 16. Reform Party candidates vehemently criticized the underlying philosophy of the YOA that, the party alleged, diminished the responsibility of young offenders for their behavior and allowed youths to hide behind procedural protections. The election result confirmed public anger about young offenders. The Reform Party won an unprecedented number of federal parliamentary seats, primarily from the western provinces where resentment toward the YOA was most intense. The Liberal Party, which won a landslide victory, began the reform of the YOA in earnest and implemented a number of crime control reforms.

The minister of justice responsible for the legislative reform endorsed the need for reform; however, he strongly opposed any fundamental philosophical changes to the YOA, arguing that rehabilitation, rather than incarceration, was the most effective way to stop recidivism and protect the public. The minister maintained that the YOA correctly attempted to balance the protection of the public with both the Charter of Rights and Freedoms protection against abuse of procedure and the special needs of young offenders.

Bill C-37, which became law in 1996, contained provisions to facilitate the transfer of those youths charged with violent offences to youth court and extended the maximum periods of confinement for young offenders convicted of murder. However, the bill also reiterated the need to both divert young offenders charged with less serious offenses and emphasize the importance of developing community-based rehabilitation programs to meet the special needs of young offenders. The justice minister refused to diminish any of the special "rights" youths have under the YOA.

The Modified Justice Model Young Offenders Act and Restorative Justice

The Declaration of Principle (s.3) in the YOA, as amended by Bill C-37, has generated considerable controversy, especially among academics, politicians, senior bureaucrats and interest groups representing professional criminal justice organizations and the helping professions. The essence of the conflict is that this declaration contains ten principles representing virtually all the models of youth justice and their underlying theories /of the causes of youth crime. This, it is argued, makes the philosophy of the YOA hopelessly complex. Crime prevention is the first principle; however, it was only with Bill C-37 amendment to s.3 in 1996 that "multi-disciplinary" rehabilitation approaches appeared to be given priority over "accountability" and "crime protection" approaches. These principles are seen to require supervision, discipline and control; however, they are to be tempered by the "special needs" determined by a youth's "state of dependency and level of development and maturity." Protection of society is explicitly identified in the declaration as "best served by rehabilitation." For restorative justice, the key principle is s.3(d): "...where it is not inconsistent with the protection of society, taking no measures or taking measures other than judicial proceedings under this *Act* should be considered for dealing with young persons who have committed offences."

A potential obstacle to the use of restorative justice approaches, however, is s.3(e) which provides young persons with all the Charter of Rights and Freedom and Canadian Bill of Rights, as well as special due process, protections and guarantees. S.3(f), as well, stipulates the "right to the least possible interference with freedom that is consistent with the protection of society."

Several issues, therefore, remain unresolved regarding restorative justice initiatives. First, does the absence of access to such initiatives in one province or smaller geographic jurisdiction constitute a violation of young person's right to equal treatment anywhere in Canada? Second, even though young persons

Table 1: Young Persons Charged with Crimes against Persons (Violence) Canada, 1986 to 1992

	1986	1987	1988	1989	1990	1991	1992	% Change 1986-92	
								Volume	Rate
Homicide*	38	35	48	48	49	42	53	N/A†	N/A
Attempted murder	63	58	62	66	61	67	78	N/A	N/A
Aggravated sexual assault‡	76	69	72	54	60	89	84	N/A	N/A
Sexual assault	983	1,151	1,175	1,425	1,548	1,812	1,988	+102%	+103%
Assault causing harm§	2,281	2,333	2,625	3,056	3,526	4,194	4,316	+ 89%	+ 90%
Assault — level 1	3,999	4,734	5,294	6,504	7,592	8,917	9,622	+141%	+142%
Robbery — firearms	155	140	174	239	311	459	562	+263%	+267%
Robbery — other weapons	458	404	519	586	572	746	1,007	+120%	+103%
Other robbery	690	660	851	1,127	1,179	1,487	1,397	+102%	+103%
Other violence**	532	581	617	681	795	956	926	+ 74%	+ 75%
TOTAL	9,275	10,165	11,437	13,786	15,693	18,769	20,033	+116%	+117%
Per capita rate††	41.5	45.8	52.0	63.3	72.0	85.5	90.0		

* Homicide includes first and second degree murder, manslaughter and infanticide.
† "N.A." means "not applicable" and refers to those categories where the volumes are so small that percentage changes are easily skewed by small changes in volume from year to year.
‡ Aggravated sexual assaults also include sexual assaults with a weapon.
§ Assaults causing harm include aggravated assault, assault causing bodily harm, assault with a weapon, and unlawfully causing bodily harm.
** Other violence includes assaults on peace officers, abduction, discharge of a firearm with intent, other assaults, and other sexual offenses.
†† Per capita rates are based on the number of 12 to 17 year olds and are calculated per 10,000.
Source: Victoria, BC: Ministry of the Attorney General of British Columbia.

Table 2: Per Capita Rates Of Young Persons Charged With Serious Violent And Weapons Offenses, British Columbia, 1986-94

	Homicide and Attempted Murder	Assaults Causing Harm	Robbery With a Weapon	Offensive Weapons	TOTAL
1986	0.3	11.7	2.5	5.5	20.0
1987	0.4	11.1	1.6	6.5	19.5
1988	0.6	12.5	2.8	6.7	22.6
1989	0.4	14.5	4.1	8.2	27.2
1990	0.8	16.9	4.6	9.4	31.5
1991	0.5	19.3	5.9	9.3	35.0
1992	0.3	19.8	6.0	8.3	34.3
1993	0.6	23.7	8.1	10.6	42.9
1994	0.8	22.6	8.1	11.1	42.6
% Change 1986-94	—	+93%	+224%	+103%	+113%

Definitions appended.

choose to participate in restorative justice programs are there sufficient procedural safeguards to avoid net-widening or violating the "least interference" principle. A related issue involves the right to counsel: what role will lawyers have in ensuring that young persons are appropriately informed and fully volunteer to participate in non-judicial proceedings? Third, the principle of accountability is usually defined by the public, especially crime control oriented-interest groups, in terms of punitive sentencing. Will restorative justice programs be limited by political and media pressure to minor property offenders?

Since the amendments to the YOA contained in Bill C-37 are too recent for there to have been case law interpretations that might begin to answer these and other questions, the amendments themselves distinctly favor restorative justice initiatives despite the far more punitive sentences for serious violent offenders. As described above, rehabilitation rather than punishment is explicitly identified as the most desired approach to crime prevention. And, in the *R. v. T.* (V) (1992) and *R. v. M* (J.J.) (1993) cases, the Supreme Court of Canada affirmed that the Declaration of Principles should be considered a substantive provision rather than a mere preamble. In effect, the underlying philosophy of restorative justice programs is consistent with not only the least-interference principle but also the rehabilitative principle. It is likely, therefore, that due process issues will not be a major obstacle.

In considering the potential for restorative justice approaches within the provincial and territorial youth justice systems in Canada, it could be argued that restorative justice can be incorporated to only a limited degree. Public concern and furor about violent and/or youth career criminals, the recent crime control reforms to the YOA, the Charter of Rights principle of equal treatment, the YOA emphasis on due process, the adversarial role of defense counsel, and, most importantly, the traditional dominant role of federal and provincial officials in controlling reform initiatives may all function to limit the scope of restorative justice initiatives.

In spite of the distractions presented by the enduring — and seemingly endless — debate over the impact of the YOA on patterns of youth crime in Canada, the federal and provincial/territorial governments have given increased attention to restorative justice, albeit, as our discussion later in this paper will reveal, without a clear understanding of the parameters and diversity of this concept. However, it is unclear, as to how — from the perspective of senior policy makers — the philosophy, principles, and practice of restorative justice will "fit" within the modified justice model reflected in the YOA. This model emphasizes the key principles of the justice model such as due process, responsibility for criminal behavior, and proportionality between current offense seriousness and the severity of sentencing. At the same time, key welfare model principles, such as addressing the special needs of young persons in terms of family problems, education, jobs, and peers, are considered essential in sentencing principles.

Crime control and corporatist models also are incorporated into the philosophy of the YOA and its substantive sections. These principles will be discussed further since they are critical in assessing how restorative justice principles can be incorporated into a modified justice model youth justice system (see Corrado, 1992).

The Federal-Provincial-Territorial Task Force on Youth Justice

The recent report of the Federal-Provincial-Territorial Task Force on Youth Justice (1996) entitled *A Review Of The Young Offenders Act and the Youth Justice System in Canada*, contains an extensive discussion of restorative justice and advocates the increased use of restorative justice practices in the youth justice process.

For restorative justice to make a more immediate and substantial impact on youth justice systems in Canada would require that its principles be included in the YOA s.(3) Declaration of Principle. This inclusion would mean that a consensus had been achieved between the federal and provincial/territorial levels of government, levels of government whose relationships and ability to collaborate on justice initiatives are often clouded by divergent ideologies and political agendas, complex constitutional issues, and disagreements over jurisdictional and fiscal responsibilities.

Given the jurisdictional spheres of the federal government (sole jurisdiction regarding the criminal law) and the provincial/territorial governments (sole jurisdiction regarding the administration of youth justice and related areas such as education, social services, and mental health), it is virtually politically impossible to make changes in the national law governing youth justice without reaching some form of consensus with the provinces. Further compounding and confusing the issue is the fact that the federal government has traditionally contributed to the funding for the administration of justice.

There appears to be an emerging consensus regarding the incorporation of several restorative justice principles to promote the integration and coordination of services to young offenders through various forms of "conferencing." While the YOA Declaration of Principle (s.3) identifies the need to meet the "special needs" of young persons, including "guidance and assistance," this law does not provide for any legislative mechanisms or processes to facilitate an integrated or even coordinated approach for meeting the multiple needs of young offenders. Regarding this situation the Federal-Provincial-Territorial Task Force on Youth Justice (1996) stated that:

> Unfortunately, the youth justice system functions in a way that monopolizes society's response to the young person. Processing through the system and the disposition tend to take priority over all other services and

interventions for the youth. Indeed, it is reported that in some jurisdictions, child welfare agencies close their file as soon as a young person is charged under the [YOA] *Act* [p.45]

The Task Force report reviewed favorably New Zealand's Family Group Conferencing model, yet it understandably did not endorse it for Canada since this would require the radical step of repeating the YOA. Instead the Task Force recommended a flexible and voluntary approach that would allow each province — and within each province, each jurisdiction — to implement its own version of conferencing on a case-by-case basis.

The task force avoided addressing the role of conferencing for serious violent offenders or those youths with extensive prior records. This despite the fact, as will be discussed below, that young offenders with extensive prior records in at least one jurisdiction are already being processed using a restorative justice approach. Nonetheless, there was consensus that restorative justice approaches should be included explicitly in the reform of the YOA, and in the provincial and territorial youth justice laws and systems. In fact, in several provinces, restorative justice initiatives have already been introduced, suggesting that local communities and justice personnel are far ahead of the policy makers and politicians in the restorative justice realm.

THE COMMUNITY CONTEXT OF RESTORATIVE YOUTH JUSTICE

As significant as any discussion of the political, legislative and public contexts of restorative youth justice is the community context. For it is at the individual community level that restorative justice can have its more significant impact. Across Canada, a myriad of restorative justice initiatives have emerged over the past decade, a movement led in large measure by Aboriginal peoples.

In recent years, Aboriginal communities in Canada have become increasingly involved in developing community-based justice services and programs that are designed to better address the specific needs of community residents, victims and offenders (Griffiths and Hamilton, 1996). This has included a number of initiatives, many undertaken in collaboration with criminal justice personnel and premised on restorative justice.

These developments are occurring against a larger political backdrop of the constitutional recognition of an inherent right of Aboriginal self-government, the assertion of control by Aboriginal peoples over all aspects of community life, and the revitalization of Aboriginal communities and cultures. Community-based restorative justice initiatives have generally been developed within the larger context of the devolution of justice services to Aboriginal communities, and the creation of community-based justice services and programs.

The impetus for the development of restorative programs for youths has been provided by the high rates of Aboriginal youth conflict with the law. Figures from the province of Alberta (Cawsey, 1991), for example, indicate that: there has been a significant increase in the number of Aboriginal youths in that province charged with offenses; Aboriginal young offenders are less likely to be referred to AM programs; all things being equal, they are more likely to receive a disposition of confinement than their non-Aboriginal counterparts; and they spend longer periods of time in custody than non-Aboriginal youths for the same offenses. Similar findings emerged in the report of the Saskatchewan Indian Justice Review Committee (Linn, 1992) which found that Aboriginal youths represented 45% of all young offenders receiving some form of disposition under the YOA; 72% of those in custody programs; 42% of those in community programs such as probation, community service and restitution; and 29% of the offenders who were assigned to an AM program. These findings led the review committee (Linn, 1992) to recommend the development of specialized programs and services for Aboriginal youths, including holistic programs in Aboriginal communities.

Similar findings were reported by Fortugno and Rogstad (1994), who found that in comparison to their non-Aboriginal counterparts, Aboriginal youths entered the justice system at an earlier age; had a rate of appearances in youth court on bench warrants three times that of non-Aboriginal youths; had twice the rate of remand into custody; entered guilty pleas at a rate four times that of non-Aboriginal youths; and, all other factors being equal, were more likely to receive custodial sentences. Remarkably, while only 8.2% of the city's population is Aboriginal, 65% of the female youths appearing in court were Aboriginal.

Aboriginal politicians and community leaders have also expressed concerns about the use of the YOA to respond to Aboriginal youths in conflict with the law, and have argued that the YOA's emphasis on procedural formalities may actually hinder the development of more informal, community-based programs to address the needs of youths. In particular, concerns have been voiced by Aboriginal and Inuit communities situated in rural and remote areas of the country that the procedures required by the YOA are such than many months may elapse between the time an offense is alleged to have occurred and the court appearance. As a recent report (Coutu, 1995:71) on Aboriginal justice in the province of Quebec concluded: "Sometimes, the delays are so long that the young offender has difficulty remembering exactly the offence he has committed. Of course, after six months, it is too late for the decision of the court to be really meaningful for the youth."

Perhaps the most significant attribute of these initiatives is that they have been developed at the community level, rather than as a result of the imposition of a "generic" model of restorative justice. Restorative justice strategies and programs have not developed within a pre;-established, governmental policy framework, but within a community framework, albeit most often in collaboration with provincial and territorial justice systems and personnel. This approach represents a sharp departure from the process by which restorative justice programs have traditionally been designed and developed. And there is evidence that even models of community decision making such as family group conferencing, are being tailored and adapted to the needs of specific communities. Perhaps nowhere else in the world has there been the creation of such a wide range of community-based justice programs than there has in Canada. A distinctive attribute of these initiatives is that they have often been developed as part of a process of cultural and community revitalization, and of the increasing movement of Aboriginal peoples and communities to reassert their authority over all facets of community life. This fact alone makes the development of restorative justice generally, and restorative youth justice in particular, in Canada unique among the world's nations.

Illustrative of the range of restorative justice programs that have emerged across Canada over the past decade, and that have been designed for either youths in conflict or both adult and young offenders are the following:

Circle Sentencing

This concept was originally developed in several Yukon territories as a collaborative initiative between several communities and territorial justice personnel. It is premised on traditional Aboriginal healing practices and has multi-faceted objectives, including addressing the needs of communities, the families of victims, and offenders through a process of reconciliation, restitution, and reparation. The majority of offenders who have had their cases disposed of through sentencing circles have been adults; however, an increasing number of cases involving young offenders have been handled as well. Circle sentencing has spawned a number of variations, including community sentence advisory committees, sentencing panels, and community mediation panels.

Community Sentencing Panels and Youth Justice Committees

These alternatives have been developed across the country in both Aboriginal and non-Aboriginal communities. The committees are generally staffed by citizen volunteers, including elders in Aboriginal communities. The committees employ a variety of restorative measures, including mediation, restitution, and reparation. This approach is illustrated in the operation of the Fort Chipewyan (Alberta) Youth Justice Committee, a post-charge committee comprised of community members. Power has been devolved to the committee by the circuit court judge, and the committee considers the behavior of Aboriginal and non-

Aboriginal youth in a holistic context. Another program example is the Teslin Tribal Justice Project, in which elders from each of the five clans of the Teslin Tlingit Band comprise a sentencing advisory committee that advises the territorial court judges on dispositions for offenders from the community. Recommendations are made within a holistic healing framework that addresses the total circumstance of the offender (Church Council on Justice and Corrections, 1996:75-78).

Aboriginal Youth Courts

The first of its kind in Canada, the St. Theresa Point (Manitoba) Youth Court developed out of a community justice committee. The court operates under the auspices of the provincial court and exercises jurisdiction over young offenders on the reserve. Dispositions are designed to address the needs of young offenders, and to incorporate elements of restitution, reparation, and reintegration.

In discussions about the potential for developing restorative justice initiatives, it is often argued that programs such as circle sentencing that involve substantive community participation in a holistic framework are suited only to rural and remote communities with a strong cultural identity and foundation. This assertion is often used to deflect suggestions that youth justice personnel in suburban and urban areas should explore the development of system-community partnerships to design strategies and programs that would better address the needs of young offenders, their victims, and the community. In Yukon, both Aboriginal and non-Aboriginal residents have participated in circles as victims and offenders, and have played community support roles Further, in 1997 an initiative was undertaken to establish a circle sentencing program in the city of Minneapolis. In addition, there are a number of successful restorative justice initiatives currently operating in urban and suburban areas of Canada that, with additional funding, could be easily adapted to accommodate young offenders (see Roberts, 1995).

CRITICAL ISSUES FOR RESTORATIVE YOUTH JUSTICE IN CANADA

The discussion in this paper has been designed to provide a case study in the development and implementation of restorative justice in one country. The primary objective of the paper has been to identify and describe the legislative, political, public and community contexts of restorative youth justice, and how each of these contexts may function either to hinder or facilitate the application of the principles of restorative justice to cases involving youths in conflict.

In the opening pages of this chapter it was noted that the contemporary political environment is one in which there is heightened political and public concern about crime among youths, particularly violent crime. There is little doubt that, through selective, sensationalistic reporting, the media has contributed to the widespread perception that serious violent youth crime is on the rise and that the operant youth justice legislation — the YOA — is not only at least partially responsible for this rise, but is not effective either as a general or specific deterrent. Public and political pressures have resulted in modifications to the YOA, which continues to attempt to balance protection of the community with the rights and needs of young offenders.

The discussion of restorative youth justice in Canada, however, extends far beyond the legislative framework provided by the YOA. As we have noted in the preceding section, Aboriginal communities across Canada have been driving the restorative justice agenda, designing and implementing programs specifically designed to meet the needs of victims, offenders, and the community.

While it is important to understand the role that the YOA may play in creating a legislative basis for restorative justice initiatives as well as the obstacles that the legislation may present to such initiatives, there are a number of other issues that must be addressed as well, and that extend far beyond the legislative framework. These include, but certainly are not limited to, the following:

Defining and Operationalizing the Principles of Restorative Justice

The emerging popularity of restorative justice, and the development of policies and programs, with a clear understanding of the parameters and requisite components for programs places restorative justice at risk of suffering the same fate as the concept of "community policing": while the majority of police departments indicate that they practice community policing, attempts to operationalize key terms and practices and the efficacy of community policing initiatives have proved elusive. In their review of the emerging models of restorative and community justice decision making, Bazemore and Griffiths (1997) compare victim-offender mediation, reparative probation, family group conferencing, and circle sentencing on a number of benchmark criteria. They find that while there are similarities between the models, there are also critical differences between them, including their mandate and relationship to the formal adversarial system, the role of the crime victim and other co-participants, and the provisions and procedures for preparation, monitoring, and enforcement. The models also differ in terms of their objectives, the extent to which the model requires that the justice system share power with community residents, and the extent to which the model is designed to empower the community as well as address the specific incident and behavior in question.

Role of Youth Justice Personnel

To date, the response of justice system personnel to the principles and practice of restorative justice across Canada can be characterized as "mixed." There are a number of factors that have functioned to limit the development and implementation of programs premised on the principles of restorative justice. Even with a legislative framework conducive to the development of restorative justice initiatives, there is no requirement that justice system personnel support or encourage such developments. While the authority for enacting criminal laws in Canada resides in the federal government, the provinces are given the responsibility for the administration of justice. This includes establishing youth justice systems, policies and programs. Across the country, there is considerable variation in the policies and programs that are applied to young offenders. Some jurisdictions have been more receptive to experimenting with restorative-based programs than others. In addition, youth justice personnel themselves have been a primary obstacle to attempts to reform the youth justice process, due to a number of factors. First, many youth court judges and probation officers may either distrust the community and/or feel that community residents, as "non-professionals," are incapable of participating in the resolution of disputes involving young offenders. Secondly, youth justice personnel may view restorative justice programs as adding to their already severe workloads. This is likely to occur as the fiscal crises of the provincial governments result in reduced budgets for youth justice agencies. In contrast to the formal youth justice system, restorative initiatives such as family group conferencing require a significant time commitment on the part of probation officers and other justice officials.

Since justice model principles have dominated the application of the YOA in all provinces except Quebec, the roles of defense and prosecuting counsel and judges are critical to determining how far restorative justice principles and programs will penetrate into youth justice systems in Canada. Crown prosecutors often decide what cases are eligible for processing through community-based restorative justice programs. They decide which youths will: be diverted; proceed to charge (to initiate formal court proceedings); be transferred to adult criminal court proceedings; and plea negotiate with defense counsel. Crown prosecutors also address sentencing considerations, and decide whether to appeal an unfavorable judicial decision. Crown counsel have also played a significant role in many of the restorative justice initiatives undertaken by Aboriginal communities across Canada.

The role of defense counsel is firmly entrenched in most jurisdictions throughout Canada, i.e., most youth courts have lawyers available or present as "duty counsel" to advise young persons at their first or second court appearance. It is not clear how lawyers as an interest group would react if restorative justice programs became widespread, particularly if this development diminished their role. Much of the discussion of the role of legal counsel in restorative justice depends to a great extent upon the specific type of program being envisioned, and the specific procedures and processes encompassed by the initiative.

Similarly, how will judges, crown prosecutors and court administrators react if, as in New Zealand, court processing of young persons dropped dramatically? How amenable are youth justice personnel, from youth court judges to probation officers, to collaborating with communities to design and operate restorative justice initiatives? To what extent will politicians and justice personnel be willing to transfer power and jurisdiction to communities to provide residents with a substantive role in processing youths in conflict with the law? These and other core questions should form a research agenda that examines the potential for developing and applying restorative youth justice.

Similarly, while the Charter of Rights and Freedoms generally —and, more specifically, the YOA — placed strict procedural requirements on the police in dealing with young offenders, the police assume a vital and central role in many restorative justice initiatives, including family group conferencing and circle sentencing. The factors that contribute to effective police involvement, as well as issues related to police powers within the various models of restorative and community justice, have remained largely unaddressed. These are issues that, heretofore in Canada, have remained unaddressed yet are vitally important to consider in any discussion of restorative justice.

The experience to date is that individual police officers, court judges, probation officers and other justice system personnel, motivated by personal interest, disenchantment with the traditional, adversarial system of justice, and a commitment to the principles of restorative justice, have evidenced a willingness to become involved in restorative justice initiatives. Others less so inclined have not and, the YOA notwithstanding, there is no requirement that they do so.. For example, while circle sentencing originated and is most extensively utilized in Yukon, not all of the judges in the territorial court participate in this initiative.

The Evaluative Framework

The development of evaluative criteria for assessing the efficacy of restorative justice initiatives is complicated by a number of factors. First, the holistic approach and multi-faceted objectives of many restorative justice programs require a broader evaluative framework than has been utilized for traditional crime control initiatives. Program objectives may encompass macro-level dimensions such as cultural and community revitalization and empowerment, as well as community, family and individual healing. The stated objectives of the Kwanlin Dun Community Justice Project (1995), which utilizes circle sentencing, are: (1) to promote community involvement in justice issues; (2) to assist with healing and wellness of community members; and (3) to establish active and equal partnerships with the formal justice system circle.

Second, many of the key principles of restorative justice are unfamiliar to politicians, policy makers, youth justice personnel (including judges), and research scholars. Terms such as "forgiveness," "community," "empowerment," "healing," and "spirituality" are not found in the YOA, and have had no role in the traditional, adversarial systems of youth justice. Workers in the community holistic circle healing program at Hollow Water First Nation have an extensive definition of the term "healing" in the context of the Community Holistic Circle Healing program. It includes the following: "Healing is a search, a search for who we are, who we have been, and who we can become. Healing is coming to feel good about ourselves as individuals, as families, as communities, and as a Nation. Healing is claiming responsibility for who we are and where we are going" (Lajeunesse and Associates, Ltd., 1996:37). Needless to say, to assess these concepts in practice necessitates the development of new, more holistic evaluative frameworks and criteria.

The critique of restorative justice initiatives has centered on the lack of empirical analyses of the extent to which these strategies have achieved their stated objectives.. Despite the widespread publicity accorded circle sentencing at the national and international levels, for example, only one self-evaluation of the program has been carried out (Kwanlin Dun Community Justice Project, 1995). In concluding their critique of circle sentencing, Roberts and LaPrairie (1996:82-83) state: "It has been claimed that sentencing circles have the following benefits: (a) they reduce recidivism; (b) prevent crime; (c) reduce costs; (d) advance the interests of victims; and, (e) promote solidarity among community members. These are all measurable objectives and they should be put to empirical test."

The Government Agenda versus the Community Agenda

It was previously noted that the development and implementation of youth justice policy in Canada has been traditionally characterized by a high degree of centralization, due in large measure to the federal government's exclusive jurisdiction over the criminal law. There is a considerable distance — spatially, politically, and often culturally — between the national capital of Ottawa and communities throughout the country, particularly Aboriginal communities that tend to be situated in rural and remote areas. These distances increase the likelihood that there will be differing interpretations given to the concept and practice of restorative justice, ranging, for example, from restorative justice initiatives as "appendages" to and support mechanisms for the adversarial justice system, to restorative justice initiatives as one component of community empowerment, self-sufficiency, and autonomy.

Community and restorative justice initiatives have the greatest potential when they are developed to address the needs of victims, offenders, and community residents in a specific community context. Governments, in contrast, prefer to develop policy through models that can then be applied on a generic basis. Historically, the policy-making process has made few allowances for the complexities of the historical, cultural, political and geographic attributes of individual communities. The success of many restorative justice initiatives across Canada can be attributed, in large measure, to the fact that these programs were designed by community residents to address specific community needs. While the tendency for governments is to routinize the process by which justice programs are developed and implemented, communities have the potential to create initiatives that utilize available resources and capabilities, and that are more effective in addressing specific community needs.

Another potential source of difficulty for restorative justice programs is the fiscal crises being experienced by the federal and provincial/territorial governments. At a time when governments are attempting to reduce deficits while being confronted by increasing offender caseloads, there is the danger that restorative justice initiatives will be seen as a "safety valve" for diverting offenders and reducing the costs of youth justice. The experience of youth diversion programs in Canada (and the U.S.) indicates that these programs generally functioned to widen the net of social control, and did not result in either a reduction in the levels of youth crime nor in cost savings. Rather, these programs became appendages to the existing adversarial system, were often staffed by probation officers, and were rarely subjected to empirical evaluation. Should the same fate befall restorative justice initiatives, they will be little more than a reproduction of the responses of the adversarial system.

Finally, there is the oft-heard refrain that community justice initiatives are appropriate only for small communities in remote and rural areas. And, more specifically, the principles of community and restorative justice are most compatible with the cultures and traditions of Aboriginal peoples. Although many of the more high-profile community justice initiatives in Canada, including circle sentencing in Yukon and community holistic healing in Manitoba, developed in rural Aboriginal communities, there are neighborhoods and communities within even the most dense urban centers that may be amenable to these practices. The recent experiment with circle sentencing in Minneapolis provides an illustration of the potential for community justice programs to be implemented in a wide range of settings. Evidence from Canada indicates that the success of community and restorative justice initiatives depends upon the persons involved and the willingness of criminal justice system personnel to share power, rather than on the specific social and demographic attributes of the community.

If communities are given the opportunity to participate as equal partners with government in the design and operation of community-based restorative justice initiatives, there is a real possibility that the agendas and interests of government may conflict with those of the community. The experience of circle sentencing in Yukon is instructive: when communities in that jurisdiction assumed ownership of the circle sentencing and all of the procedures associated with this process, there were several unanticipated consequences. One of the more significant developments was that, in identifying and screening offenders for suitability for the circle sentencing process, the community representatives selected individuals with the most lengthy offense records — persons with long histories of offending who had extensive contact with the justice system. The nine youths referred to the Kwanlin Dun community justice circle sentencing program during 1992-1995 had a total of 206 prior (officially recorded) offenses. While in this jurisdiction justice personnel have transferred to the community substantial power to determine which offenders are suitable for the circles, in other jurisdictions this may be a source of conflict. What is evident is that, when provided with such powers, communities often select those persons who have created the most crime and disorder. This is far removed from traditional diversion programs that tended to received "potato chip" thieves.

The Dynamics of Community Justice

The significant role assumed by communities in restorative justice initiatives requires a close consideration of the strengths, as well as the potential pitfalls, of community justice. Canadian observers have raised a number of concerns and identified several critical issues that, if unaddressed, can function to undermine the efficacy of restorative justice initiatives. These range from ensuring that the legal rights of offenders are protected to the general "health" of the community, including that of community leaders and of those who would assume key roles in any restorative justice initiatives; acknowledging that there are, within all communities, power hierarchies that may undermine consensus building and place certain residents, be they victims or offenders, in positions of vulnerability (see Griffiths et al., 1995; Griffiths and Hamilton, 1996; DePew, 1994). And LaPrairie (1996) has made the important observation that there are often competing and conflicting goals in community justice, and, further, that even in relatively small communities it may be difficult to establish and maintain consensus:

> On the one hand, community justice is about autonomy, empowerment, and control. On the other hand, community justice is about tradition, and, in contemporary terms, about 'healing' and the transformation of communities into healthier states of being. The reality, however, is that the

primary goal of community justice is the exercise of social control, the use of surveillance, and the dispensing of 'justice', which may or may not involve punishment...the potential for the community justice to divide rather than unite people, particularly where communities are small in size and geographically isolated, is great [p.127]

Others have offered important caveats about restorative justice. Stuart (1996), in his discussion of circle sentencing, noted that the approach is not appropriate for all offenders or crimes; that the success of the circle depends upon the cooperation of community residents and justice professionals; and that it is imperative that the needs, rights, and interests of crime victims and offenders be protected. These concerns are particularly important in considering restorative justice initiatives for young offenders, who, due to their age and status in communities, may have many vulnerabilities.

FINAL REMARKS

The discussions about and developments in restorative youth justice in Canada are occurring against a multi-dimensional political/legislative and community backdrop. Politicians and senior governmental policy makers at the federal and provincial/territorial levels have been, and continued to be, preoccupied with the debate over the implications of the operative youth justice legislation, the YOA, its fiscal implications as well as the extent to which the legislation is seen to be responsive to the perceptions of the Canadian public about youth crime. Recent amendments to the YOA, while providing for more severe responses to serious, violent offenders, have not significantly affected the potential for developing restorative youth justice initiatives.

It is at the community level, however, that the most innovative and significant developments in restorative youth justice are occurring, driven in large measure by Aboriginal communities seeking greater authority and control over all facets of justice service delivery. This has resulted in the creation of a myriad of community-based justice initiatives that hold considerable potential to more effectively address the needs of victims, offenders and communities. Despite these developments, a number of critical issues remain, and it is uncertain as to whether, in a decade's time, these initiatives will have survived the governmental and communities pressures that are certain to confront them. The survival and growth of restorative community justice will challenge both governments and communities to reach compromise, seek consensus and assume risks. If these can be accomplished, then the restorative justice movement has the potential to fundamentally, and positively, alter the way in which youth justice in Canada is practiced.

★　　　★　　　★

REFERENCES

Bazemore, G. and C.T. Griffiths (1997). "Conferences, Circles, Boards, and Meditations: Scouting the 'New Wave' of Community Justice Decision Making Approaches." *Federal Probation* 61(2):25-37.

Carrington, P.J. S. and Moyer (1994). "Trends in Youth Crime and Police Response: Pre-and-Post-YOA." *Canadian Journal of Criminology.* 36:1-28.

Cawsey, R.A. (1991). *Justice on Trial. Report of the Task Force on the Criminal Justice System and Its Impact on the Indian and Metis People of Alberta. Vol. 1. Main Report.* Edmonton, CAN: Attorney General and Solicitor General of Alberta.

Church Council on Justice and Corrections (1996). *Satisfying Justice: Safe Community Options That Attempt to Repair Harm from Crime and Reduce the Use or Length of Imprisonment.* Ottawa, CAN: Church Council on Justice and Corrections and Correctional Service of Canada.

Corrado, R. (1992). "Introduction: From Revolution to Despair to Justice?" In: R. Corrado, M. LeBlanc, R. Linden and N. Bala (eds.), *The Young Offenders Act and Juvenile Justice in Canada.* Toronto, CAN: Butterworths.

——— and A. Markwart (1992). "The Evaluation and Implementation of a New Era In Juvenile Justice in Canada." In: R. Corrado, M. LeBlanc, R. Linden and N. Bala (eds.), *The Young Offenders Act and Juvenile Justice in Canada.* Toronto, CAN: Butterworths.

——— and A. Markwart. (1994). "The Need to Reform the YOA in Response to Violent Young Offenders: Confusion, Reality or Myth?" *Canadian Journal of Criminology* 36:343-378.

Coutu, J.C. (1995). *Justice For and By the Aboriginals. Report and Recommendations of the Advisory Committee on the Administration of Justice in Aboriginal Communities.* Quebec, CAN: Minster of Justice and Minister of Public Security.

DePew, R.C. (1994). *Popular Justice and Aboriginal Communities: Some Preliminary Considerations.* Ottawa, CAN: Aboriginal Justice Directorate, Department of Justice Canada.

Federal-Provincial-Territorial Task Force on Youth Justice (1996). *A Review of the Young Offenders Act and the Youth Justice System in Canada.* Ottawa, CAN: author.

Fortugno, S.A. and M. Rogstad (1994). *A Socio-Legal Analysis of Youth Justice in Saskatoon: The Behaviour of the System Toward Aboriginal and Non-Aboriginal Youth.* Saskatoon, CAN: John Howard Society.

Griffiths, C.T. (1996). "Restorative Justice in Canadian Aboriginal Communities." *International Journal of Comparative and Applied Criminal Justice* 20:195-208.

——— and R. Hamilton (1996). "Sanctioning and Healing: Restorative Justice in Canadian Aboriginal Communities." In: J. Hudson and B. Galaway (eds.), *Restorative Justice: Theory, Practice, and Research.* Monsey, NY: Criminal Justice Press.

—— and S.N. Verdun-Jones (1994). *Canadian Criminal Justice (2nd ed.)* Toronto, CAN: Harcourt Brace.

Griffiths, C.T., E. Zellerer, D. Wood, and G. Saville (1995). *Crime, Law, and Justice Among Inuit in the Baffin Region, N.W.T., Canada.* Burnaby, CAN: Criminology Research Centre, Simon Fraser University.

Kwanlin Dun Community Justice Project (1995). *Kwanlin Dun Community Justice Pilot Project. Self Evaluation.* Whitehorse and Ottawa, CAN: Kwanlin Dun First Nation, Yukon Territorial Government Department of Justice; and Aboriginal Justice Directorate, Federal Department of Justice.

Lajeunesse, T. and Associates, Ltd. (1996). *Evaluation of Community Holistic Circle Healing. Hollow Water First Nation. Volume 1. Final Report.* Winnipeg, CAN: Manitoba Department of Justice.

LaPrairie, C. (1996). *Examining Aboriginal Corrections in Canada.* Ottawa, CAN: Aboriginal Corrections, Ministry of the Solicitor General.

Linn, P. (1992). *Report of the Saskatchewan Indian Justice Review Committee.* Regina, CAN: Government of Saskatchewan.

Roberts, J. (1994). *Public Knowledge of Crime and Justice: An Inventory of Canadian Findings.* Ottawa, CAN: Department of Justice Canada.

—— and C. LaPrairie (1996). "Sentencing Circles: Some Unanswered Questions." *Criminal Law Quarterly* 39:69-83.

Roberts, T. (1995). *Evaluation of the Victim Offender Mediation Project, Langley, B.C. Final Report.* Ottawa, CAN: Solicitor General Canada.

R. v. M. (J.J.). (1993). 20 C.R. (4th) 295 (S.C.C.).

R. v. T. (V.). (1992). S.C.R. 749 (S.C.C.).

Stuart, B. (1996). "Circle Sentencing in Yukon Territory, Canada: A Partnership of the Community and the Criminal Justice System." *International Journal of Comparative and Applied Criminal Justice.* 20:291-309.

APPENDIX A: CONFERENCING RECOMMENDATION: REPORT OF THE FEDERAL-PROVINCIAL-TERRITORIAL TASK FORCE ON YOUTH JUSTICE*

2.2.8 Recommendation

The Task Force Recommends that:

- the Act should be amended so as to enable and encourage conferencing, but not to require its use, by:

  (1) defining "conference" in a broad manner, but which should expressly include reference to family group conferences, youth justice committees, sentencing circles, and inter-agency case conferences.

  (2) authorizing the provincial director, or other party designated by the province to convene a conference for the purposes of alternative measures or case management and at specified points in the youth court process - including any report required by the court and to permit the provincial director or other designated party to make recommendations arising from these conferences to the youth court.

  (3) amending sections 14 and 28, and other relevant sections, to permit the recommendations arising from a conference to be included in a predisposition or progress report, or other report ordered by the court.

  (4) including a clause to the effect that the youth court "shall consider" the recommendations of the conference.

  (5) authorizing the youth court to recommend that the provincial director, or other party designated by the province, consider the applicability of a conference to an individual case, subject to provincial regulations or guidelines that may be established in this regard.

  (6) amending section 37 to include conferencing within the mandate of a youth worker.

* Pages 66-68

(7) establishing an enabling clause so that provinces are able to establish regulations or guidelines respecting conferencing.

(8) broadening the scope of youth justice committees by changing section 69 so that the words "young offenders" are replaced with the words "young persons".

- Conferences should have one or more of the following objectives, as appropriate to the circumstances of the case:

    (1) minimize the involvement of the young person in the youth justice system;

    (2) promote communication among youth serving agencies and the coordination of services and support programs for young persons;

    (3) hold the young person accountable for his or her actions;

    (4) foster the ability of families, extended families and the community to develop their own means of dealing with offending by their children and young persons;

    (5) involve the victim in the determination of the sanction, seek restitution and reparation for the victim and encourage reconciliation with the young person;

    (6) ensure that meaningful, equitable and proportionate sanctions are imposed; and

    (7) enable culturally appropriate processes and values to be recognized.

- Conferences should be utilized for six functions, including:

    (1) advice on the use of alternative measures or other forms of diversion;

    (2) recommending other responses to continuing proceedings under the Act or to an intrusive disposition;

    (3) recommending alternatives to pretrial detention;

    (4) advising the youth court at disposition or review;

    (5) coordinating services and support during the administration of a disposition; and

       (6) coordinating services and support at the post-release and post-disposition stages.

- Provinces and territories should promote conferencing within their jurisdictions - including representation from other youth serving agencies - and should establish protocols/guidelines or regulations respecting conferences, including with respect to:

  (1) the objectives of conferences;

  (2) target population;

  (3) at which decision points conferencing should be used, both within and outside the youth justice system;

  (4) which youth justice agency representatives, other agency representatives, and other individuals with a legitimate interest may be involved in conferencing; and

  (5) accountability and follow-up to the recommendations of conferences.

- To the extent that there are direct administrative costs associated with conferencing, that these be considered for inclusion as a cost shareable expenditure under the federal-provincial-territorial Young Offenders Cost Sharing Agreement.

It should be noted that additional recommendations regarding conferencing are included in other parts of this report. First, there is a recommendation earlier in this Chapter (2.1) to undertake a comprehensive review of the Declaration of Principle and to include within that review consideration of statements regarding the role of other youth-serving agencies; and to encourage conferencing. Second, in Chapter 9, there are recommendations to amend the information sharing-provisions of the Act so that participants in a conference may be provided and share information about young persons, and, more generally, to facilitate necessary information sharing among youth-serving agencies.

10. Legal Issues of Restorative Justice

by

Daniel W. Van Ness

INTRODUCTION

Schweigert (1997:23) proposed that "restorative justice brings the moral authority in personal communal traditions and the moral authority in impersonal universal norms together in a mutually reinforcing combination." This is the first of his three principles concerning restorative justice and moral education. Communal moral traditions are those that grow out of the relational networks we have of family, friends, work associates and so on. Universal moral norms are derived through a conscious, rational effort to rise above the communal traditions of *specific* times and places, and to speak instead to the human condition at *all* times and places. They may be articulated in philosophy, theology, law, and so forth. Traditional criminal justice processes tend to separate these two forms of moral authority. Communal values are of interest only when they conflict with the norms articulated in law, and then the concern is to prevent those communal values from unduly influencing the decision maker. Even in common law countries that accept the reality of jury nullification, for example, courts do not permit attorneys to tell jurors of that right or to directly appeal to them to ignore the law in making their decision. Restorative justice, on the other hand, brings communal and universal norms together in a way that reinforces the authority of each.

Schweigert's (1997:23) second principle is that "restorative justice focuses its efforts and process on the 'space between places' in social relations — not on individuals or families or particular institutions, but on the space where these important social bodies intersect." Restorative processes carve out a safe space within which all of the parties come together — the offender, the victim, their families and communities, and the state — to consider what is to be done. It is when all those parties are together in a space that is neither theirs nor another's, Schweigert (1997) says, that moral learning takes place. In part this is because all are present and the task is to develop a consensual response, which means all must participate fully. This is also because the task of designing a response means that the participants must take on new roles (problem solvers, for example) and hence new competencies. This is another difference between restorative processes and traditional criminal justice, in which the state creates the space which protects the accused from others while the state decides on the accused's guilt. Restorative justice creates a neutral space for all parties to participate in designing a solution.

Schweigert's (1997:23) third principle is that "restorative justice harnesses the resources of whole communities to take the actions and make the changes that can successfully address the problems that emerge as crime, rather than continuing the criminal justice system's focus on the offender only." All participants are learners, and, furthermore, the process itself is a means of learning. This leads, Schweigert argues, to community development on a number of levels, one of which is community moral development. Again, the contrast with traditional criminal justice is clear. Criminal law is also defended on educational grounds — it *teaches* and reinforces the universal norms from which it is derived. But a teaching function moves in a single direction, from the state to the offender, from the state to the victim, from the state to the community. Restorative justice creates opportunities to *learn*; it moves in multiple directions between all parties. All parties learn from the others. It is learning rather than teaching that leads to community moral development.

These three principles are a good starting point for discussion of some commonly raised legal issues related to restorative justice. Schweigert's (1997) first principle — that communal and universal norms can be brought together in a way that is mutually reinforcing — is useful because it reminds us that we need not think in terms of either/or in relation to those norms. Sometimes the debate over the legal principles and processes involved with restorative justice ends up sounding like courtroom arguments about the superiority of informal or formal law, of communal or universal norms. What we need is a more restorative way of thinking about these two sets of norms — one that honors and respects both, and that seeks to reinforce both. The first section of this paper will consider the problem of due process protections for the accused in restorative processes and sanctions.

Schweigert's (1997) second principle — that restorative justice processes carve out safe, neutral spaces for all parties to meet and to design solutions — is important because it reminds us of the "gatekeeper" function that exists in law. At various stages in the criminal justice process, someone decides whether the case should proceed along formal or informal lines, in traditional or restorative spaces. The second section of this paper will consider the problem of discretion and the principle of legality.

Schweigert's (1997) third principle — that restorative processes contribute to community moral education — is important because it helps give a framework in which to discuss a frequently raised concern in connection with restorative processes: the issue of proportionality. Retributivists justify punishment in part because of its educational function. In fact, proportionality is a major preoccupation of the retributive paradigm because it is seen as essential to demonstrating to the particular victim and offender, as well as to the observing community, that criminal behavior is wrong (von Hirsch, 1993). The third section of this paper will deal with the problem of proportionality.

This paper is not intended to offer a comprehensive survey of legal issues raised by restorative justice.[1] Nor does it deal with the particulars of enabling legislation necessary to formalize restorative processes or sanctions. It is an introductory discussion of several foundational issues related to the practice and sanctions of restorative justice: due process, discretion and legality, and proportionality.

THE PROBLEM OF DUE PROCESS PROTECTIONS FOR THE ACCUSED

It is far from evident that due process protections are provided to juveniles in the juvenile justice system. Proclaiming rights is not the same as observing them. But it is even unclear to what extent due process protections have been "proclaimed" in juvenile justice. In part this is because the "paradigm shift" from rehabilitation to retribution has been incomplete (Bazemore and Umbreit, 1995; Bazemore, 1996; Walgrave and Geudens, 1996). Elements of due process and other retributive features have been incorporated into juvenile justice, but *parens patriae* remains highly influential in the disposition of many juveniles' cases (Orlando, 1992).

Into this mixture of rehabilitation and retribution comes restorative justice. I have argued elsewhere that restorative justice theory, with its emphasis on the rights and needs of victims, offenders and communities, offers a conceptual framework in which a number of otherwise conflicting human rights standards and norms related to criminal justice might be reconciled (Van Ness, 1996). But this is not the same as arguing that restorative justice theory provides a justification for those standards and norms. In fact, some have argued that restorative justice theory, with its bias for enabling the parties concerned to repair the injuries caused by the criminal behavior, is better suited to forums characterized by broad discretion and few procedural limitations (Morris et al., 1996).

In other words, while the rehabilitation model of juvenile justice paid scant attention to due process constraints, and the retribution model brought a degree of concern that juveniles should receive the protections afforded adults, restorative justice theory does not immediately draw attention to protecting the rights of individual parties. Nevertheless, its comprehensiveness and values may help realise many of the rights that have been identified under retributive models as belonging to offenders and victims.[2]

M. Cherif Bassiouni (1993) has identified 11 fundamental rights of persons accused or convicted of criminal offenses that he argues have risen to general principles of international law. He bases that argument on an empirical study he and his associates made of the provisions of ten international agreements and 139 national constitutions. Because of the frequency with which the 11 fundamental rights appear in these documents, and because they have been identified as being basic to fairness in criminal proceedings, Bassiouni (1993) argues that they deserve great deference as general principles of international law. Without discussing the merits of these arguments for their inclusion as customary international law, let us think of them as expressions of what Schweigert (1997) calls the "impersonal universal norms" — those which transcend time and space. Five of these fundamental rights not only appear in the Beijing Rules, suggesting that they have prescriptive authority in juvenile justice, but they have also been mentioned by restorative justice critics as rights that may be violated by restorative processes. In the following pages, we will consider each category to consider whether restorative justice indeed conflicts with or reinforces those values in well-run programs.[3]

1. The right to recognition before the law and equal protection under the law.[4]

Where might restorative programs have to take precautions in order to avoid discrimination? One is in the selection of program participants. Brown (1994) has observed that early mediation programs in the U.S. involved a very high percentage of Caucasians, although she also noted that this could be attributed to the racial makeup of the communities in which the programs operated. Nevertheless, the possibility of discrimination bears watching, and selection criteria should be evaluated from time to time to explore the extent to which there may be such an impact.

A second area is in how the processes themselves operate. For example, Warner (1994) has cautioned that inconsistency may emerge in the way that family group conferences treat female and male offenders due to the patriarchal family structures of many families. A "boys-will-be-boys" attitude could result in less punitive sanctions for boys than for girls who demonstrate similar behavior. The informality of the conference may make it impossible to prove that discriminatory comments were made and appear to have influenced the outcome. Warner (1994) notes that similar issues arise in relation to race.

What responses have restorative justice advocates made to these criticisms? On one hand, they seem ready to embrace a certain amount of inconsistency based on society's pluralism of values and cultures. Rather than requiring all cultures and persons to apply a single set of values to particular conduct, Braithwaite (1994:206) notes that restorative justice "accommodates richly plural forms of subculturalism." This means that some inconsistency may result, and furthermore may be appropriate.

Program evaluators have also noted this discriminatory potential, and have suggested that mediation or conferencing programs be regularly evaluated to determine whether they produce sanctions that are unfairly burdensome to classes of offenders because of their sex, race or other characteristic. This has been identified as an area for further research (Robertson, 1996).

However, there is some evidence that restorative justice processes do respect this right. It appears that the amount of variance in the severity of sanctions negotiated in conferences that can be attributed to non-offense variables (among which may have been racial or gender discrimination) is similar to that found in adult courts (Maxwell and Morris, 1996). Furthermore, Gabrielle Maxwell has observed that in conferences, women seem to confront fewer traditional disadvantages to active participation than in other dispute resolution alternatives (Maxwell and Morris, 1996).

2. The right to freedom from torture and cruel, inhuman and degrading treatment or punishment.[5]

Perhaps the aspect of current restorative practices that raises most questions of possible cruelty, inhumanity and indignity is the practice of shaming. Massaro (1991), for example, in a lengthy article on shame and American culture, concludes that reintegrative shaming is unlikely to be effective in America, and, therefore, that sanctions intended to shame are likely to violate the Eighth Amendment of the U.S. Constitution as disproportionate, unequal and cruel. She argues that it is cruel because it constitutes a state-sanctioned assault on an individual's sense of esteem, in a context (American culture) which she believes is unlikely to lead to reintegration.

Shame is recognized by restorative practitioners as a powerful emotion, capable of producing significant change in a person's life (Leibrich, 1996). Braithwaite (1989) distinguishes reintegrative shaming, which he argues can reduce crime, from shaming that stigmatizes and thereby generates or reinforces criminal subcultures. Moore (1993) begins with the beneficial impact of family group conferencing, explores the elements (one of which is shame) that seem to make it a powerful form of intervention, and from that develops implications concerning criminological theory, moral philosophy, and political theory. When Retzinger and Scheff (1996:330) develop tactics for making conferences effective, their fifth tactic is: "Recognise that no intentional shaming is necessary." This is because the conference itself, with its focus on the misdeed of the offender, is inherently shaming. That inherent shame is sufficient.

Shaming can be done in such a way as to be cruel, degrading and stigmatizing. Community service and other arguably restorative sanctions can be implemented in ways that degrade. Restorative processes recognize this, but also acknowledge that reintegrative shame can be healing. Program guidelines and mediator and facilitator training must ensure that shaming is reintegrative rather than stigmatizing. The right to freedom from cruel, unusual and degrading punishments underscores the importance of this good practice.

3. The right to be presumed innocent.[6]

Most mediation and conferencing programs require that the offender accept some form of responsibility in order to participate in the programs; they are generally considered inappropriate forums when the defendant denies responsibility. However, programs do differ on the degree of responsibility offenders must accept. Some programs require an admission of guilt to committing a particular offense; others, only that the offender "decline to deny" guilt; and others, that the offender accept civil, but not criminal, liability for the offense (Braithwaite, 1994). Still others proceed only after there has been a judgment of guilt following a trial or plea of guilty. To further strengthen respect the presumption of innocence even after such limited expressions of responsibility, offenders could be given the right to terminate mediation or conferencing proceedings that are already under way in order to deny guilt. Permitting juveniles to appeal an agreement reached in restorative processes on the grounds of innocence would reassure those who are concerned that juveniles may admit guilt because they feel they have done something wrong when in fact they did not commit a crime, or they had legal defenses available of which they are not aware (Warner, 1994).

Two things should also be made clear to the offender prior to consenting to mediation or conferencing: first, whether agreement to participate in the program is legally construed as an admission of guilt; and, second, whether statements made in the course of the mediation or conferencing can be admitted in civil or criminal proceedings. The American Bar Association (1994:5), in its resolution recommending the use of what it called victim-offender mediation/dialogue, provided that "statements made by victims and offenders and documents and other materials produced during the mediation/dialogue process [must be] inadmissible in criminal or civil court proceedings."

4. The right to a fair trial.[7]

What is called for here is the *right* to a fair trial. Restorative processes may or may not include some of these provisions, and to the extent that they are alternatives to traditional proceedings, there is no need for them to do so. However, when participation in a restorative process means that the juvenile will waive these rights, the waiver should be made following a careful explanation of the alternatives. In conferences this is accomplished during the introductory stage, during which juveniles are told of their legal rights, of the alternative of proceeding in court, and of their continuing right to stop the conference at any point and to proceed to court (Wundersitz and Hetzel, 1996; Stewart, 1996; Moore, 1993).

What of the possibility of coercion? When this concern has been raised, it has not related to externally applied pressure in the sense that we may think of in relation to interrogation practices, for example. The coercion that has troubled critics (and some proponents) of restorative processes is more subtle: "...there is inevitably an inducement to admit responsibility to avoid the uncertainty of a court outcome and to dispose of the matter as quickly as possible" (Warner, 1994:142). In other words, the desirability of the alternative may cause accused individuals to admit responsibility that they do not in fact have.

Two responses might be made here. The first is that such inducements inherently exist when there is an alternative to a full-blown trial, whether it is diversion into a "treatment program" or a negotiated plea of guilty. Conferencing and mediation, then, fall within a category of alternatives that are understood to be potentially attractive to accused individuals, but that have nonetheless been accepted as consistent with the right to a fair trial. The second response is that conferences and mediation, with their emphasis on direct participation by the parties, and their opportunities for questions and answers, are more likely than other alternatives to elicit the true feelings of the accused concerning guilt and responsibility. It is one thing for accused individuals to permit their attorneys to guide them through the ritualized process of a negotiated guilty plea, and another thing altogether to answer direct questions put by the person who was harmed by the criminal act.

5. The right to assistance of counsel.[8]

Restorative processes have a clear bias for direct participation by the parties themselves. Consequently, it has sometimes been argued that defense attorneys would be a hindrance to restoration, and that they should not be included in the process. The underlying premise is that the lawyers' role is to insure that legal procedures are followed (Brown, 1994), which would essentially reformalize processes designed to be informal. This is not, of course, the only role that lawyers play. In fact, many lawyers understand that their client's interest is in obtaining the best outcome, and are willing to recommend to their clients that they agree to set aside procedural protections to achieve such an outcome; negotiated plea bargains are the most obvious example.

Attorneys can help accused individuals assess their options. The value of that assistance is directly related to their knowledge of the options. Consequently, it is in the interests of restorative practitioners and advocates to educate lawyers about their programs. In any event, notifying the attorney increases the likelihood of informed consent by a juvenile who chooses to participate in a restorative process. But once that decision is made, it is the juvenile — not the attorney — who should be the key participant.

Conclusion

There is no reason to conclude that restorative processes will inherently result in due process violations. Certainly restorative programs can be operated in such a way that they violate fundamental due process rights. But programs observing good practices are far less likely to do so, because of restorative values such as respect for human dignity, voluntary participation, creation of harmony that addresses underlying social injustices, and so on. Training and design are important to ensure good practices, and evaluation should be done regularly to expose problems when they happen.

In theory, a well-run rehabilitative juvenile justice process would also respect human rights, but we know that in practice many failed to do so. This is not offered as an excuse for restorative justice practitioners, who may take the universal norms less seriously than they should; instead, it should remind those practitioners of the importance of vigilance, of finding ways to reinforce those norms as they help parties to a dispute apply traditional wisdom in resolving it.

THE PROBLEM OF DISCRETION AND THE PRINCIPLE OF LEGALITY

Schweigert's second principle had to do with *space* — with creating a space between the places normally occupied by the individuals involved in a conflict in which they can safely work to resolve the conflict. What spaces might we think of, and who decides which space will be used to resolve a particular conflict? Those are the kinds of questions raised by the problem of discretion and the principle of legality.

It is possible to think of restorative justice as existing completely separately from, and antagonistically to, the official governmental criminal justice system. Nils Christie (1982), for example, argues that the state has "stolen" conflicts from its citizens in establishing the criminal justice system, and that these should be returned to the individuals involved so that they might pursue private methods of resolving the conflict. Under such a view, restorative justice would *replace* criminal justice. This substitution might be done quickly, or gradually as criminal justice processes are transformed into restorative processes (Walgrave, this volume). (See model 1; Figure 1)

It is also possible to position restorative justice as a co-existing alternative to criminal justice. Mirroring Haley's (1989) description of a dual-track response to crime in Japan, some have called for *parallel* restorative and criminal justice systems (see model 2, Figure 1), each capable of checking the abuses of the other and of competing with the other for the resolution of criminal disputes, and perhaps linked to one another for certain purposes (Van Ness, 1990; Wright, 1992; Bianchi, 1994).

There is a third possibility: that the criminal justice system will come to include restorative elements. Rather than replacing or paralleling, restorative programs are *incorporated* within the criminal justice system (see model 3, Figure 1). A recent example is police initiation of family group conferences in several countries.

Figure 1: Relationship Between Restorative and Traditional Processes

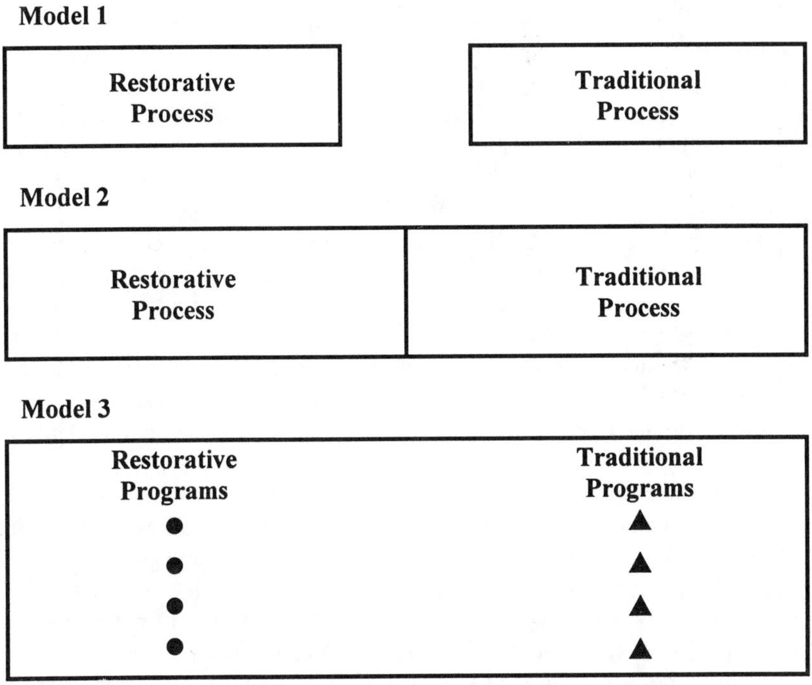

Model 1

Restorative Process	Traditional Process

Model 2

Restorative Process	Traditional Process

Model 3

Restorative Programs	Traditional Programs
●	▲
●	▲
●	▲
●	▲

These three possibilities are not mutually exclusive, but they do suggest three different "spaces" to which the conflict may be sent for resolution. One space lies outside of and is indifferent to traditional juvenile justice. A second lies outside of but paralleling, and is perhaps linked to, traditional juvenile justice. The third lies within traditional juvenile justice in programs incorporating certain restorative values and processes. To which of these spaces does a conflict go? A *gatekeeper* must be in place to make this decision. Will it be to a restorative process, a traditional criminal justice process, or some amalgamation of the two? What legal constraints are there on the gatekeeper? What considerations will guide this decision? Perhaps most importantly, who is the gatekeeper?

Traditionally, the gatekeeper is an official of the juvenile justice system, often the prosecutor. How much discretion prosecutors have in deciding whether to charge or divert a juvenile is one of the fundamental distinctions of civil law and common law legal traditions. In civil law jurisdictions, the legality principle,[9] or principle of mandatory prosecution, requires the prosecuting official to file charges when sufficient evidence of guilt has been discovered during the course of an investigation (Damaška, 1975; Pelikan, 1991; Terrill, 1992). In common law traditions, prosecuting authorities have discretion regarding whether or not to file charges (LaFave, 1970; Pizzi, 1993). The reasons for this significant difference between the two traditions have to do with the inquisitorial roots of civilian law and the adversarial roots of common law (Pizzi, 1993). La-Fave (1970) suggests that it may also relate to the structure of criminal codes in the two traditions: the legislatures in common law traditions have tended to overcriminalize, resulting in the need for prosecutors to exercise discretion in order to conserve judicial resources and to individualize justice.

There are exceptions to the legality principle in civil-law countries that offer opportunities for discretion by the prosecutor (Dünkel and Rössner, 1989; Terrill, 1992; Pizzi, 1993). Furthermore, common law prosecutors do not enjoy unfettered discretion, increasingly finding themselves more constrained by political pressures and by the growing use of informal guidelines within prosecutors' offices (Tonry, 1991; Pizzi, 1993). Nevertheless, it is clear that common law prosecutors have more discretion than their civilian counterparts (Damaška, 1975).

One obvious implication of prosecutorial discretion is that the prosecutor's stance affects the possibility of substituting restorative procedures for traditional juvenile procedures. If the prosecutor is unwilling or unable to agree to diversion of particular kinds of cases from juvenile proceedings, then a victim's and offender's desire to resolve matters in a restorative program will not prevent the juvenile processes from moving forward. Of course, failure or inability of the prosecutor to agree does not mean that there can be no mediation, since there are other later points in the process in which it can take place. For example, sentencing procedures of both traditions contain openings for apology or reparation, and mediation or other restorative practices could be used to achieve those (Dünkel and Rössner, 1989; Wright, 1991).

Clearly, there are practical implications of the prosecutor's freedom to decide where to send a case. But *should* the prosecutor be the one making the decision? If we think of a criminal conflict as involving four parties — the victim, the offender, the community and the government — we can distinguish the interests of each. The victim's interests are in being vindicated and in receiving redress; the offender's are in being treated fairly as the amount and means of recompense to the victim and community are determined, and, ultimately, in being reintegrated into the community; the community's is in building and preserving strong and peaceful relationships among its members; and the government's is in establishing a just order (Van Ness and Strong, 1997). The prosecutor does not represent the interests of the offender, nor those of the victim (Rowland, 1992). The prosecutor is a governmental employee, often claiming to represent the community as well.

A Working Party on Restorative Justice, created by the United Nations Alliance of Non-Governmental Organizations (NGOs) on Crime Prevention and Criminal Justice in New York, has adopted a series of fundamental principles concerning restorative justice (Claassen, 1996). These principles acknowledge that in the aftermath of a crime there are certain safety concerns of the victim, offender and community that must be addressed immediately. When those have been satisfied, "[r]estorative justice prefers responding to the crime at the earliest point possible and with the maximum amount of voluntary co-operation and minimum coercion, since healing in relationships and new learning are voluntary and co-operative processes" (principle 6).

This suggests several criteria to be used in determining to which space, at any point, a conflict should be directed. First, are there safety concerns that must be addressed immediately to protect the victim, the offender (and others who may be accused or suspected), and the community? Safety here should include not only physical safety, but protection of the fundamental rights of the parties. To the extent that there are, the government is probably best suited to take the necessary steps. As soon as safety is established, a second question arises: how can this matter be resolved using the maximum amount of voluntary cooperation and the minimum amount of coercion? This question governs all gatekeeping decisions thereafter.

Furthermore, this means that, in a sense, all parties become gatekeepers. Once safety is assured, the primary decision makers should be the victim and the offender, with the community and government having a voice, but a secondary one. When both the victim and the offender are willing to pursue a cooperative alternative, then the case should be sent to a restorative space. When they are not, the case should proceed according to traditional justice procedures.

This approach could be incorporated into law in both civil- and common-law traditions by requiring that restorative processes such as victim-offender mediation be offered to victims and offenders in specified cases, with subsequent judicial review and enforcement (if necessary) of the outcomes. It could permit restorative process to be used in other, more serious, cases when requested by the victim and offender, with subsequent judicial review and enforcement. In situations in which prosecutors — or any other party — believed that safety of the parties or of the community would be jeopardized by removing the case to restorative processes, a judge could make the determination after hearing from all parties, including the offender and victim.

THE PROBLEM OF PROPORTIONALITY

Proportionality has received increasing attention in recent years due to the emergence of the "just deserts" movement. In fact, the lack of proportionality helped contribute to the demise of the rehabilitation paradigm. Von Hirsch (1993:6), one of just desert's foremost advocates, has stated that the principle that "sanctions be proportionate in their severity to the gravity of offences" is a basic element of justice itself. Under a retributive model, then, proportionality has to do with relating the amount of punishment to the seriousness of the crime committed. It is retrospective, in that it is based on the seriousness of a past event: the crime (Walgrave and Geudens, 1996). I will refer to this as *retributive proportionality.*

Is there a *restorative proportionality?* This form of proportionality would derive from the principle that the offender has harmed the victim and community and now has a responsibility to make things right. It, like retributive proportionality, is retrospective, since it is based on a past event -- the crime and its resulting harm (Van Ness, 1995; Walgrave and Geudens, 1996). As Walgrave and Geudens (1996:375-376) have noted, restorative proportionality is less interested in the "retributive link between the moral-juridical severity of the offence and the degree of punishment which would restore the moral balance," and more concerned with the "link between the severity of the material, relational and social harm caused by the offence and the degree of restorative effort required by the offender." Who determines that linkage? Restorative justice processes posit that the persons best able to determine that restorative linkage in a specific case are the particular victims, offenders, and surrounding community, which is the reason that mediation and conferencing are so prominent. If restorative processes are not available or appropriate, one could argue for at least imposing sanctions that are more restorative than merely punitive in character (Walgrave, this volume).

We must then ask whether there is guidance available to those specific victims, offenders, and communities that would leave them freedom to negotiate as part of their mediation or conferencing, or to judges imposing restitution or community service sanctions, but that would also avoid unwarranted disparity. It appears that there are at least two sources of guidance.

The first is the body of tort law that has emerged in common law countries, and which addresses the translation of various forms of harm into money, as well as consideration of liability and mitigating and aggravating factors. This approach takes harm seriously, but tempers judgments based on the perpetrator's liability. In that sense, it incorporates considerations beyond the offense committed, but does that according to established principles.

A second source of guidance, based more exclusively on offense seriousness, may emerge from the deserts movement, and in particular from their work on the troubling issue of how to anchor the scale of sanctions to the scale of offenses. Von Hirsch (1993) has proposed that this anchor, or linkage, could be established by determining the seriousness of both crime and punishment based on how each impedes the standard of living of the typical person. How does a particular kind of crime infringe on the typical victim's physical integrity, material support and amenity, freedom from humiliation, and privacy? How do particular sanctions impede similar interests of typical offenders? Von Hirsch suggests that using these constructs of typical harm, cardinal proportionality can be established. Punishment equals the crime when the typical harm of a sanction equals the typical harm of the victimization that precedes the sanction. What distinguishes von Hirsch's (1993) use of harm from that of restorative advocates is that he deals with typical harm caused to typical persons. He does not individualize as restorative justice does.

Furthermore, von Hirsch (1993) suggests in his discussion of intermediate sanctions that offenders might pay their "debts" using a number of different commodities. Imprisonment need not be the only sanction; penalties with an equivalent penal bite could be substituted for one another without sacrificing retributive proportionality.

A mundane illustration might help. There are many ways in which I could pay a $1.00 debt. I could use a dollar bill, four quarters, ten dimes, 20 nickels, 100 pennies or any combination of those coins that produced a sum of one dollar. In addition, I could give my creditor a pencil we agreed was worth 35¢ together with the balance in coins. I could also substitute a bus token, postage stamps or personal service. We could agree that a particular penny has greater worth to my creditor than its face value because she collects rare coins, and that it alone will satisfy the debt. There are many ways in which the debt could be paid. In the same way, there are many ways in which the debt an offender "owes" to the victim and community might be paid, and it is at least theoretically possible that a wide range of alternatives could be constructed that would increase the likelihood of achieving *retributive proportionality* while also accomplishing *restorative proportionality*. The parties would then have an opportunity to negotiate their own resolution, which they could compare to the range of alternatives.

Either of these two sources of guidance — tort law or a future scale developed by desert theorists — could be consulted at two occasions without impeding the genuine interaction between the parties. The first occasion would be after the parties have negotiated a tentative agreement, with the "typical" sanction incorporated into the conversation for comparison purposes. They could then either decide to adjust their agreement, or could agree that specified factors justify the disparity between their agreement and the guidelines. The second occasion would be in the course of evaluation of restorative programs, to consider whether on the whole the sanctions being negotiated appear to be proportionate when compared to each other, and when compared to traditional processes.

CONCLUSION

Discussion of legal principles tends to begin (and often end) with the status quo. This is because law is so closely related to traditional approaches to dealing with crime and justice. The processes and protections are expressed in legal terms, and can reflect the assumptions and biases of formal justice processes. This complicates the discussion of restorative justice and legal principles, since it operates on different assumptions and biases.

For example, in considering how to express and protect the dignity of individuals, legal language reflects the focus of traditional juvenile and criminal justice on accused and convicted offenders. It expresses the fundamental protections in the language of rights, which reflects the adversarial and defensive posture in which those juveniles find themselves in relation to governmental authorities. Restorative processes, on the other hand, focus on both victims and offenders, and would likely articulate principles of human dignity accordingly. They also would emphasize the responsibilities, rather than the rights, of each party. This is because restorative justice seeks active, not defensive, involvement in spaces in which discussion takes place on equal footing.

This mode of thinking suggests several ways in which the earlier discussion has been incomplete. First, there has been no treatment of the legal principles and processes concerning victim involvement in restorative (and traditional) processes. Second, in discussing the due process protections of accused and convicted juvenile offenders, the "rights" language has not been paralleled with "responsibility" language; it would be informative to identify the universal norms that protect human dignity by identifying the responsibilities that community and government have rather than the rights the individual has to protection from the community and government. Third, there has been little discussion of the ways in which the community's interests and governmental interests diverge and contrast. This is particularly important in light of the multiplication of democratic governments that can be said to represent the interests of the community. Finally, there has been no discussion of other institutions (facilitator training and certifying agencies, for example), that may come to dominate restorative practices, nor of the principles that should govern their practices.

Another approach to discussing restorative justice and legal principles is to consider the extent to which current formal practices were derived from values we now describe as restorative. For example, common-law juries were originally convened to bring together members of the community familiar with the victim, the offender and the crime. Their role was to take the "universal norms" incorporated in the King's law and to apply them based on their independent knowledge of the entire situation. It may be useful to study how and why that role changed, and to consider how the jury might be adapted to recover more of its restorative potential (Van Ness, 1994). A similar effort might be undertaken in the area of comparative law in order to identify formal processes and vocabulary elsewhere that seem to capture what may be missing in our own particular traditions.

For law is not simply a set of rules and procedures, although many who participate in juvenile and criminal justice will experience it as that. Law is also an expression of values and norms. It is as those universal norms are tested, reinforced and adapted in the context of particular conflicts and communal traditions that moral education occurs; we learn better what it means to do justice.

REFERENCES

American Bar Association (1994). "Victim-Offender Mediation/Dialogue Program Requirements." Resolution adopted by the American Bar Association House of Delegates.

Ashworth, A. (1991). *Principles of Criminal Law.* Oxford, UK: Clarendon Press.

—— (1993). "Some Doubts about Restorative Justice." *Criminal Law Forum* 4:277-299.

Auerbach, J.S. (1983). *Justice Without Law?* New York, NY: Oxford University Press.

Ban, P. (1996). "Implementing and Evaluating Family Group Conferences with Children and Families in Victoria, Australia." In: J. Hudson, A. Morris, G. Maxwell and B. Galaway (eds.), *Family Group Conferences: Perspectives on Policy and Practice.* Leichhardt, AUS and Monsey, NY: Federation Press and Criminal Justice Press.

Bassiouni, M.C. (1993). "Human Rights in the Context of Criminal Justice: Identifying International Procedural Protections and Equivalent Protections in National Constitutions." *Duke Journal of Comparative & International Law* 3:235-297.

Legal Issues of Restorative Justice

Bazemore, G. (1996). "Three Paradigms for Juvenile Justice." In: B. Galaway and J. Hudson (eds.), *Restorative Justice: International Perspectives.* Monsey, NY: Criminal Justice Press.

—— and M. Umbreit (1995). "Rethinking the Sanctioning Function in Juvenile Court: Retributive or Restorative Responses to Youth Crime." *Crime & Delinquency* 41(3):296-316.

Bianchi, H. (1994). *Justice as Sanctuary: Toward a New System of Crime Control.* Bloomington, IN: Indiana University Press.

Braithwaite, J. (1989). *Crime, Shame and Reintegration.* Cambridge, UK: Cambridge University Press.

—— (1994). "Thinking Harder About Democratising Social Control." In: C. Alder and J. Wundersitz (eds.), *Family Conferencing and Juvenile Justice: The Way Forward or Misplaced Optimism?* Canberra, AUS: Australian Institute of Criminology.

Brown, J.G. (1994). "The Use of Mediation to Resolve Criminal Cases: A Procedural Critique." *Emory Law Journal* 43:1247-1309.

Butts, J.A. (1997). "Necessarily Relative: Is Juvenile Justice Speedy Enough?" *Crime & Delinquency* (43)1:3-23.

Christie, N. (1982). *Limits to Pain.* London, UK: Martin Robertson.

Claassen, R. (1996). "Restorative Justice — Fundamental Principles." Unpublished paper revised and adopted in May 1996 by the Working Party on Restorative Justice, established by the United Nations Alliance of NGOs on Crime Prevention and Criminal Justice.

Coates, R.B. (1990). "Victim-Offender Reconciliation Programs in North America: An Assessment." In: B. Galaway and J. Hudson (eds.), *Criminal Justice, Restitution, and Reconciliation.* Monsey, NY: Criminal Justice Press.

Damaška, M. (1975). "Structures of Authority and Comparative Criminal Procedure." *Yale Law Journal* 84:480-544.

Dünkel, F. and D. Rössner (1989). "Law and Practice of Victim/Offender Agreements." In: M. Wright and B. Galaway (eds.), *Mediation and Criminal Justice: Victims, Offenders and Community.* Newbury Park, CA: Sage.

Fraser, S. and J. Norton (1996). "Family Group Conferencing in New Zealand Child Protection Work." In: J. Hudson, A. Morris, G. Maxwell and B. Galaway (eds.), *Family Group Conferences: Perspectives on Policy and Practice.* Leichhardt, AUS and Monsey, NY: Federation Press and Criminal Justice Press.

Gehm, J. (1990). "Mediated Victim-Offender Restitution Agreements: An Exploratory Analysis of Factors Related to Victim Participation." In: B. Galaway and J. Hudson (eds.), *Criminal Justice, Restitution, and Reconciliation.* Monsey, NY: Criminal Justice Press.

Gelsthorpe, L. and A. Morris 1994). "Juvenile Justice 1945-1992." In: M. Maguire, R. Morgan and R. Reiner (eds.), *The Oxford Handbook of Criminology.* London, UK: Clarendon Press.

– 278 –

Gittler, J. (1984). "Expanding the Role of the Victim in a Criminal Action: An Overview of Issues and Problems." *Pepperdine Law Review* 11:117-182.

Goldstein, A. S. (1982). "Defining the Role of the Victim in Criminal Prosecution." *Mississippi Law Journal* 52(3):515-561.

Griffiths, C. T. and R. Hamilton (1996). "Sanctioning and Healing: Restorative Justice in Canadian Aboriginal Communities." In: B. Galaway and J. Hudson (eds.), *Restorative Justice: International Perspectives.* Monsey, NY: Criminal Justice Press.

Grönfers, M. (1989). "Ideals and Reality in Community Mediation." In: M. Wright and B. Galaway (eds.), *Mediation and Criminal Justice: Victims, Offenders and Community.* Newbury Park, CA: Sage.

Haley, J. O. (1989). "Confession, Repentance and Absolution." In: M. Wright and B. Galaway (eds.), *Mediation and Criminal Justice: Victims, Offenders and Community.* Newbury Park, CA: Sage.

Harding, J. (1989). "Reconciling Mediation with Criminal Justice." In: M. Wright and B. Galaway (eds.), *Mediation and Criminal Justice: Victims, Offenders and Community.* Newbury Park, CA: Sage.

—— (1996). "Whither Restorative Justice in England and Wales? A Probation Perspective." In: B. Galaway and J. Hudson (eds.), *Restorative Justice: International Perspectives.* Monsey, NY: Criminal Justice Press.

Immarigeon, R. (1996). "Family Group Conferences in Canada and the United States: An Overview." In: J. Hudson, A. Morris, G. Maxwell and B. Galaway (eds.), *Family Group Conferences: Perspectives on Policy and Practice.* Leichhardt, AUS and Monsey, NY: Federation Press and Criminal Justice Press.

Karmen, A. (1992). "Who's Against Victims' Rights: The Nature of the Opposition to Pro-Victim Initiatives in Criminal Justice." *St. John's Journal of Legal Commentary* 8:157-175.

LaFave, W.R. (1970). "The Prosecutor's Discretion in the United States." *American Journal of Comparative Law* 18:532-548.

Leibrich, J. (1996). "The Role of Shame in Going Straight: A Study of Former Offenders." In: B. Galaway and J. Hudson (eds.), *Restorative Justice: International Perspectives.* Monsey, NY: Criminal Justice Press.

Marshall, T.F. (1990). "Results of Research from British Experiments in Restorative Justice." In: B. Galaway and J. Hudson (eds.), *Criminal Justice, Restitution, and Reconciliation.* Monsey, NY: Criminal Justice Press.

Massaro, T. (1991). "Shame, Culture, and American Criminal Law." *Michigan Law Review* 89:1880-1944.

Matthews, R. 1988). "Reassessing Informal Justice." In: R. Matthews (ed.), *Informal Justice.* Newbury Park, CA: Sage.

Maxwell, G. and A. Morris (1996). "Research on Family Group Conferences with Young Offenders in New Zealand." In: J. Hudson, A. Morris, G. Maxwell and B. Galaway (eds.), *Family Group Conferences: Perspectives on Policy and Practice.* Leichhardt, AUS and Monsey, NY: Federation Press and Criminal Justice Press.

McCold, P. and J. Stahr (1996). "Bethlehem Police Family Group Conferencing Project." Paper presented at the American Society of Criminology, Chicago, November.

McElrea, F.W.M. (1996). "The New Zealand Youth Court: A Model for Use with Adults." In: B. Galaway and J. Hudson (eds.), *Restorative Justice: International Perspectives.* Monsey, NY: Criminal Justice Press.

Merry, S.E. (1989). "Myth and Practice in the Mediation Process." In: M. Wright and B. Galaway (eds.), *Mediation and Criminal Justice: Victims, Offenders and Community.* Newbury Park, CA: Sage.

Moore, D. B. (1993). "Shame, Forgiveness, and Juvenile Justice." *Criminal Justice Ethics* (Winter/Spring):3-25.

—— and T.A. O'Connell (1994). "Family Conferencing in Wagga Wagga: A Communitarian Model of Justice." In: C. Alder and J. Wundersitz (eds.), *Family Conferencing and Juvenile Justice: The Way Forward or Misplaced Optimism?* Canberra, AUS: Australian Institute of Criminology.

Morris, A., G. Maxwell, J. Hudson, and B. Galaway, "Concluding Thoughts." In: J. Hudson, A. Morris, G. Maxwell and B. Galaway (eds.), *Family Group Conferences: Perspectives on Policy and Practice.* Leichhardt, AUS and Monsey, NY: Federation Press and Criminal Justice Press.

Netzig, L. and T. Trenczek (1996). "Restorative Justice as Participation: Theory, Law, Experience and Research." In: B. Galaway and J. Hudson (eds.), *Restorative Justice: International Perspectives.* Monsey, NY: Criminal Justice Press.

Nielsen, M. O. (1996). "A Comparison of Developmental Ideologies: Navajo Nation Peacemaker Courts and Canadian Native Justice Committees." In: B. Galaway and J. Hudson (eds.), *Restorative Justice: International Perspectives.* Monsey, NY: Criminal Justice Press.

Orlando, F.A. (1992). "Mediation Involving Children in the U.S.: Legal and Ethical Conflicts. A Policy Discussion and Research Questions." In: H. Messmer and H. Otto (eds.), *Restorative Justice on Trial: Pitfalls and Potentials of Victim Offender Mediation.* Dordrecht, NETH: Kluwer.

Pelikan, C. (1991). "Conflict Resolution between Victims and Offenders in Austria and in the Federal Republic of Germany." In: F. Heidensohn and M. Farrell (eds.), *Crime in Europe.* London, UK: Routledge.

Pizzi, W. T. (1993) "Understanding Prosecutorial Discretion in the United States: The Limits of Comparative Criminal Procedure as an Instrument of Reform." *Ohio State Law Journal* 54:1325-1373.

Reeves, H. (1989). "The Victim Support Perspective." In: M. Wright and B. Galaway (eds.), *Mediation and Criminal Justice: Victims, Offenders and Community.* Newbury Park, CA: Sage.

Retzinger, S. and T. Scheff (1996). "Strategy for Community Conferences: Emotions and Social Bonds." In: B. Galaway and J. Hudson (eds.), *Restorative Justice: International Perspectives.* Monsey, NY: Criminal Justice Press.

Robertson, J. (1996). "Research on Family Group Conferences in Child Welfare in New Zealand." In: J. Hudson, A. Morris, G. Maxwell and B. Galaway (eds.), *Family*

Group Conferences: Perspectives on Policy and Practice. Leichhardt, AUS and Monsey, NY: Federation Press and Criminal Justice Press.

Robinson, P.H. (1987). "Hybrid Principles for the Distribution of Criminal Sanctions." *Northwestern University Law Review* 82:19-42.

Rowland, J. (1992). "Illusions of Justice: Who Represents the Victim?" *St. John's Journal of Legal Commentary* 8:177-195.

Schafer, S. (1977). *Victimology: The Victim and His Criminal.* Reston, VA: Reston Publishing.

Schweigert, F. "Learning the Common Good: Principles of Community-Based Moral Education in Restorative Justice." Unpublished paper dated April, 1997.

Sessar, K. (1990). "Tertiary Victimization: A Case of the Politically Abused Crime Victims." In: B. Galaway and J. Hudson (eds.), *Criminal Justice, Restitution, and Reconciliation.* Monsey, NY: Criminal Justice Press.

Shapiro, C. (1990). "Is Restitution Legislation the Chameleon of the Victims' Movement?" In: B. Galaway and J. Hudson (eds.), *Criminal Justice, Restitution, and Reconciliation.* Monsey, NY: Criminal Justice Press.

Smith, D., H. Blagg and N. Derricourt (1988). "Mediation in the Shadow of the Law: The South Yorkshire Experience." In: R. Matthews (ed.), *Informal Justice.* Newbury Park, CA: Sage.

Stewart, T. (1996). "Family Group Conferences with Young Offenders in New Zealand." In: J. Hudson, A. Morris, G. Maxwell and B. Galaway (eds.), *Family Group Conferences: Perspectives on Policy and Practice.* Leichhardt, AUS and Monsey, NY: Criminal Justice Press.

Terrill, R. J. (1992). *World Criminal Justice Systems: A Survey* (2nd ed.). Cincinnati, OH: Anderson.

Tonry, M. (1991). "Essay: Public Prosecution and Hydro-engineering." *Minnesota Law Review* 75:971-992.

Trenczek, T. (1990). "A Review and Assessment of Victim-Offender Reconciliation Programming in West Germany." In: B. Galaway and J. Hudson (eds.), *Criminal Justice, Restitution, and Reconciliation.* Monsey, NY: Criminal Justice Press.

Umbreit, M.S. (1990). "The Meaning of Fairness to Burglary Victims." In: B. Galaway and J. Hudson (eds.), *Criminal Justice, Restitution, and Reconciliation.* Monsey, NY: Criminal Justice Press.

—— (1996). "Restorative Justice Through Mediation: The Impact of Programs in Four Canadian Provinces." In: B. Galaway and J. Hudson (eds.), *Restorative Justice: International Perspectives.* Monsey, NY: Criminal Justice Press.

—— (1994). *Victim Meets Offender: The Impact of Restorative Justice and Mediation.* Monsey NY: Criminal Justice Press.

United Nations (1992). *Compendium of United Nations Standards and Norms in Crime Prevention and Criminal Justice.* New York, NY: author.

Van Ness, D.W. (1986). *Crime and Its Victims: What We Can Do.* Downers Grove, IL: InterVarsity Press.

—— (1990). "Restorative Justice." In: B. Galaway and J. Hudson (eds.), *Criminal Justice, Restitution, and Reconciliation*. Monsey, NY: Criminal Justice Press.

—— (1993). "New Wine and Old Wineskins: Four Challenges of Restorative Justice." *Criminal Law Forum* 4:251-276.

—— (1994). "Preserving a Community Voice: The Case for Half-and-Half Juries in Racially-Charged Criminal Cases." *John Marshall Law Review* 28:1-56.

—— (1995). "Anchoring Just Deserts." *Criminal Law Forum* 6:507-517.

—— (1996). "Restorative Justice and International Human Rights." In: B. Galaway and J. Hudson (eds.), *Restorative Justice: International Perspectives*. Monsey, NY: Criminal Justice Press.

—— and K.H. Strong (1997). *Restoring Justice*. Cincinnati, OH: Anderson.

Volpe, M. R (1989). "The Police Role." In: M. Wright and B. Galaway (eds.), *Mediation and Criminal Justice: Victims, Offenders and Community*. Newbury Park, CA: Sage.

von Hirsch, A. (1993). *Censure and Sanctions*. Oxford, UK: Clarendon Press.

Walgrave, L. and H. Geudens (1996). "The Restorative Proportionality of Community Service for Juveniles." *European Journal of Crime, Criminal Law and Criminal Justice* 4:361-380.

Warner, K. (1994). "Family Group Conferences and the Rights of the Offender." In: C. Alder and J. Wundersitz (eds.), *Family Conferencing and Juvenile Justice: The Way Forward or Misplaced Optimism?* Canberra, AUS: Australian Institute of Criminology.

White, R. (1994). "Shame and Reintegration Strategies: Individuals, State Power and Social Interests." In: C. Alder and J. Wundersitz (eds.), *Family Conferencing and Juvenile Justice: The Way Forward or Misplaced Optimism?* Canberra, AUS: Australian Institute of Criminology.

Wright, M. (1991). *Justice For Victims and Offenders*. Philadelphia, PA: Open University Press.

—— (1992). "Victim-Offender Mediation as a Step Towards a Restorative System of Justice." In: H. Messmer and H. Otto (eds.), *Restorative Justice on Trial: Pitfalls and Potentials of Victim Offender Mediation*. Dordrecht, NETH: Kluwer.

Wundersitz, J. and S. Hetzel (1996). "Family Conferencing for Young Offenders: The South Australian Experience." In: J. Hudson, A. Morris, G. Maxwell and B. Galaway (eds.), *Family Group Conferences: Perspectives on Policy and Practice*. Leichhardt, AUS and Monsey, NY: Federation Press and Criminal Justice Press.

Young, M. A. (1995). "Restorative Community Justice: A Call to Action." Washington, DC: National Organization for Victim Assistance.

Zehr, H. (1990). *Changing Lenses: A New Focus for Crime and Justice*. Scottdale, PA: Herald Press.

NOTES

1. Restorative justice theory has its roots in a number of reform movements of the past 25 years, including the informal justice movement, the victims' rights movement and the restitution/diversion movement. Consequently, it should be no surprise that its processes and sanctions raise legal issues that are similar to those of its antecedents. These might be categorized into four groups:

(a) *Jurisprudential concerns*, including: the principle of legality and the principle of discretion (Dünkel and Rössner, 1989); the legal status of attempted crimes that do not result in injury (Ashworth, 1993); the uneasy blending of restoration with other criminal justice purposes in any hybrid model (Harding, 1989; Grönfers, 1989; Zehr, 1990; Coates, 1990; Van Ness, 1993; Morris et al., 1996; Nielsen, 1996); the role of the lawyer in restorative processes (Maxwell and Morris, 1989); provisions concerning the independence and accountability of mediators (Merry, 1989; Ban, 1996) analogous to international provisions for the independence of the judiciary in criminal cases (United Nations, 1992); the risk of sanctions being based on attitudes or other non-offense factors (Warner, 1994; Maxwell and Morris, 1996); and the roles of governmental agencies (Matthews, 1988; Volpe, 1989; Marshall, 1990).

(b) *Rights of offenders*, including: an accused who pleads innocent (McElrea, 1996); admissibility in subsequent court proceedings of statements made in mediation issues (White, 1994; Immarigeon, 1996); achieving proportionality of sanctions (Warner, 1994; Van Ness, 1995; Maxwell and Morris, 1996); ensuring equal treatment of offenders (Warner, 1994; McElrea, 1996); protecting against cruel, inhuman, and degrading sanctions (Massaro, 1991); and protection against double jeopardy (Warner, 1994).

(c) *Rights of victims*, including: recognition of victims' interests in reparation, retribution, privacy, protection of reputation, protection from harassment and intimidation, satisfaction, and minimizing psychological trauma of criminal justice system process (Schafer, 1977; Reeves, 1989; Sessar, 1990; Van Ness, 1993; Maxwell and Morris, 1996; Netzig and Trenczek, 1996); the role of private prosecution (Goldstein, 1982; Gittler, 1984; Van Ness and Strong, 1997); the involvement of the victim in formal and informal responses to crime (Van Ness, 1986; Trenczek, 1990; Gehm, 1990); dealing with conflict between the victim and prosecutor (Rowland, 1992; Karmen, 1992) and victim involvement in a prisoner's release (Harding, 1996).

(d) *Procedural issues*, including: how to enforce restorative sanctions (Shapiro, 1990); how to ensure voluntariness and protect against coercion (Smith et al., 1988; Moore, 1993; Maxwell and Morris, 1996; Van Ness and Strong, 1997) and the related question of how to respond when one or more parties choose not to participate (Maxwell and Morris, 1996; Wundersitz and Hetzel, 1996); confidentiality/admissibility issues (Immarigeon, 1996); and power imbalances between defendant, victim, community and state (Merry, 1989; Volpe, 1989; Fraser and Norton, 1996; Griffiths and Hamilton, 1996).

2. It appears to be generally accepted that the procedural rights of victims to information, participation and recompense are more likely to be honored in restorative, rather than

traditional, processes (Young, 1995; Van Ness, 1996; Umbreit, 1990). However, concerns have been raised whether the due process rights of accused and convicted defendants are adequately protected in restorative justice processes. This paper focuses on those concerns.

3. The other six fundamental rights identified by Bassiouni (1993) are: the right to life, liberty and security of the person; the right to be free from arbitrary arrest and detention; the right to a speedy trial; the right to appeal; the right to be protected from double jeopardy; and the right to be protected from *ex post facto* laws.

4. The Beijing Rules prohibit discrimination on the basis of race, color, sex, language, religion, political or other opinions, national or social origin, property, birth or other status (2.1).

5. The Beijing Rules do not use these particular terms, but instead impose an affirmative duty on governments to provide "care, protection and all necessary assistance" to ensure that juveniles' social, educational, physical, social and vocational needs are catered to (26.1 and 2). Furthermore, they explicitly incorporate the Standard Minimum Rules for the Treatment of Prisoners, which do contain such terminology (27.1), and they prohibit the use of corporal punishment (17.3).

6. The Beijing Rules provide for the presumption of innocence and the right to remain silent in proceedings involving juveniles (7.1).

7. The Beijing Rules provide for the rights to be notified of charges, to counsel, to the presence of a parent or guardian, and to confront and cross-examine witnesses (7.1). They further provide that the case be heard "according to the principles of a fair and just trial" (14.1), and that legal assistance be provided in the event of indigency (15.1).

8. The Beijing Rules provide not only that juveniles will have the right to counsel (7.1), but also that they should have the right to apply for legal aid when that is available (15.1).

9. The term "legality principle" is also used to refer to the requirement that a law prohibiting conduct have preceded the conduct for which a person is charged with a crime. Article 7 of the European Convention on Human Rights, for example, states: "No one shall be held guilty of any offence on account of any act or omission which did not constitute a criminal offence under national or international law at the time when it was committed." For discussion of this use of the term, see Ashworth (1991), at 59-71.

PART FOUR:
RESEARCH — IMPACT ON VICTIM, OFFENDER AND COMMUNITY

11. Punitive Attitudes of the Public: Reality and Myth

by

Klaus Sessar

It is generally assumed that the public has strongly punitive views on sentencing. This belief is supported by the seemingly widespread attitude that sentences are too lenient and that criminals should be locked up for as long as possible, as well as by the marked suspicion with which any attempt to humanize the correctional systems is observed. Although perceptions of this punitive outlook are not totally wrong, little attempt is made to study the reasons behind it. Moreover, it is widely ignored that punitive attitudes play a major or even exclusive role only because alternative methods — for example restitutive approaches — have no real chance of being recognized and applied by those who administer the official philosophy of punishment.

In fact, the counterpart of punishment is restitution (*Wiedergutmachung*). Both instruments are negative sanctions that in former times were indivisible responses to what we would nowadays term a crime. Separation accompanied the introduction of the distinction between civil law and penal law, which had the well-known consequence that penal sanctions superseded civil sanctions in almost all legal systems, such that punishment came to be considered not only as social satisfaction but also as personal satisfaction. This might be one of the reasons why we tend to resort almost automatically to the usual crime-and-punishment patterns in cases of criminal victimization — without conceiving of alternatives to punishment in order to deal with crimes as social conflicts.

The hypothesis is that restitution would be accepted and perhaps even preferred by the public (and by victims of crime) if it were given a chance to prove itself. Many national and international studies have shown that *Wiedergutmachung*, restitution, compensation and the like are actually broadly accepted in lieu of punishment - not for all criminal cases, admittedly, but certainly for the majority. By contrast, with the exception of trivial misdemeanors, the judiciary rejects the notion of restitution as being an adequate response to crime. In this chapter, the findings of various German research projects will be outlined that demonstrate the acceptance of an instrument that in the minds of the public serves both the emotional and practical needs of the victim and the idea of social justice — as opposed to punishment, which instead satisfies the rather archaic requirements of retribution.

1. PRELIMINARY REMARKS

This paper deals with public attitudes toward the sanctioning as well as the procedural concept of what is called "restorative justice." Studies of this kind usually contrast sanctions that are of a conflict-solving with those of a punitive nature, although still within the criminal justice system. The most important examples are restitution (or compensation, or *Wiedergutmachung*) and community service. Restitution means more than just repairing the damage caused; it entails some sort of heart-to-heart discussion between the offender and the victim mediated by a third party, a process in fact known as "mediation." Therefore, many questionnaires focus on the usual sanctions including non-intervention (dismissal of the case), but with the addition of restitution. However, we might also be interested in whether restitution, with or without mediation, is acceptable as an alternative to punishment altogether; in other words, do we really always need the criminal justice system to guarantee social peace or to restore it just because a harmful act has been defined as a crime? More precisely, will the public accept that an agreement following negotiations between offender and victim does not merely alleviate or solve the interpersonal problem, but that it satisfies the interests of the community in restoring moral order at the same time? In such a case restitution constitutes not just another sanction but an alternative sanction; it is not an addition to the traditional penalties but is opposed to them (Sessar 1992).

One particular problem is *community service*. In Germany, its application to juvenile offenders mostly has educational (rehabilitative) purposes. It cannot be ruled out that the German Constitutional Court may declare the usage of community service in our Juvenile Court Act as an exclusive measure to compensate for the "public losses" after the occurrence of a crime as unconstitutional, because of its affinity to the repressive nature of forced labor (see *Entscheidungen des Bundesverfassungsgerichts*, vol. 74, p. 123). Indeed, it is hard to avoid the resemblance between a community service order and sanctions with retributive features precisely because the order does have retributive features, regardless of how it is defined and organized. The fact that according to the International Crime Survey of 1989 so many French, Swiss and German respondents were in favor of this sanction instead of fines, imprisonment or suspended sentences (van Dijk et al., 1990) does not necessarily mean that all of them were strong advocates of a restorative-justice system. The findings could just as well mean that many participants would like to see the offender work, perhaps very hard (but this is not how the question was put). At least this was the view of one of the participants in an American study: "Community service should be hard work which makes them [the offenders] think twice about committing a crime the next time "(Immerwahr 1993:60).

The problem of community is one with serious theoretical implications. Based on the retributive and deterrent rationale of penal law, community service was introduced in some countries as a cheaper alternative to imprisonment or as an instrument for better rehabilitation of offenders. The conception of community service as a restorative sanction is rather new. In Germany it was recommended as a symbolic form of restitution, especially where no specific victims or no material damages or damages for pain and suffering exist; community service would then be an alternative to the alternative of restitution in specific cases. One of the many theoretical difficulties is to draw a distinction between this non-punitive measure and, for example, a fine that is a penalty but also some sort of restitution — to the taxpayer. Therefore, what are the new and unconfoundable contents and purposes of community service as opposed to other non-custodial sanctions? Should it be used to compensate the loss of public safety, the damage to community values and the community's disruption caused by the crime (Van Ness, 1990). The question is how these damages differ from injuries to the state, to the legal order, or to society quite generally; and how they can be measured and how much they count for a commonly satisfying restoration without recurring to the principles of penal law? Another difficulty refers to the suitability of tasks for community service and to the matching of offenders to them: Is any task suitable to meet the restorative purposes of this measure, or is a specific (functional, emotional) link needed between the offense and the expected work? Again, in Germany, it is neither legally required nor practically possible to relate community service to the motivation of juvenile offenders or to the nature of the offenses committed. Consequently, despite the pretended rehabilitative nature of community service, this instrument is used following the ordinary scheme of "just desert." This is just another example of the criminal justice system's resoluteness to insist on penal theory underlying all types of sanctions.

The subject of this volume is restorative justice for juveniles. Many surveys on attitudes toward punitive, rehabilitative, restitutive and restorative sanctions, etc. fail to distinguish between juvenile and adult offenders. However, the gap in our information does not appear to be very large. In 1984, a postal survey entitled "Restitution or Punishment" (Sessar, 1992) was conducted using a representative sample of the Hamburg, GER population with a return rate of 44%, producing 1799 usable questionnaires. Two groups of subjects addressed identical cases, the only difference being the age of the fictitious offender, who was 30 in one group and 17 in the other group. The differences in the respondents' replies were minimal or non-existent, i.e. the juvenile and the adult offender were treated more or less equally (Sessar 1992:107-110). According to the *American Sourcebook of Criminal Justice Statistics*, only 31% of respondents thought that juvenile offenders should be dealt with differently than adults (Maguire and Pastore 1995). This underpins our approach of neglecting age differences, and therefore we will report generally on punitive and restitutive attitudes.

We shall start with some theoretical considerations about the stabilizing importance of punishment for and within the legal system in order to reflect upon the chance of changing the punitive basis of the system for restorative purposes. We will then discuss some results that might indicate that public opinion would under specific conditions accept reforms toward a system of restorative justice (although admittedly not in every country or culture). Some further information on punitive and restitutive attitudes of judges and public prosecutors will be given to show the considerable, maybe unbridgeable, gap between both groups regarding adequate reactions to crime.

2. THEORETICAL REMARKS

Equity theory teaches us that (most) harmful behavior leads to inequity in the relationship between the wrongdoer (this is, in our terms, the offender) and the victim (Utne and Hatfield, 1978). It seems to be a universal observation that any such inequitable relationship requires restoration. The wrongdoer either has to compensate the victim (through restitution or compensation), or he or she has to be punished (through vengeance or retribution). In fact, restitution and punishment are the two principal means used if something wrong or harmful has occurred in an interpersonal relationship.

In the past, these two reactions did not differ very much; instead, they were co-existing rationales for sanctions that served the reappraisal and reconciliation of victims and offenders after interpersonal disputes and violations. We know that vengeance could even be substituted by restitution because of the latter's ability to restore the broken peace — not only between the two parties involved but also in society as a whole. On the other hand, contract violations could be handled repressively, as Durkheim (1933 [1893]) has pointed out by referring to Salic law. This view has not entirely been forgotten. For example, in German civil law a *solatium* can be recovered for injured feelings; this measure is considered to be both a civil law sanction and a criminal law sanction because of its origin in a pre-medieval sanction known as *Geldbusse* (penance money), which combined both objectives (§847 Bürgerliches Gesetzbuch; see Deutler 1956; Frehsee 1987). The separation of restitutive and punitive sanctions accompanied the division of civil law and criminal law as the two main subsystems within the legal system; punishment and restitution can now be imposed simultaneously after the occurrence of a (violent) crime. Theoretically, it is interesting but also rather depressing to observe how criminal law sanctions have gained priority over civil law sanctions when it comes to preserving social peace and giving satisfaction to the victim (Frehsee 1987). It is depressing because this development has turned out to be a trap for many endeavors to restore a restorative justice.

In order to better understand this development, another theoretical approach is needed. Let me start with a scene from the play *Le Balcon* by the French poet Jean Genet. In a whorehouse one of the clients (who in reality is a banker) plays the role of a judge, a prostitute the role of a thief. The "judge" says to her: "In the beginning there was a thief. My livelihood as a judge is the consequence of your thefts....You don't deny being a thief? This would be bad. This would be a crime. You would destroy my livelihood." The scene tells us that not only are penalties needed because there are crimes — but also that crimes are needed because there are penalties (and institutions that impose the penalties). This insight is a sociological commonplace, of course. For example, Durkheim (1964 [1895]:68-69) imagines a society of saints in which usual crimes are unknown, "but faults which appear venial to the layman will create there the same scandal that the ordinary offense does in ordinary consciousness. If, then, this society has the power to judge and punish, it will define these acts as criminal and will treat them as such." Erikson (1967:15) regards deviance as an important condition for preserving stability in society and continues by asking: "Can we assume ... that forces operate within the social order to recruit deviant actors and commit them to deviant forms of activity?"

In the view of both Durkheim (1964[1875]) and Erikson (1967), some unspecified societal forces (Durkheim calls them the "collective consciousness") that are embodied by particular agencies or institutions draw and maintain the boundaries between conformity and deviance by distributing reward and punishment. Nowadays, we wouldn't locate such forces in society but would pinpoint them in specific functional systems like the legal system, and then more closely in the criminal justice system, which administers and distributes good and bad, right and wrong, justice and injustice. According to modern system theory, society is functionally differentiated. Functional systems (the economy, education, science, religion, law, etc.) are self-referential systems in that they produce and develop themselves with the elements of which they consist (also known as "autopoietic" systems; see *Luhmann* 1985, pp. 281-288).

In our example, operations within the legal system (i.e., operations that produce decisions) are of a normative and not a social nature; social conflicts which are part of society — or of the lifeworld in *Habermas'* terms — have to be digitized into system codes, otherwise they cannot be understood or read. The same happens to the participants of the conflict; they have to be transformed into legal opponents for system purposes and are then called "offender" (suspect, accused, convicted) and "victim." The binary code or binary schematization of (criminal) law is "justice/injustice" on an abstract level (Luhmann 1985, 1995);

it is not, for example, "equity/inequity" on an (inter)personal level. Consequently, the program of the criminal justice system for dealing with conflicts is
restricted to the system-specific categories of crime and punishment; the system
is unable to use and adopt conflict-solving operations (restitution, restoration,
mediation, and the like) to a larger extent because they are not part of an abstract, i.e., "victimless" program to provide normatively secured peace and justice. Even where mediation is accepted by the criminal law, it becomes part of
the punishing system: the alternative (i.e. in the case of its failure) is punishment
and not another conflict-solving procedure. At the same time mediation is also
an alternative to non-punishment (dismissal of the case) which then stresses the
big problem of "net-widening."

All this means that our problem is not something that can be changed
merely by altering criminal policy or by supplementing our penal codes; instead
it is a matter of structural differentiation and thereby structural change. This is
why, for example, the British experiment in restorative justice was not very encouraging, as Marshall (1990) pointed out almost a decade ago. Concerning
compensation orders, "the courts, seeing their job as punishing offenders, were
not geared to addressing the needs of the victims... The community service orders were more popular, but perceived solely as punitive rather than restorative.
They tended to be seen by courts as one 'appropriate' punishment ... largely on
the 'eye for an eye' principle... Restorative in form, community service orders
were retributive in practice" (Marshall, 1990, pp. 84-85). This is also more or
less the philosophy applied in German courts.

We will finish this bewildering overview with Christie's (1977) almost ir-
refutable notion that the lawyers have taken conflicts away from the parties involved; that they have stolen them. Therefore, to return to Genet's play: the
judge is also a thief. Both the judge and the thief are mutually-supporting pillars
in a recursively closed system, with punishment and crime being the essentials
for the maintenance and the development of the system. There is thus not much
scope for programs and operations without punitive features.

These remarks seem to indicate that the crime-and-punishment pattern reflects not so much the needs and interests of society, but rather the interests of
the criminal justice system. However, at first sight this is not the case. When
asked whether they favor imprisonment, a fine or restitution in the case of, say, a
burglary or assault and battery, people will usually opt for one of the penalties;
only rarely do they choose restitution as an alternative. For example, in a survey
conducted by the Criminological Research Institute of Lower Saxony in
Hanover, Germany, the respondents were asked to select one of the following
sanctions in the case of a burglary in an arbor (the offender, a 30-year-old man
with no prior record, had stolen tools worth DM 1000): imprisonment, suspended imprisonment sentence, fine, fine together with labor, labor alone, super-

vision, restitution, or no charge. Only 1.2% of the participants of the survey favored restitution, and only another 0.2% said that the case should be dismissed (Pfeiffer, 1993). In our own representative study conducted in both Eastern and Western Germany in 1993, the respondents were asked to decide between the following sanctions after a residential burglary (the offender, again a 30-year-old man without previous convictions, had stolen money and some other articles worth DM 1200): no action, private settlement, no punishment in the case of restitution, mild punishment, fine, suspended imprisonment sentence, imprisonment. In the new Länder (the area of the former German Democratic Republic), 1.7% of the respondents said that prosecution would be unnecessary in the case of restitution, while another 0.3% did not want to be the offender charged at all; the rates in the old Länder were 0.9% and 0.4%, respectively (for the methodology see Boers et al., 1997). As one can see, both studies yield similar results in spite of different samples and different research designs. At this point, a portion of a letter to the editor of the *London Times* from January 4, 1987 should be introduced: "It is a myth that the public demands tough punishment...; as several surveys have shown, a majority thinks that restorative sanctions ... make more sense than retributive ones" (see Walker and Hough, 1988:6). Is it really a myth? Judging by our two examples, isn't it really close to reality? Doesn't the system, be it closed or open, meet the interests of the general public when by applying traditional sanctions such as imprisonment or fines in lieu of restitution, compensation or *Wiedergutmachung*?

It is an old fashioned notion that criminal law represents the will of society when its system of values is protected by the use of imprisonment or fines. The reality is that the conditions determining the legal system's operations (and morals) are dictated not by the members of society but by the system itself. Conflicting interests between the criminal law and society are rarely overcome by adapting the former to the interests expressed by the society from which it was originally derived. In fact, the very reverse is true. General needs and interests mostly yield to those laid down by criminal law, such that even common belief systems became punitively oriented. Consequently, following a long tradition of successful conditioning — as a result of which most non-punitive (for example, restitutive) patterns have been extinguished while punitive patterns have been reinforced — the members of society see, define and try to solve many of their own problems within the framework of categories of criminal law. This might be one reason for the above-mentioned punitive attitudes if all that is done is to put restitution on a list together with all the familiar and well- or ill-experienced penalties.

EMPIRICAL REMARKS

We need different ways to find out the people's opinion about what should be done about punitive sanctions. Inquiring into public attitudes toward punishment and restitution means having to leave the system of penalties, and to move to the "lifeworld" in order to obtain more unbiased views of the crime-and-punishment scene. "Lifeworld," in the definition of Habermas, is "...a culturally transmitted and linguistically organized stock of interpretive patterns... This stock of knowledge supplies members with unproblematic, common, background convictions that are assumed to be guaranteed; it is from these that contexts of processes of reaching understanding get shaped, processes in which those involved use tried and true situation definitions or negotiate new ones" (1987, pp.124-125). Christie's (1977) "conflicts as property" corresponds to this conception of a world in which conflict-solving is part of steady social regeneration. Restitution belongs to these tried background convictions and experiences, however much it may have been buried over the centuries. The hypothesis is, then, that considerable acceptance of those alternatives reactions can be expected, provided it is made clear what is meant by alternative sanctions, how restitution or community service work, and what the positive and negative consequences of the given sanctions are or are expected to be. In other words, what we need for valid questioning are "informed respondents" (Sessar 1992:48; Immerwahr 1993:60).

Whom do we ask? So far, we have spoken about the public, the members of society, or just the people. Victims of crime are included, of course. Many surveys have shown that victims and non-victims share similar views of the world of crimes and criminals. One explanation could be that most non-victims are in fact victims; during the interview they simply failed to recall the crime incident suffered (*Sessar* 1990). Indeed, it is hard to believe that non-victims exist in a world where no non-offenders exist. Regardless of this, the following findings will include the victims' attitudes.

One possibility of ascertaining the importance of restitution in the minds of the people is to present cases in which the offender had indeed made restitution to the victim. The above-mentioned study conducted by the Criminological Research Institute in Hanover did in fact construct two cases of a burglary in an arbor that were then evaluated by two different groups of respondents. The description of the offense in the second case was supplemented by the information that upon the court's suggestion, the offender had returned the stolen property to the owner, paid for the damages caused and apologized to the victim for his act. Not surprisingly, the respondents' attitudes changed completely from one case to another. In the second, not only did the subjects favor milder sanctions (prison sentences became insignificant, and suspended prison sentences dropped from 12.2% to 6.6%, and fines from 35.1% to 21.8%), but most important, 25% favored dismissal of the case altogether. A similar result was found in the case of aggravated assault and battery, even though the fictitious offender was presented as a recidivist and the victim suffered serious bruises and lost two teeth (Pfeiffer, 1993; see Figures 1 and 2).

Figure 1: Attitudes toward Sanctioning for a Burglar in an Arbor (30-Year Old Offender without Previous Record); Länder of the former Federal Republic of Germany

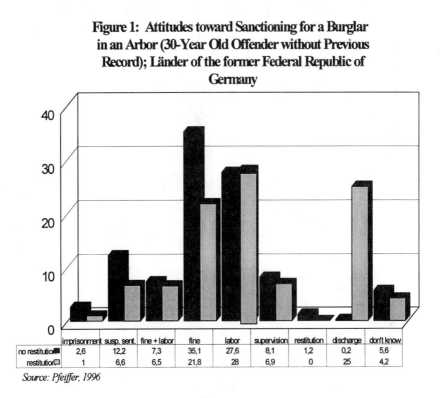

	imprisonment	susp. sent.	fine + labor	fine	labor	supervision	restitution	discharge	don't know
no restitution	2,6	12,2	7,3	35,1	27,6	8,1	1,2	0,2	5,6
restitution	1	6,6	6,5	21,8	28	6,9	0	25	4,2

Source: Pfeiffer, 1996

In our previously discussed Hamburg study (Sessar, 1995b), victims were asked how the case of "their" offender should be treated after successful restitution: on average, 48% of the victims were prepared to refrain from punishment altogether, and 35% in part. In the case of residential burglary, the figures were 32 and 44%, respectively, and 46 and 30%, respectively, for violent crimes. We then asked how the victims would decide if they were judges of their own case (open question): 42% of the respondents opted for pure restitution and another 5% for non-intervention, a further 9% chose restitution combined with labor, while the rest (44%) chose some form of punishment (Sessar 1995b.). As we can see, participants have to be familiarized with restitution in one way or the other; it is not enough merely to list it together with other sanctions.

Figure 2: Attitudes toward Sanctioning for an Aggravated Assault and Battery with Grievous Bodily Harm (30-Year-Old Offender Without Previous Record: Länder of the former Federal Republic of Germany

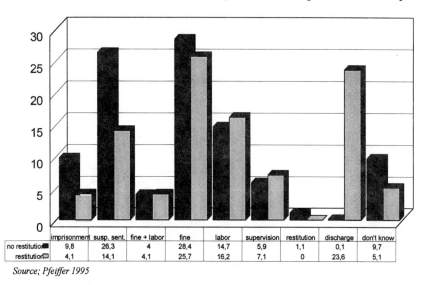

	imprisonment	susp. sent.	fine + labor	fine	labor	supervision	restitution	discharge	don't know
no restitution ■	9,8	26,3	4	28,4	14,7	5,9	1,1	0,1	9,7
restitution ▦	4,1	14,1	4,1	25,7	16,2	7,1	0	23,6	5,1

Source; Pfeiffer 1995

Another method of obtaining more valid information about the sentiments of people is to make them aware of the meaning and the effects of penalties. A number of studies have been undertaken in the U.S. to test the conjecture of Justice Marshall (in *Furman v. Georgia* [1972]) that support for the death penalty is a function of a lack of knowledge about it. *Marshall* had stated that, "it is imperative for constitutional purposes to attempt to discern the probable opiniun of an *informed* electorate" (my emphasis), and stressed that the public's choice about the death penalty must be a "knowledgeable choice" (see *Bohm, Clark, Aveni* 1991, pp. 360-361). One of the research hypotheses was that, "An informed public would generally oppose the death penalty and its effects." (Bohm et al.,1991:361).

This assumption has been used to study attitudes toward severe penalties in general. The measurement procedure very often has a pretest-posttest survey design in that the respondents (mostly students) are asked at the beginning and at the end of the experiment about their attitudes. Between these two stages, the participants attend relevant, informative courses — for example, on capital punishment or on prisons — or they might watch a video reviewing prison problems. Marshall's (1972) hypothesis is to some extent validated by the fact that many respondents displayed milder attitudes at the end of the experiments (Bohm et al., 1991; Immerwahr 1993; Lane 1997). To quote one example, in Immerwahr's (1993) study conducted in the U.S. state of Delaware, 79% of survey participants initially agreed that in the case of armed robbery, a juvenile (first-time) offender should be sent to prison. However, after watching a video on prison overcrowding and discussing alternative sanctions, this proportion dropped to 38%. For shoplifting as a third offense, the initial and final rates were 71 and 19% respectively.

Now, in order to decide whether one of the traditional penalties or restitution is a more rational or intelligent measure with which to react to a crime, the respondents need to know about the consequences of their decisions. To give you just one example, in the Hamburg study, Sessar, (1995b) constructed the case of a theft in which the victim had suffered a loss of DM 1000. The judge wished to fine the offender DM 1000 but realized that by doing so he would disadvantage the victim because the offender could not pay twice. The respondents were then asked to solve the judge's dilemma: fine the offender DM 1000, fine him DM 500 and order restitution amounting to DM 500, or sentence him to make full restitution of DM 1000. The respondents were informed that under the first alternative the money would go to the state, and that under the third alternative the offender would not be punished in the traditional way. A total of 74% of the respondents opted for full restitution; only 10% favored pure punishment (Sessar, 1995b; see also Figure 3). In another more severe case (burglary), 95% of the respondents preferred a suspended sentence to imprisonment on condition that the offender make restitution to the victim; the case account included the information that a prison sentence would cause the offender to lose his job and render him unable to repair the damage caused.

The Hamburg study then went one step further. Knowing about the difficulty of installing restitution within the framework of usual penalties without turning it into another penalty, it was contrasted with penalties. In other words, the goal was to find out whether the respondents would accept restitution not only in lieu of punishment but also in lieu of criminal proceedings. For this purpose a fixed-response menu with the following five alternatives was presented (the offender was 30 years old and had no previous convictions):

- Victim and offender should privately agree on restitution or reconciliation (with the help of a third person if needed).

- Victim and offender should agree on restitution or reconciliation mediated by an officially appointed person.

- The criminal justice system should initiate an agreement on restitution between victim and offender. The agreement should be supervised, for example, by a probation officer.

- The offender should be punished. If he provided restitution to the victim, the punishment should be dispensed with or reduced.

- The offender should be punished. Even if he or she provides restitution to the victim, the punishment should not be dispensed with or reduced.

The bias of this menu is that it starts with non-intervention and ends up with punishment. Reversing this ranking results in more punitive findings (Kury 1995) now biased in the opposite direction (Sessar, 1995a). The answers were applied to 38 different cases ranging from fare-dodging to aggravated assault and battery with serious bodily harm, burglary, and rape. Taken over the sum of the cases, the frequency of the responses to the five proposals was as follows: 23.9% for private settlement; 18.5% for private settlement with the help of a mediator; 17.4% for criminal justice system initiatives without prosecution; 18.8% for punishment to be mitigated or abolished in the event of successful restitution; and 21.4% for punishment irrespective of restitution (Boers and Sessar 1991). With respect to types of crimes, restitution inside or outside the criminal justice system was only rarely or not at all accepted in the case of rape and burglary; by contrast, restitution outside the system received substantial approval for larceny, fraud, assault, and negligent traffic accidents resulting in bruises, cuts or contusions. In the majority of cases, successful restitution made prosecution unnecessary in the minds of the survey participants, or, during trial, was accepted as a reason for reducing or even abolishing punishment.

Let us look at two examples that allow the public's attitudes to be compared with those of the judiciary. In the first case, while visiting a customer in his home, the offender sells a cheap imitation watch worth DM 20 for DM 200, pretending that this is a special offer. In the second case, while leaving a movie, the offender happens to meet his girlfriend, with whom he has recently quarreled. Because they have to go in the same direction, they decide to walk together. At a solitary spot he makes advances, the woman refuses, but he drags her into the bushes nearby and rapes her. Concerning the fraud case, 38% of the respondents from the general public opted for private agreement with or without mediation, compared to 14.5% who favored punishment regardless of restitution. Regarding the rape case, the respective rates were 4.4 and 73.4%, respectively. As can be seen, the different severity of the two acts is mirrored by the respondents' answers; the peculiarity is that restitution can lead not only to milder penalties but even to total non-intervention.

In the next step, the judicial authorities were taken into consideration. It is generally assumed that restitution only has a minor chance in the criminal justice system merely because it is not part of its program. However, there may be considerable differences between its various branches. Therefore, some of the questions from the general survey were posed to the civil judges, criminal judges and public prosecutors of the justice system of the City of Hamburg (for the methodology, see Sessar 1992). As to the case of the judge who wishes to fine the offender DM 1000, a descending order of acceptance of restitution can be detected when comparing the general population of Hamburg with judges and public prosecutors. Those most inclined toward restitution were the public, followed by civil judges and criminal judges in that order, with the prosecutors — not surprisingly, being the strongest advocates of punitive measures (Figure 3). The same can be observed of the fraud case (Figure 4), whereas no significant distinctions were found regarding the rape case (no table shown).

Figure 3: Attitudes of the General Public and the Judicial Authorities toward Fine or Restitution Sentences in the Case of Theft: City of Hamburg, 1984

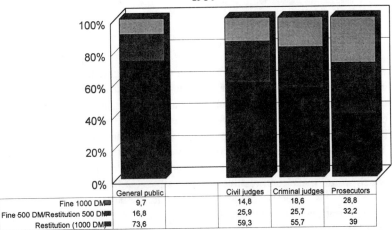

	General public		Civil judges	Criminal judges	Prosecutors
Fine 1000 DM	9,7		14,8	18,6	28,8
Fine 500 DM/Restitution 500 DM	16,8		25,9	25,7	32,2
Restitution (1000 DM)	73,6		59,3	55,7	39

Source: Sessar, 1992

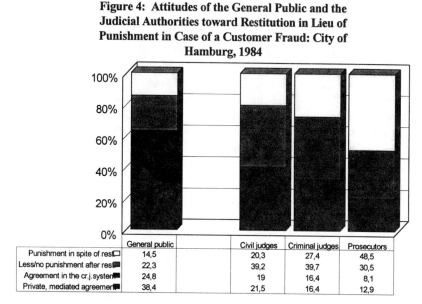

Figure 4: **Attitudes of the General Public and the Judicial Authorities toward Restitution in Lieu of Punishment in Case of a Customer Fraud: City of Hamburg, 1984**

	General public		Civil judges	Criminal judges	Prosecutors
Punishment in spite of rest□	14,5		20,3	27,4	48,5
Less/no punishment after res▨	22,3		39,2	39,7	30,5
Agreement in the cr.j.system▉	24,8		19	16,4	8,1
Private, mediated agreement▨	38,4		21,5	16,4	12,9

Source: Sessar, 1992

Let us now turn to a final example that highlights the contrast in "philosophy" between the general public and the judicial authorities in terms of restitution and punishment. Whereas in the examples so far almost none of the offenders had previous convictions, we will deal now with a case involving multiple recidivists. Such offenders are usually harshly punished (for example, by a prison sentence). The dilemma is that by doing so, the needs and interests of the victims concerned could be neglected because the offender could lose his job, which would make then restitution impossible. On the other hand, consideration of the victims' interests might lead to milder penalties (for example, to a suspended sentence on condition that the offender makes restitution to the victim) and thereby might affect the perception of justice (i.e., the general perception or that of the system). Once again the question was whether to punish without regard for the victims, or to consider the victims' interests and run the risk of inadequate punishment. In this case too (Sessar, 1995b), the Hamburg public displayed much greater concern for the victims than the judges and the public prosecutors, who were more inclined to express the traditional view of just deserts (Figure 5). Yet equally remarkable is the considerable difference between the attitudes of civil judges, criminal judges, and, especially public prosecutors. Civil judges, who have much experience with searching for compromises between the parties involved, may better understand the concepts of victim-offender reconciliation; of restitution, compensation, and mediation; and of restorative justice than criminal judges, and, of course, public prosecutors, who insist on the abstract concept that the offender has primarily violated the law, not a person.

4. CONCLUDING REMARKS

Our conclusion from all this is that the public at large displays an intrinsic acceptance of private conflict-solving following an offense. Insofar as this is the case, the conception of the public's strong punitive sentiments is a myth. However, it is also undeniable that official punishment is part of this perception in specific situations. Moreover, attitudes toward restitution and punishment are subject to social change; it cannot be ruled out that nowadays restitutive ideas might stand less chance than a few years ago. This could be related to the current conservative climate within society that favors a harsh criminal policy; it could also be linked to specific and spectacular violent crimes or to general crime waves, which make people think that punishment is an instrument designed especially to restore security (by keeping criminals out of society, for example; Maguire and Pastore 1995). However, this is not the point. Most important is the significance that has been attached to restitution by the public — and the victims! — when it comes to dealing with offenders. The impression is that whenever restitution is given precedence over punishment, it should be tried and applied before other instruments come into question; it is not or only rarely an additional sanction. This implies that in many instances, restitution substitutes not only for criminal sanctions but also for criminal procedures — meaning that restorative justice could be achieved outside the criminal justice system.

This is one side of the coin. The other side is represented by the criminal justice system. As figures show, punitive attitudes are much more prevalent on the part of judges (especially criminal judges) and prosecutors — a view that is supported by practical observations. Although the penal codes make provision for restitution and mediation for many juvenile and adult criminal offenses, these rules are rarely applied. It could be said with much caution that such findings confirm the concept of modern system theory — or at least indicate its plausibility. Restitution and mediation are foreign elements to the system because they belong to the interpersonal level of problem solving, which is paid only scant attention by the system (for example, when it has to decide upon mitigating or aggravating circumstances). My fear is that this pessimistic view is also true with respect to juveniles. The German Juvenile Court Act is based on the principle of education; consequently, most sanctions are said to have an educational purpose. A growing number of criminologists and lawyers advocate the abolition of this educational approach because it has been established that the courts use it to conceal the sole real purpose of a criminal justice system, namely, retribution.

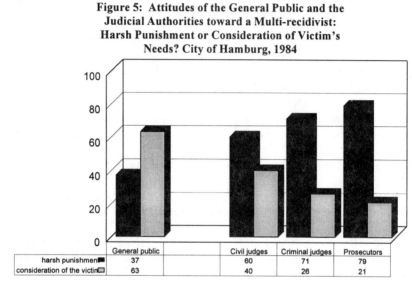

Figure 5: Attitudes of the General Public and the Judicial Authorities toward a Multi-recidivist: Harsh Punishment or Consideration of Victim's Needs? City of Hamburg, 1984

	General public		Civil judges	Criminal judges	Prosecutors
harsh punishment	37		60	71	79
consideration of the victim	63		40	26	21

Source: Sessar, 1992

Therefore, if restorative justice is to be introduced, it should not be consigned to the criminal justice system. The danger is that its instruments would not be applied, that they would be applied chiefly for decorative purposes or that they would be turned into punitive measures (as many community service orders show). The best way, without doubt, would be to introduce a separate system of restorative justice.

REFERENCES

Boers, K., G. Gutsche and K. Sessar (eds.) (1997). *Sozialer Umbruch und Kriminalität in Deutschland.* Opladen, GER: Westdeutscher Verlag

—— and K. Sessar (1991). "Do People Really Want Punishment? On the Relationship between Acceptance of Restitution, Needs for Punishment, and Fear of Crime." In: K. Sessar and H.-J. Kerner (eds.), *Developments in Crime and Crime Control Research. German Studies on Victims, Offenders, and the Public.* New York, NY: Springer.

Bohm, R.M., L.J. Clark and A.F. Aveni (1991). "Knowledge and Death Penalty Opinion: A Test of the Marshall Hypotheses." *Journal of Research in Crime and Delinquency* 28:360-387.

Christie, N. (1977). "Conflicts as Property." *British Journal of Criminology* 17:1-15

Deutler, K.-F. (1956). "Schmerzensgeld, seine Rechtsnatur und Grundsätze für seine Bemessung." Doctoral dissertation, University of Kiel, Germany.

Durkheim, E. (1993 [1893]). *The Division of Labor in Society.* New York, NY: Free Press.

—— (1964 [1895]). *The Rules of Sociological Method.* New York, NY: Free Press.

Erikson, K.T. (1967). "Notes on the Sociology of Deviance." In: H.S. Becker (ed.), *The Other Side: Perspectives on Deviance.* New York:, NY Free Press.

Frehsee, D. (1987), *Schadenswiedergutmachung als Instrument strafrechtlicher Sozialkontrolle.* Berlin, GER: Duncker & Humblot.

Habermas, J. (1987), *The Theory of Communicative Action. Lifeworld and System: A Critique of Functionalist Reason,* vol. 2. Boston, MA: Bacon Press.

Immerwahr, J. (1993). "Crime and Punishment: A New Look." *Responsive Community* 3:58-60.

Kury, H. (1995). "Wie restitutiv eingestellt ist die Bevölkerung? Zum Einfluß der Frageformulierung auf die Ergebnisse von Opferstudien." *Monatsschrift für Kriminologie und Strafrechtsreform* 78:84-98.

Lane, J.S. (1997). "Can You Make a Horse Drink? The Effects of a Corrections Course on Attitudes Toward Criminal Punishment." *Crime & Delinquency* 43:186-202.

Luhmann, N. (1985). *A Sociological Theory of Law.* London, UK: Routledge & Kegan.

—— (1995). *Das Recht der Gesellschaft.* Frankfurt/Main, GER: Suhrkamp.

Maguire, K., and A.L. Pastore (eds.) (1995). *Sourcebook of Criminal Justice Statistics 1994.* Washington, DC: U.S. Government Printing Office.

Marshall, T. (1990). "Results of Research from British Experiments in Restorative Justice." In: B. Galaway and J. Hudson (eds.), *Criminal Justice, Restitution, and Reconciliation.* Monsey, NY: Criminal Justice Press.

Pfeiffer, C. (1993). "Opferperspektiven — Wiedergutmachung und Strafe aus der Sicht der Bevölkerung." In: P.-A. Albrecht, et al. (eds.), *Festschrift für Horst Schüler-Springorum zum 65. Geburtstag.* Köln, GER: Heymanns.

Sessar, K. (1990). "The Forgotten Nonvictim." *International Review of Victimology* 1:113-132.

—— (1992). *Wiedergutmachen oder Strafen.* Pfaffenweiler, GER: Centaurus.

—— (1995a). "Die Bevölkerung bleibt restitutiv eingestellt. Eine Replik auf Kurys Replikationsversuch zur Hamburger Untersuchung." *Monatsschrift für Kriminologie und Strafrechtsreform* 78:99-105.

—— (1995b). "Restitution or Punishment. An Empirical Study on Attitudes of the Public and the Justice System in Hamburg." *EuroCriminology* 8-9:199-214.

Utne, M.K. and E. Hatfield (1978). "Equity Theory and Restitution Programming." In: B. Galaway and J. Hudson (eds.), *Offender Restitution in Theory and Action.* Lexington, MA: Lexington Books.

van Dijk, J.J.M., P. Mayhew and M. Killias (1990). *Experiences of Crime across the World. Key findings of the 1989 International Crime Survey.* Deventer, NETH: Kluwer.

Walker, N. and M. Hough (eds.), (1988). *Public Attitudes to Sentencing. Surveys from Five Countries.* Aldershot, UK: Avebury.

12. Restorative Justice, Juvenile Offenders and Crime Victims: A Review of the Literature

by

Russ Immarigeon

INTRODUCTION

Much has changed in recent years concerning the position, status and influence of crime victims in traditional criminal justice systems. Victims are now at the center of emerging crime prevention programs, criminal sanctioning policies and crime victim services. Over the past 30 years, a diverse movement for social change has focused local, national and international attention on the plight of crime victims. Initially, a major thrust of this attention was to highlight the fact that crime victims were virtually ignored by criminal justice professionals, agencies, and processes. However, victim concerns now include greater involvement at pre- and post-adjudication stages of the criminal justice process. Indeed, victims of burglary and robbery, domestic violence, drunk driving, sexual assault, street crimes and violent acts now have more advocacy, compensation, counseling, protective, remedial, shelter, and support services available to them than at any point in the history of criminal justice. Moreover, scholarship has increasingly centered on the crime victim movement (Weed, 1995). It is no longer either accurate or sufficient to say simply that victims are being ignored. As one British commentator notes: "There has been no shortage of initiatives undertaken on behalf of victims of crime over the past thirty years. In addition, there can be no doubt that the changes that have been brought about as a result of these initiatives have improved, often markedly, the situation of the victim in the criminal justice system" (Newburn, 1995:169).

Although crime victims are well-placed in legislative, media and political debates on emerging crime policies, much discussion and disagreement exists on how the lives of crime victims have improved through new victim-oriented programs and policies. In fact, the impact of different reform measures on the lives of crime victims has received insufficient attention, particularly in the shadow of adversarial efforts to assert the primacy of victim concerns over other concerns confronted by courts and communities exploring the best response(s) to crime victimization. Too little is known about how victims resist, benefit or suffer from criminal justice processes that now include them in new, often more participatory, ways.

For the last twenty years, restorative justice — a process-centered approach toward intervening in the lives of victims and offenders — has developed philosophically as well as programmatically. Initially, the main focus of this attention was on the use of "reparative" programs to humanize the treatment of victims and offenders by the criminal justice system (Wright, 1982). Later, a theoretical base emerged for some of these initiatives that essentially suggested development of a new framework, or paradigm, for criminal justice (Zehr, 1985, 1990). Recently, restorative justice has been going through a period of sudden popularity in the U.S. and elsewhere, one consequence being that the term is used to categorize a growing number of sanctions and other criminal justice interventions. Another consequence is that the very definition of restorative justice has come center stage, and concern has arisen about whether restorative justice will remain loyal to its original vision or become transformed into something else again — perhaps even a mirror image of the practices it was designed to replace.

Little has been said to date about the actual impact of restorative justice interventions on the lives and conditions of crime victims. Accordingly, the purpose of this chapter is to review what is currently known about the impact of restorative justice on victims of juvenile crime. What do restorative justice advocates claim it can do for victims? Do restorative justice sanctions actually benefit crime victims? Do these penalties reduce victim anxieties and fears? Do they "repair the damage" done to victims of crime by criminal offenders? Do they heal wounds inflicted by criminal acts? What, in fact, do we know about the impact of restorative justice sanctions on crime victims? What are the implications of this knowledge for future programs, policy and research? And, what else do we need to know?

This chapter reviews the available advocacy, evaluation, program and policy literature on restorative justice theory and practice to identify what we know about the real as well as intended influence of victim participation in restorative justice processes on crime victims themselves. The impact of restorative justice on criminal offenders is also important, and in some important ways victims is positively or negatively affected by the influence of restorative justice on offenders. This general topic is covered by Schiff's chapter in this volume.[1]

RESTORATIVE JUSTICE AND CRIME VICTIMS

Restorative justice is a process, rather than simply an option, penalty, or sanction, that brings victims and offenders together to face each other, to inform each other about their crimes and victimizations, to learn about each others' backgrounds, and to collectively reach agreement on a "penalty" or "sanction." Marshall (1996:37) gives a crisp definition: "Restorative justice is a process whereby all the parties with a stake in a particular offense come together to resolve collectively how to deal with the aftermath of the offense and its implications for the future."

An extensive literature about "restorative justice" has appeared with some suddenness in recent years (McCold, 1997). Restorative justice theory itself has emerged from numerous quarters over the past decade (for an initial effort to analyze and organize this history, see Immarigeon and Daly, 1997; Daly and Immarigeon, 1998), including interests concerned with criminological theory (Christie, 1977), victim-offender reconciliation (Zehr, 1990), reintegrative shaming (Braithwaite, 1989), the over-incarceration of juvenile and adult offenders (Maxwell and Morris, 1993; Umbreit, 1985), and the victim rights movement (Halbert, 1997).

Restorative justice theory is compelling in part because it aims to repair or return the losses to the victim and to heal the wounds of crime. Restorative justice advocates frequently raise the expectation that restorative justice can do many things that traditional retributive criminal justice approaches have not done, or even tried to do. Advocates of restorative justice often admit, however, that these are rather grand, idealistic and perhaps impractical claims. A clear indicator of the worthiness of these sanctions, however, is the positive impact on crime victims, who are, along with offenders, the intended beneficiaries of these sanctions.

What, then, are the idealized benefits of restorative justice sanctions for crime victims? In his groundbreaking tract on restorative justice, Zehr (1990) observes that victims' needs and rights should be central to the restorative justice process. In describing the typical plight of victims, he refers to feelings of violation, a sense of being at risk or being unsafe, and exclusion from the criminal justice process. Victims, he notes, have anger that is often unaddressed. They have feelings, ideas, and questions about crimes, criminals and sentencing that are often ignored or downplayed by criminal justice professionals and processes. Zehr (1990) concludes:

> We may invoke [victims] names to do all sorts of things to the offender, regardless of what victims actually want. The reality is that we do almost nothing directly for the victim, in spite of the rhetoric. We do not listen to what they have suffered and what they need. We do not seek to give them back some of what they have lost. We do not let them help to decide how the situation should be resolved. We do not help them to recover. We may not even let them know what has transpired since the offense [p.32].

Relationship between Victims and Offenders

In assessing the actual impact of restorative justice sanctioning on crime victims, it is important to discuss a number of offender-related concerns, such as ability to converse during the meeting, attitude toward participating in the meeting and eventual behavior as a consequence of the meeting. Restorative justice builds upon the crime-based relationship that is established when one stranger victimizes another stranger, or upon the personal relationship that exists when a person is victimized by another person already known to them because they are a relative, colleague, neighbor, friend, or acquaintance of any of these parties.

Peters et al. (1994) make the keen and rarely expressed observation that victims and offenders often share a similarly dissociated and powerless position within criminal justice processing:

> This system has an alienating effect not only on the victim of crime but also on its perpetrator. Penal decisionmaking remains for the criminal an almost abstract activity. The decisions which are made don't relate to his [sic] specific personal and social circumstances or at least he doesn't recognize them as such. While the victim remains for the most part excluded from the procedures, the criminal is maneuvered into an exclusive position of defense. Especially the criminal investigation and the arrest have a highly threatening effect on the criminal. The result is that neither the victim nor the criminal get the feeling of being treated as a person. This leads very often to unwanted effects: reciprocal stereotypes among criminals as well as among victims and a narrow-minded view in society about crime and the criminal justice system [p.2].

Once removed from the traditional court process and engaged in a restorative justice process, victim satisfaction may result not just from self-reported attitudes, experiences and feelings, but also from offender responses of different sorts. Theoretically, restorative justice establishes a reciprocal relationship between victims and offenders. Participation in restorative justice does not mean that victim satisfaction is wholly dependent upon offender reaction. The restorative justice process allows for specific (indeed any) victim needs to be addressed individually for the sole benefit of the victim, assuming the traditional (i.e., backup) criminal justice process follows through on them. In any case, because victims and offenders are now in this crime-based relationship, they are at least partially dependent on each other for satisfaction.

Measures of Restorative Justice

More evaluation research has been conducted on the use of community-based victim-offender mediation or reconciliation, prison-based victim-offender mediation or reconciliation, family group conferences, and victim impact panels than on other restorative processes, such as sentencing circles or Navajo peace-maker courts, which have not yet been evaluated scientifically. The objective of this chapter is to review the descriptive and empirical research literature, and to assess how these sanctions affect victims of crime. The reports and studies reviewed in this chapter will largely involve juvenile offenders. Umbreit and Bradshaw (1997) reports that, at least in the U.S., approximately 75% of the offenders in victim-offender mediation programs are juveniles.

Little information is available generally about victims of juvenile crimes, including whether these victims are adults or juveniles. Despite the importance of the impact of restorative justice on crime victims, relatively little research has been conducted on crime victim impact. Moreover, little discussion is available on how the actual or potential impact of restorative justice on crime victims should even be measured. Victimology textbooks, at least in the U.S., have been silent on this issue, giving only scant and at times misleading information about restorative justice (Doerner and Lab, 1995; Karmen, 1984, 1990, 1996; Wallace, 1998). In the studies reviewed for this chapter, the main outcome measures for crime victims have been victim participation, victim perceptions of fairness, victim satisfaction, and the completion of victim compensation or restitution requirements by offenders. I know of no chapters that address broader or longer-term outcomes for crime victims, such as changes in their perspectives on criminal justice, their feelings and outlooks on the victimization experience and their recovery from victimization.

RESTORATIVE JUSTICE RESEARCH

While intervention theory and design are important aspects of alternative sanctioning measures, evaluation research is a valuable indicator of their general viability.[2] Much research on restorative justice is contained in edited volumes (Wright and Galaway, 1989; Galaway and Hudson, 1990; Messmer and Otto, 1991; Galaway and Hudson, 1996; and Hudson et al., 1996), book-length studies (Marshall and Merry, 1990; Umbreit, 1994), and assorted journal articles and research reports. Important research can also be found in several unpublished reports.

Community-Based Victim-Offender Mediation or Reconciliation

Victim-offender reconciliation and mediation programs have been in use for approximately 20 years. Reconciliation and mediation programs share much in common with regard to their general purpose and the structure of the victim-offender meeting. There are important differences, however. Advocates of a reconciliation-oriented approach tend to hold more firmly to the religious principles that guide their work. Mediation programs are generally more secular in nature. Use of the phrase mediation instead of reconciliation emerged, historically, because of victim-based objections to being "reconciled" and of efforts by proponents of the general model to "market" the program more successfully. Umbreit (1985), an early advocate of victim-offender reconciliation programs, has conducted with various associates a series of evaluations of victim-offender mediation programs in Canada, the U.K. and the U.S. Each of these studies used the same general method. Victim-offender meetings were observed, victims and offenders were interviewed, and case files were reviewed. Umbreit's research emphasizes the importance of studying comparison groups of victims and offenders, all eligible for victim-offender mediations, although only the experimental group (as opposed to the control group) actually participates in meetings.

Canada

Umbreit (1996) studied four Canadian victim-offender mediation programs. Programs in Ottawa, Ontario, and Winnipeg, Manitoba served adult offenders and their victims; programs in Calgary, Alberta and Langley, British Columbia served juvenile offenders and their victims. Data for comparison groups suggested the following contrasts between those who met with their offenders and those who did not. Victims who met with their offenders were: more likely to receive answers to questions about the offender, the crime and their victimization (87 to 51%); more likely to value the idea of telling offenders how crime affected them (87 to 51%); more likely to value apologies by offenders (74 to 40%); more likely to negotiate restitution (88 to 52%); less likely to fear revictimization by their offenders (84 to 30%); and less likely to remain upset about the crime and the offender (53 to 66%).

United Kingdom

Umbreit and Roberts (1996) used a quasi-experimental design to evaluate victim-offender mediation programs in Coventry and Leeds, U.K. Overall, 123 telephone and in-person interviews were held with 70 victims and 53 offenders. Sixty percent of the victims were male; 94% of the offenders were male (only three offenders were female). The Coventry Reparation Scheme, established by the West Midlands Probation Service in 1985, and the Leeds Mediation and Reparation Service, initiated by the West Yorkshire Probation Service, also in 1985, were assessed for the years 1992-1993, during which the projects had 170 and 358 referrals, respectively. The study sample consisted of victims and offenders who went through a direct or indirect mediation experience, or who were referred to mediation but did not experience it.

Victims reported their experiences in the following way: victims in mediation and non-mediation samples were generally satisfied with the criminal justice system; victims with direct mediation showed greater levels of satisfaction with the system; 75% of all victims in mediation were satisfied with program outcomes; 84% of victims in face-to-face mediations were satisfied with their outcomes; 95% of victims in direct mediation and 70% in indirect mediation thought their participation was voluntary; 59% felt the mediation process was fair; victims who participated in mediation wanted offenders to answer questions about what happened to them; victims who participated in mediation found apologies important; and participating victims also deemed negotiated restitution important.

United States

Umbreit and Coates (1993) studied the use of victim-offender mediation in four U.S. states. They found that victims mainly expected to recover their losses, to help rehabilitate the offender, to tell the offender the impact of their crimes and to obtain answers to questions they had about the crime. A quarter of victims felt nervous about upcoming mediation sessions, but 90% expected that the sessions would be helpful to them. Victims were more likely than offenders to say that they participated in mediation sessions voluntarily. The most important issues for victims were the chance to tell offenders the effects of the crimes; to obtain answers about the offender, the crime, and their victimization; and to reach agreement on restitution. Victims were not as concerned, however, about actually receiving restitution payments, although 70% did in fact wish to receive their financial restitution. Other studies (Hughes and Schneider, 1989), like this one, have also found that victims who participate in victim-offender mediation have an improved chance of actually receiving their restitution. Gay (1997:31) reports that a telephone survey of 100 victims participating in a prosecutor-based victim-offender reconciliation program in Polk County, IA found that "96 percent stated that they would choose the program again, 96 percent stated they would recommend the program to other victims, and 86 percent found meeting their offender to be helpful."

Prison-Based Victim-Offender Mediation or Reconciliation

Victim-offender mediation meetings have been convened, sporadically, on a case-by-case as well as on a programmatic basis at juvenile detention and adult confinement facilities in Canada, the U.S., and the U.K. Overall, only a small number of such meetings have been held in correctional institutions, largely because the meetings are resisted by prison managers and funding for them is sparse. The Face-to-Face program in Canada, sponsored in the mid-1980s by community-based reform groups in Manitoba and Newfoundland, was perhaps the most extensive effort to date. Face-to-Face focused on adult burglars, but no longer operates. Several programs have worked with juvenile male offenders. Others, including programs in New York, Pennsylvania and Wisconsin, have worked with adult male offenders (Immarigeon, 1994).

Victims and Offenders in Conciliation (VOIC), the first program to encourage incarcerated juvenile offenders to meet with their victims, was established in 1983 by the Reverend Peter Taylor, Chaplain at Her Majesty's Youth Custody Centre in Rochester, Kent, U.K. Starting in January 1984, monthly meetings of six burglars and six burglary victims were videotaped for analysis. Each hour-and-a-half meeting featured structured discussions and extended role playing, and police and victim support staff often participated. A prison psychologist attending these meetings applied attitude and personality scales to all parties after each meeting. Offenders and victims agreed on many matters, including their poor treatment by the criminal justice system. Perhaps the most notable finding of this exercise was victims attitudes toward financial restitution, an objective of the mediation sessions:

> While some victims were happy to make a purely financial agreement, other victims demanded a convincing expression of regret and/or some form of guarantee that the offenders would not offend again. In at least one role-play, no agreement was possible, the victim refusing, in her words, 'to make a private deal.' She considered that the compensation for her burglary was of secondary importance compared to the needs of the community (for example, protection from the offender) and the needs of the offender (for example, treatment/ punishment) which she did not feel qualified to judge [Launay, 1985, p.207]

The Victim Offender Mediation Program (VOM), started in 1991 by the Fraser Region Community Justice Initiatives Association in Langley, B.C., CAN, worked with offenders and victims involved in serious crimes such as armed robbery, aggravated sexual assault, serial rape and murder. Offenders in the program were confined at several federal prisons in the Lower Mainland of the western Canadian province. The primary goal of the program was to promote the "healing" of both victims and offenders. A wide range of interventions were used, including individual support or counseling and direct as well as indirect victim-offender communication through videos, letters, and face-to-face meetings. An independent consultant evaluated VOM cases from February 1991 through July 1994. Face-to-face or telephone interviews were held with 22 offenders, 24 victims and 23 criminal justice system professionals. The study included a literature review, a quantitative analysis of the demography and activity of 130 referrals made to the VOM over the study period, and an analysis of videotapes of 15 offender interviews, 3 victim interviews, and 15 face-to-face meetings.

The major general findings of this study were the following: victim-offender mediation was a new concept for victims; referral agents did not describe the program to victims adequately; confidentiality was properly maintained; victims wanted to participate; victims trusted program staff, victims wanted to learn about their offenders and the crimes; victims wanted to communicate the impact of the crime; victims exerted considerable discretion about desired services; victims delayed or stopped participating because thinking about the crime again upset them, spouses expressed concerns or fear, family events or holidays intervened, they wanted more time to think about the program, or they feared meeting their offenders; victims did not see the program as therapeutic; victims felt videos were useful for answering questions, assessing offender sincerity and personality, and learning about the process; and victims were satisfied with preparations for the meeting.

This research had a strong impact on crime victims:

For most victims, there was a sense of completeness, of having completed a journey one had set out on, or of having closed a chapter in their lives. This could be a chapter of emotions, of not knowing, of fear, loss or power-lessness. For example, victims said they had finally been heard, the offender no longer exercised control over them, they could see the offender as a per-son rather than a monster, they felt more trusting in their relationships with others, they felt less fear, they weren't preoccupied with the offender any more, they felt peace, they would not feel suicidal again, and they had no more anger. [Roberts, 1995, p.104].

Finally, a small-scale evaluation of victim-offender meetings held at a juvenile facility in Anchorage, AK suggests some benefits for victims of institution-based victim-offender meetings. In this study, Flaten (1996:399) describes scenarios for seven cases involving serious crimes, including attempted murder and burglary: "All the victims felt strongly," she notes, "that the mediation process should be available to everyone who desires to participate, and that this information [about the availability of the program] should be made available to other victims." Further-more, all victims agreed that victim-offender mediation was appropriate for serious crimes.

Family Group Conferences

Family group conferences are primarily used with young and youthful offend-ers. The first formal use of family group conferences for juvenile offenders began in New Zealand shortly after passage of the Children, Young Persons, and Their Families Act 1989. Family group conferences are used with juvenile offenders extensively in Australia and New Zealand and to lesser extents in Canada, the U.K. and the U.S. Scotland, South Africa and Sweden are currently developing plans to use family group conferences with juvenile offenders (Immarigeon and Daly, 1997).

Maxwell and Morris (1993) have completed the most comprehensive evalua-tion of the use of family group conferences. According to these researchers, in the mid-1980s New Zealand began expanding various options, such as victim impact statements, and services such as support services, improved court procedures, and reparative sentences. Even with these reforms, however, little room was available for victim-offender reconciliation meetings or for other forms of victim participa-tion in the sentencing process. Maxwell and Morris (1993) note that the Children, Young Person, and Their Families Act 1989 afforded victims both these possibili-ties.

Maxwell and Morris (1993) assessed approximately 700 cases from five re-gional districts throughout New Zealand. Among the positive victim-related find-ings of the study are the following: approximately 60% of participating victims found family group conferences helpful, positive, and rewarding; positive evaluations of the conferences by crime victims were generally related to: the extent that their roles in and their expectation of the conference were discussed before the conference; their satisfaction with the sanctions developed at the conference; and their original reasons for attending the conference; victims felt better because they were included, rather than excluded, from the sentencing process; the conference itself was a cathartic experience that released anxieties and fears about crimes and the offenders; victims found benefit in having their voices recognized through the process; and meeting with offenders and their families allowed victims to assess the cause of the offense, the attitudes of offenders and their families, and the likelihood of further victimization.

Maxwell and Morris (1997) also identify some negative impacts of family group conferences, such as: one-fourth of victims felt worse after attending the conference because they were either dissatisfied with conference outcomes, or their reasons for attending were not positive; victim dissatisfaction with the conference did not concern offense seriousness (in fact, higher levels of satisfaction were reported after conferences involving more serious crimes); and victim dissatisfaction resulted in depression, fear, distress, and unresolved anger.

Maxwell and Morris (1997: 39) identify other important levels of victim dissatisfaction with family group conferences: "Eighty-five percent of the victims who did not attend a family group conference gave reasons which related to poor practice: they were not invited, the time was unsuitable for them, or they were given inadequate notice of the conference." Maxwell and Morris (1997) argue, however, that these findings challenge the *implementation* of more than the *value* of family group conferences:

> The Children, Young Persons, and Their Families Act 1989 was amended in 1995 to ensure that victims are consulted about the time and venue of family group conferences; and the proportion of victims attending family group conferences has now certainly increased in some areas. There will always be a minority of victims who choose not to participate in a restorative process but our research found that only 6 percent of victims, when asked, said they did not wish to meet the offender" [p.39].

Victim Impact Panels

Victim impact panels were initiated in the U.S. by Mothers Against Drunk Driving (Lord, 1989). At victim impact panels, victims of drunk drivers tell driving-while-impaired offenders stories about the consequences of their victimization. Victim impact panels make use of "surrogate" victims, persons who are not actual victims of participating offenders but instead persons who have experienced either similar experiences or who are family or friends of the victims. In either case, the offenders hear directly from victimized persons.

Victim impact panels involve neither direct face-to-face meetings (mediated by interpersonal dialogue) nor discussions about specific sanctions. Offender participation in the panels is ordered by the court and is usually not voluntary. Victim (or surrogate victim) participation, however, is voluntary, usually organized by an anti-driving-while-impaired group.

Mercer et al. (1994:3) report: "In this program, offenders are sentenced to listen to a panel of bereaved and/or injured victims of drunk drivers describe the impact of their crashes on their lives. The purpose of the panels is to help offenders individualize and humanize the consequences of drunk driving to the crash victims, to change their attitudes and behaviors, to deter drinking and driving, and to reduce drunk driving recidivism."

Research on victim-impact panels is hard to locate and rather rudimentary. Lord (1989) reports findings from studies conducted in Dallas; Washington County (OR), Clackamas County (OR), and Portage County (OH). She reports primarily offender attitudes or recidivism rates, but not victim impact after attending these panels. Mercer et al. (1994) have collected data from 1,784 persons (largely affiliated with a Mothers Against Drunk Driving chapter) who either participated or did not participate on a victim impact panel. A three-wave mail survey was used to collect this data. The second wave was mailed eight months after the first (the third wave had not been completed when this preliminary report was issued). Mercer et al. (1994) reported that panel members:

- experienced fewer intrusive thoughts;
- engaged in fewer avoidance behaviors;
- had better psychological well-being;
- felt less anxiety and depression; and
- suffered fewer posttraumatic stress disorder symptoms.

Over all, the authors found, panel members "scored similar to non-victims on measures of self-esteem, locus of control, hostility, and well-being. Additionally, panelists were less angry at the perpetrator of their traumas than were non-panelists" (Mercer et al., 1994:4).

Other Restorative Justice Processes

Victim-offender mediation, family group conferences, victim impact panels and prison-based victim-offender meetings are not the only forms of restorative justice. Other approaches include: Navajo peace maker courts (Zion, 1983), sentencing circles (Stuart, 1996), expressions of forgiveness (Gehm, 1992; Jaeger, 1983), and, in New Zealand, *marae* justice (Tauri and Morris, 1997). No scientific evaluations have been completed on these interventions, although there is much generally favorable anecdotal evidence of their positive impact on crime victims.

IMPLICATIONS FOR FUTURE POLICY, PROGRAMMING, AND RESEARCH

This brief review of available evaluation research on the impact of restorative justice on crime victims has a number of implications for future restorative justice policy, programming and research. An umbrella that covers all three areas is the maturing of the crime victims' movement. Like all movements, the crime victims' movement has gone through stages of development. It is a movement that remains complex, diverse and emotional. The crime victims movement is experiencing significant growth in its understanding and willingness to address issues previously avoided, neglected or resisted. Increasingly, for example, crime victim advocates are talking about and advocating the use of restorative justice (Halbert, 1997).

Policy Implications

The restorative justice movement is gaining greater acceptance among mainstream criminal justice agencies. A critical question, however, is how restorative justice options and processes can be integrated into generally retributive state policies. Other issues are how restorative justice-centered policies can: help crime victims, focus more concretely on the role of victims within the pursuit of restorative justice, assess the impact of restorative justice processes on victims, and elaborate the parameters of what crime victims might gain from restorative justice sanctioning. Further thought should also be given to how crime victims can help shape emerging criminal justice policy. In North Carolina, for example, a local prosecutor recently tried, unsuccessfully, to have a jury sentence to death a man convicted of killing two women while driving under the influence of alcohol. Families of the victims, who were interviewed by journalists but did not testify in court, asserted that they did not want the death penalty. Their daughters, they said, believed in forgiveness and would not have wanted the man executed. The "policy tug" in this case (and others) is that victim interests, regardless of the severity of the crimes and the apparent suitability for restorative justice, do not always fit well with the interests and objectives of prosecutors. Over all, it seems that perceived state interests are not necessarily mirror images of victim interests. How will this conflict affect restorative justice policy development?

Program Implications

Research on the implementation and operation of restorative justice programming has tended, minimally, to focus on the satisfaction of program staff (Hughes and Schneider, 1989). However, more recent studies have found crime victims expressing opinions and preferences about the need for and quality of specific aspects of restorative justice preparations, process and follow-through. Training is vital: "To assume that victims and offenders can simply be brought together and reconciled without careful briefing of the parties first and without considerable training of the coordinators to manage such emotional and, by their nature, unpredictable meetings is a mistake but one which is remediable" (Maxwell and Morris, 1993:120) Finally, program managers, particularly those running new programs, need to incorporate a research protocol into their planning and implementation efforts. Calling a program "victim-centered" does not necessarily mean that it is helpful to victims. Moreover, in the long run, victims benefit to a greater extent when more is understood about their needs and the types of services required to address those needs.

Research Implications

While some excellent evaluation research has been completed on restorative justice, little is actually known about the impact or influence of this sanctioning process on either offenders or victims. A number of areas for further research suggest themselves. The extent of victim impact on criminal justice decision making is an important area of inquiry. We need to learn more about not only the extent of victim involvement in official, public policy decisions, but also the degree to which crime victims wish their feelings and perspectives to determine sanctioning decisions. Also, we need to learn about different methods of informing crime victims about the availability and possible consequences of certain sanctions.

Restorative justice options should be compared with other victim-oriented reform for effectiveness. Some research, for example, shows that victims are dissatisfied with their participation in presenting victim impact statements (Erez, 1990). To what extent does this dissatisfaction reflect the process imposed upon victims?

Research should be conducted on the ability of specific offenders to participate meaningfully in restorative justice settings. Restorative justice sanctions, like intermediate and incarcerative sanctions, generally focus more on the violent or nonviolent nature of the offense or the bureaucratic procedures of the penalty than on the physiological, psychological, and sociological nature of the offender. Restorative justice sanctioning is used with some offenders who have committed violent offenses. Gustafson (1997) and Umbreit (1995), among others, have shown that victim-offender mediation is used effectively in some of these cases. It is important, however, to develop methods for identifying whether particular offenders have physiological, psychological or sociological limitations that prevent them from participating in restorative justice processes in a meaningful way. Lewis (1998), for example, has found that certain offenders have suffered physical trauma that influences their affective behavior. Many of the subjects of her studies have been involved in capital cases, which by their nature would be excluded from restorative justice processes. But offenders with affectional disorders need not commit simply violent offenses. How are these offenders identified?

Research on offender-based concerns or circumstances is also relevant to victim interests. Some time ago, Umbreit (1987) wrote that victim-offender mediation was of interest to victims because it provides greater assurance that victims will actually receive their restitution than they would through routine court processing in a more adversarial setting. Skeptics about restorative justice and other penalties that require offender involvement often argue that offenders participate only for selfish or self-aggrandizing reasons. Research that looks more carefully at the motivations of offenders in restorative justice processes, or at the methods by which offenders are brought to restorative justice, could aid understanding of how victims can benefit, what they might expect from a victim-offender mediation or a family group conference, and so forth. Official acceptance of restorative justice may increase as a consequence.

Research should be conducted on the timing of restorative justice processes and their impact on crime victims. In the course of preparing defender-based presentence reports, Henderson and Gitchoff (1983), in one of the only studies of its kind, examined the responses of crime victims to alternatives to incarceration at various time periods after their victimization. Their method, exploratory in nature, was the following:

> When conducting our interviews with victims, our general procedure was to introduce ourselves with mention of our credentials, state that we were retained by the defense attorney, and that we were writing a pre-sentence evaluation to assist the court in providing the appropriate punishment or sentence for the case. We then stated our concerns in providing a recommendation which would serve the interests of society (community), the offender, and the victim. We asked the victims if they had considered what might have been an appropriate punishment and whether they would share their feelings with us on this issue. We also told them that we had investigated the case and had begun to formulate some ideas. If they preferred, we would share these ideas with them to determine their interests and concerns. We then proceeded to discuss the various possible dispositions of the case. [Henderson and Gitchoff, 1983, p.49]

The Henderson-Gitchoff (1983) approach shares a general restorative justice concern with the reparation of offender, victim and community. But it differs from the customary restorative justice process on several levels: their researchers' concern about victim, offender and community was expressed vaguely enough that it could have come from a textbook on standard, adversarial criminal justice. In addition, they assumed a decision-making — or at least controlling — role at the expense of victim or offender empowerment, and there was no face-to-face contacts between victim and offender.

Still, their findings are quite interesting. Like any number of surveys conducted on public opinion about crimes and punishment (see, for example, Flanagan and Longmire, 1996 or Roberts and Stalans, 1997), Henderson and Gitchoff (1983) learned that if they gave victims information about the offender and the possible sentencing options, victims were likely to suggest alternatives to incarceration, which was frequently their initial thought on the matter. Most significantly, they found that

> ...the time from occurrence of the crime was important in determining the victim's feelings about the sentence that should be imposed. In this case when victims were interviewed twice, once immediately after the crime and again several weeks later, they were generally more amenable to alternatives to incarceration during the second interview. This also appeared to hold in the case of single interviews. In this instance, those who were interviewed directly after the crime were more inclined to favor prison than those who received their initial interview a month or two after the crime was committed [Henderson and Gitchoff, 1983, p.49-50].

Flaten (1996) also offers evidence that victims, at least victims of serious crimes, feel that time — perhaps up to a year — should pass before mediation is attempted. "Having the opportunity to vent anger, sorrow, and other feelings," she found, "were variables cited as important in aiding the success of the mediation" (Flaten, p.399). Umbreit and Bradshaw (1997), it should be noted, has found strong victim support for holding mediation sessions sooner rather than later.

The role of victims in restorative justice has received too little attention. Roberts (1995) suggests that victims are a key factor in offender responses to restorative justice processes. "It appears subjectively," he has noted, "that those who were willing to very strongly hold the offenders accountable and to talk about the impacts with some force, while at the same time weaving a thread of compassion or understanding and a willingness to hear the offender, had the greatest potential positive impact on the offender" (p.130). It is also necessary to better understand the impact on offenders of victims who react with less empathy and helpfulness. But it is important, too, to assess the impact of these processes, where victims respond variously, on victims themselves. Further, what sort of offender behavior and physical or verbal communications at these meetings affect victims themselves in different ways?

In addition, long-term follow-up studies should be completed on the actual and possible changes victims experience as a result of their participation in restorative justice sanctions. Roberts (1993) observes the following:

We have presented victim impacts in terms of feelings of "closure," "putting something behind one," and "getting on with one's life." It is our feeling that, even in the long term, the primary effect of VOMP [victim offender mediation programs] will be this pivotal change which allows victims to free themselves from any of the negative and traumatic impacts of the offense. What they then *do* with their future will have less to do with VOMP (and would be difficult even to attribute to VOMP), and much more to do with their environment, their skills and their persona. Nonetheless, a sense of what and how substantial these changes are would be important in assessing the ultimate significance of achieving some closure with the offender. [p.129].

Finally, Roberts (1993) suggests that long-term follow-up studies with participating victims would be helpful in determining "...any relapses, flashbacks or loss of confidence that victims feel in the longer term, and the adequacy of their support network (including [the] VOMP) in dealing with those differences in long-term sense of well-being and security (and other indications) between victims who actually meet their offender (if any) prior to and after release (e.g., attendance at National Parole Board hearings, correspondence through [the] VOMP with the offender, comfort/ discomfort with release, post-release contact") [p.139].

CONCLUSION

The actual impact of restorative justice sanctioning on crime victims is important for the well-being of both crime victims and restorative justice theory. Restorative justice reflects an ancient literature and practice, but it is an innovation, nonetheless, in contemporary criminal justice. Use of restorative justice sanctioning is relatively recent, occurring only within the past 20 years. Much confusion and uncertainty still exists about the definition and practice of restorative justice. It is a new endeavor struggling to make its way in the world. Empirical research on its impact is slight and narrowly focused. The major restorative justice interventions that have been evaluated — with some emphasis on their impact on crime victims — are family group conferences and victim-offender mediation programs. Other potential restorative justice interventions, from victim impact panels to sentencing circles, have yet to receive substantial research evaluation. In short order, important evaluations will appear from the Reintegrative Shaming Experiments (RISE) Project in Australia (Braithwaite and Sherman, 1997) and the Bethlehem Police Family Group Conferencing Project in the U.S. (McCold and Stahr, 1996; McCold and Wachtel, 1998) that hopefully will shed further light on the impact of restorative justice on crime victims. Other research is also being conducted in Belgium, Sweden, and other nations on victim-offender mediation. At this point, the initial results of research on restorative justice are encouraging, but they only touch lightly on the myriad concerns and questions of interest to crime victims. It would behoove the field to dig deeper into not just the desired impact of restorative justice on crime victims, but also the actual short- and long-term consequences of this immensely intriguing and promising intervention.

★   ★   ★

Acknowledgement: An earlier version of this paper was delivered to the international conference, "Restorative Justice for Juveniles: Potentialities, Risks and Problems for Research," held at Belgium's Catholic University of Leuven on May 12-14, 1997. The conference paper, and subsequent revisions, have received critical and immensely helpful commentary from the following persons: Gordon Bazemore, Irwin Epstein and Gretchen Stevens. In addition, I have benefited from a day-long discussion of invited papers for the conference that was organized by Lode Walgrave and his colleagues at the Department of Criminal Law and Criminology, Catholic University of Leuven. Finally, other conference participants — those who gave papers as well as those who patiently sat through and constructively commented upon aspects of these papers — provided valuable context and input. I thank them all for their assistance in making this a better chapter. Any shortcomings are of my own making.

REFERENCES

Braithwaite. J. (1989). *Crime, Shame and Reintegration.* New York, NY: Cambridge University Press.

—— (forthcoming). "Restorative Justice: Assessing an Immodest Theory and a Pessimistic Theory." In: M. Tonry (ed.), *Crime and Justice - A Review of Research.* Chicago, IL: University of Chicago Press.

—— and L.W. Sherman (1997). *RISE Working Papers, Papers #1 to #4. A Series of Reports on Research in Progress on the Reintegration Shaming Experiments (RISE) for Restorative Community Policing.* Canberra, AUS: Australian National University.

Christie, N. (1977). "Crime as Property." *British Journal of Criminology* 17(1):1-14.

Daly, K. and R. Immarigeon (1998). "The Past, Present, and Future of Restorative Justice: Some Critical Reflections." *Contemporary Justice Review* 1:1-25.

Doerner, W.G. and S.P. Lab (1995). *Victimology.* Cincinnati, OH: Anderson.

Erez, E. (1990) "Victim Participation in Sentencing: Rhetoric and Reality." *Journal of Criminal Justice* 18:19-31.

Flanagan, T.J. and D.R. Longmire (1996). *Americans View Crime and Justice: A National Public Opinion Survey.* Thousand Oaks, CA: Sage.

Flaten, C.L. (1996). "Victim-Offender Mediation: Applications with Serious Offenses Committed by Juvenile Offenders." In: B. Galaway and J. Hudson, (eds.), *Restorative Justice: International Perspectives*. Monsey, NY: Criminal Justice Press.

Galaway, B. and J. Hudson (eds.) (1990). *Criminal Justice, Restitution and Reconciliation*. Monsey, NY: Criminal Justice Press.

—— and J. Hudson (eds.) (1996). *Restorative Justice: International Perspectives*. Monsey, NY: Criminal Justice Press.

Gay, F. (1997). "Restorative Justice and the Prosecutor." *ICCA Journal on Community Corrections* 8:30-32.

Gehm, J. (1992). "The Function of Forgiveness in the Criminal Justice System." In: H. Messmer and H.U. Otto (eds.), *Restorative Justice on Trial: Pitfalls and Potentials of Victim-Offender Mediation: International Research Perspectives*. Dordrecht, NETH: Kluwer.

Gustafson, D. (1997). "Facilitating Communication Between Victims and Offenders in Cases of Serious and Violent Crime." *ICCA Journal on Community Corrections* 8:44-49.

Halbert, E. (1997). "I Can Remember a Time...A Crime Victim's Journey to Restorative Justice." *ICCA Journal on Community Corrections* 8:40-43.

Henderson, J.H. and T.G. Gitchoff (1983). "Victim and Offender Perceptions of Alternatives to Incarceration: An Exploratory Study." *South African Journal of Criminal Law and Criminology* 7:44-53.

Hudson, J., A. Morris, G. Maxwell and B. Galaway (eds.) (1996). *Family Group Conferences: Perspectives on Policy and Practice*. Leichhardt, AUS and Monsey, NY: Federation Press and Criminal Justice Press.

Hughes, S. and A. Schneider (1989). "Victim-Offender Mediation: A Survey of Program Characteristics and Perceptions of Effectiveness." *Crime & Delinquency* 35:217-233.

Immarigeon, R. (1993). "The Problems and Promises of Community Service." *IARCA Journal on Community Corrections* 5:5-6.

—— (1994). *Reconciliation Between Victims and Offenders: Program Models and Issues*. Akron, PA: Mennonite Central Committee U.S.

—— and K. Daly (1997). "Restorative Justice: Origins, Practices, Contexts, and Challenges." *ICCA Journal on Community Corrections* 8:13-18.

Jaeger, M. (1983). *The Lost Child*. Grand Rapids, MI: Zondervan.

Karmen, A. (1984). *Crime Victims: An Introduction to Victimology*. Monterey, CA: Brooks/Cole.

—— (1990). *Crime Victims: An Introduction to Victimology*. Monterey, CA: Wadsworth.

—— (1996). *Crime Victims: An Introduction to Victimology*. Belmont, CA: Wadsworth.

Launay, G. (1985). "Bringing Victims and Offenders Together: A Comparison of Two Models." *Howard Journal of Criminal Justice* 24:200-212.

Lewis, D.O. (1998). *Guilty By Reason of Insanity: A Psychiatrist Explores the Minds of Killers*. New York, NY: Fawcett Columbine.

Lord, J. (1989). *Victim Impact Panels: A Creative Sentencing Opportunity*. Dallas, TX: Mothers Against Drunk Driving.

Marshall, T.F. (1996). "The Evolution of Restorative Justice in Britain." *European Journal on Criminal Policy and Research* 4:21-43.

—— and S.E. Merry (1990). *Crime and Accountability — Victim/ Offender Mediation in Practice*. London, UK: Her Majesty's Stationery Office.

Maxwell, G. and A. Morris (1993). *Families, Victims and Culture: Youth Justice in New Zealand*. Wellington, NZ: Department of Social Welfare and Institute of Criminology.

Maxwell, G. and A. Morris (1997). "Family Group Conferences and Restorative Justice." *ICCA Journal on Community Corrections* 8:37-40.

McCold, P. (1997). *Restorative Justice: An Annotated Bibliography*. Monsey, NY: Criminal Justice Press.

—— and J. Stahr (1996). "Bethlehem Police Family Group Conference Project." Paper presented at the annual meeting of the American Society of Criminology, Chicago.

—— and B. Wachtel (1998). *Restorative Policing Experiment: The Bethlehem Pennsylvania Police Family Group Conferencing Project*. Pipersville, PA: Community Service Foundation.

McDonald, D.C. (1986). *Punishment Without Walls: Community Service Sentences in New York City*. New Brunswick, NJ: Rutgers University Press.

Mercer, D., R. Lorden and J. Lord (1994). "Sharing Their Stories: What are the Benefits? Who is Helped?" Unpublished paper, Chicago, IL.

Messmer, H. and H.-U. Otto (eds.) (1992). *Restorative Justice on Trial: Pitfalls and Potentials of Victim-Offender Mediation — International Research Perspectives*. Dordrecht, NETH: Kluwer.

Newburn, T. (1995). *Crime and Criminal Justice Policy*. Essex, UK: Longman Group Ltd.

Peters, T., J. Goethals and I. Aertsen (1994). "Corrections and Restorative Justice." Paper presented at the "Prisons 2000" conference, Leicester, U.K.

Roberts, J.V. and L.J. Stalans (1997). *Public Opinion, Crime, and Criminal Justice*. Boulder, CO: Westview Press.

Roberts, T. (1995). *Evaluation of the Victim Offender Mediation Project*. Langley, CAN: Focus Consultants.

Singleton, J. (1993). "CASES: The Community Service Sentencing Project." *IARCA Journal on Community Corrections* 5:6-8, 17.

Strang, H. and L.W. Sherman (1997). "The Victim's Perspective. Working Paper #3. In: J. Braithwaite and L.W. Sherman (eds.), *RISE Working Papers*, Papers #1-4. Canberra, Australia: Australian National University.

Tauri, J., and A. Morris (1997). "Re-forming Justice: The Potential of Maori Processes." *Australian and New Zealand Journal of Criminology* 30:149-167.

Umbreit, M.S. (1985). *Crime & Reconciliation: Creative Options for Victims and Offenders*. Nashville, TN: Abingdon Press.

—— (1987). "Mediation May Not Be as Bad as You Think; Some Victims Do Benefit." *NOVA Newsletter* 11(3):1-2.

—— (1994). *Victim Meets Offender: The Impact of Restorative Justice and Mediation.* Monsey, NY: Criminal Justice Press.

—— (1995). *Mediation of Criminal Conflict: An Assessment of Programs in Four Canadian Provinces.* St. Paul, MN: Center for Restorative Justice and Mediation, University of Minnesota.

—— (1996). "Restorative Justice Through Mediation: The Impact of Programs in Four Canadian Provinces." In: B. Galaway and J. Hudson (eds.), *Restorative Justice: International Perspectives.* Monsey, NY: Criminal Justice Press.

—— and W. Bradshaw (1997). "Victim Experiences of Meeting Adult vs. Juvenile Offenders: A Cross-National Comparison." *Federal Probation* 61(4):33-39.

—— and R.B. Coates (1993). "Cross-Site Analysis of Victim Offender Mediation in Four States." *Crime & Delinquency* 39:565-585.

—— and A. Roberts (1996). *Mediation of Criminal Conflict in England: An Assessment of Services in Coventry and Leeds.* St. Paul, MN: Center for Restorative Justice & Mediation, University of Minnesota.

Wallace, H. (1998), *Victimology: Legal, Psychological, and Social Perspectives.* Boston, MA: Allyn and Bacon.

Weed, F. (1995). *Certainty of Justice: Reform in the Crime Victim Movement.* Hawthorne, NY: Aldine de Gruyter.

Wright, M. (1982). *Making Good: Prisons, Punishment and Beyond.* London, UK: Burnett Books.

—— and B. Galaway (eds.) (1989). *Mediation and Criminal Justice: Victims, Offenders and Community.* London, UK: Sage.

Zehr, H. (1985). "Retributive Justice, Restorative Justice." *New Perspectives on Crime and Justice, Issue #4.* Akron, PA: Mennonite Central Committee Office of Criminal Justice.

—— (1990). *Changes Lenses: A New Focus for Crime and Justice.* Scottsdale, PA: Herald Press.

Zion, J.W. (1983). "The Navajo Peacemaker Court: Deference to the Old and Accommodation to the New." *American Indian Law Review* 11:89-109.

NOTES

1. Braithwaite (forthcoming) offers a concise, comprehensive, international summary of research findings concerning the impact of restorative justice models on victim participation, victim satisfaction, the honoring of offender obligations to victims, and symbolic reparation. He does not, however, separate the research according to whether it evaluated programs focusing on adult or juvenile offenders. The restorative justice research covered in this

chapter, it should be noted, involves only programs with juvenile offenders. Programs with adult offenders have been excluded from this review.

2. In the U.S., community service and restitution received much research attention when they were federally funded. But, as these options have gone from demonstration project to common practice, the number of research evaluations has dropped dramatically. The major exception is a study by McDonald (1986) of the community service program operated by the Vera Institute of Justice and now the Center for Alternative Sentencing and Employment Services (Singleton, 1993). A more recent overview of community service in the U.S., however, found little empirical research. Beyond the U.S., sound baseline research has been conducted on the use of community service orders in Canada, Finland, Scotland, and the United Kingdom (Immarigeon, 1993).

13. The Impact of Restorative Interventions on Juvenile Offenders

by

Mara F. Schiff

INTRODUCTION

This chapter is about evaluating the effects of restorative justice interventions on juvenile offenders. In the context of a theory and practice that defines itself as focusing on the reparation of harm done *by* offenders *to* victims and communities (Bazemore, 1997; Van Ness and Strong, 1997; Zehr, 1990), attention to the impacts of such interventions on offenders may seem incongruous. However, if justice system interventions are leaving offenders more (or even equally) bitter, angry and violence-prone after they leave the system than when they entered, then something is wrong with the strategy and restorative outcomes must be examined in this context. Moreover, offenders *are* members of the community (and are often victims themselves); failing to examine the effects such interventions have on them only furthers the disintegrative nature of current justice system approaches (Braithwaite, 1989).

This chapter distinguishes between restorative justice processes and sanctions. Restorative justice processes deal with the means through which the offender and the victim agree to some form of compensation for the harm caused or damage done. Such processes may include victim-offender mediation, family group conferencing, circle sentencing, reparative probation and possibly victim awareness or victim impact panels. *Sanctions*, on the other hand, refer to the actual agreements reached through such processes. These include strategies such as restitution, community service and other responses to delinquency designed to repair harm to victims and communities.

While it makes conceptual sense to separate restorative processes from sanctions, in practice these distinctions are not so clear-cut, and evaluating their discrete effects is difficult. There is considerable overlap, for example, between victim-offender mediation (VOM) and restitution, as restitution is often the outcome of VOM.[1] In examining the research, deciphering whether the process of mediation or the act of making restitution has had the greater impact on the offender may be next to impossible.

It is also important to recognize that the mere existence of such programs does not guarantee that they are part of a comprehensive restorative approach to juvenile or criminal justice. For example, many community service programs were designed as part of the pre-trial diversion and alternative-to-incarceration movements of the 1970s and 1980s (e.g., Hillsman and Sadd, 1981; Hillsman, 1982; Feeley, 1983; McDonald, 1986; Morris and Tonry, 1990). These programs were not meant to, and did not, include explicitly restorative objectives, and thus should not be reviewed in the same context as programs explicitly designed to be restorative (e.g., Walgrave and Geudens, 1996a; 1996b). To date, there have been few published empirical evaluations of justice processes or programs implemented in a restorative context, and even fewer that have examined the impacts of such programs on offenders.

This chapter examines the outcomes of restorative justice processes and sanctions for juvenile offenders, looking first at the results of *processes* and then at the impacts of the *sanctions* subsequently imposed through such processes. Significant gaps in the literature are examined, and recommendations are made for future research on restorative justice. In addition, some outcome measures to help standardize empirical evaluations are suggested. Given the limited data on restorative justice programs, it would be impractical for this review to completely exclude programs that fail to explicitly articulate restorative objectives, or that deal with both adults and juveniles; there is still much to be learned from the experiences of such programs. Therefore, this review is slightly broader in scope than its title implies, although its focus remains on restorative programs for juvenile offenders.

RESTORATIVE JUSTICE PROCESSES

The primary restorative justice processes on which research has been conducted include victim-offender mediation and family group conferencing. In addition, circle sentencing, reparative probation and victim impact panels are increasingly gaining recognition in some jurisdictions. These strategies all aim to increase contact between victims and offenders as a means of "humanizing" the justice system (Umbreit and Coates, 1992b), as well as involving victims, offenders and the community equally in the justice process.

Victim-Offender Mediation

This section examines the effects of VOM on offenders, and then considers some of the results achieved through the process. As mentioned previously, distinguishing the impacts of the VOM process on offenders from those of the subsequent sanction (such as restitution or community service) is difficult, and the reader is cautioned to bear such considerations in mind during this review.

Overview

Much VOM research has focused on victim impact (see Immarigeon, this volume) rather than on offenders (Nugent and Paddock, 1995). Program goals, however, often include offender rehabilitation, reduced recidivism, diversion of cases from the courts and prevention of further "trouble" (Marshall and Merry, 1990). In fact, one survey found that most programs saw their primary goal as offender accountability, followed by restitution to victims, offender rehabilitation, victim reparation, reconciliation between victim and offender, and the avoidance of a custodial term (Hughes and Schneider, 1990). VOM is designed to allow victims and offenders an opportunity to reconcile and mutually agree on solutions. The object is to deal with crime as a conflict to be resolved between the persons directly affected, rather than as an opportunity for state intervention (McKnight, 1981; Hughes and Schneider, 1990).

Most VOM programs evaluated have tended to handle primarily white, male, first-time juvenile offenders (Kigin and Novak, 1980; Coates and Gehm, 1985; Umbreit and Coates, 1992a; Warner, 1992; Zehr and Umbreit, 1982), though some programs have served a higher proportion of prior offenders (Kuhn, 1987). Bussman (1987) found that about half of the offenders in selected programs in Canada, the U.S. and Germany were first-time offenders. In Great Britain, Marshall and Merry (1990) found most programs to include mostly single, white, unemployed male offenders, with a prior police or court record. Many offenders who participate in VOM programs have had a previous relationship with the victim (Kuhn, 1987; Marshall and Merry, 1990); such acquaintance is more likely in violent cases (Marshall and Merry, 1990). VOM cases typically deal with property crimes such as theft, burglary, criminal damage or vandalism (Marshall and Merry, 1990; Umbreit and Coates, 1992a), although a small but growing trend toward applying VOM in more serious, violent cases is apparent (Umbreit, this volume).

The following sections examine reasons for VOM participation, satisfaction with the process, compliance rates, the effect of the process on court imposed sanctions, and subsequent recidivism rates.

Reasons for Participation

When confronted with the prospect of facing their victims, some offenders have felt shame and embarrassment or humiliation; some have perceived double punishment and/or feared violent assault from the victims (Smith et al.,1988). The vast majority of offenders studied felt that VOM was a difficult and demanding experience (Smith, 1986; Marshall, 1992; Umbreit and Coates, 1992b; Umbreit, 1996); those who participated often did so with the hope that it would help in court or to get a job, be an opportunity to demonstrate remorse, offer an apology, and/or repair a relationship (Kuhn, 1987; Marshall and Merry, 1990; Coates and Gehm, 1989; Warner, 1992).

In some cases, offenders felt more resentment toward the victim when he or she was a family member or a neighbor (Warner, 1992). Others felt that negotiating and paying restitution, discussing the event with the victim, and apologizing were important, and were concerned what the victim thought of them (Umbreit and Coates, 1992a; Umbreit, this volume). Some research has found high rates of voluntary participation (Umbreit and Coates, 1992a, 1992b, 1993), while other studies indicate more evidence of coercion (Coates and Gehm, 1989; Warner, 1992).

Marshall and Merry (1990) conducted one of the most comprehensive and methodologically sound evaluations on the effects of mediation in several U.K. Home Office funded mediation and reparation projects. Examining three juvenile diversionary programs operated by the police and six programs originating in the formal court system (primarily for adult offenders), they found that mediation increased offenders' sense of responsibility. Marshall and Merry (1990:83) also found, however, that because the system inherently favors offender interests by focusing on "fairness" and due process, programs had trouble equally involving victim and offender, and "had difficulty maintaining their restorative focus in the face of a dominating criminal justice system." Moreover, some offenders were unclear about the purpose of VOM, and many juveniles in the police diversionary programs participated because they believed they would be prosecuted if they did not. Such perceptions of coercion may have resulted in more passive participation in the process (Marshall and Merry, 1990).

Marshall and Merry (1990) found that in the court-based programs, some offenders believed the program was primarily intended to assist them, but most saw advantages for both parties and regarded the meeting as a chance to achieve understanding with the victim (see also Umbreit, this volume). Reparation, however, was not necessarily seen as part of this process. The extent to which offenders thought participation might reduce their sentence varied across programs, and most offenders saw the incident as "opportunistic" and expressed regret. The most important impact felt by offenders was the opportunity to see the actual human and material consequences of their actions (Marshall and Merry, 1990).

Satisfaction with the Process and the Outcomes Achieved

Most research indicates offender satisfaction with both the process and the outcome of VOM (Coates and Gehm, 1985, 1989; Smith et al., 1985; MacKay, 1986; Marshall, 1990; Dignan, 1990; Umbreit and Coates, 1992b, 1993; Rock, 1992; Umbreit, this volume). However, not all offenders have been satisfied with their level of input (Smith et al., 1985). Juveniles who met their victim were more likely to perceive the process as fair (Umbreit and Coates, 1992a) and to experience mediation as "humanizing the justice system response" (Umbreit and Coates, 1992b). Most offenders surveyed who were unable to participate stated that they would have liked to if given the choice (Marshall, 1990; Umbreit, this volume). Participants found the VOM process to be fair and no less demanding than the traditional court response (Umbreit, this volume).

Similar to earlier findings (Coates and Gehm, 1985), Umbreit and Coates (1992a, 1992b, 1993) found that most offenders were happy with the contract achieved through VOM. Novak et al. (1992) found offenders to be most satisfied with the program when required to complete *both* financial and community service restitution, and that most offenders found restitution requirements to be fair. These findings highlight the difficulty in identifying if such satisfaction is a result of the actual mediation process or its outcome. It is possible that the process of mediation is less important than achieving the right mix of subsequent sanctions. Or, conversely, that the sanctions imposed are of less actual importance to the offender than the process through which they were realized. Such findings do suggest, however, that when offenders believe they have been treated fairly, they are not averse to being held accountable, even when this may result in a seemingly more difficult agreement. It is important to recognize, however, that the perception of coercion may affect how fair and useful the process seems (Coates and Gehm, 1989).

Compliance With Agreements Achieved Through Mediation

Umbreit and Coates (1992a, 1992b) found that most VOM cases result in financial restitution, followed by community and personal service. They also found that completion rates have been significantly better following VOM participation than after other, more traditional, processes.

Compliance with agreements achieved through mediation varies from program to program, generally hovering around 80% (Galaway, 1983; Ivari, 1987; Kuhn, 1987; Pate, 1990). Some research found higher completion rates and increased involvement in the process when there was a relationship between the parties (Pearson, 1982; Marshall and Merry, 1990), while other studies found *less* compliance when the parties were acquainted (Warner, 1992). This suggests that while the relationship between the victim and the offender affects completion and compliance rates, the exact nature and direction of this relationship is unclear and may be important in determining successful outcomes. Marshall and Merry (1990) found that repeat juvenile offenders who knew their victims were more likely to make reparation, although this was least likely in violent or sexual assault cases, and Warner (1992) found completion rates highest among employed offenders.

Effects on Court Sentences

There is some evidence that VOM in Britain has resulted in decreased use of custody, conditional discharge, probation and community service orders (Marshall, 1990). This same research indicates a higher use of compensation orders (the British term for court-ordered restitution) for offenders who participate in VOM than among the general court population (Marshall and Merry, 1990). Offenders who participate in VOM may be treated more leniently by judges, perhaps because of the appearance of regret and willingness to "put things right." In addition, it is possible that taking material responsibility (through restitution) for the harm caused might decrease the judiciary's perception that a retributive punishment is required (Marshall and Merry, 1990). In one German study, the vast majority of cases referred to mediation were dismissed either by the prosecutor or the judge, with about one-fifth resulting in a judgment or verdict (Kuhn, 1987).

On the other hand, some research has found that a poor mediation outcome may negatively impact the subsequent sentence, and one study found that an antagonistic victim more than doubled the likelihood of a custodial sanction (which may also have been related to the severity of the offense and subsequent victim response; (Marshall and Merry, 1990). This may reflect how little control offenders (and victims) actually have over outcomes, and how much decision-making power continues to rest, finally, firmly within the traditional judicial process.

VOM may increase public and state awareness of the effect that minor offenses have on victims, resulting in net widening as the state's ensuing desire to control petty offenders intensifies. In restorative justice, net widening (Austin and Krisberg, 1982) can be distinguished as either governmental- or community-based (Braithwaite, 1994; Polk, 1994), and while expansion of "government nets" may have detrimental implications for juvenile offenders, strengthening "community nets" may be beneficial and serve to (re)integrate the offender into the community. Diverting first-time offenders to community sanctioning processes such as mediation may reduce future offending, as community groups and citizens become more aware of the needs and risks presented by such offenders. This may, in turn, induce the community to take responsibility for preventative action at the neighborhood and institutional levels (Bazemore, 1997).

Some evidence has suggested that VOM may ultimately increase offender accountability as court sentences include reparative *as well as* other, more traditional, sanctions (Marshall and Merry, 1990). This may increase the overall scope and severity of sanctions, suggesting governmental *net strengthening* rather than *widening* (Austin and Krisberg, 1982; Warner, 1994).

Recidivism

Although there is limited data on reoffending following VOM, available research has found decreased recidivism among VOM participants when compared with similar offenders going through the traditional juvenile justice system process (Pate, 1990; Umbreit and Coates; 1992b, 1993; Nugent and Paddock, 1995). One study concluded that not only were recidivism rates lower among juveniles who participated in VOM, but those who did reoffend committed less serious offenses than a comparable control group (Nugent and Paddock, 1995). Rock (1992), however, found no significant difference in recidivism rates among offenders who did and did not participate in VOM in Texas.

A variety of structural and demographic factors have been found to influence recidivism rates following VOM. For example, in some cases, a face-to-face meeting between the victim and the offender is either impossible or unwise, and a third-party will instead shuttle between the principles; Dignan (1990) found that the number of reconvictions following the VOM process in Kettering, U.K. was lowest following face-to-face meetings. Nugent and Paddock (1995) identify family size, and particularly the number of siblings, as an important influence on rearrest rates among juveniles who went through a traditional juvenile justice process. The same factor was not significant for comparable juveniles who participated in a VOM program, suggesting that participating in the program may minimize the effect of family size on reoffending.

O'Haley (1992), who examined programs in the U.S., Canada and the U.K., and reported that while none had adequate control samples, recidivism rates of 25% or less emerge in each country, with the lowest overall rates in the U.K. Without control groups, however, it is difficult to know if this represents any improvement over traditional processes, and what specific legal or extra-legal variables might account for such differences.

VOM Conclusion

Over all, research suggests that VOM has positive impacts on offenders. Offenders seem to benefit from and be satisfied with the process, to feel themselves to be held appropriately accountable and subject to fair and equitable outcomes, and to tend to commit fewer subsequent crimes. Moreover, compliance rates are generally good, suggesting that offenders tend to hold themselves accountable for accomplishing goals agreed upon through this process. Court sentences also tend to be reduced following participation in VOM. While the evidence is limited and may or may not be generalizable, the overwhelming sense is that there are more positive than negative impacts of VOM, and that, given a choice, juveniles prefer this approach to more traditional processes.

Family Group Conferencing

Family group conferencing (FGC) has been emerging as a promising restorative intervention (for a description of the process, see Braithwaite and Parker, this volume).[2] In both New Zealand and Australia, FGC has been institutionalized through legislative acts requiring that it be used either in place of, or in addition to, more traditional juvenile justice methods (Fraser and Norton, 1996; Robertson, 1996; Maxwell and Morris, 1996; Wundersitz and Hetzel, 1996; Ban, 1996). Other countries are also experimenting with the process, in both juvenile justice and in child welfare (Marsh and Crow, 1996; Immarigeon, 1996; Longclaws et al., 1996; Pennel and Burford, 1996; McCold and Starr, 1996). There is, however, little research on the process itself, and even less on the effects of FGCs on participants (Maxwell and Morris, 1996). Moreover, little systematic data collection is occurring that might facilitate such comprehensive research (Robertson, 1996).

Concerns about the Process

Important concerns have been cited about the potential for FGC to widen the net of social control, in addition to being coercive, inconsistent, not proportional and ignorant of the principle of parsimony in sanctioning (von Hirsch, 1993; Braithwaite, 1994; Polk, 1994; Moore and O'Connell, 1994; Warner, 1994; Maxwell and Morris, 1996; Umbreit and Stacy, 1996; Bazemore, 1997). While these specific concerns are untested, available research does suggest a decrease in the number of cases processed through the court system as well as placed in residential custody (Moore, 1995; Maxwell and Morris, 1996; Moore and O'Connell, 1994). In fact, some evidence has indicated that offenders *themselves* may argue for tougher penalties in an effort to demonstrate their willingness to earn respect (Moore and O'Connell, 1994). Some advocates caution that due process may be threatened when youths are not adequately apprised of their rights (Maxwell and Morris, 1996; Braithwaite and Parker, this volume), while other research highlights the fear that FGC may result in punitive, rather than restorative, sanctions, and/or be insensitive to victims (e.g., Warner, 1994; Umbreit and Stacy, 1996). There is no conclusive evidence either for or against these hypotheses (McCold and Starr, 1996).

Offender Satisfaction with the Process

Research in New Zealand (Maxwell and Morris, 1993; Morris, 1993; Moore, 1995) has found high levels of participant satisfaction with the FGC process and its subsequent outcomes, although victims were somewhat less satisfied than offenders (Maxwell and Morris, 1993; Maxwell and Morris, 1996). Preliminary reports from the U.S. suggest similar findings (McCold and Starr, 1996). In New Zealand, the youth court has typically supported outcomes achieved through FGC, suggesting official as well as participant satisfaction with agreements reached (Maxwell and Morris, 1993; Morris et al., 1993; Olsen et al., 1995).

One concern has been that only a limited number of the youths have reported feeling "involved," "partly involved" or "a party to the decision making process" (Maxwell and Morris, 1993). This may simply reflect traditional norms holding adults as primary decision makers, although the study's authors argue that while low, the figures are still considerably higher than the proportion of youths who exit the traditional juvenile court process feeling involved.

Current research in Canberra, Australia (RISE: The Reintegrative Shaming Experiments) has been randomly assigning separate groups of adult drunk drivers and youthful offenders to either FGC or court. This research is finding that offenders do not see FGC as a "soft" option, and youthful offenders spend an average of 71 minutes in a conference as compared with about 13 minutes in court (Sherman and Strang, 1997; Sherman and Barnes, 1997).

Offenders in the Australian RISE experiments (both adults and youths) were more likely than those processed through the court to believe that the outcome of their case was fair (72 versus 54%); adult drunk drivers were over three times more likely to leave the process feeling "bitter and angry" following court than after a conference (Sherman and Strang, 1997; Sherman and Barnes, 1997). Youthful offenders sent to conferences were more likely than court-processed offenders to believe that they would be caught for a reoffense, and that the prospect of being later sent to court represented a significant threat (Sherman and Strang, 1997). Sherman and Strang (1997:3) offer that perhaps "once the offender has put family and friends to all the trouble of attending the conference, they generally become more committed to helping the [offender] avoid repeat offending." Youthful offenders also said they felt significantly more likely to obey the law following a conference than after court (Sherman and Strang, 1997).

Sherman and Barnes (1997) report that youthful offenders felt they understood conference proceedings better than court, that their rights were respected "a lot," and that they were treated both fairly and with respect and courtesy in the FGC. Offenders processed through FGC in the Australian experiments were also more likely than those processed through the court to report fair treatment by, and increased respect for, the police and the justice system process (Sherman and Barnes, 1997).

In the only controlled study of the effects of FGC in the U.S., McCold and Starr (1996) found virtually no difference in youth perceptions of fairness between FGCs and the court process. However, more youths in the U.S. felt they were "held accountable" for their actions following a FGC than did members of a control sample processed through the court (McCold and Starr, 1996). In an uncontrolled New Zealand study, about 70% of youths believed the outcomes of the FGC process to be fair and appropriate (Maxwell and Morris, 1993).

Rates of Compliance with Agreements Achieved Through Family Group Conferencing

Only two studies to date have examined compliance, both finding rates of 85% or better (Wundersitz and Hetzel, 1996; Maxwell and Morris, 1996). This highlights a critical gap in the research. More work must be undertaken to understand whether FGC results in similar, higher or lower compliance with sanctions than court processing.

Recidivism Rates

It is impossible to draw any valid conclusions from the limited data on recidivism following participation in FGC. One study suggested a 42% reconviction rate, but the lack of a control group or pre-test sample makes it impossible to know whether this figure was lower or higher than expected (Maxwell and Morris, 1996). About one-quarter of the youths in this New Zealand study became "persistent offenders," but this seemed more related to the offender's prior criminal history and the imposition of a custodial placement than the FGC process itself (Maxwell and Morris, 1993). In general, however, New Zealand has reported a decrease in juvenile offending rates following the implementation of FGC that has not been observed among court-processed adults during the same period. It remains unclear how much of this can be attributed to the FGC process itself.

Family Group Conferencing Conclusion

Over all, FGC represents a promising restorative alternative to traditional justice system processes. There is, however, little comprehensive research from which to draw conclusions about its effectiveness. Concerns about net widening, the fairness of the process and consistent outcome measures should dominate future research agendas, with particular attention to the results of the process and its effects on compliance rates and subsequent offending.

Other Restorative Processes

Circle sentencing has been in use in the Yukon and other parts of Canada since approximately 1992, and is among the most recent restorative interventions to be applied outside its traditional native environment (Stuart, 1996; Melton, 1995). It represents an innovative adaptation of traditional Native American sanctioning processes wherein members of the offended community collectively determine an appropriate response to the harm caused. Circle sentencing can be used as a diversion or an alternative to formal court proceedings, and depends on an admission of guilt by the offender and demonstration of a sincere willingness to change.

There has been virtually no research documenting outcomes from this process; preliminary unpublished anecdotal evidence suggests positive results (Stuart, 1996).

Another model currently being tested in Vermont is reparative probation (Dooley, 1995). This strategy is grounded in the traditional probation model and is directed primarily at non-violent probationers. It is implemented by a reparative coordinator on the staff of the department of probation, and carried out by a community reparative board that collectively determines appropriate restorative sanctions (Bazemore, 1997). While a study is under way to document the effects of this strategy, no data have yet been published.

A final though also not well-documented process is the victim awareness or victim impact panel (Mercer et. al, 1994). In these panels, meetings are arranged between offenders and victims (or surrogate victims when necessary and/or appropriate) to educate the offender. There are no reliable data on this process from which to draw conclusions about its efficacy.

RESTORATIVE JUSTICE SANCTIONS

To date, restorative justice sanctions have been primarily limited to restitution and community service, although there are many other responses to delinquent behavior that may arise within a restorative context. Conditions such as direct service to the victim, payment into a compensation fund, attending victim impact classes, or other non-traditional sanctions may result from negotiated agreements or restoratively intended court requirements. None of these possible sanctions are reviewed here due to the lack of reliable research about their impacts on juvenile offenders. Only restorative sanctions on which consistent and reliable research has been performed are presented here.

Restitution

Overview

Restitution aims to simultaneously hold an offender accountable for his or her actions, while also making amends to the victim for the harm and/or damage done. When properly implemented, restitution seeks to restore the victim (and/or the community) to the state of wholeness that existed prior to the offense. Ideally, restitution enables the offender to both make reparation and "put things right" with the victim.

This section examines program compliance, recidivism rates and offender perceptions of restitution's effectiveness. Again, it is important to recognize that the mere existence of a restitution program does not signify its inclusion as part of a comprehensive restorative scheme. Because the number of programs actually implemented within a restorative context is limited, restitution programs reviewed here are broadly defined and may include some that do not have explicitly articulated restorative goals but that, nonetheless, have restorative implications.

Offender Attitudes and Satisfaction with Restitution

Schneider (1990) found that while incarcerated juveniles were more remorseful and felt their sanctions to be less fair than those subject to restitution, they also felt that incarceration was not as severe as restitution. The lower degree of remorse shown by youths under restitution orders may have resulted from restitution's emphasis on accountability and making amends, as opposed to a more traditional focus on repentance; in other words, "feeling bad" may ultimately be a less meaningful component in restitution programs than accepting responsibility for one's actions (Schneider, 1990).

Reports conflict on the degree of punitiveness experienced by offenders in restitution programs. Research has stressed that some offenders experience restitution as more punitive than restorative, especially when the experience is limited to just making payments rather than being involved in a more comprehensive support system (Zehr and Umbreit, 1982). Schneider (1986), on the other hand, found most restitution programs studied rated relatively low on a scale of punitiveness. Coates and Gehm (1985:127) found fewer offenders who viewed restitution as "excessively punitive" than who considered it a "reasonable alternative to incarceration." Again, the degree to which these findings reflect sentiments about the process though which the sanction was imposed, or the sanction itself, is ambiguous, but it appears that juveniles did not perceive restitution as "soft."

Compliance with Restitution Orders

In general, success rates in juvenile restitution programs studied have been over 75%, and often as high as 86% (Schneider and Schneider, 1980; Schneider and Bazemore, 1985; Schneider, 1986; Zehr and Umbreit, 1982). Schneider et. al (1982) found that restitution ordered and imposed as a sole sanction was more effective than when combined with other, more traditional, sanctions such as probation or a suspended commitment. This may reflect the possibility that restitution holds offenders more directly accountable for their actions, a less apparent component of more traditional sanctions. Additionally, Schneider and Schneider (1984b) found that restitution was considerably more effective when delivered through a formal restitution program, rather than through *ad hoc* court-appended projects. Restitution completion rates in this study were about 40% higher than those achieved by the probation department, suggesting that the success of restitution may depend as much on program structure as on conditions of the order itself.

Schneider et. al. (1982) found that most program-specific features had only a modest effect on successful completion of restitution. Rather, research has found that size of the order, closer offender monitoring and the process through which the sanction is ordered are more likely to affect compliance rates (Softley, 1978; Schneider and Schneider 1980; Schneider et. al., 1982; Schneider and Schneider, 1984a; Schneider, 1986; Wheeler et al., 1989; Ervin and Schneider, 1990; Davis et. al., 1991; Umbreit and Coates, 1992a; 1992b; Davis and Bannister, 1995; Smith et al., 1996).

Smaller orders, in either monetary or community service terms, tend to increase compliance rates, although there is some difference in the effects for adults and for juveniles (Smith et al., 1996; Schneider et. al., 1982; Softley, 1978). For example, Smith et al., (1996) found that non-payment for adults was not related to the size of the order or time given to pay, while Schneider and Schneider (1980) found the opposite effect for juveniles.

Closer offender monitoring has also been found to increase compliance rates (Davis et al., 1991; Davis and Bannister, 1995), which may derive from better enforcement mechanisms in comprehensive restitution-only programs. Such monitoring and enforcement is unlikely in traditional probation departments facing large caseloads and multiple offenders with diverse sanction obligations.

Finally, some research has found higher compliance rates when the sanction is ordered through a restorative process, such as VOM, rather than through a more traditional criminal justice process (Schneider and Schneider, 1984a; Schneider, 1986; Wheeler et al.,1989; Ervin and Schneider, 1990). Offenders who negotiate directly with their victims are more likely to complete restitution than those so ordered through the court (Umbreit and Coates, 1992a; 1992b). Over all, the effectiveness of restitution appears linked to program structure, specific sanction characteristics and the process through which it is imposed, with program enforcement and follow-up important contributors to the overall efficacy of the sanction.

Recidivism Rates

In general, research has found lower recidivism rates resulting from restitution than from other, potentially more severe, justice system sanctions such as incarceration or probation (Hudson and Chesney, 1978; Cannon and Stanford, 1981; Hofford, 1981; Heinz et al., 1986; Schneider, 1986; Rowley, 1990; Ervin and Schneider, 1990; Butts and Snyder, 1991).[3] Again, this is particularly true when restitution was successfully completed as part of a comprehensive restitution-specific program (Schneider and Schneider, 1984b), implying that direct accountability for repayment, with enforcement and follow-up mechanisms, may result in lower subsequent offending. Schneider (1986) stressed that while restitution programs may not always significantly decrease recidivism, they certainly do not increase it; Guedalia (1979) found lower recidivism rates among juveniles who had more contact with victims coupled with lower restitution amounts. Schneider (1986) also found that completing the restitution order was itself a strong predictor of decreased recidivism, which was in turn related to the strength of the program structure.

Contrary to expectation, Schneider (1990) found that sanctions perceived to be more severe, as well as the perceived likelihood of being caught, resulted in increased recidivism.[4] Moreover, reduced recidivism was also related to perceptions of being a "good citizen." Juveniles who did not think of themselves as "criminals" tended to reoffend less than those with a more negative self-image, and this more positive image may have resulted from being given the opportunity to make reparation through restitution (Schneider, 1990; Ervin and Schneider, 1990).

During the three-year follow-up period of Schneider's study (1986), juveniles in restitution programs were more likely to have jobs or be in school than youths sentenced to incarceration or probation. Not surprisingly, staying in school was negatively related to recidivism (Ervin and Schneider, 1990). Lawrence (1990) reports lower unemployment rates among youths completing restitution as compared with their levels of employment prior to the program, which may relate to opportunities for offenders sentenced to restitution to have "real job" experiences (Schneider, 1986).

Finally, some research has not found decreased recidivism rates following restitution (Bonta et. al., 1983; Wax, 1977), or has found that the effect of restitution on subsequent recidivism rates was not sufficiently isolated to enable drawing conclusions (Roy, 1995). That is, while much research suggests that youths sentenced to restitution programs may have lower recidivism rates, it is not clear that such results derive from the restitution program itself; it is possible that other factors — such as the type of defendants selected for participation, other services simultaneously offered, or the process through which the sanction was determined — may have been responsible for the outcome.

Restitution Conclusion

In sum, these findings imply that there are some clear benefits of restitution, but that these benefits may be related to other program elements such as academic or employment services, or the process through which the sanction is determined or delivered. Ervin and Schneider (1990) found that an important characteristic of restitution programs was that successful program completion required specific, tangible positive action by youths that was not the case in traditional programs offering no such opportunities.

Over all, restitution has the potential to be a meaningful restorative sanction, from which both offenders and society in general can derive multiple benefits. The primary obstacle is the ease with which restitution can be imposed in the absence of a comprehensive restorative framework, facilitating the appearance — but not the actual development — of a restorative agenda. Moreover, distinguishing the effects of restitution as separate from other services provided, program structure, and the process through which it was imposed is important, and research must strive to isolate these separate effects. Finally, research must identify differences in outcomes when restitution is imposed as a fully restorative sanction (including reparation to the victim and meaningful competency-building skills for the offender), rather than simply as a court-ordered retributive sanction. Such studies must control for: (1) offenders sentenced to traditional sanctions, (2) offenders sentenced to restitution through a variety of processes, and (3) restitution imposed within and outside of a comprehensive restorative structure. Such studies will enable policy makers and practitioners to distinguish the value, or lack thereof, of restitution as a restorative intervention.[5]

Community Service

Overview

While a number of community service programs exist, very few have been implemented in a restorative context. In fact, many community service programs have been implemented in the absence of *any* theory relating program activities to desired objectives, limiting the degree to which restorative, or any other, effects can legitimately be claimed (Bazemore and Maloney, 1994; Walgrave, 1995). For example, Morris and Tonry (1990) comment that community service is simultaneously expected to be punitive, deterrent, reparative and rehabilitative, and while some programs are designed to be rehabilitative in nature (Schneider, 1985; Walgrave, 1995), others focus on punishment as the central objective (Pease, 1985; McDonald, 1986). Such conflicting goals may result in multiple, diffuse and/or ambiguous program objectives and structure (Harris, 1986). Marshall (1990) noted that community service orders intended to be restorative in Great Britain became routinized as one of a variety of available punishments that had little rehabilitative or reconciliatory potential.

While community service for juveniles was originally designed to be rehabilitative (Schneider, 1985; Rubin, 1986), there are more recent case studies of restorative community service projects (Bazemore and Maloney, 1994). However, research on the effects of such programs on offenders is still limited, and the lack of standards for such programs (Schneider, 1985; Bazemore, 1991) has led some to conclude that such services should not be included as a part of a reparative sanctioning system (Pease, 1985; Harland and Rosen, 1991).

Most community service research has not looked for, and hence not found, explicit restorative effects. Walgrave and Geudens's (1996a) review of literature on community service for juvenile offenders in the U.S., Europe, Canada and New Zealand found that only 11 of 25 projects mention restoration as an explicit goal, mostly in conjunction with rehabilitation, and eight (8) explicitly refer to punitive goals. Only one study specifically refers to restoration of damage caused (van der Laan, 1991).

The best known study of community service in the U.S. was McDonald's (1986) examination of community service for adult offenders in New York City, a program developed and implemented under expressly retributive assumptions. Many of the original community service programs followed this model, predominantly focusing on diverting offenders from jails and prisons as a cost saving device (U.K. Home Office, 1970; Harland, 1980; Harris, 1984; McDonald, 1986). As such, the effectiveness of community service has not typically been gauged in terms of offender, victim or other social benefits. Programs typically offer few restorative benefits, and offenders are often restricted to menial and sometimes humiliating tasks specifically designed to be punitive (Harland, 1980; Krajick, 1982).

The following review highlights some of the central findings about community service and its impact on juvenile offenders. Because of the limited information on programs implemented under restorative conditions, the research reviewed discusses findings from available research on the impact of community service on juvenile offenders, even though not all of these can be considered restorative programs.

Offender Satisfaction and Completion Rates

Varah (1981) found that most offenders studied saw community service as a serious sanction, and that the vast majority felt they were given meaningful work to do. Most of these same offenders believed they learned useful skills, and among those who had previously been to prison, most felt that community service benefited others and enabled them to feel good about having done something for society (Varah, 1981). Thorvaldson (1978) found more favorable attitudes among offenders toward community service than toward fines and probation.

Completion rates have generally been between 70 and 90% (Skinns, 1990; Klein, 1990; McIvor, 1991; Van der Zande, 1987; Vallieres and Simon, 1982; Bol and Overwater, 1986; Rowley, 1990). An important component of community service seems to be the extent to which the offender believed he or she was doing something useful. In Scotland, offenders viewed the experience differently, depending on whether or not they were able to acquire a new skill, have contact with the beneficiaries of the work, or see that the work had social value (i.e., whether the work had a "restorative" focus). Such experiences led to increased compliance rates, and sometimes even resulted in continuation of the work after the community service order was completed (McIvor, 1991).

Recidivism Rates

Some studies have found lower recidivism rates among offenders sentenced to community service than among comparable control groups (Schneider, 1986; van der Laan, 1991; Rowley, 1990), while others have not (Pease et al., 1977). Examining one community service program implemented as a restorative sanction, Geudens (1996) finds lower recidivism among youths sentenced to community service in Belgium than among a similar group receiving more traditional sentences. These differences remained over 18 months, with no apparent increase in the rate of subsequent offending over time for the community service-sentenced juveniles.

Community Service Conclusion

The lack of restorative intent in most community service programs has had some negative impact on offenders. When sentenced to perform only menial labor that has no clear benefit for the victim, the community or the offender, offenders can be expected to derive little benefit from a community service sentence. However, when community service is imposed as a restorative sanction that meets real victim and community needs, and where input from the victim and the community is included in the sanctioning process, the possibility that community service will benefit offenders, victims and the community is considerably increased.

GAPS IN EXISTING RESEARCH

While extant research clearly implies promising effects of restorative interventions on juvenile offenders, the lack of controlled studies, absence of consistent effectiveness measures, and paucity of research on some of the more recent interventions tends to engender more questions than answers. In part, this reflects the newness of some of the restorative interventions in juvenile justice from which final evaluation results have yet to be published (e.g., the RISE experiments in Australia or the FGC project in Bethlehem, PA, or the reparative probation project in Vermont). Additionally, some innovative sanctions have simply not, to date, been subject to rigorous review and evaluation (e.g., circle sentencing processes in the Yukon Territory, or some of the newer mediation and conferencing processes that have arisen in various U.S. states).

In part, this abundance of questions also arises from the tension of trying to distinguish the impact of restorative processes from those of restorative sanctions. Focusing developmental attention on processes over sanctions may often mean that existing retributive sanctions, such as restitution and community service, are simply relabeled as restorative with little substantive change. In other words, the importance of implementing restorative processes may be overshadowing the need to assure that associated sanctions are indeed restorative. Even when restoration is considered an explicit goal, there is a tendency to concentrate on program-specific rather than systemic interventions, leaving little changed in the overall structure, operation or philosophy of the juvenile justice system.

A research agenda for the future must first develop a language that speaks directly to the concerns of skeptics who would dismiss restorative justice interventions as simply another fad in the long history of failed rehabilitative programs (see Bazemore, this volume). Such cynics argue that restorative justice is unresponsive to concerns about increased recidivism (Wundersitz, 1994; Polk, 1994); proportionality constraints (Warner, 1994); concerns for "punishment" and censure (von Hirsch, 1993); and the fear of net widening and/or strengthening (Warner, 1994; Polk, 1994). Such a language must be grounded in methodologically sound empirical research that both demonstrates the benefits, and meaningfully addresses the deficits, of such interventions.

Specific research challenges for the next decade can be divided into two categories: broad systemic issues and program-specific empirical issues.

Broad Systemic Issues

Research on systemic issues must identify the extent to which a program is truly restorative in nature and not simply a transmogrified retributive approach. It must clarify precisely what characterizes restorative processes and sanctions, as well as present such findings in terms that are meaningful to advocates and skeptics alike. Two particularly important systemic concerns include the potential for discrimination in restorative processes, and the degree to which net widening and net strengthening result from such interventions.

First, some evidence suggests that more white, middle-class offenders are sent to VOM and thus receiving restitution, while minorities subject to traditional processes may end up in custody (Kigin and Novack, 1980; Coates and Gehm, 1985; Umbreit and Coates, 1992; Warner, 1992); Zehr and Umbreit, 1982); Warner, 1994). If this is true, then programs must be made aware of such potential discrimination in order to correct it. Careful attention must be paid to social demographic characteristics of offenders in restorative programs as compared with those processed through more traditional mechanisms, and formative process evaluations must continually inform program operations and structure.

Second, if restorative programs are increasing the number of juveniles coming under official control, i.e., expanding government nets (Braithwaite, 1994), then the extent to which program goals may have been co-opted to serve broader social control objectives must be explored. However, if it is community nets that are being expanded or strengthened (Braithwaite, 1994; Polk, 1994), then the overall effect might be positive. Research must examine if official over-control occurs because restorative sanctions are imposed *in addition to* other, more traditional, sanctions, as well as what happens in cases of non-compliance and subsequent recidivism. In particular, there must be safeguards against subjecting offenders to significantly harsher sanctions upon resentence after either "failing" to complete, or reoffending during or after, a restorative program. This can significantly increase the number of juveniles subject to custodial terms, drastically altering the system's restorative intent. Specific outcome measures here are less meaningful than are the presence of rigidly selected and carefully monitored control groups, as well as study designs that permit long-term effects to be examined. Specific measures might include the types of sanctions imposed, the types of offenders involved and attention to the specific process involved.

Other systemic concerns worthy of research attention include:

- *Identifying whether restorative processes or sanctions are having the greatest impacts on juvenile offenders.* It is important to identify whether it is the process in which the offender participates, or completion of the sanction itself, that results in the most positive impact. Important indicators here include the type of process, the type of sanction, completion of the process, completion of the sanction and time to completion.

- *The extent to which offenders develop empathy for the victim, a sense of justice and fairness, and feelings of responsibility and accountability.* It is not only important to identify whether such characteristics may result from participation in restorative processes, but also if such attributes can be linked to increased program compliance, decreased recidivism rates, and other successful outcome measures. Indicators here should rely on qualitative criteria derived from offender interviews and questionnaires, with specific definitions to indicate the presence of such attributes. These must then be related to more concrete outcome indicators, such as completion and recidivism rates.

- *The extent to which participation in restorative programs is voluntary or coerced and the impact this has for program "failure" and participant satisfaction.* Research findings that restorative programs are less effective when participants feel coerced into a process must either be confirmed or rejected. Measures here must address offender perceptions of coercion, paying careful attention to consistent measurement and unbiased interview questions.

- *The extent to which interventions are restorative for the victim and the community, while also holding offenders accountable and helping them to develop valuable skills.* Research presented in this chapter has suggested that offenders benefit most when they are held accountable by a targeted, comprehensive program, can perform meaningful work and are held directly accountable to the victim. These factors are not only important in increasing compliance and decreasing recidivism rates, but are also fundamental to the restorative model. Research must examine the extent to which these conditions are met, and identify what elements that may prevent the achievement of such goals. Process evaluations would be particularly useful here, enabling mid-course corrections whenever possible.

- *The extent to which programs are implemented in isolation or in the context of a comprehensive restorative framework.* As suggested by much of the research reviewed here, as well as other literature on restorative justice (Bazemore and Schiff, 1996; Bazemore, 1997), research must identify the extent to which programs are developed and implemented comprehensively or in isolation from a restorative framework. Such research must clarify whether and how programs are operating outside of the restorative context, and the impact this has on the evolution of the restorative model.

Program-Specific Empirical Issues

Program-specific empirical issues are important insofar as they demonstrate actual impacts of restorative interventions on victims, communities and offenders. Such outcome measures are particularly important because they can communicate the impacts of restorative interventions in terms that are meaningful to both supporters and opponents alike. The following specific empirical indicators are suggested by the existing literature:

- *Recidivism rates.* Research must demonstrate that recidivism following a restorative intervention is, if not significantly reduced, at least no worse than what occurs following traditional juvenile justice methods. Policy makers and the public must both be convinced that they are no worse off, and potentially significantly better off, under a restorative juvenile justice system than a retributive one. Rearrest, reconviction and reincarceration rates should all be examined, with particular controls for time at risk to assure comparable follow-up periods.

- *Compliance rates.* Studies should look to see if and how compliance rates may be related to recidivism. If higher completion rates result in lower recidivism, than programs should concentrate resources on increasing compliance as a means of reducing juvenile crimes rates and increasing public perceptions of safety. Specific outcome measures here should include: program and sanction completion rates, time to completion, and the relationship of program compliance to recidivism and offender satisfaction.

- *Victim and offender satisfaction rates.* If an important aspect of the restorative model includes satisfaction with the process and with the outcomes, consistent indicators that can be applied across different types of programs and jurisdictions must be developed. To date, "satisfaction" remains a somewhat ambiguous term subject to the definition of the evaluator. Satisfaction measures must distinguish between perceptions of the process and of the outcome. They must also precisely define the parameters of victim, offender and community satisfaction.

- *More methodologically sound, controlled evaluations of some of the newer processes and sanctions.* These evaluations should focus on FGC, circle sentencing and victim impact panels, as well as on evaluations of some of the more traditional interventions undertaken in restorative contexts.

CONCLUSIONS AND DIRECTIONS FOR THE FUTURE

Restorative justice is a "holistic" approach to justice (e.g., Zehr, 1990). In a holistic model, no part of the system nor actor in the process is presumed to function independent of the others, but rather the success of any individual component is contingent on that of the others. In terms of restorative justice, this means that the actions of each participant are directly related to those of the others, and only through shared interaction, communication and commitment between the victim, the offender and the community can "justice" in fact be served (for a more complete description of the restorative model, see Walgrave and Bazemore, this volume). To date, most discussions have been in language that lends itself to existing retributive models rather than clarifies appropriate definitions and terms for a restorative discussion. To this end, it is important to develop a "language of restorative justice" that defines its own unique and precise terminology.

Holistic restorative models clearly show great promise for juvenile justice, and seem to offer some significant advantages over current retributive strategies for both offenders and victims. Considerably more research remains to be undertaken, however. Current limitations in the research make it difficult to unequivocally argue the benefits of restorative programs, suggesting that the time is ripe for developing a systematic research agenda dedicated to showing both the benefits and shortcomings of restorative interventions for juvenile offenders.

Finally, the community must be directly involved in the research process, as well as in the design and implementation of specific restorative justice programs. As people are more likely to support policy solutions once involved in their formulation (e.g., Carpenter and Kennedy, 1988; Madigan et. al., 1990), communities must be invited to participate in research design, as well as in the planning and implementation processes of restorative models. Researchers must identify the specific concerns of judges, victims, offenders, policy makers and especially communities, and design relevant and responsive research investigations. Results must then be communicated effectively to policy makers. Developing impact measures for restorative justice interventions in isolation from those actors most directly affected by such strategies would be senseless, and separating the research process from the overall axioms of restorative justice does a disservice to the precise values on which the concept is founded. Essentially, a research agenda for the twenty-first century must work to apply restorative justice principles to the very study of restorative justice itself.

REFERENCES

Austin, J. and B. Krisberg (1982). "The Unmet Promise of Alternatives-to-Incarceration." *Crime & Delinquency* 28:374-409.

Ban, P. (1996). "Implementing and Evaluating Family Group Conferences with Children and Families in Victoria Australia." In: J. Hudson, A. Morris, G. Maxwell and B. Galaway (eds.), *Family Group Conferences: Perspectives on Policy and Practice.* Leichhardt, AUS and Monsey, NY: Federation Press andCriminal Justice Press.

Bazemore, G. (1991). "On Mission Statements and Reform in Juvenile Justice: The Case of the Balanced Approach." *Federal Probation.* 65(3):64-70.

—— (1997). "The Community in Community Justice: Issues, Themes and Questions for the New Neighborhood Sanctioning Models." *Justice System Journal* 19(2):193-228.

—— and D. Maloney. (1994). "Rehabilitating Community Service: Toward Restorative Sanctions in A Balanced System." *Federal Probation* 58(1)24-35.

—— and M. Schiff. (1996). "Community Justice/Restorative Justice: Prospects for a New Social Ecology for Community Corrections." *International Journal of Comparative and Applied Criminal Justice.* 20(1):311-335.

Bol, M.W. and J. Overwater (1986). *Dienstverlening: Einrapport van het Onderzoek Naar de Vervanging van de Vrijheidsstraf Voor Volwassenen.* (Community Service: Report of and Investigation into the Replacement of Detention for Adults.) Cited in L. Walgrave and H. Geudens (1996). "Community Service as a Sanction of Restorative Juvenile Justice: A European Approach." Paper presented at the annual meeting of the American Society of Criminology, Chicago, November.

Bonta, J.L., J. Boyl, L.L. Motiuk and P. Sonnichsen (1983). "Restitution in Correctional Half-Way Houses: Victim Satisfaction, Attitudes And Recidivism." *Canadian Journal of Corrections* 20:140-152.

Braithwaite, J. (1989). *Crime, Shaming and Reintegration.* New York, NY: Cambridge University Press.

—— (1994). "Thinking Harder about Democratising Social Control." In: C. Alder and J. Wundersitz (eds.), *Family Conferencing and Juvenile Justice: The Way Forward or Misplaced Optimism?* Canberra, AUS: Australian Institute of Criminology.

Bussman, K-D. (1987). "Mediation Programs as a New Paradigm for a Restorative Juvenile Justice: Different Experiences and Models of Conflict Resolution Programs in the U.S., Canada and Germany." Paper presented to the International Seminar on Mediation, Finland, September.

Butts, J. and H. Snyder (1991). *Restitution and Juvenile Recidivism.* Monograph. Pittsburgh, PA: National Center for Juvenile Justice.

Cannon A. and R.M. Stanford (1981). *Evaluation of the Juvenile Alternative Services Project.* Unpublished paper. Florida Department of Health and Rehabilitative Services.

Carpenter, S. and W.J.D. Kennedy. (1988). *Managing Public Disputes.* San Francisco, CA: Jossey-Bass.

Claassen, R. (1996). "Restorative Justice – Fundamental Principles." Unpublished paper revised and adapted by the Working Party on Restorative Justice, established by the United Nations Alliance of NGOs on Crime Prevention and Criminal Justice. New York, May.

Coates, R. and J. Gehm (1985). *Victim Meets Offender: An Evaluation of Victim Offender Reconciliation Programs.* Valparaiso, IN: PACT Institute of Justice.

—— (1989). "An Empirical Assessment." In: M. Wright and B. Galaway (eds.), *Mediation and Criminal Justice.* London, UK: Sage.

Davis, R.C. and T. Bannister (1995). "Improving Collection of Court-Ordered Restitution." *Judicature* 79:30-33.

Davis, R.C., B.E. Smith and S. Hillebrand. (1991). "Increasing Compliance with Restitution Orders." *Judicature* 74:245-249.

Dignan, J. (1990). *An Evaluation of an Experimental Adult Reparation Scheme in Lettering, Northamptonshire.* Sheffield, UK: Centre for Criminological and Legal Research, University of Sheffield.

Dooley, M.J. (1995). *Reparative Probation Program.* Waterbury, VT: Vermont Department of Corrections.

Ervin, L. and A. Schneider (1990.) "Explaining the Effects of Restitution on Offenders: Results From a National Experiment in Juvenile Courts." In: B. Galaway and J. Hudson. (eds.), *Criminal Justice, Restitution and Reconciliation.* New York, NY: Criminal Justice Press.

Feeley, M. (1983). *Court Reform on Trial.* New York, NY: Basic Books.

Fraser, S. and J. Norton (1996). "Family Group Conferencing in New Zealand Child Protection Work." In: J. Hudson, A. Morris, G. Maxwell and B. Galaway (eds.). *Family Group Conferences: Perspectives on Policy and Practice.* Leichhardt, AUS and Monsey, NY: Federation Press and Criminal Justice Press.

Galaway, B. (1983). "Probation as a Reparative Sentence." *Federal Probation* 46(3):9-18.

Geudens, H. (1996). "The Impact of Community Service on Juvenile Offenders: The Recidivism Rate." Paper presented at the annual meeting of the American Society of Criminology, Chicago, November.

Guedalia, L.J. (1979). *Predicting Recidivism of Juvenile Delinquents on Restitutionary Probation From Selected Background, Subject and Program Variables.* Rockville, MD: National Criminal Justice Reference Service.

Harland, A. (1980). "Court-Ordered Community Service in Criminal Law: The Continuing Tyranny of Benevolence" *Buffalo Law Review* 29:428-429.

—— and C. Rosen. (1991). "Impediments to the Recovery of Restitution by Crime Victims." *Violence and Victims* 5(2):127-140.

Harris, M.K. (1984). "Rethinking Probation in the Context of the Justice Model." In: P.D. McAnany, D. Thompson and D. Fogel (eds.), *Probation and Justice: A Reconsideration of Mission.* Cambridge, MA: Oelgeschlager, Gunn and Hain.

—— (1986). *The Goals of Community Sanctions.* Washington, DC: U.S. National Institute of Justice.

Heinz, J., B. Galaway and J. Hudson (1986). "Restitution or Parole: A Follow-up Study of Adult Offenders." *Social Service Review* 50:148-156.

Hillsman, S.(1982). "Pretrial Diversion of Youthful Adults: A Decade of Reform and Research" *Justice System Journal* 7:361-387.

—— and S. Sadd (1981). *Diversion of Felony Arrests: An Experiment in Pretrial Diversion* Washington, DC: U.S. Department of Justice.

Hofford, M. (1981). "Juvenile Restitution Program." Unpublished final report. Trident. Charleston, SC.

Hudson, J. and S. Chesney (1978). "Research on Restitution: A Review and Assessment." In: B. Galaway and J. Hudson (eds.), *Offender Restitution in Theory and Action.* Lexington, MA: Lexington Books.

Hughes, S. and A. Schneider (1990). *Victim Offender Mediation in the Juvenile Justice System.* Washington, DC: U.S. Office of Juvenile Justice and Delinquency Prevention.

Ivari, J. (1987). "Mediation as a Conflict Resolution: Some Topic Issues in Mediation Project in Vantaa." Paper presented to International Seminar on Mediation, Finland, September. Cited in T. Marshal and S. Merry (1990). *Crime and Accountability: Victim Offender Mediation in Practice.* London, UK: U.K. Home Office.

Immarigeon, R. (1996). "Family Group Conferences in Canada and the United States: An Overview." In: J. Hudson, A. Morris, G. Maxwell and B. Galaway (eds.), *Family Group Conferences: Perspectives on Policy and Practice.* Leichhardt, AUS and Monsey, NY: Federation Press and Criminal Justice Press.

Kigin, R. and S. Novak (1980). "A Rural Restitution Program for Juvenile Offenders and Victims." In: J. Hudson and B. Galaway (eds.), *Victims, Offenders and Alternative Sanctions.* Lexington, MA: Lexington Books.

Klein, A.R. (1990). "Restitution and Community Work Service: Promising Core Ingredients for Effective Supervision Programming." In: T. Armstrong (ed.), *Intensive Interventions with High Risk Youths.* Monsey, NY: Criminal Justice Press.

Krajick, K. (1982). "Community Service: The Work Ethic Approach to Punishment." *Corrections Magazine* 8:5.

Kuhn, A. (1987). "Koperverletzung als Konflikt, Zwischenbericht (zum Project Handschlag)." Unpublished paper cited in T. Trenczek (1990). "A Review and Assessment of Victim-Offender Reconciliation Programming in West Germany." In: B. Galaway and J. Hudson (eds.), *Criminal Justice, Restitution and Reconciliation*. Monsey, NY: Criminal Justice Press.

Lawrence, R. (1990)."Restitution as a Cost-Effective Alternative to Incarceration." In: B. Galaway and J. Hudson (eds.), *Criminal Justice, Restitution and Reconciliation*. Monsey, NY: Criminal Justice Press.

Longclaws, L. B. Galaway and L. Barkwell (1996). "Piloting Family Group Conferences for Young Aboriginal Offenders in Winnipeg, Canada." In: J. Hudson, A. Morris, G. Maxwell and B. Galaway (eds.) *Family Group Conferences: Perspectives on Policy and Practice*. Leichhardt, AUS and Monsey, NY: Federation Press and Criminal Justice Press.

Madigan, D., G. McMahon, L. Susskind and S. Rolley (1990). *New Approaches to Resolving Public Policy Disputes*. Washington, DC: National Institute for Dispute Resolution.

Marsh, P. and G. Crow (1996). "Family Group Conferences in Child Welfare Services in England and Wales." In: J. Hudson, A. Morris, G. Maxwell and B. Galaway (eds.), *Family Group Conferences: Perspectives on Policy and Practice*. Leichhardt, AUS and Monsey, NY: Federation Press and Criminal Justice Press.

Marshall, T. (1990). "Results From British Experiments in Restorative Justice." In: B. Galaway and J. Hudson (eds.), *Criminal Justice, Restitution and Reconciliation*. Monsey, NY: Criminal Justice Press.

—— (1992). "Restorative Justice on Trial in Britain." In: H. Messmer and H.-U. Otto (eds.), *Restorative Justice on Trail: Pitfalls and Potentials of Victim-Offender Mediation — International Research Perspectives*. Dordecht, NETH: Kluwer.

—— and S. Merry (1990). *Crime and Accountability: Victim Offender Mediation in Practice*. London, UK: Home Office.

Maxwell, G. and A. Morris (1993). *Family, Victims and Culture: Youth Justice in New Zealand*. Wellington, NZ: Victoria University.

—— (1996). "Research on Family Group Conferences with Young Offenders in New Zealand." In: J. Hudson, A. Morris, G. Maxwell and B. Galaway (eds.), *Family Group Conferences: Perspectives on Policy and Practice*. Leichhardt, AUS and Monsey, NY: Criminal Justice Press.

Morris, A., G. Maxwell and J. Robertson (1993). "Giving Victims a Choice: A New Zealand Experiment." *Howard Journal* 32(4):304-321.

McCold, P. and J. Starr (1996). "Bethlehem Police Family Group Conferencing Project." Paper presented at the annual meeting of the American Society of Criminology. Chicago, November.

McDonald, D. (1986). *Punishment Without Walls: Community Service Sentences in New York City*. New Brunswick, NJ: Rutgers University Press.

McIvor, G. (1991). *Sentenced to Serve.* Aldershot, UK: Avebury.

McKnight, D. (1981). "The Victim-Offender Reconciliation Project." In: B. Galaway and J. Hudson (eds.), *Perspectives on Crime Victims.* St Louis, MO: C.V. Mosby.

Melton, A. (1995). "Indigenous Justice Systems and Tribal Society." *Judicature* 70(3):126-133.

Mercer, D. , R. Lorden and J. Lord (1994). "Sharing Their Stories: What are the Benefits? Who is Helped?" Paper presented at the International Society for Traumatic Stress Studies. Chicago, November.

Moore, D.B. (1995). *A New Approach to Juvenile Justice: An Evaluation of Family Conferencing in Wagga-Wagga.* A Report to the Criminology Research Council. Wagga-Wagga, NSW, AUS: Centre for Rural Social Research, Charles Stuart University-Riverina.

—— and T. O'Connell. (1994). "Family Conferencing in Wagga-Wagga: Communitarian Model of Justice." In: C. Alder and J. Wundersitz (eds.), *Family Conferencing and Juvenile Justice: The Way Forward or Misplaced Optimism?* Canberra, AUS: Australian Institute of Criminology.

Morris, A., G. Maxwell and J. Robertson (1993). "Giving Victims a Choice: A New Zealand Experiment." *Howard Journal* 32(4):304-321.

Morris, N. and M. Tonry (1990). *Between Prison and Probation: Intermediate Punishments in a Rational Sentencing System.* New York, NY: Oxford University Press.

Novak, S. B. Galaway and J. Hudson (1992). "Victim and Offender Perceptions of the Fairness of Restitution and Community Service Sanctions." In: J. Hudson and B. Galaway (eds.), *Victims, Offenders and Alternative Sanctions.* Lexington, MA: Lexington Books.

Nugent, W.R. and J.B. Paddock (1995). "The Effect of Victim-Offender Mediation on Severity of Reoffense." *Mediation Quarterly* 12(4):353-367.

O'Haley, J.O. (1992). "Victim-Offender Mediation: Japanese and American Comparisons." In: H. Messmer and H-U Otto (eds.), *Restorative Justice on Trial: Pitfalls and Potentials of Victim Offender Mediation — International Research Perspectives.* Dordrecht, NETH: Kluwer.

Olsen, T., G. Maxwell and A. Morris (1995). "Maori and Youth Justice in New Zealand." In: K. Hazelhurst (ed.), *Popular Justice and Community Regeneration: Pathways of Indigenous Reform.* Westport, CT: Prager.

Pate, K. (1990). "Victim-Offender Restitution Programs in Canada." In: B. Galaway and J. Hudson (eds.), *Criminal Justice, Restitution and Reconciliation.* Monsey, NY: Criminal Justice Press.

Pearson, J. (1982). "An Evaluation of Alternatives to Court Adjudication." *Justice System Journal* 7:420-444.

Pease, K. (1985). "Community Service Orders." In: N. Morris and M. Tonry *(*eds.*)*, *Crime and Justice: An Annual Review of Research,* vol. 6. Chicago, IL: University of Chicago Press.

—— S. Billingham and I. Earnshaw (1977). *Community Service Assessed in 1976.* U.K. Home Office Study, #39. London, UK: Her Majesty's Stationery Office.

Pennel, J. and G. Burford (1996). "Attending to Context: Family Group Decision Making in Canada." In: J. Hudson, A. Morris, G. Maxwell and B. Galaway (eds.), *Family Group Conferences: Perspectives on Policy and Practice.* Leichhardt, AUS and Monsey, NY: Federation Press and Criminal Justice Press.

Polk, K. (1994). "Family Conferencing: Theoretical and Evaluative Questions." In: C. Alder and J. Wundersitz (eds.), *Family Conferencing and Juvenile Justice: The Way Forward or Misplaced Optimism?* Canberra, AUS: Australian Institute of Criminology.

Robertson, J. (1996). "Research on Family Group Conferences in Child Welfare in New Zealand." In: J. Hudson, A. Morris, G. Maxwell and B. Galaway (eds.), *Family Group Conferences: Perspectives on Policy and Practice.* Leichhardt, AUS and Monsey, NY: Federation Press and Criminal Justice Press.

Rock, J. (1992). "An Evaluation of the Juvenile Offender Mediation Program." Masters Thesis, University of Houston, Clear-Lake.

Rowley, M.S. (1990). "Recidivism of Juvenile Offenders in a Diversion Program Compared to a Matched Group of Offenders Processed Through Court." In: B. Galaway and J. Hudson (eds.), *Criminal Justice, Restitution and Reconciliation.* Monsey, NY: Criminal Justice Press.

Roy, S. (1995). "Juvenile Restitution and Recidivism in a Midwestern County." *Federal Probation* 59:55-62.

Rubin, T. (1986). "Community Service by Juveniles: Also in Need of Guidance." *Juvenile and Family Court Journal* 37:1.

Schneider, A.L. (1982). "The Effects of Deinstitutionalization of Status Offenders: A Review Essay." *Criminal Justice Abstracts* 182-195.

—— (1985). *Guide to Juvenile Restitution.* Washington, DC; U.S. Department of Justice.

—— (1986). "Restitution and Recidivism Rates of Juvenile Offenders: Results From Four Experimental Studies." *Criminology* 24:533-552.

—— (1990). *Deterrence and Juvenile Crime.* New York, NY: Springer-Verlag.

—— and P.R. Schneider (1980). "Policy Expectations and Program Realities in Juvenile Restitution." In J. Hudson and B. Galaway (eds.), *Victims, Offenders and Alternative Sanctions.* Lexington, MA: Lexington Books.

—— and P.R. Schneider (1984a). *The Effectiveness of Restitution as a Sole Sanction and as a Condition of Probation: Results from an Experiment in Oklahoma County.* Stillwater, OK: Policy Sciences Group, Oklahoma State University.

—— and P.R. Schneider (1984b). "A Comparison of Programmatic and 'Ad Hoc' Restitution in Juvenile Courts." *Justice Quarterly* 529-547.

Schneider, P.R., A.L. Schneider, W.R. Griffith and M.J. Wilson (1982). *Two Year Report on the National Evaluation of the Juvenile Restitution Initiative.* Washington, DC: National Institute of Juvenile Justice and Delinquency Prevention, U.S. Department of Justice.

—— and G. Bazemore. (1985). "Research on Restitution: A Guide to Rational Decision Making." In: A.L. Schneider (ed.), *Guide to Juvenile Restitution.* Washington, DC: Office of Juvenile Justice and Delinquency Prevention, U.S. Department of Justice.

Sherman, L. and G. Barnes. (1997) "Restorative Justice and Offender's Respect for the Law." RISE Working Paper #3. [online]. Available: http://ba048864.aic.gov.au. links.rise.risepap3.htm

—— and H. Strang. (1997). "Restorative Justice and Deterring Crime." RISE Working Paper #4.[online]. Available: http://ba04886.aic.gov.au.links.rise.rispap4.htm

Skinns, C.D. (1990). "Community Service Practice." *British Journal of Criminology* 30(1):65-80.

Smith, D., H. Blagg and N. Derricourt (1985). *Victim-Offender Mediation Project.* Report to the Chief Officers' Group, South Yorkshire Probation Service. Cited in T. Marshal and S. Merry (1990). *Crime And Accountability: Victim Offender Mediation in Practice.* London, UK: Home Office.

—— H. Blagg and N. Derricourt, (1988). "Mediation in South Yorkshire." *British Journal of Criminology* 28(3):378-395.

—— R. Davis and S. Hillebrand (1996). "Restitution: Promising Practices." Application for funding submitted to the U.S. Office for Victims of Crimes,.Washington, DC: Fund for Justice and Education. American Bar Association.

Smith, J. (1986). "Mediation in Practice: An Example of Victim-Offender Mediation from the South Yorkshire Scheme." *Mediation* 2(2):2-4.

Softley, P. (1978). *Compensation Orders in Magistrates Courts.* London, UK: Home Office Research Study #43. London, UK: Her Majesty's Stationery Office.

Stuart, B. (1996). Unpublished presentation to the Society for Professionals in Dispute Resolution, Anaheim, CA, October.

Thorvaldson, S. (1978). "The Effects of Community Service on the Attitudes of Offenders." Doctoral dissertation, Cambridge University.

U.K. Home Office (1970). *Noncustodial and Semi-Custodial Penalties.* London, UK: Her Majesty's Stationery Office.

Umbreit, M. (1996). "Restorative Justice through Mediation: The Impact on Programs in Four Canadian Provinces." In B. Galaway and J. Hudson (eds.), *Restorative Justice: International Perspectives.* Monsey, NY: Criminal Justice Press.

—— and R. Coates (1992a). "The Impact of Mediating Victim Offender Conflict: An Analysis of Programs in Three States." *Juvenile and Family Court Journal* 43(1):21-28.

—— and R. Coates (1992b). *Victim-Offender Mediation: An Analysis of Programs in Four States of the U.S.* Minneapolis, MN: Citizens Council Mediation Services.

—— and R. Coates (1993). "Cross-Site Analysis of Victim-Offender Mediation in Four States." *Crime & Delinquency* 39(4):565-585.

—— and S. Stacey (1996). "Family Group Conferencing Comes to the U.S.: A Comparison with Victim-Offender Mediation." *Juvenile and Family Court Journal* 29-39.

Vallieres, S. and H. Simon. (1982). *L'Evaluation d'une Nouvelle Mesure Penale: Les Travaux Communitaires au Quebec.* Montréal, CAN: School of Criminology, University of Montréal. Cited in L. Walgrave and H. Geudens. (1996). "Community Service as a Sanction of Restorative Juvenile Justice: A European Approach." Paper presented at the annual meeting of the American Society of Criminology, Chicago, November.

van der Laan, P. (1991). *Eperimenteren met alternatieve Sancties Voor Jeugdigen.* (Experimenting with Alternative Sanctions for Minors.) Cited in L. Walgrave and H. Geudens. (1996). "Community Service as a Sanction of Restorative Juvenile Justice: A European Approach." Paper presented at the annual meeting of the American Society of Criminology, Chicago, November.

Van der Zande, C. (1987). *Een Vergelijkende Studie van 2 Alternatieve Sancties in Nieuw Zeeland: Community Service en Community Care.* (A Comparative Study of Two Alternative Sanctions in New Zealand: Community Service and Community Care.) Dissertation in Criminology, Katholieke Universiteit Leuven, BEL.

Van Ness, D. and K.H. Strong. (1997). *Restoring Justice.* Cincinnati, OH: Anderson.

Varah, M. (1981). "What About the Workers? Offenders on Community Service Orders Express Their Opinions." *Probation Journal* 120-123.

von Hirsch, A. (1993). *Censure and Sanctions.* Oxford, UK: Clarendon Press.

—— M. Wessex and J. Greene. (1989). "Punishments in the Community and the Principles of Desert." *Rutgers Law Review* 20:595-618.

Walgrave, L. (1995). "Restorative Justice for Juveniles: Just a Technique or a Fully Fledged Alternative?" *Howard Journal* 34(3):228-249.

—— and H. Geudens (1996a). "Community Service as a Sanction of Restorative Juvenile Justice: A European Approach." Paper presented at the annual meeting of the American Society of Criminology, Chicago, November.

—— (1996b). "The Restorative Proportionality of Community Service for Juveniles." Paper presented at the annual meeting of the American Society of Criminology, Chicago, November.

Warner, K. (1994). "The Rights of the Offender in Family Conferences." In: C. Alder and J. Wundersitz (eds.), *Family Conferencing and Juvenile Justice: The Way Forward or Misplaced Optimism?* Canberra, AUS: Australian Institute of Criminology.

Warner, S. (1992). "Reparation, Mediation and Scottish Criminal Justice." In: H. Messmer and H.-U. Otto (eds.), *Restorative Justice on Trial: Pitfalls and Potentials of Victim-Offender Mediation— International Research Perspectives* Dordecht, NETH: Kluwer.

Wax, M.L. (1977). "Effects of Symbolic Restitution and Presence of Victim on Delinquent Shoplifters." Doctoral dissertation. Washington State University Pullman.

Wheeler, G., A.S. Rudolph and R.V. Hissong. (1989). "Do Probationers' Characteristics Affect Fee Assessment, Payment and Outcome?" *APPA Perspectives* 13:12-17.

Wundersitz, J. (1994). "Family Conferencing in South Australia and Juvenile Justice Reform." In: C. Alder and J. Wundersitz (eds.), *Family Conferencing and Juvenile*

Justice: The Way Forward or Misplaced Optimism? Canberra, AUS: Australian Institute of Criminology.

Wundersitz, J. and S. Hetzel. (1996). "Family Group Conferencing for Young Offenders: The South Australian Experience." In: J. Hudson, A. Morris, G. Maxwell and B. Galaway, eds.), *Family Group Conferences: Perspectives on Policy and Practice.* Leichhardt, AUS and Monsey, NY: Criminal Justice Press.

Zehr, H. (1990). *Changing Lenses: A New Focus for Crime and Justice.* Scottsdale, PA: Herald Press.

—— and M. Umbreit (1982). "Victim-Offender Reconciliation: An Incarceration Substitute?" *Federal Probation* 46(4):63-68.

NOTES

1. Early VOM programs have also been referred to as victim-offender reconciliation programs (VORPs). This terminology is no longer popular because it implies a goal of reconciliation between the victim and the offender, which is often offensive and insensitive to the victim. Although many of the programs reviewed in this chapter were originally referred to as VORPs, I will use the term VOM here as it is more current and victim-sensitive. The reader should bear in mind that some of the programs herein reviewed originally referred to themselves as VORPs.

2. Family group conferencing is a process whereby offenders and their families meet with victims and their families in a structured process. The so-called Wagga-Wagga model is a front-end, police-driven process wherein the parties discuss the impacts of the action and mutually decide on appropriate reparation; the New Zealand model is not sponsored by the police and can serve as an alternative to the dispositional process at any point during the case.

3. It is possible, however, that this is because of the type of offender likely to be sanctioned by restitution; more serious offenders posing greater risks may be sentenced to more severe sanctions.

4. Schneider (1990) suggests that one possible explanation for this may be that higher risk offenders are simply more realistic about their chances of being caught and punished.

5. Claassen (1996) has developed a broad set of indicators that can help delimit the parameters of restorative interventions. However, these need considerably more detail in order to become tangible and specific measurement indicators that are useful in designing research evaluations. (See Umbreit, this volume, for some dimensions related to victim sensitivity.)

PART FIVE:
TOWARD THE FUTURE

14. Reflections on the Future of Restorative Justice for Juveniles

by

Lode Walgrave

and

Gordon Bazemore

By now readers of this text will understand that restorative justice, as a fully-fledged alternative response to youth crime, is a "work in progress." As a vision for a distinctive *future* juvenile justice system, restorative justice is clearly "in the air" in Europe, North America, Australia, Canada and a number of other countries around the world. Implementation of restorative juvenile justice is best seen primarily in small experiments, but restorative justice is also "on the ground" as a systemic model in New Zealand as the primary means of carrying out the disposition of juvenile cases. Restorative justice is also now the primary intervention model for adult community corrections in the state of Vermont, and the preferred means of responding to crimes of a wide range of seriousness in many Aboriginal communities in Canada. Its principles are increasingly being used in European jurisdictions as the model for a holistic alternative juvenile justice system, one of which is now under discussion in Belgium. Restorative justice is also being utilized as the general framework for reform of both juvenile and adult corrections systems in several jurisdictions in the U.S.[1]

The insistence in this text on the need for restorative justice advocates to articulate and begin to implement systemic models should not diminish the value of the many small, non-systemic experiments that have been conducted. Indeed, if the principles that distinguish restorative justice as a fully-fledged model from traditional punitive and social welfare approaches are to be fully developed and widely understood, a much greater number of tightly designed and administered (presumably small-scale) intervention prototypes will be needed. Yet, we are aware that even the most well-managed, well-established and carefully evaluated restorative programs are likely to remain on the margins unless these are presented not as "add-ons" to retributive and/or treatment/welfare systems, but as part of a coherent and primary intervention model. We have argued that a fully-fledged model will first require a definition of restorative justice that is at once inclusive enough to accommodate emerging and evolving interventions and also exclusive enough to limit practices and processes labeled "restorative" to those that meet certain principle-based criteria. Such criteria would exclude "new" programs that are actually retributive or treatment interventions in restorative clothing. Second, a fully-fledged restorative juvenile justice presumes the development of viable processes and reparative interventions at all levels and stages of both the community and formal system response to all criminal incidents, as well as distinctively restorative approaches to accomplishing essential system functions (e.g., public safety, sanctioning). Third, a restorative model for youth crime requires the development of a strategic focus that offers practical restorative justice solutions to some of the crises and seemingly unresolvable problems currently facing juvenile justice systems.

After completing this text, readers are likely to have a number of lingering concerns. Many questions about the normative theory underlying the restorative response and what a systemic restorative justice might look like in practice remain unanswered. In addition, the preceding chapters have only partially addressed issues such as: what implementation approaches and standards for practice should be developed; what theories of restorative intervention can guide research aimed at assessing offender, victim and community impact; and what role is anticipated for "the community" and how might this role may reshape the role of government in the justice process.

1. WHY RESTORATIVE JUSTICE?

The purpose of this chapter is to explore some of these questions in greater depth as we look to the future of restorative juvenile justice, while also reviewing the current state of thinking and practice as expressed by the authors of the preceding chapters. First, it is important to revisit two dominant agendas that currently drive juvenile justice policy, place limits on protocols for reform, and consume a great deal of energy and resources.

1.1. Justice as Uniformity of Punishment: The Limits of "Just Desert"?

The "nothing works" slogan, together with the "just deserts" approach, has led some authors to opt for a radical change in juvenile justice, by remodeling it according to the traditional penal justice system. Feld goes furthest in this direction, arguing in his chapter for the abolition of juvenile courts and the incorporation of youthful offenders in a criminal justice system, in which age would be recognized as a mitigating factor in sentencing. This would, in theory, safeguard the legal rights of juvenile offenders and at the same time allow for consideration of age as it relates to socio-psychological and moral development differences. This so-called "youth discount" in the criminal court is one increasingly prominent response to the juvenile justice crisis, but it is not our option.

There are many reasons to challenge the just deserts ideology behind this approach (Braithwaite and Pettit, 1990). The argument goes that punishment should restore a balance, for example, a balance of benefits and burdens. Such a balance is difficult to maintain in societies with gross inequalities of wealth and power, wherein the punitive system obviously administers more burdens to those who already receive the least societal benefits. Others defend punishment as a social good because punishing wrongdoing is said to restore a moral balance. But the kind of morality that lies behind this kind of "getting even" balance can be questioned. And, at minimum, it must be viewed as more oriented toward public order, personal security, and property, than toward solidarity and social and economic equity. The position that denunciating wrongdoings is necessary to preserve the legal order is acceptable, but punishment is not the only possible way to achieve such denunciation. What is important is a response to a violation of the rule or norm, and confirmation that its transgression will be followed by a sanction and its enforcement. Viewed as an obligation, rather than as a means of inflicting pain or imposing threats, a sanction can be different from punishment (e.g., Packer, 1967). Reprobation through reintegrative shaming is one of many possibilities, for example, apart from or together with various reparative obligations.

In addition, several instrumental claims made by advocates of traditional penal responses to crime appear to be more cosmetic than supported by empirical research. Prevention through deterrence is only effective under specific circumstances, and for limited categories of offenses and offenders (Piliavin et al., 1986; Schneider, 1990; Lab, 1997). Personal improvement of the offender under the influence of the penal sanction is the exception rather than the rule. Psychological learning research convincingly demonstrates that the effectiveness of punishment or of negative reinforcers is dependent on specific conditions, which are certainly not present in the context wherein penal sanctions are typically imposed (Gendreau and Ross, 1981; Gendreau, 1989, Gendreau, 1996).

A question raised by Feld's proposal to provide for a "youth discount" is whether the differences between adolescents and adults would be reflected only in the quantity of punishment. Moral development appears not to evolve from "less" to "more" moral judgment, but to evolve over several stages that include different criteria for moral appreciation (Kohlberg, 1969). Moral evaluation of the option to commit an offense, and appreciation of the formal response, will therefore vary according to age. Hence, if youthfulness of the offender has to play a role in sentencing, it should not be in the sense of mitigating a possible punishment, but rather in differentiating the content of the sanction (e.g., its educative purpose). The idea of changing the quantity of punishment according to the age of the offender is thus too narrow a response to the broader and more complex question posed by age.

However, Feld's questions for advocates of restorative justice in chapter 1 are good ones. We address these later in this chapter.

1.2 Revitalizing Treatment: Seeking "What Works"?

The other major competing agenda for juvenile justice reform is to attempt to improve the efficiency of the individual treatment or social welfare mission of the juvenile court. While there are many variations of this effort, which may actually involve combining many attributes of just desserts, crime control, and corporatist philosophies (Corrado et al., 1992; Torbet et. al., 1996), the most dominant theme in defense of individual treatment has been that it has not been given a fair chance. The now-discredited claim that nothing works has, according to proponents of the "what works" perspective in corrections, caused a decline in confidence and investment in effective treatment. In reaffirming a treatment agenda as the primary mission for a revitalized juvenile justice, these advocates argue that the problem has not been with the limits of treatment. Rather, they say, it has been with the failure of policy makers to distinguish effective from ineffective programs, to provide adequate support for programs that are effective, and to appropriately match the needs of offenders with adequate programs.

While acknowledging the value of research that can distinguish program models with some prospects for positive impact from those that may even be harmful, Bazemore (this volume) argues that treatment programs have been oversold as a remedy for preserving a viable and effective response to youth crime. First, the singular focus on offender treatment is no longer politically or ethically adequate as a rationale for a distinct justice system, or as a rationale for intervention itself. Like punishment, treatment offers a one-dimensional response that, even when effective, fails to attend to community expectations that justice systems will give at least equal attention to other essential needs. Communities need, and expect their justice systems to engage in, a variety of efforts to promote peace and public safety, and to guide a sanctioning response to crime that offers constructive consequences for victims, communities and offenders.

Second, the treatment model, even as expressed in newer forms with due regard for the what works research, is practically, conceptually, and empirically limited even as a complete approach to rehabilitation and reintegration. Some treatment programs are demonstrably effective in producing statistically significant changes in attitudes and behavior, at least within a limited context in which offenders who end up in these programs are compared with other similar offenders under correctional supervision who are referred to other interventions (Gendreau, 1996). However, a growing body of research on resiliency and maturational reform confirms that the vast majority of young offenders are "rehabilitated" by the onset of adulthood. Such rehabilitation appears to be a consequence of more naturalistic community processes (e.g., starting a family, getting a job) that have little or no relationship to formal treatment intervention (e.g., Elliott, 1994).

Finally, these arguments should not be used as justification to stifle the search for more effective treatment interventions, which could also incorporate a focus on involving crime victims and community members and attempting to address their needs. However, there are other concerns about the hegemony of the treatment paradigm in juvenile justice. Most salient for proponents of restorative justice — who envision a more community-based, participatory and less professionalized approach to justice intervention — is the concern that the growth of professionalized services and the expansion of the justice apparatus may be undercutting the responsibility of communities to prevent and control crime. Moreover, expanded investment in this apparatus and service bureaucracy seems to be viewed increasingly as a substitute for strengthening those community socializing institutions (e.g., school, family, work, religious) that are ultimately responsible for the conventional maturation of young people (Polk, 1994; McKnight, 1995).

Since the beginning of this century, the debate about the most appropriate social reaction to youthful offending has fluctuated between the retributive and the rehabilitative responses, reflected in the positions mentioned above. Arguments have been exchanged, experiments carried out, minimum procedural rules determined internationally, and rhetorical constructs developed. Yet, in fact, the basic incompatibility of treatment concerns with legal safeguards remains unresolved. As one example, advocates of individual treatment as the guiding philosophy for juvenile justice have been unable to reconcile the assumed need to base the length of treatment on the relative responsiveness of offenders to the intervention, rather than on fixed limits beyond which state control cannot be extended. This problem, and the aforementioned inability of the current treatment paradigm to involve community members and victims in the justice process, is why a real alternative is needed, that would go further than most diversionary models and special programs.

1.3. The Need for Restorative Justice as a Systemic Alternative

Although the available experiences are not very encouraging due to net widening, loss of legal safeguards, and stigmatization by extra-judicial treatment programs (Lemert, 1981; Walgrave, 1995a), diversion may, theoretically, remove a large number of cases from the juvenile justice system. However, the diversion concept leaves the "non-divertible" cases to a system that is now widely considered to be unpropitious. Rather than divert cases from the system, reformers might instead seek to *divert the system itself* from its current retributive and/or treatment focus. The fully-fledged, systemic alternative to both the retributive and the social welfare responses to crime we wish to see developed should offer as many legal safeguards as the traditional criminal justice system. But it should be socially more constructive, provide more standing and support for crime victims, and offer (at a minimum) no fewer opportunities for offender reintegration and rehabilitation than systems grounded in individual treatment assumptions.

As part of a general motivation to unburden the criminal and juvenile justice systems and/or to affirm and expand victims' rights and needs, a restorative justice paradigm seems to be emerging that is gaining increasing confidence and support. Although the restorative justice response is not confined to youth crime, a majority of current experiments are being carried out with juveniles. Authorities, as well as the public, in general appear to be more open to the idea of new, less familiar responses to juvenile rather than adult crime. As existing systems of juvenile justice around the world come under increasing pressure, it is therefore timely to critically explore the potential of restorative justice for juveniles.

2. MAIN CONCLUSIONS

Can restorative justice avoid the negative side effects of the retributive response to crime, while maintaining the commitment to legal safeguards? Can restorative justice offer a more socially constructive and realistic response than the programs and practices of the individual treatment model? As we look back on the chapters in this volume, we consider whether the ideas, theories, experiences, and scientific results presented provide support for affirmative answers to these questions, and whether the goal of developing restorative justice as the dominant response to juvenile crime is realistic. What specifically has been achieved, where are the problems, which kind of practices and research are needed in the future, how can we influence the social and societal context wherein restorative justice is to be implemented? To what extent have restorative justice advocates begun to address the challenges of articulating a coherent, common definition; developing a holistic set of restorative responses to crime at all system levels and for all justice functions; and responding to emerging questions of those professionals who must operate within existing youth justice systems? The chapters of this volume have yielded important conclusions relevant to these challenges and questions.

2.1. A Tradition of Restorative Justice

The idea that the response to norm transgression should primarily be oriented to restoration is not new. Weitekamp has shown that restoring the harm caused by an offense is deeply rooted in human communal life. It was the dominant way of reacting in the so-called acephalous (non-state) societies, wherein restitution to the victim and his or her kin frequently took precedence over action against the offender. Reestablishing peace in the community was of utmost interest. Also in the early state societies, restitution and compensation were important tools for resolving conflicts. But as medieval kings and lords consolidated and centralized power, they also took an increasingly interested and active role in the resolution of trouble. As this occurred, the needs of crime victims were gradually replaced by the interests of the state in the emerging retributive response to crime. By the end of the twelfth century, the erosion of restorative justice elements was virtually complete and the state had taken control over the criminal law. But the idea of restoration was not lost, as is obvious in the writings of Thomas Moore, Bentham, Garofalo and others. Several International Prison Congresses by the end of the 19th century had also underlined the importance of restitution and compensation.

The observation that the restorative response to crime was in fact the first, and that this approach had its authoritative defenders throughout history, is a challenge to those who pretend that the need for punishment is naturally given and cannot be avoided. But, of course, things have changed since then, and we cannot simply turn back the clock to earlier times. In our urbanized, industrialized, (post)-modern societies, communities have lost much of their earlier capacity to maintain informal social control. In some situations, one might even wonder whether communities do still exist. At present, the state has overruled communities and has become the dominant force in the reaction against crime. Powerful institutions like the police and the judiciary have been established for that purpose.

Thus, while the idea of restoring the harm caused by a crime is not new, the cultural and structural context in which it has to be implemented today is completely different. The restorative justice ideal can no longer rely on the assumption of strong communities, and it must "compete" with other, now well-established, criminal justice models.

2.2. Restorative Justice and the Other Responses to Crime

Restorative justice has to position itself for comparison with both existing dominant formal approaches to reacting to crime: the retributive and the rehabilitative models. Restoring is not the same as punishing or treating, though it can be (mis)used in both these ways. Striving for more clarity in the focus of restorative justice, however, does not mean that all other models and their objectives are completed rejected.

The purely punitive response to crime is rejected for reasons mentioned earlier. Yet even here, Feld's chapter clearly underlines the importance of the legal principles and safeguards that have been traditionally associated with the retributive model. Due process and the right that interventions be gauged in proportion to the seriousness of the offense are important legal warrants, basic to democratic societies. Feld rightly links the credibility of the restorative justice model to its ability to "address fundamental issues of procedure and substance."

But restorative justice can hardly be viewed as a challenge to the rule of law or to "tenets of individual liberty," as Feld suggests in chapter 2. Several chapters in this volume, and especially those by Walgrave and by Van Ness, deal explicitly with problems of legal rights and guarantees, and share the concern with specifying the government versus system role in implementing restorative justice. These chapters suggest that apparent juridical problems are not intrinsic to the restorative justice paradigm, but are rather a function of the lack of experience in implementing restorative justice within a legalistic framework and the scarcity of systematic experimentation and reflection on legal topics (see also Van Ness and Strong, 1997). In addition, proponents of restorative justice may question the hegemonic dominance of lawyers and their capacity to provide "justice" as a satisfying resolution to the problems of victims, offenders and communities in the aftermath of crime (e.g., Stuart, 1995). There is an acknowledged need, however, to find new solutions for new juridical problems that may be associated with the emerging restorative justice paradigm.

Moreover, restorative justice is compatible with juvenile justice efforts to address community expectations to enhance public safety, sanction youth crime and promote offender reintegration. As the chapters by Guarino-Ghezzi and Klein, Walgrave, and Bazemore suggest, each of these expectations can be addressed in a restorative model, albeit through different processes and practices that in one way or another give priority to the need to repair harm and rebuild, or build, interpersonal and community relationships. Moreover, these different approaches, according to research and experience, are typically viewed by victims, offenders, and other citizens as more satisfying on a variety of dimensions (see chapters by Umbreit, Immarigeon, Schiff, and Sessar, respectively).

Bazemore demonstrates that restoration is not contradictory to rehabilitation, for example, if rehabilitation is considered in its 'naturalistic' form. "Relational," or "restorative," rehabilitation would be grounded in the communities where victims and offenders live. Such rehabilitation would be aimed at restoring both the victim and the offender by strengthening the offender's relationship with conventional adults and institutions, for example, though competency development rather than simply therapy and remediation (Bazemore and Terry, 1997). Such efforts to strengthen social and community relationships link reintegration with more direct efforts to repair harm and promote safer, more peaceful communities. The possible combination of reintegrative with restorative options also clearly appears in Braithwaite's chapter. That restorative processes and sanctions can yield rehabilitative effects on offenders is not just theoretically conceived. In her chapter on the impact of restorative interventions on offenders, Schiff concludes that extant research indicates promising rehabilitative effects of restorative interventions on juvenile offenders in terms of compliance, satisfaction and recidivism rates. However, well-controlled studies have been scarce, in part due to the recency of the restorative approach.

An important issue here will be to make sure that restoration is not subsidiary to the rehabilitative goal. This threat is especially significant in juvenile justice, with its dominant tradition of treatment. Some authors, like Feld (this volume), seem even to fear that the restorative justice movement could become little more than an attempt to "revive rehabilitation" or "return to a pre-Gault system of informal, discretionary coercive social control." If this occurs, the danger from a restorative perspective is that victim needs, for example, would not be considered in their own right, but would be (mis)used as essentially didactic materials in the treatment of the offender. But, while it will be difficult to prevent justice professionals from labeling otherwise traditional practices as "restorative," we do not believe that any careful review of the restorative justice literature would locate any arguments against the right to counsel or any suggestion that due process rights of juvenile offenders should be weakened.

Moreover, restorative justice is almost equally critical of the individual treatment model as it is of retributive justice (Bazemore, 1997a; Walgrave, 1993). And understanding the difference between restorative policy and practice and offender-driven individual treatment is not nearly as difficult as Feld (this volume) and other critics suggest. Where in the traditional treatment model, with its sole focus on the presumed needs of the offender, for example, is the crime victim? And where is the focus on repair and reconciliation? Just deserts advocates may continue to depict interventions that do not fit the mold of traditional punishment as signs of a return to *parens patriae* or "best interests" ideology. Yet, such characterizations are no more convincing than the efforts of some advocates of traditional treatment to lump restitution and community service in the same category as boot camps and shock incarceration (see Bazemore, this volume).

2.3. Restorative Justice, Community and Society

Restorative justice is more than just a program or technique. Changing the current system into a restorative justice system presupposes more than passing new laws or amendments to existing statutes and providing new training for juvenile justice professionals. As the chapter by Braithwaite and Parker clearly illustrates, restorative thinking departs from a different view of individuals and society. In their terms, restorative justice can only be achieved completely within the context of a wider "republican" politics of non-domination. While the adjective 'republican' might be misunderstood as a reference to the Republican political party in the U.S., Braithwaite would categorize Republican Party members within what he calls the "liberal" tradition, conceiving freedom as absence of interference. Such freedom is in fact individualized freedom, wherein other actors, and collectives, are viewed as a threat to one's own freedom. In contrast, Braithwaite's republican conception of freedom is freedom as non-domination (see also Braithwaite and Pettit, 1990).

Critical in republican society is a rule of law and a regime of rights that guarantee freedom as non-domination. Such freedom is only possible in a society striving for greater equality and stronger communities, wherein lies the assurance against domination by others and against arbitrary exercise of power. This is the freedom to be found in caring, mutually supportive societies, wherein other actors are not a threat to liberty but are indeed a guarantee of one's own freedom. In societies striving for the former concept of freedom, restorative justice would risk perpetuating the oppressions of community, trying to restore an equity and peace that never existed. It would, for example, be paradoxical to demand that young offenders restore the harm that their offenses have caused to victims, while remaining blind to the (often greater) victimization that results from social and economical inequalities.

For Braithwaite and Parker (this volume), the implication is that restorative justice is only achievable in such a republican society. While many societies in which the restorative justice movement is an emerging force (including the U.S.), are not clearly there yet, the basic precondition to assure that society moves in the republican direction is the existence of a "vibrant social movement politics that percolates into the deliberation of conferences, defends minorities against tyrannies of the majority and connects private concerns to campaigns for public transformation" (Braithwaite and Parker, this volume). Even short of massive and macro social change, this should allow for greater interaction between the formal rule of law and restorative justice in the community.

The restorative justice movement, in fact, needs an active political commitment to more equality and stronger communities, which provide fruitful soil for what Umbreit (this volume) calls "another legal culture." This entails an extensive program of cultural, social and economic change, and the objectives of such a program will not be achieved very soon. But, as Braithwaite (this volume) notes, "Rome was not built in a day." Restorative justice advocates must ensure that they are actually building *their Rome*, and not a chaotic bunch of ugly buildings. What is needed to prevent the latter occurrence is good theory, well-established and evaluated practice, much perseverance and, over all, good strategic actions that depart from the existing societal and juridical context.

2.4. Assessing Practice and Evidence

Thus far, practice seems to justify positive expectations for restorative justice. The available descriptive and evaluative research indicates that the processes and outcomes of restorative interventions are achieving promising results, and no decisive counter-indications have been observed.

Umbreit (this volume) convincingly demonstrates that victim-offender mediation may now be viewed as appropriate for a wide range of types and seriousness of crimes. Chapters by Umbreit and Immarigeon show that victims who participate in a mediation process are mostly more satisfied than those who go through traditional court procedures. Such satisfaction is reflected in attitudes about the quality of the process, the concrete results of the agreements, the feelings of equity and fairness, and reduction in fear. According to Schiff's review of the literature on offender outcomes, offenders who take part in a victim-offender mediation or in a family group conference, or who have been ordered to complete restitution or community service obligations, generally comply with restorative agreements when properly monitored and supported in these efforts. In addition, participants display greater feelings that just outcomes have been achieved, and offenders exhibit generally lower rates of recidivism. Small variations in these findings are mostly due to the social context of specific interventions and to variation in implementation, program design, and management. An important danger here, however, is that these encouraging results might lead to the proliferation of "fast food" mediation and settlements focused only on the material consequences of an offense. Also, today many of these efforts persist at the margins of existing judicial systems and are too often reserved for easy cases. Both individual and community healing and other restorative impacts are thereby minimized, if not completely lost (see Umbreit, this volume).

Guarino-Ghezzi and Klein (this volume) observe that traditional public safety and law enforcement policies are detrimental to the cohesiveness of communities. Instead, juvenile justice agencies should aim at "protective restoration" i.e., (re-) creating community cohesion through enhancing informal social controls and participation in a justice process focused on repairing past harms. These authors describe examples in neighborhoods and schools illustrating that communities that engage in partnerships with juvenile justice agencies in such "protective restorative" actions are better off with regard to safety, feelings of security among citizens, and overall sense of effectiveness and potency. Experiences with restorative initiatives in Aboriginal jurisdictions in Canada and elsewhere, described by Griffiths and Corrado (this volume), point to the same conclusions.

Sessar (this volume) reviews available research on the public's attitudes toward punishment and other possible responses to crime, and then presents his findings from citizen surveys of sanctioning alternatives. Based on those previous studies and his own surveys in which respondents were asked to choose, in specific offense scenarios, between restitution (with or without mediation) and punitive sanctions, Sessar (this volume) concludes that "the perception of the public's strong punitive sentiments is a myth." Generally speaking, respondents are in favor of restorative sanctions (and more favorably inclined toward ensuring victim restoration than are criminal justice professionals). These preferences hold even when these obligations are imposed in the absence of a punitive (incarcerative) sentence, and even for more serious offenses generally expected to receive such punishments. This finding is indeed surprising, given that the public is far less well-acquainted with this kind of response, and is bombarded by the media on a daily basis with assertions and "evidence" that crime can only be controlled by increasing the threat and severity of punishment. Again, Sessar's research raises questions about the widely accepted claim that punishment is "natural" and unavoidable.

Despite these general results and assessments in support of restorative experiments thus far, many problems persist. These present a primary list of topics for further examination and research, to which we turn in the next section.

3. AN AGENDA FOR RESEARCH AND CRITICAL EXAMINATION

Certainly, restorative justice is both a vision for a better way of responding to crime and a *movement* focused on more widespread implementation of restorative practices. But restorative justice must also remain a field of research and critical inquiry. As one of its most authoritative critics suggests, restorative justice advocates are strong on enthusiasm, but in need of more reflection (von Hirsch, 1997).

In our opening chapter, three challenges to implementing restorative justice were presented. We believe that the strategic challenge to thoroughly integrate restorative justice into the international youth crime debate has been addressed as completely as possible by various authors in this text, and in some detail in our own chapter 2 on restorative justice principles. In the light of what the preceding chapters have taught us, we now therefore reconsider challenges one and three: to develop a more workable definition, and an approach to implementing restorative justice as a systemic alternative in the response to youth crime.

3.1. Challenge One: Clarifying the Definition and Normative Theory of Restorative Justice

One of the most threatening problems for restorative justice is its disparity in concepts and emerging theories. Because the tradition is young and the development of the restorative justice idea needs openness for new reflections and reformulations based on emerging practice, it is appropriate to insist that the concept must necessarily remain flexible. Such flexibility, however, creates at the same time weakness and vulnerability in the face of criticisms and possible misuses.

It is obvious that many differences remain in the understanding of restorative justice. Indeed, a wide variety of practices — in very different legal and/or communal contexts with very different intents, processes, and outcomes — are presented as examples of "restorative" interventions. Because restorative justice as a paradigm is emerging in a societal context that is dominated by polarized thinking and practice, its advocates must therefore engage proponents of both retributive and rehabilitative models, as well as other approaches. While they must develop and maintain some degree of discipline in defining their own position, restorative justice advocates must also avoid the rigidity that would limit creativity in emerging restorative justice practice. Yet, currently, agreement over the need for discipline about the parameters of restorative justice is far from self-evident. Tentative statements and provisional experiments from proponents of the young restorative tendency are quickly and easily challenged by retributivist or rehabilitative stand-points, which are sustained by a long tradition as well as by professional interests (e.g., von Hirsch, 1993; Feld, this volume). Several authors of chapters in this volume (Van Ness, Braithwaite and Parker, Walgrave) have made headway toward a more disciplined conceptualization of restorative justice as a systemic alternative that also allows for flexibility capable of encompassing an emerging informalism within a broader system that includes a different type of formalism.

Rigid definitions or a set of strict rules for recognizing experiments as exam-ples or "models" of restorative justice would limit development and no doubt lead to "schools" and conflicting tendencies. But if the words "restorative" and "justice" have a meaning, it must be possible to find principles common to all interventions and experiments that define themselves as restorative justice. What is needed is a commonly acceptable "core," or normative theory, about restorative justice that can allow for development of minimum standards and criteria in order to select out those practices that obviously misinterpret or misuse the restorative justice para-digm.

The development of such normative theory can build upon existing attempts to come to grips with the essence of restorative justice. Current tentative efforts should be inventoried and compared. Regarding this, McCold (1998) has under-taken a Delphi-analysis of concepts and interpretations among leading scholars. It reveals some essential commonalities, but also important divergences. Another interesting initiative has been undertaken by SINRJ (Standards in Restorative Justice), a British collaborative consisting of advanced practitioners and policy makers. It "has been formed in order to extract lessons to be learned from the past and thereby establish principles and standards for the guidance of the future" (SINRJ, 1997:1). The Declaration of Leuven (1997), composed by a number of prominent scholars at a meeting of the International Network for Research on Restorative Justice for Juveniles, compiles what participants agreed to consider as the essential elements of restorative justice, as a recommendation to policy makers. Finally, our own ideas about challenges or necessary conditions for a fully-fledged alternative, as outlined in chapter 2, should also be debated as minimum standards, as well as discussed for their implications for implementation.

3.1.1. Good Ideas Often Lose their Credibility by Bad Implementation

Restorative practices are carried out in organizational environments that are grounded in other rationales and designed for other purposes. Proponents of the restorative approach have to cope with systems that are not appropriate for such actions, and with professionals who are neither trained nor motivated to be gov-erned by restorative principles. As a consequence, their experiments are often weakly, and even subversively, sustained and may have to accept so many compromises that they are hardly representative of what restorative justice is and can be (see Umbreit, this volume).

In other situations, restorative practices are lumped together — under a general category of "alternative sentences" or intermediate sanctions — with programs such as boot camps, which must be viewed even by the most lax definitions as nonrestorative (Higgins and Snyder, 1996). Sometimes, techniques that are restorative in origin are reinterpreted in implementation. Processes of mediation and sanctions such as restitution or community service are simply added to a group of interventions in the rehabilitative "tool kit," adapting these schemes solely to the treatment needs of the offender while neglecting victim claims for restoration, satisfaction, and possible opportunities for resolution and healing. Restitution and community service are also often misused as additional punishments (Duenkel, 1990), in which case community service assignments are selected because of their painfulness and/or humiliating character rather than their potential to repair harm to victimized communities (Bazemore and Maloney, 1994). An example of the ideological assumptions underlying this approach is found in a recent public-opinion study conducted in North Carolina, where a majority of the respondents surveyed preferred community service to be "long, tough, and visible" in order to deter would-be criminals (Higgins and Snyder, 1996:14). These new ways of making the societal reaction to crime more painful to offenders are to be understood merely as an extension of the retributive tradition of responding to wrongdoing by inflicting harm to the wrongdoer.

3.2. Challenge Two: Developing Restorative Justice as a Systemic Alternative

So far, restorative justice proponents have focused on the mediation process and have emphasized the informal, while too often neglecting formal system issues. But the ambition to develop restorative justice as a systemic approach makes urgent in-depth reflection on the juridical, societal, and community status of its implementation. Essentially, restorative justice must be prepared to take its place within the broader sociolegal structure, and to, in turn, incorporate the basic principles of a constitutional democratic state.

3.2.1. Restorative Informalism: Responding to Critics

First, it is important to explore how to retain the rich, humanistic, and user-friendly features of informal settings, as well as the opportunities for emotional expression and exchange associated with community mediation and restorative conferencing, within a juridical framework. The value of such accessibility and emotional exchange between parties affected by crime in an informal setting is no reason to remain blind to the possible misuses in such settings. Mediators can exert informal but very strong pressure according to their subjective opinions and preferences; victims may be secondarily victimized by poorly facilitated mediation processes; offenders may undergo harsher stigmatization and exclusion than if the traditional procedures were followed (Umbreit, this volume); communities may be divided into "camps" as a result of citizen involvement in the resolution of local conflict and responses to crime (Griffiths and Hamilton, 1996). The human rights of all parties concerned are threatened if there is no legal and structural framing of restorative justice interventions. Because this might be a very frightening prospect, especially for the poor and powerless in our society, restorative justice advocates and scholars must respond to several concerns here.

In this respect, Feld's chapter is especially challenging. Writing from the perspective of just deserts, and as a youth advocate concerned about the juvenile court's capacity to ensure due process and enforce limits on coercive intervention, Feld raises several important questions for restorative justice proponents. Many of these questions have been addressed in this text or have been dealt with elsewhere (e.g., Bazemore and Umbreit, 1995b; Van Ness, 1993; Walgrave and Geudens, 1996; Van Ness and Strong, 1997). However, because they represent key issues frequently raised about the viability of restorative justice, Feld's concerns justify a detailed response.

One of Feld's questions — whether restorative justice is formal or informal, inside or outside the system — is easily answered. It is both. The informal, community-based implementation of restorative justice is most desirable, because it is more capable of minimizing coercion and maximizing space for dialogue, negotiation, and meaningful participant input. However, as Walgrave (this volume) makes clear, much more extensive development of the formal side is absolutely essential if restorative justice is to become more than pre-judicial "window dressing."

How then, Feld asks, does informal restorative justice differ from current diversion efforts? Diversion as currently practiced is meant to provide a "second chance" for offenders, to minimize the negative impact of formal processing, and to reduce court workloads, while accepting the formal retributive system as the dominant institution for intervention. In restorative justice, the primary objective is to provide a more open and satisfying way for victims, offenders, and citizen stakeholders to repair harm and resolve conflict, ideally, though not exclusively, in informal contexts. As a consequence, "diversion" is perhaps a misnomer for informal restorative justice processes, whose primary purpose is neither to help the current system solve its problems, nor to allow offenders to avoid or minimize their obligations.

But restorative justice advocates are as much concerned about net widening, coercion and discrimination in such informal interventions as Feld and other advocates are of just deserts restrictions on intervention (see Walgrave, Braithwaite and Parker, Bazemore and Van Ness, this volume). There are, however, important differences in the ideology and "intervention lenses" that frame informal restorative justice and current diversion practice respectively, and these differences may produce distinctly different results in terms of net widening. Restorative justice questions the presumption underlying most diversion programs that professional intervention (e.g., placement in special treatment programs) is necessarily likely to help troubled or pre-delinquent youths. Hence, the restorative goal is ultimately one of less system intervention, and more community intervention of a type carried out by local citizens and socializing organizations. While the libertarian critique of government intervention (and the obsession with net-widening as the sole criterion of concern in considering harmful impact) is rejected, the goal is instead to redefine and/or minimize professional roles to support expanded involvement of citizens (including victims, offenders and their supporters; Bazemore, 1997a) and to build capacity in community organizations (Pranis, 1997; McKnight, 1995). There is then, in restorative justice, a desire to strengthen "community nets," while challenging the hegemony of "government nets" under sponsorship of service and criminal justice bureaucracies (Braithwaite and Mugford, 1994; McKnight, 1995).

It may be that restorative justice is no *more* successful in preventing net widening or reducing the threat of informal coercion than current diversion programs. In the latter, both of these unintended consequences can now be viewed as virtually institutionalized side effects that no amount of advocacy for just deserts restrictions or rights-based reforms has been effective in reducing (Ezell, 1992; Polk, 1984)[2]. But why should restorative justice be immediately required to achieve higher standards than current practice, especially if restorative interventions would produce greater benefits in term of outcomes for participants? Yet, a failure to define limits on system intervention and identify threats of coercive practice could become primary obstacles to implementing restorative justice. To address these concerns, a formal system also based on restorative justice principles would be charged with protecting and "empowering" the informal system, as Braithwaite and Parker (this volume) suggest, by developing various checks (including monitoring and appeals) to prevent excess and abuse.

Restorative justice is an emerging paradigm, and is therefore not well-positioned to answer the questions of its critics by appeal to legal precedent as a primary standard. To some degree, new statutes or alternative legal frameworks will need to be crafted to encourage use of restorative justice processes as a primary rather than ancillary option. But this crafting will need to be carried out not by lawyers and court professionals alone, but also by those who have a stake in justice outcomes. Victim advocates and citizens groups, for example, must have input in designing community justice processes tailored to *their* needs, rather than the bureaucratic needs of justice systems (Stuart, 1995a; Dooley, 1995; Griffiths and Hamilton, 1996). Hence, restorative proponents should avoid the trap of attempting to provide too many details of specific designs for restorative justice models. While retributivists can provide such designs based on rules and precedent, restorativists must take account of the unique needs of victims, communities and offenders in each case in a way not required when the sole concern is with just punishment. This does not mean that outlines of both prototypical and real restorative systems are unavailable (Walgrave, this volume, 1995a; Belgrave, 1995), or that basic ground rules should not be developed that provide upper limits (Van Ness and Strong, 1997; Van Ness, 1993). It simply means that restorative systems will by definition be built and operated in a different way that allows greater diversity of input, participation and focus.

Does restorative justice, as Feld suggests in chapter 1, require the develop-ment of "an entirely new procedural and substantive framework?" This question seems odd unless one assumes, as some critics seem to, that restorative justice is an attempt to displace formal adjudication procedures with informal fact-finding processes in which guilt or innocence is determined by a kind of informal "jury." Because restorative justice processes do not begin until guilt has been established or admitted, restorative justice advocates have no interest in limiting due process rights, and would be no less interested in procedural formality and the rule of law to protect the accused. On the one hand, restorative justice advocates are as con-cerned as retributivists with establishing responsibility for the crime. For both practical and ethical reasons, there is also a strong commitment to minimize coer-cion. As can be seen in efforts to prevent potential harm to victim and offender in mediation and other restorative processes when participation is not at least some-what consensual on the part of both parties (and absolute on the victim's part), (Umbreit, Van Ness, this volume), restorative justice advocates are very concerned that victims and offenders are fully informed of risks, as well as opportunities. On the other hand, whenever the accused is willing to admit guilt and is informed of the risks, restorative justice advocates would indeed wish to substitute a *restorative informal process* (e.g., mediation) for a retributive one (i.e., plea bargaining), (Bazemore and Umbreit, 1995). And restorative justice advocates would question a lawyer-driven process that seems (at least in rhetoric) to rely exclusively on rules that often exclude stakeholders from meaningful input into sentencing or disposi-tion.

But it is in the outcome sought in the aftermath of an admission or finding of guilt that restorative justice can be most clearly distinguished from the retributive model. [3] Specifically, restorative justice questions whether an outcome can be called "just" if it has only ensured that a defendant received the same punishment as all other similar defendants. Although retributivists correctly claim that restorative justice advocates lack the encoded precedent of just deserts and have yet to think through all the implications for gauging the upper limits of a reparative obligation, the fundamental difference between restorative and retributive models is what the offender is required to do (i.e., take the punishment versus take responsibility for repairing the harm). [4]

Where *process* rather than outcome is the concern, a key distinguishing premise of restorative justice is that citizens, victims and offenders can usually come up with more meaningful and satisfying dispositions — guided by a set of rules meant to guard against excess — than those developed by judges, prosecutors, defenders and other "experts." Such legal experts currently operate within the limits of a vision of justice as the equivalent of uniform punishment. In addition, they are themselves generally limited by a lack of both knowledge of and connection to the parties affected by crime (Stuart, 1995b), and are therefore incapable of meeting the real needs created in its aftermath.

Interestingly, recent innovations in restorative justice conferencing (e.g., circle sentencing in Canada and family group conferencing in New Zealand) allow for a merger of the formal and informal on the micro level. When sentencing or disposition of serious or indictable offenders occurs in these cases, judges, defenders, and prosecutors participate in what remains for the most part an informal process. While these legal professionals play their assigned formal roles within this more meaningful formal/informal context, participants are empowered by this process to come up with an appropriate sanction and plan for attending to the needs of victim, offender and community in the future (e.g., Stuart, 1995a; Belgrave, 1995). [5]

To summarize our reply to Feld's most important (and also most easily answered) questions, a primary core difference between restorative and retributive models is that, in the restorative view, equivalence of punishment is not the be-all and end-all of justice system intervention. This premise, and the idea that victims, offenders and other citizens can be actively involved in a more satisfying justice process, frame both a formal and an informal response that is clearly distinguishable from either the treatment or punishment response. This response is different from retributive or treatment model responses regardless of whether it occurs at diversion, disposition, or any point thereafter in the process. In addition, restorative justice advocates ask whether "justice" is an abstraction that can only be understood and achieved by lawyers. Or might justice instead have something to do with the real sense of fairness and resolution experienced by victims, offenders, and other participants in a process which can offer healing and repair? Regarding this, questions raised by just deserts critics about the empirical grounding of restorative justice can be tossed back at them. Is there any research basis that could demonstrate that the almost singular concern with uniformity is justified by any public definition of equality of punishment as a social good, or by the feelings of participants that such equivalence is a satisfying outcome of the justice process? Transposing Feld's (this volume) challenge to restorativists: can its proponents reconcile *retributive justice* with justice? Indeed, is retributive "justice" an oxymoron?

3.2.2. Implementation, Community and Other Difficult Questions

But Feld raises other concerns that are somewhat independent of just deserts ideology, and also less easily addressed because they go to issues of implementation in a system and societal context that work against restorative justice. His most salient question in this regard is whether restorative obligations will be used as alternatives or dispositional add-ons to current punishments. Such misuse and distortion in implementation is an important issue that just deserts advocates in the U.S. themselves have had to face in the past two decades, as they watched their own efforts to limit and rationalize punishment become subsumed within a more dominant crime control movement in juvenile justice. While this movement eschewed limits in favor of expanded incarceration, just deserts logic meanwhile gave new legitimacy to policy makers' urges to "get tough" on youth crime by expanding punishment (Castellano, 1986, Bazemore and Umbreit, 1995). The degree to which restorative justice can be implemented with integrity is an empirical question, but it can hardly do worse than just deserts — whose legacy has generally been longer periods of confinement, mandatory minimums, etc.

Feld (this volume) also wonders appropriately why an offense should be the primary trigger for restorative intervention. Should not other individuals harmed by actions that do not involve violation of criminal law have equal claims to restoration as crime victims? Indeed, Feld is not alone in asking this question, and restorative advocates of "community healing" interventions have drawn on the indigenous and Aboriginal experiences in North America and New Zealand to suggest that distinctions between the response to crime and a variety of community problems are often artificial ones (e.g., Stuart, 1995a; Griffiths and Hamilton, 1996; Bazemore, 1997b). Restorative principles are thereby used frequently as the basis for preventive, problem-solving processes aimed at addressing broader social ills as well as responding to crime. As discussed in chapter 2, though we applaud those efforts, we prefer (at least provisionally) to limit the concept of restorative justice to something that occurs subsequent to the commission of a crime, as a means of repairing harm caused by that crime (see also Walgrave, this volume). We shall come back to that topic in the next section.

Perhaps the most provocative, substantive questions Feld (this volume) raises have to do with the role of the "community" in restorative interventions. In part because the formal justice system has historically been unable to engage citizens in constructive, reconciliatory or reintegrative processes, many restorative justice proponents reject it as in any way representative of the community. Given this, it remains for these restorativists to define their "community," and to specify what kinds of groups will be accepted as its members for purposes of restorative decision making. As more than a century of unresolved debate among sociologists and other experts over how to operationalize this concept attests, identifying the community, defining its role, and deciding who will be allowed to speak and negotiate on its behalf will be no easy task. More practically, restorative justice advocates will need to develop models for determining how courts and formal agencies will relate to various community groups and their decision processes, and what kinds of specific injuries to said communities will be addressed. All these issues have been insufficiently considered so far, and there are certainly unlikely to be "cookbook" answers.

For the moment, restorative practitioners find pragmatic solutions. "Community" is indeed being defined daily in various forms of restorative conferencing as "those with a stake in the aftermath of a crime," and/or as those "personal communities" that emerge in support of offender and victim (Braithwaite and Mugford, 1994; Stuart, 1995b). While practitioners seem to be effectively engaging appropriate participants, and seeking to ensure the presence of members of the "communities of care" of both offender and victim (Bazemore, 1997c; Stuart, 1995a), there are valid concerns with regard to power imbalances and "tyranny of community" (Griffiths and Hamilton, 1996; Braithwaite and Parker, this volume).

On the one hand, if restorative justice is to become a systemic alternative, advocates will inevitably have to respond to these concerns, perhaps by developing guidelines that place some parameters on the community's role. On the other hand, it is important not to "overstructure," or become too quick to judge, informal community processes that may yield satisfying (if unusual) results through what appear by traditional standards to be unorthodox methods. The community involvement task for restorative justice is to find the right balance between the formality needed to guarantee legal rights, and the informality required to encourage unique and genuine exchanges and satisfying resolutions arrived at with maximum stakeholder input. This should be achieved, whenever possible, through the use of consensus-based processes.

What needs also to be more fully developed here is the "community-building" agenda of restorative justice. Years of service system "colonization" of neighborhoods, and a tendency to describe community members and subgroups in terms of need and deficit rather than capacity, has imposed blinders on our ability to recognize the real potential of community involvement in justice processes (McKnight, 1995). As is being demonstrated almost daily — even in some of the most devastated Aboriginal communities in Canada, for example (see Griffiths and Corrado, this volume) — the key to engaging the community in restorative justice processes may be a willingness and ability to *recognize* community in its myriad forms, and to remain open to the capacity of "damaged" individuals and collectives to heal and ultimately thrive.

3.2.3. The Role of Coercion

Third, considering restorative justice as a systemic alternative obliges us to also examine the term in its coercive form. Since limiting restorative justice to an informal process, entered into voluntarily by all parties, would at a minimum make restorative options unavailable to most crime victims, restorative sanctions will also have to be imposed — not only negotiated or proposed. If the use of force is accepted, its limits must be clearly indicated. Establishing procedural rules, as proposed earlier, is one way of accomplishing this. The idea of restoration as such also poses a strong relationship of content between the act and its consequences, because the term "restoration" means making up for the wrong or harm that has been done.

But there should also be a relationship between the offense and the amount of intervention. Although an equal amount of restorative action should, theoretically, make up for a specific amount of harm, this is not always straightforward in practice. One can assume that mediation and/or other restorative processes can lead to a negotiated agreement about the amount of restitution or compensation. The very agreement of the parties concerned presupposes their feeling of equity or fairness. But even here, imbalances of power and/or pressure may lead to more or less forced "agreements," that may appear to be disproportionate. We do not know of research on victim-offender mediation that specifically examines this problem, though it is an important theme to be explored.

The problem of upper limits to the intervention is of course still more acute with regard to efforts to restore the community or even society. Problems here include defining the kinds of collective harm that can be considered as part of an agreement, developing standards for gauging such harm, and determining how such harm can be repaired. These concerns are obviously among the most critical and difficult issues in developing a general normative theory of restorative justice (von Hirsch, 1997; Feld, this volume).

Although proportionality is one of the key characteristics that anchor the judicial safeguards for citizens in a retributive justice system, retributive proportionality is not naturally given either. Historically, it is a relatively recent sociolegal construction (von Hirsch, 1993), essentially based on two centuries of tradition, practice and precedent. Although restorative justice does not have such a long and firmly institutionalized tradition, this does not mean that standards for gauging harm could not be developed that are at least as equitable as the often arbitrary "rough equivalencies" for assigning, say, a two-year sentence to someone who commits a burglary (Walgrave and Geudens, 1996; Walgrave, this volume; Robinson, 1987). Restorative proportionality can be similarly constructed, because, like retribution, restoration basically is retrospective (Feld, 1993): it refers to an event in the past (the harm caused) to define an actual intervention. Also, from a restorative point of view, concepts like "intentional" causation of harm or "competency" to appreciate the harm caused by one's actions could also mitigate the accountability of the offender and thus the obligation for restoration. At the moment of the intervention, a theoretical yardstick is available to measure the maximum extent of possible deprivation of liberty (Walgrave and Geudens, 1996). That this kind of reasoning has yet to produce any *actual* yardstick for proportionate "restorative" sanctions is due to the short tradition with institutionalized restorative justice, and also to the lack of interest of restorative proponents in the formal aspect. While such apparent accommodations to retributive proportionality might not be accepted by all restorativists, the urgent task to develop standards should begin with a critical description and comparison of current practices, and an explicit discussion of the legal, ethical and social principles behind them.

To conclude, socioethical and juridical research is apparently badly needed, in order to fully insert restorative justice practices into a constitutional democratic state. Restorative justice researchers have to cope with the tension between the informality needed to support human emotional processes aimed at repairing harm and the formal rules that hold essential guarantees against misuses of power. Researchers must not repress this tension.

3.3. Research Focused on Intermediate Outcomes of Restorative Justice Practices for Victims, Communities and Offenders

The restorative justice literature advances many arguments as to why restorative interventions would be better than the alternatives. Victims would be better off psychologically if they participated in a restorative process, for example, and they would enjoy more complete reparation than in a traditional procedure. Restorative processes within communities would lead to more constructive solutions to local conflicts and safer neighborhoods. Offenders are expected to more easily accept restorative sanctions, to more often complete these obligations and to be more readily reintegrated after doing so. The public in general is also said to be more willing to accept restorative interventions than is usually assumed. Whether these premises will hold true in practice over the long term remains to be proven. Previous chapters by Bazemore, Umbreit, Immarigeon, Klein and Guarino-Ghezzi, Griffiths and Corrado, Schiff, and Sessar have compiled a significant amount of positive experience and empirical data that point to the opportunities of restorative approaches, but much remains to be done.

3.3.1. How Do We Know Restorative Justice When We See It?

One of the most important concerns is to make sure that practices presented as being restorative, really are. As mentioned in section 3.1, many experiments take place within non-restorative contexts, under inappropriate conditions, with insufficient support and unskilled staff. On the one hand, empirical research on experiments presented as "restorative" should first of all examine whether they really are acceptable as "case studies" in restorative justice, or are simply examples of new extensions of treatment or punishment models. On the other hand, practices that do not explicitly advance restoration, nor refer to the restorative justice paradigm can often be considered as *de-facto* restorative by virtue of the way they are conceived and carried out. As argued previously, a normative "core theory" and a set of "minimum conditions" can help to distinguish between those practices that can be considered restorative and those that cannot.

Impact evaluation can only take place when it is clear what really has been carried out. Many reparation schemes, conferencing or community service interventions do not conform in their daily practice with what has been theoretically conceived. They are obstructed by the quality of the conceptualization and concrete preparation, the quality and preparation of staff, the dynamics of cooperation with relevant agencies and authorities, financial support, the adequacy of goal-oriented strategies, and subjective interpersonal staff differences. Experimental outcomes are partially dependent on unplannable and uncontrollable events, personal creativity and coincidence. This may explain a great deal of the differences in outcomes of previously evaluated experiments. Therefore, empirical research on such practices should include detailed process analyses of what really happened, and of the cultural and structural features of the implementation context. Such research should seek to discover the minimum environmental conditions that must be met to allow a restorative program to function reasonably according to principles.

However, empirical research on restorative justice processes and outcomes for victims, communities and offenders cannot be conducted without an intervention theory (Weiss, 1997; Bazemore, 1997c). Such theory should provide a conceptual link between participants in restorative processes, the quality of the process itself, intermediate changes in participants (e.g., initial victim satisfaction or increased empathy on the part of the offender), and more long-term restorative outcomes. It should specify the conditions under which restorative processes would result in better outcomes (recidivism, social networks, peace in community, satisfaction, feelings of equity, etc.), and why this result would be expected. Such intervention theory would provide the primary blueprint for empirical research.

3.3.2. The Challenge of New Outcomes

Outcome evaluations always pose several basic methodological questions. These include finding and composing an appropriate control or comparison group, determining the right outcome criteria, and designing a realistic follow-up period (Hagan, 1993; Taylor, 1994). Results of research focused on the general willingness of crime victims to participate and on victim satisfaction with the results of mediation programs provide some cause for optimism about the possibility of conducting such experiments, as well as their promising outcomes. However, comparison of experimental and comparison groups thus far have often been vulnerable to various biases. Victims who agree to participate in a mediation program probably are intrinsically different from those who refuse. The observed differences in satisfaction may have to do with preexisting differences in both groups. Moreover, many mediation programs are carried out by highly motivated, often highly skilled, experimental staff, whereas the traditional justice responses are delivered in very routinized, often malfunctioning, settings. Part of the difference in victim satisfaction in experimental and control groups, for example, may not be easily attributable to differences between restorative interventions and the alternative, but rather to differences in staff motivation and commitment. Because mediation programs have generally been reserved for less serious crimes, results may not be generalizable to victims of more serious crimes. Ultimately, better measures of victim impact are also needed that include cognitive, emotive and behavioral indicators. Such measures as those related to perceptions of justice and overall well-being in the aftermath of crime must be utilized in controlled studies, in which victims involved in restorative processes of varying intensity are compared with victims who go through traditional processes that also vary in the extent to which victims have input, receive information, and are simply treated with respect.

To the extent that community peace and safety is advanced as one of the main objectives of restorative justice, evaluation research also should address this issue. Unfortunately, there is little available research that examines community-level outcomes. The first of many problems in carrying out such research is how to measure community peace and safety. Survey research and/ or qualitative methodologies might be considered here, but both must be tailored for this specific research purpose. A more difficult problem is to delimit the community wherein a specific restorative program is expected to have an impact. Do we consider possible changes in only those community members directly involved in restorative processes and their intimates, in the immediate neighborhood where the restorative actions are taking place, or also those changes in the broader community where several such programs are carried out and propagated? Do we examine the effects of restorative programs on the functioning of the justice system itself vis-a-vis the community, and, if so, what kind of changes should we expect? Finally, the most precarious task here would be to observe changes in peace and safety in a given community within a given period of time, and to link these changes to the increasing presence of restorative initiatives in that same community.

Also still difficult is defining the role and focus of research aimed at assessing the impact of restorative intervention on offenders. From a purist point of view, such research may seem somewhat surprising as part of the restorative agenda. While restoring the harm caused by an offense is not a consequentialist rationale, a focus on offender impact is. Nevertheless, the impact of restorative initiatives on the offender remains important for several reasons. First, an absolute non-consequentialist position is untenable. Even pure retributivists, who claim to be interested only in the desert value of punishment and to be unconcerned with the effects of retribution, ultimately view deserved punishment as a means of achieving a just and safe society and are called to answer critics if their punishment agendas lead to much higher crime rates (Braithwaite and Pettit, 1990). In the same sense, giving priority to restoring the harm is a goal-oriented (as well as normative) choice aimed at achieving a more harmonious and peaceful community. Second, the basic reparative aim of restorative justice is better served when intervention has a constructive impact on the offender. Indeed, it would be difficult to imagine that restorative interventions would contribute to peace and harmony in the community in the absence of a concern for possible reoffending and reintegration of offenders. Third, from a more strategic perspective, any large-scale and systematic introduction of restorative intervention would be impossible and unwise if the impact on offenders should prove to be inferior to outcomes achieved by conventional sanctions. Finally, even if changing offender behavior is not the prime objective of restorative justice, it is an important secondary goal, and restorative justice provides unique theoretical rationales for the expectation that restorative actions can result in positive offender outcomes (Bazemore, this volume).

To date, most available research on offender impact is rather simplistic, and conclusions are necessarily tentative and incomplete. The only truly firm conclusion thus far is that offenders who complete restorative obligations are no more likely to recidivate, and appear to be generally "better off" on a variety of dimensions (e.g., sense of fairness and justice, empathy), than young offenders who go through traditional programs and processes. To improve on the precision of impact research, it is first important to begin to specify one or more explicit sets of theoretical expectations of possible intermediate effects of restorative intervention, the specific conditions under which these impacts would be expected, and for what kind of offenders. [6]

Second, because recidivism is a necessary but not sufficient outcome, clarity is needed in testing claims of restorative justice proponents that their interventions are less stigmatizing, more likely to strengthen social bonds, better able to improve empathy and generally more reintegrative. And it is these intermediate changes in the personal and interpersonal situation of the offender in the aftermath of restorative intervention that may provide the link to reduced recidivism that has been apparent in some studies (Schneider, 1986; Butts and Snyder, 1990; Umbreit, 1994). The nature of the presumed causal linkage between participating in a family group conference or completing community service needs to be fully specified and empirically examined.

Third, whereas control groups are needed to draw clear conclusions about impact, random assignment has proven to be very difficult to implement, in part because it requires close cooperation by judicial authorities. Close cooperation presupposes that those authorities are positively motivated to risk allowing significant numbers of cases to be referred to restorative programs on a random basis.

Finally, some reflection is needed on what kinds of interventions should be used to compare the impact of restorative justice actions on offenders. Because treatment programs explicitly and primarily advance the improvement of the offender as their goal, in that portion of the evaluation focused on offender impacts restorative programs should be first compared with these rehabilitative interventions. On the other hand, retributive approaches primarily present themselves as being just and legally well-defined. Traditional punishments should therefore be compared with restorative sanctions and processes regarding their impact on offenders' feelings of equity and fairness.

3.3.3. Gaining Public Support

Finally, more empirical research is also needed with regard to the broader societal context in which restorative justice is to be implemented. In a democratic society, the introduction of restorative programs or even systems is not thinkable without public support. Information on public attitudes about crime and justice issues is therefore crucial, and may point to problems in understanding that provide opportunities to clarify the focus of specific strategies.

But public attitudes are not naturally given. They are influenced by socialization, direct experience and the media. Sessar's (this volume) findings and his conclusion, for example, that public punitiveness is a myth are not without parallel even in the U.S., where recent opinion research suggests that given practical alternatives to punishment, citizens prefer reparative sanctions to incarceration, at least for property offenders (Doble and Associates, 1994; Pranis and Umbreit, 1991; Schwartz, 1992). The public punitiveness hypothesis should be further elaborated and explored with a focus on examining what underlying needs may influence support for punishment, the kinds of influences that shape people's ideas about crime and justice, and how these influences give rise to different opinions in different sub-populations. Comparisons of media-saturated societies like the U.S., with cultures where the influence of media is less intense could be interesting, for example. Special attention should also be given to population groups whose unique experiences have direct implications for the successful implementation of restorative policies and practices. The views of individuals with victimization experiences, social workers, judicial agents, policy makers and others will have critical influence, and it is also important to examine empirically those factors that influence their positions. To conclude, restorative justice is not only a matter of choices and principles. Its *de facto* feasibility and results have to be examined very closely.

3.4. Explore the Limits of Restorative Justice

Developing restorative justice as the dominant model for reacting to crime does not mean that restorative objectives will be the only outcomes pursued. For some crimes, in certain situations, with certain victims, offenders and communities, other sentencing goals may assume greater priority (e.g., public safety). This is, in fact, also the case for the retributive and rehabilitative models.

At present, while the retributive model is clearly dominant, it is not mono-lithic. Societies seem to accept that retribution cannot be applied to everybody, and they allow for the pursuit of rehabilitative or other objectives within this framework. Most societies have also created separate judicial systems or separate processes for juveniles and for the insane, and most make deliberate choices not to prosecute a large proportion of offenses and offenders. The rehabilitative model, though weakened, plays a dominant role in the judicial approach to juveniles. But the treatment agenda is limited by the demands for legal safeguards (which are often neglected), by the need for cooperation by juvenile offenders (which is often hidden behind the illusions of "coercive assistance" and "educative penal interventions"), and by public safety concerns and the retributive derivation of punishment. Simi-larly, it will be necessary in a system in which restorative justice is dominant to define the boundaries beyond which the pursuit of restorative objectives end, in order for the concerns of other models to begin to receive greater consideration or take precedence. At first glance, we can think of four possible factors that define the parameters of the restorative justice approach and/or influence the nature and priority of the restorative response: crime seriousness, coercivity, public security and rehabilitation.

3.4.1. Crime Seriousness

Experiments with restorative justice models have on the whole been overly cautious, dealing primarily with cases that present minimal risks for further victimi-zation and minimal harm to victims and communities. But as these experiments evolve, the potential of restorative justice to deal with a wider variety of cases appears to be increasing, and the need to appeal to traditional dispositional proto-cols and goals appears to be decreasing. We do not know yet how far this evolution may lead us.

In more serious crimes, a simple victim restitution will typically be insufficient as a sole response. The impact of the offense extends beyond its effects on the concrete victim to include the community and even the society as a whole. But it is also difficult to find a good reason to exclude serious offenders from community service (Walgrave, 1994, 1995b), or from the obligation to make restitution or other forms of reparation to individual victims (Schneider, 1990; 1985). Indeed, for serious crimes, far more extensive restoration of individual victim and community is needed.

The idea that serious offenders must undergo a highly punitive response is grounded in the purely retributive interpretation of penal justice, and we have already developed our arguments against this approach. The statement that "the public" would not accept the imposition of community service or restitution for serious offenders relies on a stereotype that is increasingly contradicted by public opinion studies. Moreover, as Umbreit (this volume) has shown, a growing number of victims of serious and violent offenses wish to participate in a restorative response instead of a purely punitive one.

The assumption that serious offenders cannot be positively influenced by community service, or other restorative interventions, rests upon a naive etiological supposition that is not confirmed by empirical research. Up to now, there is a lack of experience with serious offenders, but the available data, reviewed in the chapter by Schiff, do not suggest that the seriousness of crime would necessarily be a discriminating factor in compliance with reparative sanctions, or that seriousness alone would predict greater recidivism for offenders assigned restorative obligations.

3.4.2. Coercivity

It is also possible to insist on the voluntary participation of all parties concerned as a limiting factor in the application of restorative justice. Of course, if the victim refuses to participate in mediation or in another face-to-face encounter, this choice must be accepted. However, victim refusal is not a stable nor a purely objective element, and, in many cases, may be simply a function of the manner in which a proposition has been made and the timing of that proposition. Moreover, refusal of mediation or conferencing does not necessarily remove the possibility for compensation or restitution, and the victim may wish to be involved or give input in other ways.

But even if the victim still refuses, restorative possibilities have not run out. As we opt for a systemic alternative, the response to an offense may not depend purely on individual victims or on a local community's wishes. A restorative system would provide for restorative opportunities and obligations that may operate independent of the voluntary participation of these parties. It is here that community service, a variety of victim assistance programs, victims awareness education and a variety of other interventions are possibilities. If the offender him or herself does not voluntarily accept community service or another reparative obligation, the problem of coerciveness is posed; we have previously developed our arguments for accepting coercive restoration as a part of restorative justice. Even if a non-custodial community service were excluded, one could consider the possibility of imposing service within a residential environment.

3.4.3. Public Security

Security concerns are often cited as reasons for restricting the implementation of restorative techniques. Because many restorative programs are carried out in free contact with the community, it is argued that this could entail too much risk for chronic or serious offenders. However, risk management involving even the highest levels of incapacitation does not eliminate the possibility of a restorative response. Incarceration does not, in itself, exclude restorative objectives, and several authors have proposed restorative actions during a period of imprisonment (e.g., Immarigeon, this volume). Such actions can take the form of restitution or even mediation, service to the community, or payment into victim support funds.

Public safety is an important consideration under any justice model. The question, however, is whether the traditional penal reaction would lead to more community security than restorative approaches. Recidivism rates following imprisonment are very high, and it is doubtful whether these rates and the cost of incarceration are offset by the temporary safety achieved through incapacitation. In view of developments in the U.S., it is difficult to claim that the purely punitive response to crime, including its massive expansion of imprisonment, has been a success in achieving security in society (Haen Marshall, 1996).

Preceding chapters, especially the one by Guarino-Ghezzi and Klein, provide many reasons to believe that the generalized option for restorative justice would not decrease safety in communities. General deterrence through penal justice is overestimated, and the crime-reduction impact of restorative actions, voluntary as well as coercive, is underestimated. Moreover, the reintegrative impact of restorative actions, and certainly the community-building impact, is probably much higher. That is not to say that security concerns would receive less emphasis under a restorative system. However, risks for serious recidivism are often overestimated, as is illustrated through the great diversity in prison regimes. Many of them, for example, allow substantial periods of unsupervised contacts with society. The fact that relatively few incidents occur provides empirical verification that many currently imprisoned offenders could participate in reparation or community service in the community, without serious risks for security. Under a retributive model, unfortunately, the demand for punishment increases the use of incarceration almost independent of risk (Irwin and Austin, 1993).

3.4.4. Rehabilitation

The priority given to the need for offender treatment could also hamper the introduction of a fully-fledged restorative justice approach. Rehabilitation of the offender is a worthy objective. But it need not limit the larger, overarching focus on restoration. Rehabilitative concerns can be introduced in the restorative framework, and restorative interventions themselves should be viewed as core features of a holistic approach to reintegration. The opportunity or obligation to make things right, the content of the act itself, the process of taking responsibility and facing one's victim, and the social context in which these take place all can promote and mobilize community reintegrative social networks, and can rehabilitate both the self-image and public image of offenders who participate in a kind of "earned redemption" ceremony. The restorative option, however, must also ensure due process and provide upper limits on the intensity of intervention.

Moreover, even coercive restorative interventions within the formal justice system do not exclude rehabilitative possibilities outside the justice process. One can imagine that the judicial obligation to restore could run parallel to an offer of support by individuals, community groups, socializing institutions or social welfare agencies. The problem historically with the sole emphasis on individual treatment based on medical-model assumptions has been the tendency of treatment regimes to overwhelm other concerns and minimize the role of victim and community.

In fact, the limits of the restorative justice interventions are not yet known, and experimentation is still in its infancy. Although most experimentation has been cautious — targeting relatively benign offenses, offenders with good prognoses and cooperative victims — as the experience increases, confidence in restorative practices is likely to grow. Scientific reflection and research should challenge unsubstantiated claims, both pro and con, with regard to possible feasibility. Many counter-arguments are in fact advanced by fear of the unknown, because of stereo-typical ideas, or to hide actual lack of willingness to seriously consider restorative options or change of any kind. The role of research here is to carefully design and carry out restorative experiments with serious and non-cooperative offenders, in order to compare the gains and losses for public security of restorative practices with those of more traditional alternatives and to examine further the rehabilitative impact of restorative actions.

3.5. Develop Strategies for Improving the Quality and Range of Restorative Justice Intervention

The limits of restorative justice are of course also imposed by the skills of those who implement restorative justice programs in the field. Bringing victims and offenders together and facilitating dialogue and negotiation is quite different than counseling offenders, visiting a family in need of support, or managing the application of a correctional punishment. Helping to design and facilitate the execution of a restorative community service project is quite different than doing casework with a young offender, or monitoring his or her school attendance.

Experience with monitoring restorative processes, and with facilitating and supporting compliance with reparative agreements or sanctions, is relatively recent. Program protocols and technical skills are still in the developmental stage. Many practitioners proceed tentatively, based on a few available specific guidelines, their own experience with other restorative practices, their own intuition, ad hoc exchanges with colleagues doing comparable work, and (in the best cases) a strong grounding in restorative principles. In recent years, programmatic guides have emerged (Balanced and Restorative Justice Project, 1997, 1998; Wachtel and Wachtel, 1997), and some seem to have become primers for restorative methodology. Based on extensive experience with specific practices (e.g., victim-offender mediation) in specific contexts, they provide more general lessons for other practices and therefore offer an important base for developing training protocols and implementation standards (see, for example, Schneider, 1985, Umbreit, 1994; Wright, 1991; Church Council on Justice and Corrections, 1996).

Yet, much remains to be done here. Existing practices evolve, and new variations in restorative practices emerge. New problems become visible as evaluations are available, and practitioners need to confront many questions. How do proponents develop good program methodologies as a support and frame of reference for practice, while avoiding rigidity or the reduction of restorative practice to a set of purely technical skills meant to be applied only by paid, "certified" professionals? How do they select and motivate victims, offenders, and/ or community members to participate in restorative processes without resorting to coercive pressure? How can concerns for community feelings of safety and peace be part of the debate in restorative processes, while avoiding tendencies to exclude or stigmatize offenders? What kind of relationship is preferable between informal restorative processes and the system of formal social control and sanctioning?

The goal should not be to develop one single intervention manual consisting of compulsory directives and techniques. What is needed is a variety of different possibilities and options, and a description of intervention choices and the consequences that these choices may entail. Practitioners should have the opportunity to benefit from knowledge of earlier successes and failures, and to draw lessons for their own practices, in their own contexts, with their own clients.

Research focused on the relative effectiveness of various practices and procedures can help to construct frameworks for programmatic reflection and decision making. As available practical experience increases, professionals and non-professionals alike will be able to deal with more difficult cases, and thereby extend the limits of restorative justice. Especially in an emerging field grounded in the inclusive and non-authoritarian principles of restorative justice, scientific research is highly dependent on practitioners. In an evolving movement, those implementing restorative interventions should first be given the floor to communicate their trials, successes, failures, and knowledge obtained from both positive and negative experiences. The role of scientific work, in turn, seems to be to promote: communication among program staff; managers, and participating stakeholders; learning from these communications; comparison and attempts to synthesize experience and develop theory; posing of questions; and identification of possible new paths for improving practice.

3.6. Develop Strategies for Enhancing the Acceptability of Restorative Justice

Restorative justice is more than a field of academic research. It is also an ideal of justice, grounded in a set of socioethical beliefs and values. It may also be viewed as a movement toward a new way of achieving justice in the response to crime that is also ultimately directed at social change. A movement generally requires a strategy and a coherent set of substrategies (see Van Ness and Strong, 1997).

However, thinking in terms of a "strategy for a movement" raises the question as to whether a restorative justice movement really exists. We certainly cannot speak of one single conceptualization of restorative justice goals, and the coherence of various practices and processes is not really striking. But we cannot deny either that restorative justice has a common core-meaning (see chapter2, this volume; and section 3.1, this chapter), and that many practitioners and scholars at least occasionally assume the role of activists with the objective of moving intervention closer to what they consider to be restorative justice. At a minimum, there are several "informal network-like associations" (Scott, 1990) that interact with each other in the context of a general objective of strengthening restorative justice practice, theory and research. Generally, these groups share what may be loosely described as a communitarian social ethics. In that respect, restorative justice has some characteristics of what sociologists call a "new social movement." Variations within this broad configuration of restorative justice activism are unlikely to allow for the possibility that one single strategy could emerge that would be unanimously sustained by all its proponents. We must instead advance a set of general strategic considerations that may guide restorative justice advocates in their efforts to broaden the acceptance and application of the new paradigm.

Basic in an implementation strategy is clarifying the vision and goals to be achieved, and then carefully assessing the existing situation. In our situation, setting goals seems easy at first glance. As maximalists, who view restorative justice as a systemic alternative to both the retributive and rehabilitative responses to juvenile crime, we promote the establishment of restorative justice as the dominant response to juvenile crime — including a restorative juvenile justice system — as the ultimate (utopian) goal. Sub-goals may consist of all those steps that move systems closer to this ideal or that help to bring about the conditions that move us closer.

3.6.1. Confronting Challenges

Looking at the existing situation, many interacting elements challenge the introduction of restorative justice. Current juvenile justice systems were not designed with restorative justice practices in mind. They are based on acts of power and submission: identifying the person who has committed an offense, stigmatizing the offender, inflicting punishment and/ or imposing treatment. Agents of existing justice systems develop ideologies to protect such approaches (see e.g., Sessar's chapter), and professional groups at times rigidly defend their prerogatives. Restorative justice is mostly considered as an ornament or exceptional "gadget," at the margins of the "serious work" of mainstream judges and advocates.

Media, supported by commercial interests, favor simplistic, sensationalist news items. Moreover, because broadcasted images and values are aimed at pleasing consumers, they generally conform to and reinforce public stereotypes and beliefs. As a consequence, the public is bombarded with crime and justice issues, but is not well-informed about what is at stake. Media accounts invite citizens to think in stereotypes and to believe in quick and simplistic solutions. Such solutions are almost always punitive, and little if any information is provided about the potential of restorative justice options.

Many politicians, driven by media and its version of public opinion, do not take risks and tend to go along with this simplifying punitive tendency. They try to score electoral points by boosting the "war against crime," which in some cases has come to resemble a civil war against specific segments of the population. In addition, the dominant cultural climate in much of the industrialized world is not really favorable toward restorative justice. The general climate is neither communitarian nor moving toward Braithwaite's (this volume) republican vision. Community, as far as it is recognized, is not valued as a focus of responsibility and a source of support. Networks are fragmented in varying subgroups of conflicting concerns, and individualistic interests predominate. Restorative justice is not easily promoted in such an atmosphere. Restorative processes run the risk of being reframed to fit an agenda aimed at hardening conflicts between victims and offenders, as has been the case in some more politicized factions of the victims' rights movement, rather than promoting constructive solutions that would serve victims and communities and preserve opportunities for reintegration of offenders. All these forces work together in a way to enhance a punitive "carousel" in the struggle against crime.

3.6.2. An Agenda for Moving Forward

Can the restorative justice movement stop this carousel, or even make it begin to move in another direction? Good strategic planning for implementation is needed (Van Ness and Strong, 1997), based partly on the principles of planned social change (see, e.g., Bennis et al., 1976) and grounded in the fundamental insights of restorative justice principles. Few restorative justice proponents, or even enlightened practitioners, currently occupy positions of power in our societies. As a consequence, a confrontational approach is inappropriate; the restorative justice movement would simply lose in such a confrontation.

If it has no structural power, the restorative justice movement must then seek to gain advantage through moral influence. This may be achieved through three interdependent "strategic attitudes" that must guide all implementation efforts: develop the restorative justice paradigm into a coherent set of theory, practice and empirical data of high quality; make sure that this high quality is observed by the appropriate groups and agencies at the appropriate moments in time; and take the concerns of needed collaborating groups seriously.

(1) *Make restorative justice stronger, in order to construct a vigorous countervailing power against punitive movements.* This is, of course the most important issue (for example: "The best argument for a salesperson is the quality of the products she sells)." The restorative justice movement should rest on reflection and research of high quality. This should be done by: developing a normative restorative justice theory as a coherent set of beliefs and standards; carrying out good experiments on key questions with regard to the feasibility and the range of restorative justice intervention; developing methodologies for facilitating, "coaching," and monitoring restorative justice processes; and carrying out methodologically rigorous empirical research. A body of high-quality theory and research is fundamental to a strategy for several reasons. First, coherent theory sustained by enlightened practice and rigorous research is needed to make the ultimate strategic goals more concrete, and therefore provides the basic guideline for all strategic actions. Second, high-quality data is needed to support the strong vision of restorative justice and, especially, debates with opponents and skeptics. Third, a well-elaborated vision of restorative justice offers an opportunity to check practices, and, therefore, helps to protect the restorative paradigm against misconceptions and misuses in political and practical contexts.

(2) *Make restorative justice practice and research more visible.* Good scientific and practical work does not necessarily reach the public. Restorative justice proponents have to make sure that the quality of their work is known by those who may be relevant for the development of the approach. The persistent gap among social scientists, practitioners and the general public requires a strategy of communication: valid and clear information relayed through the right communication channels to the right target groups.

Target groups include local and national policy makers, government professionals, the judiciary, social work practitioners, the general public, victims and local community groups. Most of these groups are characterized by different sets of beliefs, interests and values. Though they all have to play a role in the emergence and the propagation of restorative justice, some are more crucial than others. In addition, each target group makes use of different communication channels. Communication strategies must therefore be differentiated, according to the kind of information to be disseminated and the kind of group addressed. Messages transmitted through the general media, specific journals and reviews, conferences, training programs, participation in work groups and study circles, and very focused communications to governments, judicial, and other authorities should all be part of a well-reflected strategy.

The content of the information should be clear without being simplistic. Moreover, it should consider the fact that some target groups have a distrust of social scientists and social practitioners. Parts of the general population, and too many policy makers, for instance, simply do not believe either social scientists or practitioners because they suspect bias due to ideological and/or naive prejudices.

(3) *Take the concerns seriously*. Even if high-quality information is easily available, it may fail to persuade one or more target audiences, often for reasons that are irrational. Crime is also a mythical image, engendering curiosity and fear. Criminal justice policy is often grounded in beliefs, folklore, ideologies and symbols — as well as professional interests. Thinking about crime and making criminal justice policy is, in many ways, a non-rational endeavor.

It is crucial that restorativists keep this reality in mind. The restorative justice approach is still relatively unknown, and the unknown always causes anxiety and resistance. Even if public concerns for safety are exaggerated, they are real in their capacity to hamper the acceptance of new approaches to crime. Common knowledge about crime is based on exaggerated accounts of the most extreme cases, which become part of a kind of folklore. Restorative justice strategy must therefore incorporate not only a strategic and data-based approach to dealing with citizen concerns for public safety that responds to fear, but also must provide case studies of restorative justice interventions that can be shown to promote safety. Such examples can begin to provide the basis for developing an *alternative* folklore. Short-term reactive approaches, on the other hand, should be stripped of their self-serving rhetoric and confronted with their negative impacts on longer term peace and safety. Professional interests behind the opposition should be identified, so that they can then become part of the dialogue and negotiation when restorative experiments are introduced. The fears and distrust of some victims' advocates provide a challenge to restorativists to make the potential advantages for crime victims real and clear, while also ensuring that restorative strategies are indeed designed to involve and meet victim needs.

Of course, strategic actions will need detailed and more concrete considerations, tailored to local implementation contexts. However, we believe that the three "strategic attitudes" should underpin all actions. Restorativists will be listened to and will provide hope in the search for a more constructive response to crime if they: further develop their option into a well-reflected, coherent and empirically supported systemic alternative; find the appropriate communication channels and the right messages; and indeed respect the fears and concerns of necessary partners.

CONCLUSION

As a comprehensive model guiding the response to youth crime, restorative justice is a work-in-progress. But while restorative justice does not provide all answers to all questions and will probably never do so, it must be said that the retributive and rehabilitative models also fall short in providing such answers.

Based on the materials this volume has brought together, we conclude that the restorative justice option is the most promising pathway along the journey to find a more humane and effective way of responding to youth crime. The restorative response is at once healing and just for victims, strengthening for communities, reintegrative for offenders, and constructive in enforcing community norms and promoting peaceful relations.

But there is so much still to do. Practical experiments, theoretical reflection, systematic empirical research and well-conceived implementation strategy together must enhance the development and the replication of restorative justice experiments. We hope that this volume may contribute to both the implementation and evaluation agenda for a restorative juvenile justice. An evaluation protocol will be necessary to allow for a valid and reliable assessment of the implementation and impact of restorative justice, but at this stage, we can only begin to speculate about the specific components of practical research designs. Clearly, a restorative justice evaluation, like implementation itself, could not be top-down but would need to be developed by researchers in collaboration with key stakeholders. Such evaluation would ultimately be geared toward measuring those outcomes that are important to victims, communities and offenders seeking common ground in an effort to repair the harm crime causes.

★   ★   ★

REFERENCES

Balanced and Restorative Justice Project (1997). *A Framework for Juvenile Justice in the 21st Century*. Washington, DC: U.S. Office of Juvenile Justice and Delinquency Prevention.

—— (1998). *Guide for Implementing the Balanced and Restorative Justice Model*. Washington, DC: U.S. Office of Juvenile Justice and Delinquency Prevention.

Bazemore, G. (1997a). "What's New About the Balanced Approach?" *Juvenile and Family Court Journal* 48(1):1-23.

—— (1997b). "The 'Community' in Community Justice: Issues, Themes and Questions for the New Neighborhood Sanctioning Models." *Justice System Journal* 19(2):193-228.

—— (1997c). "Evaluating Community Youth Sanctioning Models: Neighborhood Dimensions and Beyond." In: *Crime and Place: Plenary Papers of the 1997 Conference on Criminal Justice Research and Evaluation, NIJ Research Forum*. Washington, DC: U.S. National Institute of Justice,

—— and D. Maloney (1994). "Rehabilitating Community Service: Toward Restorative Service in a Balanced Justice System." *Federal Probation* 58:24-35.

—— and C. Terry (1997). "Developing Delinquent Youth: A Reintegrative Model for Rehabilitation and a New Role for the Juvenile Justice System." *Child Welfare* 65(5):665-716.

—— and M. Umbreit (1995). "Rethinking the Sanctioning Function in Juvenile Court: Retributive or Restorative Responses to Youth Crime." *Crime & Delinquency* 41 (3):296-316.

Belgrave, J. (1995). "Restorative Justice: a Discussion Paper." Wellington, NZ: New Zealand Ministry of Justice.

Bennis, W., K. Benne, R. Chin and K. Corey (1976). *The Planning of Change* (3rd ed.). New York, NY: Holt, Rhinehart and Winston.

Braithwaite, J. and S. Mugford (1994). "Conditions of Successful Reintegration Ceremonies: Dealing with Juvenile Offenders." *British Journal of Criminology* 34(2):139-171.

—— and Ph. Petitt (1990). *Not Just Desert. A Republican Theory of Criminal Justice*. Oxford, UK: Clarendon.

Butts, J. and H. Snyder (1990). *Restitution and Juvenile Recidivism*. Monograph. Pittsburgh, PA: National Center for Juvenile Justice.

Byrne, J., A. Lurgio and J. Petersilia (1994). *Smart Sentencing*. Newbury Park, CA: Sage.

Castellano, T. (1986). "The Justice Model in the Juvenile Justice System: Washington State's Experience." *Law and Policy* 8:479-506.

Church Council on Justice and Corrections (1996). *Satisfying Justice: Safe Community Options that Attempt to Repair Harm from Crime and Reduce the Use or Length of Imprisonment*. Ottawa, CAN: author.

Corrado R.R., N. Bala, R. Linden and M. Le Blanc (1992). *Juvenile Justice in Canada*. Toronto, CAN: Butterworths.

Declaration of Leuven (1997). *On the Advisability to Promote the Restorative Approach to Juvenile Crime*. Leuven, BEL: International Network for Research on Restorative Justice for Juveniles/Onderzoeksgroep Jeugdcriminologie.

Doble, J. & Associates, (1994). "Crime and Corrections: The Views of People of Vermont." Montpelier, VT: Department of Corrections.

Dooley, M.J., (1995). *Reparative Probation Program*. Monograph. Montpelier, VT: Department of Corrections.

Duenkel, F. (1990). "Médiation Delinquant-Victime et Réparation des Dommages. Nouvelle Evolution du Droit Pénal et de la Pratique Judiciaire dans une Comparaison Internationale." (Victim-Offender Mediation and Reparation of Damages. A New Development in Penal Law and in Judiciary Practice According to an International Comparison.) In: F. Duenkel and J. Zermatten (eds.), *Nouvelles Tendances dans le Droit Pénal des Mineurs. Mediation, Travail au Profit de la Communauté et Traitement Intermédiaire*, vol. 42. Freiburg, GER: Kriminologische Forschungsberichte aus dem Max-Planck-Institut.

Elliott, D. (1994). "Serious Violent Offenders: Onset, Developmental Course, and Termination." American Society of Criminology 1993 Presidential Address. Reprinted from *Criminology* 32(1):1-18.

Ezell, M. (1992). "Juvenile Diversion: The Ongoing Search for Alternatives." In: I. Schwartz (ed.), *Juvenile Justice and Public Policy*. New York, NY: Lexington.

Feld, B. (1993). "Criminalizing the American Juvenile Court." In: M. Tonry (ed.), *Crime and Justice: A Review of Research*, vol. 17. Chicago, IL: University of Chicago Press.

Gendreau, P. (1989) "Programs that Do Not Work: A Brief Comment on Brodeur and Doob." *Canadian Journal of Criminology* 31:193-195.

—— (1996) "The Principles of Effective Intervention with Offenders." In: Alan Harland (ed.), *Choosing Correctional Options that Work: Defining the Demand and Evaluating the Supply*. Thousand Oaks, CA: Sage.

—— and R. Ross (1981). "Correctional Potency: Treatment and Deterrence on Trial." In: R. Roesch and R. Corrado (eds.), *Evaluation and Criminal Justice Policy*. Beverly Hills, CA: Sage.

Griffths, C.T., and R. Hamilton (1996). "Spiritual Renewal, Community Revitalization and Healing. Experience in Traditional Aboriginal Justice in Canada." *International Journal of Comparative and Applied Criminal Justice* 20(1):285-310.

Haen Marshall, I. (1996). "How Exceptional is the United States? Crime Trends in Europe and in the U.S." *European Journal of Criminal Policy and Research* 2:7-35.

Hagan, F. (1993). *Research Methods in Criminal Justice and Criminology* (3rd ed.). New York, NY: Macmillan.

Higgins, D. and R.C. Snyder (1996). "North Carolinians Want Alternative Sentences for Nonviolent Offenders." *Overcrowded Times* 7(4):1,12-15.

Irwin, J. and J. Austin (1993). *It's About Time: America's Imprisonment Binge*. Belmont, CA: Wadsworth.

Kohlberg, L. (1969). "Stage and Sequence: The Cognitive-Developmental Approach to Socialization." In: D.A. Goslin (ed.), *Handbook of Socialization Theory and Research*. Chicago, IL: Rand McNally.

Lab, S. (1997). *Crime Prevention. Approaches, Practices and Evaluations* (3rd ed.). Cincinnati, OH: Anderson.

Lemert, E. (1981). "Diversion in Juvenile Justice: What Hath been Wrought." *Journal of Research in Crime and Delinquency* 22:34-46.

McCold, P. (1998). "Restorative Justice: Variations on the Theme." In: L. Walgrave (ed.), *Restorative Justice for Juveniles. Potentials, Risks and Problems for Research.* Proceedings of the International Conference, Leuven, May 1997. Leuven, BEL: Katholicke Universiteit University Press.

McKnight, J. (1995). *The Careless Society: Community and Its Counterfeits.* New York, NY: Basic Books.

Packer, H. (1968). *The Limits of the Criminal Sanction.* Palo Alto, CA: Stanford University Press.

Piliavin, I., C. Thornton, R. Garten and R. Matsueda (1986). "Crime, Deterrence and Rational Choice." *American Sociological Review* 51:101-119.

Polk, K. (1984). "When Less Means More." *Crime & Delinquency* 30:462-480.

Pranis, K. (1997). "From Vision to Action: Some Principles of Restorative Justice." *Church & Society* (Presbyterian Church Journal) 87(4):32-42.

—— and M. Umbreit (1993). "Restorative Justice: Back to the Future in Criminal Justice." Working Paper. Minneapolis, MN: Minnesota Citizens Council.

Robinson, P. (1987). "Hybrid Principles for the Distribution of Criminal Sanctions." *Northwest University Law Review* 19:34-6.

Schneider, A. (ed.). (1985). "Guide to Juvenile Restitution." Washington, DC: U.S. Office of Juvenile Justice and Delinquency Prevention.

—— (1986). "Restitution and Recidivism Rates of Juvenile Offenders: Results From Four Experimental Studies." *Criminology* 24(3):533-552.

—— (1990). *Deterrence & Juvenile Crime: Results from a National Policy Experiment.* New York, NY: Springer-Verlag.

Schwartz, I.M. (1992). "Public Attitudes Toward Juvenile Crime and Juvenile Justice: Implications for Public Policy." In: I. Schwartz, (ed.), *Juvenile Justice Policy.* Lexington, MA: Lexington Books.

Scott, A. (1990). *Ideology and the New Social Movement.* London, UK: Urwin Hyman.

Standards in Restorative Justice (1997). Unpublished leaflet.

Stuart, B. (1995a). "Circle Sentencing. Mediation and Consensus — Turning Swords into Ploughshares." Unpublished paper. Territorial Court of the Yukon.

—— (1995b). "Sentencing Circles — Making 'Real' Differences.' Unpublished paper. Territorial Court of the Yukon.

Taylor, R. (1994). *Research Methods in Criminal Justice.* New York, NY: McGraw-Hill.

Tonry, M. and N. Morris (1992). *Intermediate Sanctions.* Chicago, IL: University of Chicago Press.

Torbet, P.R. Gable, H. Hurst, I. Montgomery, L. Szymanski and D. Thomas (1996). *State Responses to Serious and Violent Juvenile Crime.* Office of Juvenile Justice and Delinquency Prevention research report. Pittsburgh, PA: National Center for Juvenile Justice.

Umbreit, M. (1994). *Victim Meets Offender: The Impact of Restorative Justice and Mediation.* Monsey, NY: Criminal Justice Press.

Van Ness, D. (1993). "New Wine and Old Wineskins: Four Challenges of Restorative Justice." *Criminal Law Forum* 4(2):251-276.

—— and K.H. Strong (1997). *Restoring Justice.* Cincinnati, OH: Anderson.

von Hirsch, A. (1993). *Censure and Sanctions.* Oxford, UK: Clarendon.

—— (1997). "Penal Philosophy: How Much to Punish?" In: M. Tonry (ed.), *Oxford Crime and Justice Handbook.* New York, NY: Oxford University Press.

Wachtel, B. and T. Wachtel (eds.), (1997). *Real Justice Training Manual: Coordinating Family Group Conferences.* Pipersville, PA: Piper's Press.

Walgrave, L. (1993). "Beyond Retribution and Rehabilitation: Restoration as the Dominant Paradigm in Judicial Intervention Against Juvenile Crime." Paper presented at the International Congress on Criminology, Budapest, Hungary.

—— (1994). "Beyond Rehabilitation: In Search of a Constructive Alternative in the Judicial Response to Juvenile Crime." *European Journal of Criminal Policy and Research* 2:57-75.

—— (1995a). "Diversion? It Depends on What We Divert to: Some Comments on Diversion and the Restorative Alternatives." In: G. Albrecht and W. Ludwig-Mayerhofer (eds.), *Diversion and Informal Social Control.* New York, NY: Walter de Gruyter.

—— (1995b). "Restorative Justice for Juveniles: Just a Technique or a Fully-Fledged Alternative?" *Howard Journal of Criminal Justice* 34:228-249.

—— and H. Geudens (1996). "Community Service as a Sanction of Restorative Justice: A European Approach." Paper presented at the annual meeting of the American Society of Criminology, Chicago, November.

Weiss, C. (1997) "How Can Theory-Based Evaluation Make Greater Headway?" *Evaluation Review* 21(4):501-524.

Wright, M. (1991). *Justice for Victims and Offenders.* Buckingham, UK: Open University.

NOTES

1. There are possibly even more highly developed restorative justice initiatives in Asia, Africa and in other parts of the world. We thus acknowledge that our unfamiliarity with literature and possible emerging practices in countries of this region limits our ability to present a truly "international" perspective.

2. The goal of minimizing state intervention and stigma has therefore been frequently subverted by the overarching aim to provide early intervention to "help" at-risk youths (Lemert, 1981; Polk, 1984). Once established, diversion programs *need* a steady influx of troubled or pre-delinquent youths in order to survive. Historically, to ensure this client supply, diversion's professional service providers appear to have gradually displaced youth supervision and development functions once assumed by informal community networks, as well as formal socializing institutions.

3. Indeed, it is this difference in outcome that also provides an answer to Feld's (this volume) question about the difference between a restorative response and the existing array of intermediate sanctions. Intermediate sanctions aimed primarily at replacing a period of incarceration by inflicting the maximum amount of punishment possible in the community (e.g., Tonry and Morris, 1992) have different objectives than those with the intent of repairing harm to victims or repaying the community. Such sanctions (e.g., boot camps, intensive supervision and electronic monitoring) may accomplish punishment, surveillance or even some treatment goals--but have nothing to do with such repair. The "conceptual alternative" Feld (this volume) seeks could be captured in a formal reframing of the purpose of community-based sanctioning, from inflicting pain on an offender (or avoiding prison) to repairing harm to victim and community. In doing so, however, the offender may still experience pain that is indistinguishable from the "bite" of purely retributive sanctions, and therefore limits must of course be imposed (see Byrne et al., 1994, for discussions of problematics in imposing such restraints under *current* application of intermediate sanctioning).

4. The question of whether primary criteria for gauging the restorative obligation could be based on the amount of harm caused to victims and victimized communities, and the extent to which offender culpability for this harm could be taken into account is far from resolved (see later discussion in this chapter). But a rough scale gauging the size and duration of a restorative obligation based on the amount of harm an offender's action caused to a specific victim would seem no more arbitrary than a designated prison sentence of, for example, three years for a home burglary. And it does not seem improbable that restorative justice as a goal of disposition could not co-exist with at least the most general retributive standards for setting upper limits on the offender's obligation to repair harm based on the seriousness of the offense. The specific nature of harm to the victim could also shape the nature of the restorative requirement, and to some degree guide the determination of the intensity of the burden placed on a specific offender to "make it right" with the victim.

5. Such a process may indeed be viewed by some as "lawless" (Feld, this volume) in the sense that attorneys are given much less power to propose and negotiate a disposition. But if participation by non-experts in sentencing is the problem, one may well raise fundamental questions for retributivists about the lawlessness of the current jury system, which uses citizens not only to make sentencing decisions but also to weigh often very technical evidence regarding guilt or innocence.

6. It must be said here that we view as a given the need for similar intervention theories to guide research on victim impact and community impact (Bazemore, 1997b). Since recidivism is not at issue in assessing victim impact, researchers need to develop meaningful and relevant victim outcome measures that address long-term well-being, the absence of trauma, feelings of closure, etc. The long-term outcomes need to be linked empirically to more intermediate feelings of satisfaction with the process, as well as with the quality and amount of reparation achieved, which must in turn be linked more specifically to program processes and interventions.